TERROR IN THE CITY OF CHAMPIONS

ALSO BY TOM STANTON

The Final Season
The Road to Cooperstown
Hank Aaron and the Home Run That Changed America
Ty and The Babe

TERROR IN THE CITY OF CHAMPIONS

Murder, Baseball, and the Secret Society
That Shocked Depression-Era Detroit

TOM STANTON

Guilford, Connecticut

An imprint of Rowman & Littlefield

Distributed by NATIONAL BOOK NETWORK

British Library Cataloguing in Publication Information Available

Library of Congress Cataloging-in-Publication Data

Names: Stanton, Tom, 1960– author.
Title: Terror in the city of champions : murder, baseball, and the secret
  society that shocked Depression-era Detroit / Tom Stanton.
Description: Guilford, Connecticut : Lyons Press, 2016. | Includes
  bibliographical references and index.
Identifiers: LCCN 2015043482 (print) | LCCN 2016005240 (ebook) | ISBN
  9781493015702 (hardcover : alk. paper) | ISBN 9781493018185 (ebook) | ISBN
  9781493018185 (e-book)
Subjects: LCSH: Murder—Michigan—Detroit—History—20th century. | Black
  Legion. | Professional sports—Michigan—Detroit—History—20th century. |
  Baseball—Michigan—Detroit—History—20th century. | Detroit
  (Mich.)—History—20th century.
Classification: LCC HV6534.D6 S73 2016 (print) | LCC HV6534.D6 (ebook) | DDC
  364.152/30977434—dc23
LC record available at http://lccn.loc.gov/2015043482

♾™ The paper used in this publication meets the minimum requirements of American National Standard for Information Sciences—Permanence of Paper for Printed Library Materials, ANSI/ NISO Z39.48-1992.

For my sister Janis Stanton-Peterson,
who gave me my first typewriter and so much more

CONTENTS

Prologue xi

PART I: SOMETHING AFOOT, 1933–1934

Mickey and Dayton 3
A Friend Disappears. 15
Spring in Lakeland. 16
Major-General Bert 22
A Future Together 30
The Bee Is Buzzing 32
Neither Threats Nor Bribes 36
It Hurt for Days 43
The Little Stone Chapel 52
The Superstitious Schoolboy and His Gal 60
Happy Rosh Hashanah, Hank. 69
Oh, Those Dean Boys 77
The Attorney down the Street 87

PART II: GRAND PLANS, 1935

A New Year 101
Mr. Hoover, Investigate 103
Harry's Caravan 113
The Radio Priest 121
The Killing of Silas Coleman 128
Worries. 135
Unwanted Attention 145
Zero Hour 153
Louis vs. Baer 159

CONTENTS

World Champions 165
Amid the Joy, Punishment 178
The Pastor Who Said No 182
Uncle Frank 189
Come to Detroit, Lindbergh 192

PART III: JOY AND TERROR, 1936
Case Closed 203
City of Champions 214
Rumors 222
Poole and Pidcock 230
Secrets 236
Black Legion Hysteria 244
Frenzied Nerves 255
Dayton Dean and the Negro Reporter 257
The Captain 260
Wyoming 267
The Cover-Up 270

Epilogue 277
Acknowledgments 283
Notes 285
Bibliography 309
Index 315
About the Author 329

This is the Detroit of the Detroiters: first, of course, the automobile capital of the world . . . then, the city of champions—Joe Louis, the Tigers, the Redwings . . . the parish of the priest with the largest congregation ever . . . the financial center that produced the most prodigious banking crash of the Depression . . . the city that calls itself Detroit the Dynamic.

—AUTHOR JAMES STEVENS IN
THE AMERICAN MERCURY, NOVEMBER 1935

The Black Legion probably is the craziest and most dangerous mob ever formed in the United States. Police are not fighting gangsters. We are fighting a low type of mentality, men easily incited by mob psychology, who have taken a silly pledge and gone through a crazy ritual apparently created by a fanatic who seeks power.

—DETROIT POLICE INSPECTOR
JOHN A. HOFFMAN, MAY 1936

PROLOGUE

When I was a boy in the early 1970s, my aunts and uncles came to our house every December for the annual family holiday celebration. Amid clouds of cigarette smoke, the basement aglow with Christmas lights, they reminisced about their early years in Detroit. I heard of a magical time when even personal tragedies—the deaths of two infant sisters, the funeral of a grandfather, the slow demise of pal Beezie—were rendered soft and sweet. Most of their stories related to family: Aunt Bernice singing with a Big Band, Uncle Herbie leading a pack of neighborhood toughs, Uncle Teddy taking a church parishioner's car for a joy ride.

My father and his brothers had been athletes, playing on sandlots, outdoor rinks, and cemetery football fields. They captivated me with their tales of the triumphant teams and heroes of their younger days. In the 1970s only one team I followed came close to winning anything. But my dad and uncles evoked an enchanted era of nonstop triumphs. Mickey Cochrane, Charlie Gehringer, Hank Greenberg, Schoolboy Rowe, Joe Louis, Dutch Clark, Normie Smith—the names danced from their youthful hearts. Within a six-month period in 1935 and 1936, the Tigers, Red Wings, and Lions all captured titles as Detroit's own Joe Louis reigned as boxing's uncrowned champion. Detroit remains the only city to score the trifecta of a World Series, a Stanley Cup, and an NFL championship in one season. The fact that it happened during the Depression—when my grandfather was unemployed, the family risked losing its home, and the children subsisted on watery soups and bacon-grease sandwiches—only added to its mystical significance. That it took place in a Detroit that was no longer recognizable made it all the more enticing. Through the eyes of a boy, it seemed a glorious time to be alive, a *Little Rascals* episode of endless escapades.

And it was at a family gathering that I first heard of the Black Legion. Clements Maximilian Stone was the eldest of my father's nine siblings, one of several who changed his last name from Stankiewicz. On a summer evening in 1936, Clem was walking near Hastings Street in Detroit's black district with his brother Bucky and two friends. They were white, left-leaning, aspiring writers and artists in their early twenties. Their presence in jazzy Paradise Valley spoke to their progressive nature, their sense of adventure, and, likely, their desire to score reefer. As they made their way down a side street, a car carrying two men slowed beside them. A white man in the driver's seat asked why they were in the neighborhood.

"What's it to you?" said Bucky, feisty and fierce.

"You don't belong here," the guy answered.

In Uncle Clem's retelling, Bucky tensed his meaty biceps, raised his bulldog shoulders, and stepped toward the car.

"Who the hell are you?" he snapped.

The driver flashed a police badge. Bucky, already a veteran of several protest marches, had heard rumors of activists being abducted and killed. He didn't believe the men were actually cops—they were in street clothes and their car was unmarked—so he barked out a challenge. The two men pulled revolvers and ordered the four into the backseat. As the car sped off, Clem imagined the two gunmen to be Black Legion night riders. Clem thought he and his comrades were heading to a bloody end. Instead, they wound up at a police precinct, where they spent a night in jail, angry but relieved to have not encountered the Black Legion's infamous thugs. In his 1970s recitation my uncle provided only the vaguest sense of the organization, enough to intrigue but not terrify an eleven-year-old.

Most of my uncles died years back. In the seasons that followed, while researching other books, I would occasionally stumble upon references to the Black Legion and the true, horrific, nonromanticized, adult version of the secret society would come into focus. With tens of thousands of members across the Midwest, the legion harbored grand, sinister ambitions.

Its eventual exposure—and the revelation that its tentacles reached into police forces, court systems, and elected offices—spawned hysteria.

Neighbors turned on neighbors. Officials selectively purged public payrolls of accused members. Terrified citizens flooded J. Edgar Hoover with demands for action. For months the legion dominated page one, even prompting a Humphrey Bogart movie.

The rise and fall of the Black Legion paralleled, intersected, and overlapped that of the City of Champions. One of Detroit's darkest hours became entangled with one of its grandest. Much of this story has faded into history, passing with the men and women who lived it. Some of it has never been told until now.

Tom Stanton

PART I:
SOMETHING AFOOT

1933–1934

Mickey and Dayton

MICKEY COCHRANE STEPPED OFF THE TRAIN INTO THE NIGHT AIR AT Michigan Central and grinned for the press photographers. As he removed his fedora, he revealed the two physical features everyone always noticed about him: his helmet of brilliant black hair, dark as coal smoke and glimmering like obsidian in the camera flash, and his protruding ears, which over the years had been compared to a mule's and a dairy cow's and to the handles of a milk jug and a sugar bowl, and had been said to be so large that they could cast a shadow over Philadelphia's Shibe Park.

Cochrane looked older than thirty. It might have been his decade as a catcher, baseball's most physically demanding position, with games spent crouching behind a mask, or maybe his days as a boxer at Boston University, where as 160-pound "Kid" Cochrane he absorbed punches from true heavyweights. His fiery nature—the burning competitiveness, the flaming anger—also might have aged him. Cochrane wore his intensity on his prematurely creased face. It smoldered in his eyes, which columnist Jimmy Powers of the *New York Daily News* described as a window into "a soul of torment." It was Cochrane's forceful temperament, steeped in his success with Connie Mack's Philadelphia Athletics—two World Series championships, three pennants, six seasons of ninety or more wins—that earlier in the week had prompted Detroit Tigers owner Frank Navin to acquire him as manager. Mickey Cochrane was a winner, and Navin needed desperately to win.

The rousing, heroic story of Gordon Stanley Cochrane—only his parents called him by his given name; fans knew him as Mickey, friends and teammates as Mike or Black Mike, for his moods—was familiar to every baseball-obsessed kid in America. He grew up outside Boston in the small town of Bridgewater; aspired to be an Olympic runner, sprinting, frightened, past rural cemeteries late at night; loved to hunt and fish; studied hard; earned a partial scholarship to Boston University; through vigor and zeal became the star of the football team, practicing beside the rail yards; demonstrated flashes of valiance in day-to-day life (rescuing a teen who had fallen through ice, for one example); chose baseball against all odds; through more vigor and zeal learned to be a catcher; rose to the position with Philadelphia at age twenty-two; drove his team to victory; and worked furiously until he became the game's best, winning the Most Valuable Player Award at twenty-five and being selected three years on for a baseball tour of Japan with Lou Gehrig and other luminaries. And as if all that weren't enough, Cochrane liked to sing, played saxophone in jazz bands, dressed about as fashionably as anyone in the game, and, being a good sport, had even tried his hand at Shakespearean acting.

As he headed into the grand vaulted lobby of the train station, Cochrane exuded an optimism that defied the reality of life in Detroit. It was a Thursday evening, December 14, 1933, within the final weeks of a dreary year. Outside, the temperature hovered in the teens. Two inches of snow covered Theodore Roosevelt Park. The Great Depression had devastated the whole nation, but Detroit had suffered more than most. The year had brought bank panics and closures, unemployment of 45 percent, winding food lines, burgeoning public-relief rolls, and severe wage cuts for surviving auto workers. Car sales fell by four million units between 1929 and 1932. Almost half the city's population qualified for assistance, limited as it was.

In rough times Detroiters had often found comfort in their sports teams. But in 1933 no one had found solace in the Tigers. They had finished in fifth place, twenty-five games out, closer to the bottom than to the top. The Tigers—the papers had taken to calling them Kittens—hadn't lifted anyone's spirits. Not in a long time. It had been almost a quarter-century since the team had captured first place. Long gone were the heady days of Ty Cobb.

Frank Navin felt it, not only in his weakening, sixty-two-year-old heart, but also in his pocketbook. Attendance had plummeted to barely 4,000 per game, 321,000 for the year—the lowest since the war and a steep drop from the one million who had come in 1924, the last time the Tigers had seriously contended. Weary of waiting for a champion, fans belittled Navin as a cheap, complacent loser. Even longtime friend and *Detroit Free Press* editor Malcolm Bingay, who as a cub reporter had covered the Tigers during their heyday, urged his old pal—in newsprint—to produce a winner. "If baseball is a sport, then Frank Navin should bestir himself to present to the public some form of competition," he wrote. "It's up to Mr. Navin to show some sporting blood, take a gambler's chance, spend some money."

"Gambler's chance"—a sly choice of words by "Bing." As a young man, Frank Navin had worked taking bets for a bookie and dealing cards in a gaming house. There, he learned the art of poker. He still loved to gamble. Schooled to become an attorney, he eventually bet stacks of bills, reportedly parlaying a $5,000 prize at an all-night poker party into a greater share of the Tigers. But wagering on cards paled beside his love of horses. He rode daily at the Detroit Riding and Hunt Club, followed the thoroughbreds passionately, studied racing forms, owned a box at two tracks across the river in Windsor, and went almost annually to the Kentucky Derby. Once firmly established as a baseball executive, he bought a racing stable near Lexington, Kentucky, and raised horses as a pastime. Navin bet smartly and heavily, and he won regularly. When he did lose, he did so without remorse. In gambling, money came and went.

But with his business it was different. The team provided Navin's income. Unlike his sometimes-silent partner, automotive tycoon Walter O. Briggs, Navin didn't have a gushing stream of nonbaseball revenue. The team was mostly it. When it came to running his club, Navin guarded his money. He bordered on miserly, shunned expensive prospects, and claimed poverty in negotiations, bickering over small amounts. Players found him cold, unsmiling. They called him a "nickel-nurser." Cobb referred to him as "Old Stone Face." With his ball club Navin the frugal business owner kept Navin the gambler in check.

Until Mickey Cochrane.

Since arriving in the major leagues, Cochrane had been part of the Philadelphia team that for nine straight seasons finished ahead of the

Tigers in the American League. Navin could not have helped but notice him. Cochrane pulsed with energy. He needled opponents, dove for foul balls, and expended every ounce of himself on the field. He abhorred losing and after avoidable defeats flew into tantrums. When Cobb, long believed to be the most competitive man in the game, was finishing his career with the Athletics, he saw the young Cochrane up close. "He put on one of the greatest examples of what it means to be a 'hard loser' that I've ever seen," said Cobb.

Cochrane wasn't only a hothead. He had the ability to motivate teammates, to keep the game loose at the right moment, and to inspire and arouse. "Men fall naturally into his groove, particularly young men who are still impressionable and who unconsciously ape a leader," wrote H. G. "Harry" Salsinger, the formidable dean of Detroit baseball writers, a man so sage that his august column could legitimately carry the tag "The Umpire."

Yet for all of his achievements, Mickey Cochrane had never managed a club. And there, for Navin, lay the gamble. He was putting his team in the hands of a rookie manager and it was a costly experiment. The Depression had eroded Navin's finances, as well as Connie Mack's. Mack had been selling his stars to stay in business. Ballplayers had little say in such matters. Owners bought and unloaded them as they pleased. If he hadn't found a buyer for Cochrane, Mack would have had to cut Cochrane's wages, which gave the catcher reason to be receptive to Detroit's inquiries. To purchase him Navin borrowed $100,000, backed by a bank and the much-wealthier Briggs, who had wanted Cochrane for years. During such dire economic times, the transaction posed significant risks to Navin.

Navin Field occupied a corner six blocks from the train station, just east along Michigan Avenue at Trumbull. On Friday morning Cochrane went to Navin's office to talk of the coming season. Age-wise the two men could have been father and son. But they looked nothing alike. At six feet Navin stood two inches taller than Cochrane. He was portly, a fact accentuated by his bald, moonlike head, circle-framed glasses, and three-piece suits that skirted over his troubled stomach. Those features combined with his narrow, squinting eyes—friends nicknamed him Jap, a term used commonly in the press—to make him appear eternally suspicious.

The lack of a championship clung to Navin like a cocklebur. It wasn't as if he had been a failure. He had been with the Tigers for three decades, working up from bookkeeper to owner, building the team from vulnerable fledgling to established club. He had already secured his place in baseball history by signing eighteen-year-old Ty Cobb to his first contract. If he did nothing else, that was enough. He had also launched other young stars, including one of Babe Ruth's drinking buddies, Harry Heilmann; handsome Heinie Manush; and silent Charlie Gehringer, the current Tigers veteran. Plus, he had built a steel-and-concrete ballpark, and along the way risen in stature within the American League, serving as vice president and as one of the sport's top spokesmen. He had much to be proud of. Only one thing made his career incomplete.

The absence of a World Series title ate at Navin. Truly ate at him, not symbolically. For a dozen years doctors had been treating him for stomach ailments. For the past three years, friends, family, and physicians had been urging him to sell the ball team. It was costing him his health, aggravating his stress, and provoking needless worry. Compounding the problem, Navin seldom showed emotion in public. His poker face rarely betrayed him. "I wish I could let my feelings out like some other men," he said, "but I just can't." Navin told his doctors that he wouldn't consider parting with the team until he won a World Series.

With Cochrane beside him, Navin lingered over the photographs that decorated his office walls. The pictures conjured warm memories. He reminisced more regularly these days, about old friends and players, about the teams of 1907, 1908, and 1909, all of which had made it to the World Series only to lose. Amid the good cheer Navin did not lose sight of what was at stake. Cochrane would be catching as well as managing, and he would be making more money than anyone on the team. Navin needed to know that his top man was in top shape. So he put Cochrane through a physical, which he passed. Then Navin hedged his bet by purchasing a $100,000 insurance policy on Cochrane. "Now we can shove him off a diving board . . . if we have a bad season," he said with a laugh.

Later that night, after less than twenty-four hours in town, Cochrane headed back to the train station. The snow had melted; the temperature had jumped forty degrees into the unseasonably high fifties. Cochrane boarded the Ambassador train for Philadelphia, where he lived with his wife, Mary, his sweetheart since high school, and their two children, Gordon Jr. and Joan.

If Cochrane had stayed the night, he could have taxied over to the Naval Armory, where twenty-eight amateur boxers were fighting in a charity exhibition benefitting poor children. Among the ten local winners was a little-known Detroit Golden Gloves champion, nineteen-year-old Joe Louis Barrow, who knocked out Chris Schussler of Chicago in two rounds. If Cochrane had stayed two additional nights, he would have been in town when the governor signed away Prohibition, allowing Detroiters to legally party publicly for the first time in thirteen years. The celebration jammed bars and flowed into the streets. The city exploded in revelry, a fitting toast to a promising weekend. Harbingers of brighter days abounded.

For some, anyway.

Before the market crash Detroit had been booming. Between 1910 and 1929 it had added one million residents, catapulting past Pittsburgh, Baltimore, Boston, St. Louis, and Cleveland to become the nation's fourth-largest city. Ornate skyscrapers exploded into the sky. The Fisher Building with its three-story marble hall opened along Grand Boulevard near General Motors headquarters. The salmon-colored, elaborately tiled Union-Guardian debuted closer to the waterfront months after the mountainous Penobscot, then the tallest building outside New York or Chicago.

Workers erected a soaring suspension bridge to connect Detroit to Windsor, Ontario, and drilled an international tunnel beneath the Detroit River. The opulent 5,000-seat Fox Theatre debuted, along with Olympia Arena, home to the city's hockey team. These buildings were preceded by the Institute of Arts on Woodward Avenue, across from the main branch of the public library, onto which the names of thinkers—Plato, Aristotle, Justinian, Archimedes—had been chiseled.

Detroit was awash in money. It adopted "Detroit the Dynamic" as its nickname. The auto industry propelled the prosperity and residents embraced it as their own. Car companies weren't faceless entities. They carried the names of entrepreneurs whose lives and deaths, marriages and divorces, successes and failures, unfolded on the pages of newspapers and magazines. There was Henry Ford, of course, but also Ransom Olds, James Packard, David Dunbar Buick, Walter Chrysler, Louis Chevrolet, and brothers Horace and John Dodge.

"Why Detroit?" asked Bingay of the *Free Press*. "That question has been asked throughout the world for the past twenty-five years. . . . Chicago was inevitable. Chicago grew like a callous on a hand. . . . Detroit was unique. . . . Word swept over America about a new strange thing that was happening. . . . A group of Detroiters were making wagons that could run without horses."

Automotive jobs drew tens of thousands to the city. Newcomers came from other parts of Michigan and the Midwest, from throughout the country. "In the South they had labor trains bringing people north," recalled one Alabama native. Immigrants came from Europe. Between 1920 and 1930 Detroit's population not only added more than half a million people, rising to 1.5 million, its mix changed substantially. Fewer than 60 percent of Michigan residents had been born in the state. Eighteen percent had come from another country, 9 percent from Ohio or the South. Blacks accounted for more than 7 percent and their presence was growing. In ten years the black population had tripled to 120,000. The result of this broad influx was a city divided by ethnicity, faith, race, economics, political beliefs, and complicated allegiances. When the Depression hit, those divisions grew sharper. Detroit was a cauldron. "It is a city of strangers," observed writer Forrest Davis. And then the market crashed and the taloned beast of the Great Depression grabbed hold of the great city.

On a visit novelist John Dos Passos found thousands of jobless men living on the streets and in parks, fretting over their futures, debating the right paths, and pondering revolt amid men hawking copies of the *Labor Defender*. "They are everywhere, all over the vast unfinished city, the more thrifty living in shacks and shelters along the waterfront, in the back rooms of unoccupied houses, the others just sleeping any place . . . ," he wrote. "In the evening they stroll up and down Woodward Avenue and look at the posters on the all-night movies and cluster around medicine shows and speakers in back lots where you hear the almost forgotten names of old-time labor parties like the Proletarian Party and the Socialist Labor Party."

Mickey Cochrane moved his family into the Walbri Court Apartments in northern Detroit. His three-bedroom unit was one of seventeen in a five-story complex built by Tigers co-owner Walter O. Briggs. Much earlier, when he was a young father, Briggs had been unable to find an apartment that allowed children. He vowed to someday construct a building that would welcome families. Walbri was born, the name a contorted contraction of his own. The Cochranes and their two children occupied apartment number five. Walter Briggs's twenty-two-year-old son, Spike, was in number ten.

The area was lovely. Across the street lay the three-hundred-acre Palmer Park with ponds, a fountain, tennis courts, a public golf course, and an historic log cabin where Senator Thomas Palmer and his family had summered. Verdant and uplifting, the park had become a destination, anchoring an affluent section of the city. To its west was Detroit Golf Club, with private grounds bordered by sprawling houses. To its north sat Palmer Woods, one of the two addresses—the other being Boston-Edison—preferred by city and industry leaders. Palmer Woods counted among its residents Senator James Couzens, Kresge president Charles Van Dusen, two of the Fisher Body brothers, future GM president William Knudsen, Briggs's brother Mirt, and Roman Catholic bishop Michael Gallagher, the Detroit diocese head who lived in the city's largest dwelling, a donated 39,000-square-foot, sixty-two-room mansion. (Joseph Burnstein, one of the founding brothers of the criminal Purple Gang, also lived in the neighborhood in a lovely English Tudor home with awnings emblazoned with the letter "B.")

For all its prestige, Palmer Woods stood across Woodward Avenue and about three-quarters of a mile from a plain, nameless, working-class area. It was there Dayton Dean lived. Dean, thirty-three, rented a place along State Fair Road with his common-law wife, Margaret O'Rourke, her two adolescent daughters, and his two children by his first wife, Geneva and Bobby. Dean and O'Rourke had been together nearly a decade. Born in Vassar in the thumb area of Michigan, he had lived in Detroit since the age of eight, moving to the city after his father died and his mother married Clarence Nacker. Dean left school early, labored as an office boy for the Electric Light Company, and bounced between physically demanding jobs before and after joining the Navy during the Great War. He liked to tell drinking buddies how in July 1919 during the Washington, D.C., race riots he and several sailors on patrol obeyed an officer's directive and opened fire on a group of blacks. "We shot them down. Quite a few of them." It wasn't the targeting of the blacks that filled Dean with pride. The racial aspect was secondary. Dean liked the notion that he was a good soldier, a man who could be depended upon. "I always obey orders," he said.

Dean had worked for Packard, Ford, and Briggs Manufacturing before settling into a job with the Detroit Public Lighting Commission. He wrapped pipes in asbestos and considered himself the city's best at it. For a while he belonged to the National Guard and the Orangemen, a Protestant fraternal organization. Many nights you could find him smoking oversized cigars—he loved big cigars—and drinking beer at the Blinking Eye on John R Road. The bar was just beyond the railroad tracks amid cinderblock machine shops and plumbing, auto-parts, and lumber stores.

Dean was stocky at five-eight and round-faced, like actor Edward G. Robinson, but with a wide, flat forehead. Some described him as dim-witted, with the intellect of an eleven-year-old. He had his qualities though. He had always been good with guns. He liked to sit on his back porch taking his weapons apart, oiling them, and reassembling them. He could also muster charm with the ladies, some of whom were susceptible to his twinkly eyes and broad, white, straight-toothed smile. He owned a superb memory too. Years on, he could recall details of mundane moments, faces, names, locations, peculiar traits, and makes of cars.

In March 1933, nine months before Mickey Cochrane stormed into town, Whitney Fleming, one of Dean's co-workers at the lighting commission, asked him if he'd like to join a political organization similar to the Ku Klux Klan. The idea intrigued Dean. He and Fleming, fifty-one, had belonged to the Klan years earlier, and Dean had enjoyed his time as a member. In the 1920s the Klan flourished throughout Detroit. An estimated 30,000 people belonged. In an intimidating show of force, Klan supporters gathered on Christmas Eve 1923 to burn a cross on city hall grounds. More substantially, they nearly elected their candidate mayor of Detroit in 1924. By the end of the decade, the Klan itself had faded but the sentiments it evoked remained.

One evening not long after the invitation, Fleming and three other men picked up Dayton Dean at his home. The five headed north on Van Dyke Avenue to Washington Township, a rural community twenty miles outside the city. Lights from occasional homes interrupted the darkness. It was late in the evening and their car's headlamps striped the road and illuminated the budding trees as they drove. Soon they spotted a red signal flashing across the night landscape of a secluded field. As they approached, a band of guards waved them deeper into the woods. They parked and walked farther yet. Along with several other men, Dayton Dean was about to begin his initiation into an organization that would alter his life—an organization he knew nothing about.

It started innocuously enough with the signing of cards labeled "insurance prospect." The cards served as a decoy. If discovered, they could not possibly be incriminating, the organizers felt. Each man recorded his name, address, phone number, car make, and occupation. Questions followed: Are you native-born? White? Protestant? An American citizen? Dean was informed he was joining a secret militaristic group that some viewed as outlawed. Guards searched him and the others for weapons and then administered a preliminary oath. Dean promised to never reveal anything about the organization. "If I should fail in keeping of this, my oath, may the fearful punishment of the Black Knights be meted out to me," he repeated. "The punishment is death."

The mood grew even more serious when the guards ushered Dean and the other recruits toward a grove of trees, where a throng of black-robed men waited with guns. Dean could see their eyes through the holes in their hoods. He didn't recognize any of them. The high-ranking officers wore capes with gold trim. One man walked with a halting limp. Until that moment, Dean had never heard of the Black Legion. Few people other than its members had, and some of them knew it by other names: Black Knights, Black Guards, Bullet Club, Night Riders, Malekta Club, or United Brotherhood of America. Dean was about to join a brutal secret society with tens of thousands of members spread across several states.

The robed men interrogated each recruit at length. Dean was asked his name, age, religion, and whether he could ride a horse, fire a rifle, and drive a car. (He could do it all.) As a member, he would need to acquire a gun; Dean already had one. But for those who didn't, the legion had connections in city and county offices. Recruits were lectured about the legion's "chivalry and daring." They heard a lengthy diatribe against blacks, Catholics, Jews, immigrants, anarchists, and communists.

"At the present time, neither of the two great political parties stands for the liberties and privileges that the founders of this country intended us to enjoy," said an officer. Another series of questions followed, each ratcheting up the inductees' level of commitment: "Will you take an order and go to your death if necessary to carry it out? . . . Will you accept for your roof, the sky; your bed, the earth; and your reward, death? . . . You may be required to perform some duty on a higher plane other than the routine night riding. This would require a blood pact. Are you willing to sign your name in your own blood?"

Dean said yes promptly. Some men were reluctant. Most were terrified. They had been tricked into coming to the meeting and now they were ensnared in an organization that was apparently capable of a multitude of atrocities. To what degree they could not have guessed. There were passwords and secret gestures to remember. "Put none but Americans on guard," they were instructed to say. Or "Until Death," which would be answered with, "Under the star of the guard." A member could identify himself in two ways: by making three and a half circles with a lighted match or by tipping back his hat once and, if answered with the same, repeating the movement and, if answered again, doing it a third time to be certain. In times of distress a member could signal for help by clicking his flashlight on and off three times or by drawing three half arcs with a torch.

As ordered, Dean kneeled and covered his heart with a hand. A colonel directed an armed legionnaire to draw his loaded pistol and train it on Dean as he repeated a final oath, the Black Oath, "in the name of God and the Devil," pledging his life to his peers in the organization, promising never to betray any of them, and inviting that his own heart be roasted, his brain split and spread, his bowels disgorged, and his body ripped asunder should he violate the promise. "And, lastly, may my soul be given to torment . . . through all eternity. In the name of God, our Creator. Amen." Finally Dean, like every new member, was handed a .38-caliber bullet cartridge and told an identical one would be used on him should he violate his vow of secrecy.

This was the stuff of movies and radio shows and Dean delighted in it. It infused his mundane life with a sense of importance and excitement. He quickly threw himself into the organization, his fervor making him a favorite of local leaders. He was assigned to Detroit's third regiment, one of four in the city, and also to a regiment in nearby Highland Park, where he enthusiastically accepted orders to assist Mayor N. Ray Markland, a member who would be facing a tough reelection.

Soon after, Dean and other legionnaires followed George Washer home in their cars after he heckled Markland at a council meeting. On Church Street they pulled to the curb. Dean emerged first and surprised Washer with a punch to the jaw. Washer fell, and the pummeling continued with fists, feet, and a blackjack.

Dean rose rapidly through the ranks, from sergeant to first lieutenant to captain to major. "It was his religion, his whole life," said Margaret, his wife. "He thought of nothing else." Legion officials liked Dean's passion. More assignments followed quickly. The first significant one—his chance to really elevate his stature—involved a crusading newspaper editor, Art Kingsley, who was causing trouble for Mayor Markland. Dean's mission: Kill him.

A Friend Disappears

THE FIRST DAY OF 1934 WAS DRAWING TO A CLOSE.
Edward J. McGrath sat having dinner with Art Kingsley and Sidney Michaelson in a restaurant along Woodward Avenue. Kingsley was the publisher of the *Highland Parker* weekly newspaper. His friend McGrath, sixty and unmarried, was active in fraternal organizations. He served as the secretary of the Highland Park Masonic Temple and belonged to the Knights Templar and Moslem Temple Shrine.

Around eight o'clock McGrath bid Kingsley farewell. McGrath lived on Waverly Avenue, a block from Kingsley's residence. He said he would be heading home "to get a good rest." An hour later, he was spotted reading papers in a local drugstore, as was his habit. He looked dapper at five-foot-five, standing there in a velvet-collared black overcoat with a white scarf draped over his shoulders and a tan felt hat atop his head.

It was the last report of anyone seeing him.

Spring in Lakeland

FRANK NAVIN'S CHAUFFEURED CAR PULLED UP TO THE TERRACE HOTEL in Lakeland, Florida, on a Saturday night. It had been four years since Navin had bothered to go to spring training. But this season felt different. He wanted to see the confident Mickey Cochrane in action. The two had grown close over the winter. Married but childless, Navin had introduced Cochrane around Detroit as if he were a son. They had gone to a Red Wings hockey game, where word of Cochrane's presence blew like a polar gust through the packed Olympia stadium, bringing the audience to its feet. They had been to speaking engagements together, with Cochrane entertaining gatherings of grocers, car sales agents, fire chiefs, boys' club members, Rotarians, Optimists, yacht owners, and Kiwanists. Everywhere, Cochrane had enthused fans and impressed newsmen. He had also intrigued Navin with his high expectations. Last year had been miserable financially for the club and Navin desperately needed to see an increase in revenue. Cochrane was helping to sell tickets with his fervor.

In Lakeland Navin paused when he stepped from his vehicle into the muggy night air and onto the brick-paved road. Even in Florida, he wore a vested suit and starched hat. From the hotel emanated the raucous clatter of men and women singing and cheering. It sounded like a party. *" . . . In all my dreams, your fair face beams. You're the flower of my heart, Sweet Adeline."* Navin groaned. For a moment he remembered the rowdy, drunken gatherings of ballplayers in the days of his former manager Hughie Jennings. Wary of what he might find, he headed into the hotel. In the lobby with its white-and-black checkered floor and to-the-ceiling arched windows, Navin saw Cochrane and several players holding court.

To his great relief the men were entertaining a group of elderly tourists. The cheering ladies were gray-haired matrons, not babes, broads, or dolls.

"What do you say if we all sing 'Mammy'?" shouted Gee Walker, who at twenty-five could often be found at the center of team commotions. It would be said that in any discussion with Walker on one side and everyone else on the other the volume would be roughly the same.

Cochrane had a Hollywood-worthy cast, a veritable circus of characters. There was a Flea, a Firpo, a General, and a Chief, as well as a talisman-carrying, hard-drinking son of an absent trapeze artist, an outfielder branded "The Madman from Mississippi," a reserve who subsisted on bananas and donuts, and a 155-pound pitcher named for both a Founding Father and a confederate president: Thomas Jefferson Davis Bridges. The 1934 Tigers were nearly as varied as their fans and like them they carried their biases and prejudices everywhere. They were sons of miners, doctors, and tobacco farmers and they came from Dixie and Jersey and Texas, from privilege and homeless poverty. Among them were college fraternity brothers, elementary school dropouts, and, in at least one case, a raised-by-the-streets orphan. There were whiskey guzzlers and teetotalers. Most smoked. Some liked to brawl and some kept to themselves. There were Baptists, Methodists, Lutherans, Catholics, a Quaker, and a Jew, which made for complicated allegiances for the many Black Legionnaires who rooted for the Tigers. Two of the team's most prominent players—Charlie Gehringer and Hank Greenberg—belonged to faiths abhorred by the secret society.

In the burgeoning Catholic community, mothers saw the devout Gehringer as an athlete worthy of their sons' adulation, a figure they imagined as close to earthly sainthood as any they would find on a professional sporting field. "There's never been another like him," said Navin, a fellow Catholic. Gehringer was also co-owner Briggs's favorite player—a "perfect model for the [clerical] collar ads," according to the *Detroit Times*. Gehringer had grown up in a large farming family in Fowlerville, shirking his duties in favor of the game. He spent two semesters at the University of Michigan studying physical education before being discovered as a ballplayer. In 1926, his first year with the

Tigers, he fell under the tutelage of Ty Cobb, who recognized his hitting talent but wished Gehringer were more fiery. Now entering his ninth full season, Gehringer was regarded as the game's best second baseman. Still he remained quiet and humble.

One of the city's most famous Catholics—only radio priest Father Charles Coughlin, Bishop Michael Gallagher, and former mayor Frank Murphy could compete—Gehringer possessed a dry sense of humor, delivering cutting lines softly and subtly. His style would soon be on display on Monday nights on WJR, where his radio show, "Gehringer at Bat," would be debuting. Gehringer lived with his diabetic mother and attended church daily, vowing to remain single while she was alive, believing it unfair to bring another woman into the household. He glowed as husband material, one of the city's most eligible bachelors.

Hank Greenberg was another. A year ago, at age twenty-two, Greenberg had become the Tigers' first baseman—and, along with boxer Max Baer, one of the best-known Jewish athletes in the country. If not for Lou Gehrig and his consecutive games played streak, Greenberg might have signed with the Yankees. "I had to pick a team on which I was reasonably sure of obtaining a regular job," he said. The decision, according to *Free Press* baseball writer Charles P. Ward, showed Greenberg had a mind of his own. "Like most members of his race," Ward wrote, "he is also a smart businessman." Such stereotyping was a daily part of Greenberg's life. Jews and blacks—"darkies" in some stories—regularly endured such indignities and typecasting. (Ward had recently published what he no doubt viewed as a complimentary article about an honorable black Baptist deacon whom he praised for recovering foul balls for the Tigers. Ward peppered the piece with cartoonish dialogue: "Dah she comes. . . . Yassah, I preaches to 'em and sing to 'em . . .")

In his first season Greenberg, six-foot-three, had hit twelve home runs and knocked in eighty-five runs, a solid showing for a rookie. But he had also led the team in strikeouts and often looked as unsteady as a rangy colt. At camp Cochrane worked with Greenberg. He modified his stance, shortening his swing. Doing so, he reasoned, would help him hit more home runs. Not knowing that Greenberg was self-motivated, Cochrane brought

Harry Davis to camp to pressure Greenberg to improve. Davis had lost his job the previous season to Greenberg. He was the fallback.

Greenberg's faith was an issue for some teammates. It usually simmered beneath the surface. After a disappointing loss in Bradenton, Florida, Gee Walker boarded the team bus and noticed a grim expression on Greenberg's face. As he passed him, Walker waved his hand in front of Greenberg.

"Get that sour look off your puss, Greenberg," Walker said.

Greenberg wasn't in a pleasant mood, having gone hitless against Dizzy Dean's Cardinals. As the bus departed, cold air rushed through Greenberg's window. Near the back team trainer Denny Carroll yelled for Greenberg to close the window because it was getting cold. Carroll had a thing about drafty air and the health of his players. Greenberg didn't respond. Carroll asked again. Still no response. Rip Sewell was two seats behind Greenberg. In the row between them sat minor leaguer Jelly Collier.

Sewell tapped Collier's shoulder. "Hey, Bush," he said. "Pull the window."

"Bush" was slang for "minor leaguer."

Greenberg thought Sewell was talking to him.

"Who you calling a Bush, you southern son of a bitch?"

"Well, you—you big Jew bastard," said Sewell.

Greenberg told Sewell he was going to beat his ass once the bus stopped. When it arrived at the Terrace Hotel, Greenberg followed through. He and Sewell fought in the street for several minutes before a plainclothes cop interrupted their battle. Greenberg had won. The next morning Mickey Cochrane, who hadn't been on the bus, told Sewell that though he respected him for standing up to Greenberg, he was cutting him from the team. He needed the big first baseman. A day later, he announced Sewell's release.

The team was entirely white, of course. Black athletes were prevented from playing in the American and National Leagues. Instead, they competed in all-Negro leagues. The Stars had been Detroit's local entry but had moved to Columbus, Ohio, after the 1933 season. The semi-pro black Cubs would draw some of their fans in the coming year. But the Tigers had black fans too. They sat mostly in the informally segregated sections in the bleachers.

The Tigers were youthful. The club featured seven men twenty-five or younger who figured to contribute substantially. At camp those players received the bulk of Cochrane's attention. Like other player-managers, Cochrane found himself in the tricky position of leading several men who were his age or older. With them he adopted a mostly hands-off approach, bolstering their confidence but affording them the respect he felt they had earned.

Cochrane's greatest challenge was mental, getting his players to see themselves as something other than second-tier. "You're better than any team in the league," he told them repeatedly. "No club ever had the chance that you've got. You can hit and you can field and you've got pitching. . . . You can go around without that hang-dog expression that you've carried all these years." The speech, delivered over and over again, began to penetrate the young players' minds. This was the renowned Mickey Cochrane after all. A winner. He knew what it took. The guys in their twenties mostly ate up his encouragement. But with a few veterans, the pep talks provoked mental eye-rolling.

Leon "Goose" Goslin was the other champion who had been to the top. One day at camp, he came upon two older players doubting Cochrane's expectations. Goslin confronted them, calling them quitters. "You've been a second-division team for years because you believe you're a second-division team," he said. "No man is ever better than he thinks he is, and neither is any ball club."

Cochrane had plenty of projects at camp. But his major concern stood an inch taller than anyone else. Arkansan Schoolboy Rowe had impressed baseball observers in his 1933 debut season. But he had appeared in just one game after injuring his arm in July. Rowe arrived late to camp with the arm still sore. "It feels like it's going to fall off," he told trainer Denny Carroll, who rubbed him down. Two days later, the pain returned. Cochrane was growing frustrated. He remarked that Rowe might be sent to the minor leagues to rebuild his strength. The comment, combined with his glowing remarks about other prospects, amounted to psychological gamesmanship: Work through it or be replaced. The Tigers sent Rowe to Miami to be checked by a specialist. Cochrane's view of Rowe worsened when he learned from the doctor that Rowe had only minor inflammation. Nothing serious. Injuries he could deal with, but Cochrane had no respect for those he viewed as milking their ailments. Even if his arm were hurting, Rowe should be energetically going about his other duties.

Complicating matters was that Cochrane didn't fully believe in sore arms. Pitchers were losing their virility, he thought. "They've been babied so much that they've become a lot of mollycoddles," he confided to a reporter. "Pitchers are always complaining. They complain of this and they complain of that. They generally complain of sore arms. I get tired hearing about sore arms. . . . Sore arms have become ultra-fashionable among pitchers. They think they don't belong unless they have sore arms. It wasn't that way before. . . . These sore arms are mainly in the mind."

As the spring progressed, Cochrane lost sleep over Rowe. So much of the season hung on Rowe's pitching success. Cochrane tried to motivate Rowe by implying that other players resented him. "He is no star," he said. "He is only a rookie who has won seven games in the major league. I grant that we can use him and that he has great potentialities. But unless he gets in there and hustles like the rest of the gang, he will have to make room for somebody else. I am going to give him his choice."

Major-General Bert

THREE THOUSAND OR MORE BLACK LEGION MEMBERS, MOST OF THEM
armed, converged on a farm outside Oxford, Michigan, on a pleasant, dry
spring Saturday for a two-day general muster. Men roasted pigs and oxen,
and at midnight conducted skull-and-crossbones induction ceremonies.

Held a few times a year, musters were staged mostly at rural sites.
Locations changed because legion officials didn't want nonmember
police officers snooping around. Gatherings were held in Saline, south of
Ann Arbor, and outside Monroe, between Toledo and Detroit, and in the
Irish Hills area, below Jackson Prison, and in border states. Oxford, on
its way to becoming the gravel capital of America, sat forty-three miles
from Detroit and even closer to Flint and Pontiac, industrial cities with
significant populations and strong legion presences.

At the center of every muster stood Virgil "Bert" Effinger, the portly,
suspender-wearing major-general of the Black Legion. A veteran of the
Spanish-American War, Effinger made a modest living as an electrician.
He didn't have much in the way of money, managing the legion from
the basement and porch of his simple, five-room house in Lima, Ohio.
The legion didn't require dues of its members; Effinger wasn't in it for
the profit. Married and a father of four, including two teenage daughters,
he was in his early sixties. While overseeing the secret society, he ran for
sheriff as a Republican in Allen County. "I will shoot square with everybody," he declared, "and avoid if possible shooting at anybody." It was his
second campaign. In 1932 he had lost in the party primary. The eventual
winner was Democrat Jess Sarber, later killed by John Dillinger's posse
when they broke the gangster out of the Lima jail. Sarber's death did not
deter Effinger.

Effinger's proudest achievement, aside from his children, was the Black Legion and its exploding membership. Effinger boasted to his troops that their ranks had swelled into the millions. Three million, he said one time; six million, another. Both numbers amounted to wild exaggerations, but they served Effinger. By the early 1930s Effinger was the uncontested leader of the secret society. But he had not started it. Dr. Billy Shepard had.

In Bellaire, Ohio, where Shepard based his medical practice and served as the low-paid city health officer, residents regarded him as a "big wind jammer," a blowhard, and a braggart. Townsfolk had heard his angry rants against Catholics and foreigners, but they didn't fear him. Some mocked him. Most viewed him as about as dangerous as fermented cabbage. Even when he quipped about blowing up the local bank because it loaned money to European immigrants, the bank president did not take him seriously. "Doctor Billy," in the words of one observer, qualified as nothing more than a "drugstore orator."

Still, he had followers. Shepard had begun his secret organization in the 1920s after being kicked out of the Ku Klux Klan for establishing his own fiefdom. Back then he believed the Klan's ways had become pedestrian. The group lacked mystery and thrills. Shepard convinced a group of followers to replace their white KKK robes with black ones and to brand themselves the Black Guard. For a short while they caused trouble in eastern Ohio, western Pennsylvania, and northern West Virginia, whipping a local laborer who violated their sense of decency, threatening to hang a young man and tar his girlfriend, and forcing a black man onto a railcar headed south after he was seen socializing with a white woman. By 1929 FBI director J. Edgar Hoover had been made aware of the night-riding organization, but he had no name to attach to it and nothing came of the investigation. The legion withered quietly—until Effinger, two hundred miles west in Lima, visited Shepard and arranged to breathe new life into it. He shuffled Shepard into the role of a powerless figurehead and began to reorganize the group.

Using his old Klan connections, Effinger founded branches throughout the Midwest. At legion events he talked as if it were a national outfit, but it actually took root only in Michigan, Ohio, Indiana, and Illinois, with scattered activity in a few border states. The legion's unremarkable "Doctor Billy" origins could not inspire romantic life-and-death loyalty. Effinger fashioned more glorious histories. One traced its roots to colonial days, claiming Paul Revere and the Minutemen as early members and tying it to the Boston Tea Party. While Shepard's name still surfaced (as "Shotgun Shepard"), he had no real role in the current legion.

At musters, some of which stretched over three days, men slept in tents or cars or under the stars. A few had campers. Effinger stayed in the brigade headquarters, emerging from a trailer, often with a black fedora atop his balding head. A blustery man, he could—and did—talk for hours about true Americans and the danger of a multitude of "isms": communism foremost, but also socialism, fascism, Nazism, Trotskyism, Marxism, anarchism, radicalism, unionism, Catholicism, Judaism, Negroism, and more.

He regaled members with declarations of the legion's reach, saying it extended into all branches of government, including the FBI and state guards. The legion had absolutely infiltrated many police, court, and prosecutor's offices. In Detroit and Pontiac, legion members honeycombed the police forces. (Dayton Dean estimated one hundred officers belonged in Detroit alone.) Effinger claimed access to a vast array of weapons. On occasion at his home, he would bring down from the rafters an oversized map that he said showed the nation's hidden military installations, including one within the Statue of Liberty. "The first prerequisite of a prospective member is that he be a real patriotic American citizen," he said. (And a white Protestant, he should have added.) "The object of the Black Legion is preservation and perpetuation of our American ideals and social order."

The legion expanded aggressively through deception, threats, and brutality. Required to bring others into the organization, members invited friends who soon found themselves in a frightful predicament. Surrounded by armed men cloaked in ebony hoods and gowns, they took the legion's Black Oath, acknowledging the sentence of death for betrayal. Many went to their first legion meetings believing they were headed to political affairs. If they knew anything truthful beforehand, it was most often that the gathering would be for those opposed to communism. The issue resonated across wide swaths of America. "Nobody wants to see a red flag floating around," member Riley Sparrow said. "I thought the outfit was out to fight the reds."

Talk of communism surfaced continuously in the news and in discussions at work and home. In the Detroit area in 1932, in one of the region's defining moments, thousands participated in the communist-organized Ford Hunger March, which saw Dearborn police and Ford security forces, under the charge of Harry Bennett, Henry Ford's top lieutenant, open fire and kill four individuals. The funeral march that followed attracted tens of thousands. Taken against the backdrop of the Russian revolution fifteen years earlier and the current unrest throughout the region, the sight shook the city's political foundation.

During the Depression hints of rebellion pulsed through neighborhoods. Candidates who were neither Republican nor Democrat drew significant votes. In some local municipalities they were elected. Communists, socialists, and anarchists joined and led fledgling unions. *The Daily Worker* debuted a Michigan edition. Around the same time famed artist Diego Rivera, a Mexican Marxist, and wife Frida Kahlo lived in Detroit. He was laboring over his controversial Industry murals at the Detroit Institute of Arts, a project funded by Edsel Ford but deemed anti-capitalist by critics.

The Black Legion's dislike of leftists motivated many of its actions. Two members, one a Pontiac police sergeant, went undercover to a lecture intending to assassinate a celebrated communist speaker. But the event was so well attended that they didn't attempt it. At their meetings legionnaires heard from "White Russians," men who had fought the Bolsheviks in the 1910s. Legionnaires infiltrated enemy groups too, joining labor, socialist, and communist organizations as spies.

At the Oxford muster Major-General Bert Effinger complimented his underlings on the turnout. It was good, he said, "But not good enough." He implored them to do better. He emphasized the necessity of electing candidates who would support the legion's goals. He told of a mayor who had betrayed the legion by naming a Catholic to a top position. "A few weeks later, the mayor got tangled up with some gangster bullets and was found dead," he claimed.

Perhaps no legion leader spoke more passionately against communism than Arthur Lupp, who was the Michigan commander. Even more than Effinger, the nearly forty-year-old Lupp had a talent for delivering long monologues. He carried an air of self-righteousness and he looked more polished than his peers, often in suit and tie, his hair slicked back, his face smoothly shaven, wire-rimmed glasses polished and perched primly on his nose. Stump speeches came easily to Lupp. He spoke frequently at the legion's clandestine meetings about the principles that united legionnaires. His voice rose when he made an argument. Like a handkerchief-waving tent preacher, he could work himself to the point of hoarseness and perspiration. The legion, he said, gave men hope and purpose.

"When men have pledged themselves to be loyal to that flag," he said, pausing to salute for effect, "their days of service begin." Once he got rolling, he almost couldn't stop himself. His own voice stirred him like a rhapsody. "Now, I'm not in the habit of making speeches," he liked to say, but "on this one subject I have made many. I have gone among the farmers and I have preached the doctrine of Americanism, the doctrine of the flag, and the counteracting of communism. . . . We are opposed to all 'isms.' . . . We believe first, last, and always in pro-Americanism and support the Red, White, and Blue."

Raised in poverty on a farm outside Evansville, Indiana, Lupp had made something of himself professionally. He had acquired money and land, only to lose them before the market crash. In Detroit he built a new life. For a while he served as a sheriff's deputy. Now he worked for the city of Detroit as a health department milk inspector. Weeknights and weekends he devoted to the legion, planning, plotting, and recruiting. A letter to a Lansing man attests to his persuasive abilities. The man had promised to host meetings at his house but harbored second thoughts. He viewed the legion as a violation of his faith. Twice legionnaires drove two to three hours from Detroit to his home, only to find it locked and unoccupied. Lupp chided him:

I have had many disappointments in men during the last few years and still have managed to retain some faith in my fellow men. But when we find men who profess to be good clean Christian men and

*yet cannot be depended upon to serve their country, one loses faith. . . .
Our boys are not all Christians but when we give our word we make
every effort to keep in this fight for the preservation of our country,
homes, and all the ideals of freedom and liberty. Sometimes we become
even bitter at the thought of unreliable and incompetent men on every
hand, but we must remember the father of our country also had the
same things to contend with at Valley Forge and Denton. We too have
leaders who can kneel in the snow if necessary asking help from above.
But we must then be ready to fight. Prayer alone will not do the work.*

Effinger and Lupp were two of three key figures at the Oxford muster.
The third qualified as the least eloquent and the personally nastiest of
the trio. His walk always drew notice. Low-level legionnaires might not
recall his name, but they never forgot him. One Michigan man described
him typically as "some one-legged fellow." A chap in Indiana reported,
"The speaker at the meeting was a peg-legged man." Another related,
erroneously, that the lecturer, a former Detroit policeman, had lost a leg
in battle with the bootlegging Purple Gang.

Isaac "Peg-Leg" White, born in Canton, Ohio, had come to Detroit
in 1911. He found work guarding the homes of the wealthy before being
hired by city police. His law enforcement career did not last long. At age
thirty tragedy struck White while on the job. A police car accident (not
a gun-wielding gangster) cost him his leg below the knee. It also took
one of his thumbs. The year was 1916. White retired with half pay and
a lot of time on his hands. Over the next decades he kicked around as
a carpenter and an odd-jobs man and picked up extra money offering
security and information to manufacturers, including some targeted by
mobsters in a Prohibition-era malt tax racket. Through the Ku Klux
Klan's boom decade of the 1920s, he devoted himself to the Klan. In his
forties White remarried, this time to a woman twenty years younger from
the hills of Pennsylvania. She and White had a son, Teddy, now a toddler.
A confidant of Major-General Effinger, White had risen to become one
of the top Black Legion recruiters in the Midwest. He remained active
in manufacturing circles as an informant. Wherever communists or labor
organizers surfaced in the Detroit area, White seemed to surface as well.

In Lincoln Park, a suburb south of Detroit populated by workers from the massive, 70,000-employee Ford Rouge complex, White became a familiar presence, hobbling about on his shoeless stump, which was concealed beneath the baggy bell of a long left trouser leg. Councilman George Shanley reported that White threatened his life after Shanley asked for a police investigation into the mob beating of two leftist men who had sought to use a school auditorium for a political meeting. Not long after, someone shot at Shanley as he walked along Fort Street. Shanley complained to Lincoln Park police chief Charles Barker who, it turned out, belonged to a group that fronted for the legion.

Several times White had threatened George Marchuk, an officer of Local Seven of the communist-led Auto Workers' Union in Lincoln Park. Married and the father of a six-year-old daughter, Marchuk had been arrested over the years as an agitator. He had participated prominently in the Ford Hunger March. On a Friday morning three days before Christmas 1933—a week after the Tigers had hired Mickey Cochrane—two boys going to school discovered his body in a field beside a road. Marchuk had been shot once in the head. He had been on his way to a union meeting. Neither the police nor the dailies showed much interest in the crime. A small story played on the inside pages. RED's SLAYING STILL MYSTERY, said one headline. Police focused their minimal investigation on Marchuk's peers in the union and publicly blamed the killing on leftists. It was practically the same as closing the case.

During the time of the Ford Hunger March and in the years after, White worked for the Citizens Committee, a business-sponsored agency that supplied rosters of suspected radicals to auto-plant officials, who used the lists to fight the organizing of unions. White delivered lists to numerous factories, including Ford and Budd Wheel—"in fact," he said, "to all the plants that had strikes or threats of strikes." With two other Black Legion members, White carried one of those lists to the personnel department of Hudson Motor Company. It included the names of five men he identified as communists and saboteurs. One of them was John Bielak.

By the time of the Oxford muster, White's star was dimming in the eyes of Effinger. A few jobs hadn't gone smoothly and White may have been drawing too much attention to himself and jeopardizing the legion's stealthy nature. White moved his young wife and son hours from Detroit to Lyons, a little farming town northwest of Lansing, an area with an active Black Legion element. In 1931 Earl Little, father of the future Malcolm X, had bled to death on the streetcar tracks of Lansing. His wife, Louise, thought the Black Legion was responsible.

Peg-Leg White and family lived in a small frame house on a three-acre plot. He did odd jobs for neighbors, all while keeping his one foot in the legion. White's diminished role coincided with Arthur Lupp's soaring stature. Lupp took on more responsibilities and Effinger came up from Ohio regularly to confer with him, one time bringing a suitcase containing several grenades, which he flashed to legionnaires. Lupp was beginning to explore how he might use his job as milk inspector to further the legion's mission.

Among the thousands attending the Oxford muster was Dayton Dean. He loved the camaraderie and being in the center of the action. It was his sort of thing.

A Future Together

JOHN "JACK" BIELAK DROVE A SPORTY BLACK FORD COUPE WITH RED racing stripes and red wire wheels. Gregarious and likeable, he had come to Detroit from Toledo in the late 1920s, quickly meeting and marrying Wanda Wadelik. Soon after they had a daughter, Dolores. Wanda adored Jack, but he had trouble holding a job and too freely gambled away their money. She found that she couldn't live with him, so they separated but remained friendly. She still cared for him. So did her parents, who liked that he was Polish, a fact he disguised at the Hudson plant, where they knew him as Bailey.

By March 1934 Bielak, twenty-seven, had matured, and he and Wanda, a waitress, had reconciled. She appreciated that he had kept his job at the Gratiot factory, risen to be head of the metal finishers, successfully pushed for a wage increase for his department, and gotten his younger brother Joe a job there too. All of these signs pointed to a brighter future. Bielak acted almost giddy about his success in persuading co-workers to join the union local. One week he gathered ninety membership applications. Just recently, the men at the plant had stood with him, threatening to walk off the job when higher-ups tried to fire him for his union activities.

He and Wanda picked out a house along Six Mile Road, a little place with a yard for their four-year-old daughter. They planned to move in together. On the evening of Thursday, March 15, Bielak met her for dinner at her parents' place in Hamtramck. He discussed their future with her father, who approved of the reunion. That night, all of the Wadeliks thought John Bielak sweet. But he had rushed off early to meet his plant foreman. En route, he stopped to talk with his best friend about a develop-

30

ing strike action at the plant. His bosses knew him to be an organizer. Not long ago one of his friends had gotten a job at the factory, only to be fired the same day he was seen laughing and joking with Bielak.

After Bielak picked up his foreman, the man asked to be dropped off at a political meeting. It was being held less than a half mile from the Jefferson Avenue apartment that Bielak shared with his brother. Both places were close to the union hall. The meeting turned out to be a gathering of the Black Legion.

Later that night, thirty-seven miles south along a rural road in a small town near Monroe, a driver saw two cars stop abruptly. He braked and then heard the repeated pop of a gun and saw the flash of a shot. He grabbed his crankshaft, thinking he might be next. But the two cars fled past, leaving the scene silent, save for the mournful whistle of a train. Bielak's body—badly beaten and shot through both arms, the chest, and head—was discovered along the road, a union application tucked beneath his bloody head and fifty blank memberships cards stuffed in his pockets. A card for the Wolverine Republican League was also found on him. Bielak's foreman convinced Detroit Police that the killing had been committed by communists as part of an intra-party squabble.

Mystery solved. Case closed.

The Bee Is Buzzing

MICKEY COCHRANE'S INTENSITY HUNG OVER SPRING CAMP IN FLORIDA. He demanded his players hustle. When outfielder Frank Doljack moseyed toward first base on an easy out, Cochrane yelled: "We're running out everything this year. It's going to be expensive loafing to first." He wasn't joking. To reinforce the point, he started the Fine Club and appointed old-timer Fred Marberry as judge. If you didn't hustle, you'd pay ten bucks. That was the lighthearted punishment. In actuality if you didn't hustle, you might lose your job.

Cochrane wasn't above his own rules. In a spring game against Cleveland, with Charlie Gehringer on first, Cochrane lined to the shortstop. It was an easy catch, but the fielder trapped the ball, allowing him to double up Cochrane, who had stopped running. Gee Walker charged out of the dugout. "That'll just about cost you ten dollars, Mike," he said. Walker was beaming. "You would have been safe if you had run out that hit." Cochrane agreed and paid the money.

The first-year manager tried to inspire his charges with Knute Rockne speeches. "Now fellows, we're down here to work and get ready for a big season and no monkey business," he said. "I want every man to bear down and give all he's got. I want every man to be hustling all the time. I want every man out there on that field giving all to win ball games. . . . You're a better ball club than you think you are. You belong up there (in the standings) and you're going to be up there by hustling all the time and bearing down. Now let's hop to it."

Cochrane encouraged his players to be cocky and chesty. He favored those with spirit, like rookie Steve Larkin. When Cochrane asked him whether he'd be willing to pitch in relief, Larkin didn't just say yes.

"Willing?" he responded. "Why, I'll be sitting on that bench every day hoping you will send me into the game." That's what Cochrane liked to hear. That's what he wanted from hard-throwing Schoolboy Rowe, rather than Rowe's warped notion that he should be experimenting with the whimsical knuckleball, a dalliance that Cochrane quickly crushed.

After games Cochrane held "skull sessions" with his players, talking over opponents' strengths and weaknesses and looking for ways to improve. He worked on team unity. He wanted his men to socialize together. Many guys played pool across from the hotel and most golfed in the late afternoon, with Cochrane joining them. There were factions of course. The southern boys tended to hang together. Some of the veterans too. Roommates often grew close: Elden Auker and Tommy Bridges, Gehringer and Elon Hogsett, Rowe and Pete Fox, Flea Clifton and Billy Rogell. Everyone had a roommate except Goose Goslin, a fifteen-year veteran who had nine times driven in a hundred or more runs and whom Cochrane had picked up within days of becoming manager. Goslin stayed in a private hotel room, even when the team was at home. Goslin was prickly. (Later in the summer, bothered by pokey service in a dining car, he would hurl a water decanter through a train window.)

As the start of the regular season approached, the Tigers began to jell. Gehringer and Goslin looked ready. Greenberg, though suffering through hitless spells, settled in at first base. Cochrane bounced back from a bout of appendicitis, and Marv Owen won the third base job, his manager predicting that he would be the best in the league. Gee Walker was showing improvement on defense, and Bridges and Auker were impressing on the mound. As for Schoolboy Rowe's spring training, one day he would have a sore arm—prompting alarmist declarations from columnists: "his fate is in the lap of the gods and no one can tell now just what it will be"—and the next he would be painting the corners of the plate.

Frank Navin, in full suit and hat, turned out to watch the team daily. He ruminated about seasons past, recalling how he learned early not to interfere with his managers. He liked to tell how he had once ordered Hughie Jennings to start a pitcher against Jennings's judgment. The other team battered the man, costing the Tigers a game. Navin said that he had resisted the temptation to intrude ever since. "This is my thirty-first year in baseball and I'm still what I've always been, a grand-stand manager," Navin said. "And there are a few million of us scattered around the country."

In late March Navin arrived at the ballpark to see the recovering Rowe finally test himself. Schoolboy opened up and gunned several pitches at full speed. "Not so hard—not so hard," the owner admonished. "Wait until you have had a little more work before you begin to bear down that way." But Rowe was feeling good. He blazed several more fastballs. "It's all right, Mr. Navin," Rowe said. "It feels great. Tonight, Schoolboy Rowe is going to do some serious sleeping. It's a long time since I've been able to do that."

Rowe frustrated Cochrane. It wasn't just his sore arm and perceived laziness. Rumors were flying. A club official accused Rowe of violating training rules. The official said that a priest had spotted Rowe drinking and gambling and living a wild nightlife. "The priest" reported that Schoolboy had been ejected from several saloons. Rowe denied it all, saying it was "a pack of lies." Team officials didn't believe him. With a friendly disposition and a laid-back nature, Rowe was easily swayed by men and women of questionable character, they felt.

Vexed, Cochrane had earlier turned over Rowe's day-to-day super-vision to his coaches. Cochrane couldn't deal with him. It felt as if they were riding on different tracks. But finally the manager got behind the plate and caught Rowe for the first time. It was in a scrimmage against Montreal. In six innings Rowe allowed only two balls to leave the infield. Encouraged by the possibilities, Cochrane's earlier criticism melted like a Charleston chocolate on summer sand. "There isn't a pitcher in baseball today with a better fastball than Rowe's . . . it was unhittable," he said. Teammate Gehringer added, "I've never seen anything like it."

Owner Frank Navin remained with the Tigers as they headed north, which was unusual. After they swept Cincinnati in several scrimmages, he decided to go to the opening game at Chicago's Comiskey Park. When was the last time he had been on the road to witness the start of a Tigers season? He couldn't remember. Usually, he retreated to his own ball field and prepared for the home debut. Perhaps sensing that something special was underway, Navin made an exception. The Tigers rewarded him with a convincing 8–3 victory. He headed back to Detroit as Cochrane's team finished its road trip. After four games the Tigers were 3–1. The last victory was a ninth-inning win in Cleveland. It raised expectations almost overnight. "The championship bee is buzzing in the ears of Detroit fandom," noted *Free Press* sports editor M. F. Drukenbrod. The season wasn't yet a week old.

In his office Navin spoke with uncharacteristic exuberance. He couldn't say enough about Cochrane. He could hardly believe what he had witnessed in Florida and in the first game in Chicago—how the new manager had fired up the team, got the players thinking differently, envisioning themselves as winners, not as perennial, sure-to-fall-short, not-quite-good-enough entrants in a pointless crusade. And then there was Goose Goslin, the other veteran acquisition, the other proven champion. What an impression he had made on the whole team by insisting, against doctor's orders, that he be allowed to play in the opener—with a fractured nose and two black eyes. "When the rest of the fellows saw this sort of spirit, they became imbued with it," Navin said.

At his grand desk, ornamented with an oval-framed picture of his wife in her youthful days, Navin grinned at a reporter. Cochrane stirred something in him. He summoned Navin's early years with the team, back when he was a robust man, a go-getter relatively fresh out of law school. Cochrane reminded him of those glory days.

"He's the nearest thing to Hughie Jennings I have ever seen," said Navin. "He's got the same flaming spirit that made Hughie famous—the same unbounded enthusiasm and seemingly unlimited energy. He's up and at them all the time, setting the pace and leading the fight every minute of the way. . . . Jennings was always raring to go. He liked nothing better than a battle. Mickey is the same way."

Coming from Navin, there was no higher praise than to be compared to Hughie Jennings. During Navin's tenure eight men had guided the Tigers on the diamond. Jennings was the only one to have taken Detroit to the World Series. He had done it three times. Navin did not come out then and say it, but one needn't read much into his enthusiasm to know what he was hoping by invoking Jennings's name: Cochrane might indeed be the man to finally deliver a world championship.

Neither Threats Nor Bribes

ART KINGSLEY, NOT LONG OUT OF AN ILLINOIS COLLEGE WHERE HE HAD been a football star, visited Highland Park, Michigan, in the early 1910s while working for Western Newspaper Union. He found a town that thanks to Henry Ford was booming. Kingsley, a short man who smoked aggressively, wanted to be part of it. He started a local paper, the *News*, and began building his future. Not long after, the Great War interrupted, temporarily derailing his dream. When he returned in 1919, Kingsley relaunched the publication, bought his competition (*The Times*), and merged the two into the *Highland Parker*.

An enclave literally surrounded by Detroit, Highland Park swelled in population between 1910 and 1920, increasing tenfold. Families flocked to the community, drawn by well-paying manufacturing jobs at Ford's 120-acre Woodward Avenue complex. New Model Ts rolled off the assembly line in mesmerizing numbers, one every three minutes. In 1925, just blocks away Chrysler christened its new headquarters, close to the railroad lines, attracting even more residents to the bungalows and apartment complexes that lined leafy streets.

A lifelong bachelor, Kingsley devoted himself to his work. He relished his role as publisher and enjoyed the allegiance of employees who fondly called him The Boss. Every Thursday his newsboys blew their whistles as they delivered to subscribers. "The whistle means your paper is on the porch," proclaimed the weekly's tagline. As his *Highland Parker* grew, Kingsley—friends called him Art, but his byline, Arthur L. Kingsley, carried a more regal flair—became a powerful force in city politics, aggressively pursuing stories and ardently endorsing favored candidates and crusading against opponents. So strong was his newspaper that even those he mocked had to advertise on his pages.

Kingsley had known N. Ray Markland since 1928, when "Billy Ray," as chums called him, became a city commissioner. He did not impress Kingsley. "He is not very smart," he once wrote of the councilman. When Markland sought a promotion to mayor in 1932, Kingsley took aim with a barrage of ink-filled bombs. In a special "Edition of Progress" days before the election, he published two long front-page editorials against Markland, without ever mentioning his name. POLITICIANS CANNOT MUZZLE THIS NEWSPAPER read the banner headline. It charged that elected officials were dangling the city printing contract in exchange for endorsements. "Neither threats nor bribes can purchase our support," he wrote. "Spinelessness does not happen to be our weakness." Kingsley endorsed former judge James Ellmann for mayor, describing him as "vastly better equipped." Kingsley noted that Markland had admitted he wasn't a bright man, a statement the editor echoed in print. "His modest appraisal of his own mental equipment may be quite correct," Kingsley wrote. Markland's campaign ads, in fact, seemed to hint at such, touting no qualifications and highlighting mainly this promise: "I shall do what I think is right." In public Markland referred to Ellman as "a damn Jew." "Watch me take that hook out of his nose," he said. Kingsley, a Catholic, chided Markland, saying his prejudice rendered him unfit "for any office in this democracy." He added, "Intolerance of race or religion, or bigotry of belief, conclusively establish this fact always—whoever admits them, denies his own right to represent all races and all religions in the city government in any capacity. . . . We are peculiarly in a position to know the qualifications for office of the men now seeking election, and on the basis of our knowledge, we are urging the election of the one we consider immeasurably superior in every respect."

Kingsley was not alone in his low opinion of Markland. A reporter for a Detroit daily also characterized him as "not an intellectual giant or a man of any marked brilliance." A native of Indiana, Markland also could not be accused of being debonair in appearance. His meaty shoulders set off a jowly face that featured wild, wiry eyebrows, deep, asymmetrical eyes, and a smile flecked with gold teeth. Regardless, Markland had the secret support of the clandestine Black Legion, and Highland Park voters elected him mayor. The outcome wasn't so much a rousing endorsement as a judgment against the faith of his Jewish opponent.

The election did not end the war between Kingsley and Markland. When Mayor Markland ousted several department heads, Kingsley ran their photos with the notation: "Sacrificed at the altar of political ambition." Throughout Markland's term, Kingsley took aim, blasting him relentlessly for a bond deal that cost the city $19,000. "I have always been critical of the city fathers when I thought they were not competent," said Kingsley. For good measure he added that Markland lacked "the ability to be mayor of any city."

After a year in office, Markland had weathered all the criticism he could handle and began to plot more elaborately against Kingsley. One day he got a supporter to arrest Kingsley and editor Curtis Swanwick on a charge of criminal libel. They were held in the county jail for a few hours before a judge released them. Another time Markland confronted Kingsley at a meeting and snarled a vague threat. He promised to get him. Kingsley, accustomed to such warnings, took it to mean that Markland would get him politically, but Markland had other ideas. He wanted Kingsley out of the way. Permanently.

The Black Legion—called the Bullet or Malekta Club in Highland Park—wielded significant municipal power. Numerous city figures and their followers belonged, including a councilman, police officers, and fire officials. Their biases spread along a spiteful scale from serious (attempts to block blacks from moving into neighborhoods) to silly (qualms about renaming Six Mile Road for Father John McNichols, the late Jesuit president of the nearby University of Detroit). Mayor Markland, a central figure in the local legion, turned to his friends for help in dealing with the troublemaking editor. Among them was Black Legion state commander Arthur F. Lupp.

When legion leaders wanted action, they filtered their orders down through their military-style ranks, reminding members of the life-and-death pledges they had made to fulfill their assignments. Lower-level members got "picked" to handle the dirtiest work. In July 1933 at his cottage at Lake Orion, thirty miles outside of Detroit, Markland assigned Gordon Smith to bump off Kingsley, promising him a job with the city fire department if he succeeded. Later Lupp gave Smith a .45-caliber army pistol. Another man handed him fifty dollars to help with expenses. Smith used the money to rent a room under the alias Willis Hudson at a small hotel not far from where Kingsley lived. While Smith had completed some assignments for the legion—infiltrating a communist group, for example—he drew an unspoken line at murder. He had no intention of killing Kingsley. Eventually Lupp got wise to him and told him it would be his own fault if he got shot "through a window with a rifle that had a silencer attached."

Somebody else would have to do the job. On a chilly evening Col. Roy Hepner, a metal finisher by day, took Dayton Dean and several other legionnaires to a field north of Eight Mile Road. There the men entered into a pact. Each cut his hand, dipped a matchstick in his own blood, and signed his name to paper. They resolved to do as told, whatever the assignment. It was a test of their commitment, an attempt to flush out the squeamish. They all signed and on the drive back Hepner revealed that publisher Art Kingsley needed to die and that Dean must do the job. The others were tasked with ensuring that he did.

Dean received a blackjack from Markland and a pistol from Lupp. He built a compartment in the floor of his car to conceal the weapons. He had never seen Kingsley and did not know him by sight. It fell to a fire department captain to point out the journalist to Dean while sitting with him in a restaurant between Kingsley's apartment and office. Kingsley lived in a third-floor unit about a block from the Woodward Avenue home of the *Highland Parker*, which stood next to Sievert's Radio Store and across from Koslow's Grocer and Manufacturers National Bank. While waiting for Kingsley, the fire captain ordered himself a meal. He got Dean just a glass of milk. (Such rudeness would not be forgotten.) Kingsley entered the diner and sat three tables over.

"There's your man," the fire official said quietly. "Look him over good."

In the weeks that followed, Dean waited for Kingsley outside his apartment, near his office, and in the restaurant. The circumstances were never quite right and the publisher always managed to slip away. Lupp and Markland tired of the delays. They reminded Dean that three men had been assigned to kill him should he let them down. At a Black Legion meeting they chastised Dean for his failures. They also discussed a variety of new approaches. They could try to lure Kingsley on a hunting trip and Dean could kill him en route. Or Dean could tail Kingsley to Lefty Clark's gambling establishment and shoot him when he exited. (Kingsley had a fondness for cards and craps.) Or Dean could join the local American Legion, in which Kingsley was active, to get a better sense of his comings and goings. Easily manipulated, Dean admitted that he had failed and promised to do better.

With money provided by his superiors, Dean began attending American Legion meetings. He asked fellow veterans about Kingsley. What he heard intrigued him. They all respected the man. They described him as one of the post's finest, and they applauded his efforts to help veterans. A Navy man himself, Dean liked what he heard. During Christmas week, days after Mickey Cochrane had become the Tigers' manager, Dean and another man were following Kingsley. They pulled alongside his car near Woodward Avenue. Dean had a clear shot but didn't take it, claiming that he was too close to the main thoroughfare and might hit an innocent person. The driver was furious.

Two Highland Park police officers, also legion members, were drawn into the Kingsley plot. Dean met with them in a patrol car near the railroad tracks. They told him that after he killed Kingsley they would help him escape the city limits. In truth they had orders of their own: to shoot Dean as he fled. Doing so meant that Kingsley would be dead, the assassin killed, and the cops glorified. The plan fizzled when Dean skipped the follow-up meeting.

On another evening Dean and two companions drove to Kingsley's place and waited for him to exit. Kingsley noticed their car and pointed it out to friends. He was aware someone had been following him. It was an effort to scare him, he figured. He had made a habit of always checking his rearview mirror and maneuvering onto side streets to gauge whether he was being shadowed. Dean and company chased Kingsley that winter night as snow glistened in the streetlights. Given the presence of other Black Legion members, Dean knew that if they got close he would have to shoot Kingsley or be shot. For six miles—through the streets of Highland Park and into Detroit—Dean and company tailed the publisher. They nearly caught him, but Kingsley turned abruptly and blew through traffic lights. He owned a new car and it was faster than theirs. The pursuit lasted fifteen minutes. A few blocks from Detroit's mammoth Masonic Temple, Kingsley lost the legionnaires.

Through the winter and into the spring of 1934, Dean hosted small Black Legion initiations in his home. He wore his gun in a holster around his waist and kept a suitcase with rawhide whips and nooses under his bed. He borrowed chairs from a local undertaker, sometimes two dozen, sometimes fifty, and set them up in the basement. Before the men began arriving at night through a side door, Dean's wife would leave the house. If their four children—her two and his two—hadn't fallen asleep, she would take them with her, returning only after the men had left, usually around midnight. The Black Legion had become a daily affair for Dean.

As the spring 1934 vote approached in Highland Park, with Kingsley still hammering Mayor Markland in print, a fake newspaper appeared with a special pre-election issue. Banner headlines crowded its pages. Rather than targeting Markland's opponent, it took aim at publisher Kingsley. SHALL 'DICTATOR' KINGSLEY RUN HIGHLAND PARK? WILL KINGSLEY RULE HERE? Stories referred to him as Boss Kingsley and Czar Kingsley and compared him to Mussolini and Hitler.

Mayor Markland and the Black Legion lost the election on April 5, 1934, to Joseph "Honest Joe" Hackett, whom Kingsley had endorsed. In the days after, Arlington Jones, a city employee, came to Kingsley with a bizarre story. He told him how he had been tricked into joining a secret society, enticed to a meeting by word that a black family was moving onto a nearby street. He said he had been forced to take an oath at gunpoint. He now feared he would be killed. After his initiation Jones had told an acquaintance that he didn't like the group and wanted no part of it. Mayor Markland and others had heard and confronted him. They had warned that he would face serious trouble if he didn't keep his mouth shut. Jones told Kingsley all of this and recalled parts of the Black Oath, the threats of floggings and murder, and the evil things happening within the group.

Kingsley found the story unbelievable but shared it with the new mayor. He thought it inconceivable that anyone in their city would resort to murder over politics. Still, he told Jones to report it to the office of county prosecutor Duncan McCrea. He did. But no one there was interested. Jones went to the Detroit bureau of the Federal Department of Justice. Agents viewed his story as a bag of mumbo jumbo. No one believed "Little Arly" Jones. They wondered if he had been hallucinating. Agents directed Jones to file a complaint with the Highland Park Police. Weeks earlier, Jones had spotted Highland Park cops at a Black Legion gathering in the basement of a church, two blocks behind Mickey Cochrane's apartment. The cops belonged to the secret society. He knew better than to complain to them. So he let it go.

Not long after his defeat, former mayor Markland found work as an investigator—for Prosecutor Duncan McCrea.

It Hurt for Days

EARLY SPRING'S OPTIMISM WILTED AFTER THE TIGERS FELL INTO FIFTH place. Mickey Cochrane juggled his lineup throughout April and May, trying to find a combination that could win consistently. Every few days he gave someone new a whirl in the leadoff spot: first Billy Rogell, then Jo-Jo White, then Pete Fox, then back to White, then Frank Doljack, then Fox again. When Cochrane made out a lineup, the only players assured to be hitting in the same positions were the last two, Marv Owen and whoever was pitching. For a long while Cochrane batted himself third, the spot frequently reserved for the team's best hitter. But he struggled, hitting sixty, seventy, and eighty points below average. Midway through the fifteenth game, he pulled himself out of the lineup. He stayed out only for a day and a half. Cochrane's frustrations mounted. Aside from Charlie Gehringer, none of the stars started strongly. Greenberg managed one home run in the first twenty-seven games. Goslin scuffed out a hit every four at bats or so. The pitchers faltered too. Even psychologically.

Schoolboy Rowe faced booing from Tigers fans in his third appearance. The greeting staggered him as he charged toward the mound in the ninth inning of a relief assignment. He said he felt like running straight to the train depot and jumping a car to Arkansas. "Boy, I'm just telling you, it was terrible," he said. "I could feel those cold chills playing leapfrog up and down my spine. I like to died." Fox, one of his friends, said Rowe had been longing for Edna, his sweetheart back home. They had been together for eight years. She was his first love and he hers. In school they used to write love notes behind their textbooks. Rowe hinted that they might marry. "I'm going to surprise all of you guys," he said. Two weeks later, with Rowe still floundering, Cochrane debated whether to demote him to the minor leagues.

Mental mistakes plagued the team. Forgetting there were two outs, rookie pitcher Steve Larkin fielded a grounder and pivoted to throw to third base. When he realized he had no chance to get the runner, he turned in a rush and flung the ball wildly beyond Greenberg at first. A run scored. Base runner Heinie Schuble also lost count of the outs, thinking there were two when Fox hit an easy pop to second. Schuble, running full throttle toward home, got doubled off third base.

And then there was Gee Walker. No one could set off Cochrane like Walker. On May 21 he got picked off second base—the third time he had been caught in a month. Another ten dollar fine followed. The Tigers had decided that the penalty money would go to the clubhouse teen at the end of the season. "Unless the [Tigers] change their ways," noted a reporter, "the lad will probably step right out and buy the ball park from Mr. Navin as soon as he receives his dough."

Cochrane couldn't catch a break. The streak of aggravation even touched his personal life in a minor way when his son's bike was stolen. Hoping the thief would return it, police portrayed the disappearance as possibly a mistake, noting that nine-year-old Gordon might have lost his ride. But he hadn't. The twenty-eight-inch, red-and-white, chrome-wheeled bike with electric lights on the front and rear had been pilfered as more of the Cochranes' belongings were transferred from Philadelphia to their apartment near Palmer Park. It was the kind of bike that not every family could afford, especially during the Depression.

Cochrane was gloomy, tense, and often angry. Connie Mack, his beloved old boss, noticed it when his Philadelphia Athletics came to town on Wednesday, May 23. Mack was seventy-one, a year older than Henry Ford, whom he had met during spring training. Mack stood out on the ball field in part because of his age—nearly two decades older than anyone else in the dugout—but also because of his clothes. Mack wore a business suit on the field. His public persona was that of a wise old grandfather. After his team blistered the Tigers 11–5, Mack headed over to the Detroit Yacht Club, where he was being honored. Cochrane was sitting in the high-ceilinged, chandeliered lounge looking glum.

"What's the matter, Mickey," said Mack. "Don't you feel well today?"

"I'd feel better if we'd won that game this afternoon," Cochrane replied.

Mack had long ago learned to move on after a loss.

University of Michigan football coach Harry Kipke, Athletics slugger Jimmie Foxx, and Red Wings coach Jack Adams were sitting with Cochrane. All had come to hear Mack speak. Kipke told Cochrane he had a "hunted look" in his eyes.

"What's the matter?" he asked. "Are the wolves out already?"

Cochrane didn't laugh. He admitted that he had been getting nasty letters. "Some of them are tough, and it's tough on the boys," he said. "Hell knows they're trying."

Adams tried to cheer him. "Bet you five bucks that for every letter you get calling you a tramp, you get a dozen telling you you're okay," he said.

It didn't work. Cochrane began listing his team's failures. Before he got far, Kipke cut him off. "It's a mystery to me why a manager like you with a team in third place in a tough league should worry. . . . Here's what I'm worrying about: Where will I crawl next fall after Michigan takes a beating from Ohio State, Illinois, and Minnesota? Now, there's something to worry about." (He was right to be worried; the Wolverines would lose all of those games and more, scoring only twenty-one points all season.)

At the banquet in front of a thousand club members, Mack talked of Cochrane without mentioning the encounter in the lobby. Mack recalled how he had motivated his team during a slump years ago. Cochrane was the hardest-working player on the Athletics and all of his teammates knew it. Mack contrived to rally the others by scolding Cochrane publicly for the team's flop. He figured the lecture would force Cochrane's teammates to reflect on their own lackluster contributions. In that long-ago outburst, he placed the blame squarely on Cochrane.

"I want to apologize for saying that to Mickey," he told the crowd on Belle Isle. Mack noted, however, that that the ploy had worked and the team had rebounded. More seriously, he added, "I let Mickey come to Detroit because I didn't want to stand between him and a career as a manager. That was the real reason why I allowed him to leave. I believe he is going to be one of the really great managers of the game. Like all new managers, he is trying too hard at present. He is taking baseball too seriously. Fifty years as a manager of a baseball team has taught me a lesson that Mickey has yet to learn."

———

Boxing teams from twenty states converged on St. Louis for the national Amateur Athletic Union championships. Of the hundreds competing one boxer was drawing the most attention by far. Word had been spreading about the promising fighter from Detroit's Black Bottom neighborhood. In a short time he had risen from the city's Golden Gloves competition to the top tier of American amateurs. No one wanted to miss this emerging phenom, this "baby-face Negro," as some writers were calling him. As Joe Louis, a light-heavyweight, slipped into the ring for his title match, aficionados of the sport rushed to their seats.

Joe Louis Barrow came to Detroit at age thirteen in 1926 after his mother and stepfather, Lillie and Pat Brooks, had moved north from Alabama with their oldest sons. A close call with the Klan had prompted Brooks to head to Michigan to seek a better life for his family. "The Ku Klux Klan stopped them and was going to pull them from the car," recalled Louis's sister Vunies. "Someone in the crowd recognized my stepfather. He said, 'That's Pat Brooks. He's a good nigger.' . . . My stepfather . . . made up his mind that night he was leaving Alabama." After Brooks had settled into a job, he and his wife sent for their children, who were staying with family. In Detroit Joe floundered in school but got work. He shoveled snow. He sold ice in the summer and coal in the winter from a horse cart. Later he operated a lathe. When he discovered boxing at the Brewster Center—famously redirecting the money his mother had given him for violin lessons—he began to see his future take shape. As Louis plowed through opponents, others took notice.

"When he hit you, it hurt for days," said Eddie Futch, who had sparred with him.

In Missouri the AAU match did not last long. Louis dropped his opponent, Arlo Soldati of Princeton, Illinois, three times in two rounds. His final punch, a right to the head, put Soldati on the mat, unconscious, for five minutes. Nat Fleischer, covering the bout for *Ring* magazine, called Louis "the most promising heavyweight prospect" he had seen since Max Schmeling in 1926. James Zerilli, writing for Louis's hometown fans, said Louis had honored himself as "the classiest and most finished boxer" at the tournament. The black press lavished attention on Louis as a posse of trainers, managers, and racketeers pushed to get a piece of his lucrative future. They wanted to take Louis into the professional ranks. He wasn't yet twenty.

The Tigers exploded at the end of May. They swept the Boston Red Sox at Navin Field, split a four-game series in St. Louis against the Browns, and then won eight of ten games against Cleveland and Chicago, scoring more than ten runs in five of those contests. In a cycle of three games, they accumulated forty-three runs—twenty in one thrashing of the Indians. By the end of the second week of June, Detroit sat in first place, ahead of New York.

But the Yankees were also playing well. Thirty-nine-year-old Babe Ruth was winding down his tenure in pinstripes. He would last one more season in the majors. After the previous campaign New York had tried to unload Ruth, offering him as a playing manager and a gate draw. Frank Navin had considered him for a while, but the deal grew complicated with demands and delays, and ultimately Navin favored Cochrane. Ruth could still hit on occasion. In a two-game series against the Tigers, he popped three home runs. But he was becoming a liability overall. Sports editor Harry Salsinger, who had witnessed Ruth's entire career, offered a blunt assessment. He described Ruth as a "distinct handicap" in the field and on the bases. "The Babe is fatter than before and slower, and Joseph McCarthy, the manager of the Yankees, dislikes to think of what will happen after the middle of June when the scorching sun dries the base paths and hardens them and steams the vim and vigor out of the ball players."

The Tigers' victories cheered Mickey Cochrane, but not for long. He was bracing for a critical fifteen-game road trip to Boston, New York, Washington, and Philadelphia. "If we finish our present swing through the east with an average of .500 or better, we will be in an excellent spot for the dash down the stretch," he said. "Just give us an even break or better now and the boys will find us very, very tough when we get back on our own lot."

Cochrane settled on a lineup in early June. He deviated occasionally, but most often he batted Fox first, placed himself second, and followed with Goslin, Gehringer, Rogell, Greenberg, Walker, Owen, and the pitcher. After games at Fenway Park and Yankee Stadium, the Tigers were on target to meet Cochrane's goal of breaking even on the road trip. Detroit arrived in Washington on June 19, the day before they were to face the defending American League champions. Goose Goslin offered a bold prediction. He said Detroit would take four of five games at Griffith Stadium. Goslin had played with the Senators last year and despised some of them. The Tigers were able to pry him away because of his clashes with manager Joe Cronin.

Leading the league and being a major leaguer carried responsibilities, Cochrane believed. One of them was to represent your club in a dignified fashion. The Tigers stayed at the elegant Wardman Park Hotel, not far from the National Zoo. One morning, Cochrane headed into the fancy main dining room for breakfast. He was astounded to discover four of his young players wearing unclean club sweaters. He expected them in sports coats. "This sort of stuff belongs in a Class B league," he told them at a team meeting that afternoon. "From now on act like champions off the ball field as well as on, and pay a little attention to your appearance. Make people respect you outside the ball park as well as inside the park. Don't ever forget that you are the top team in the American League and act like it."

The Tigers played like a first-place team. They proved Goslin correct and took four of the five Washington games. Goslin contributed by scoring eight runs and knocking in six. It was onto Philadelphia next, where Detroit took two out of three—and would probably have taken another had Connie Mack not canceled the fourth game. He called it for wet conditions, but seeing as it had not rained, the more likely reason was dismal ticket sales. Mack figured he'd be better off hosting a doubleheader later.

The road trip was a flag-waving success. Hank Greenberg stood out, driving in twenty-four runs in fifteen games. Gehringer scored twenty-one times. Goslin got twenty-five hits. And Gee Walker, the high-spirited buck who tested Cochrane's patience, launched a 400-foot home run, chased down a long fly with a remarkable over-the-shoulder catch, and raised his average twenty points. The trip filled Walker with confidence. A bit too much.

The Tigers headed into St. Louis, home of the lowly Browns, with a half-game lead over New York. The next week would be telling. The Tigers would be playing three doubleheaders in five days. Two would be back-to-back—in different cities. The schedule promised to be exhausting, but Cochrane hoped to put distance between his team and the Yankees. In the eighth inning on June 30, with the game tied 3–3, the Tigers saw a chance to pull ahead. Greenberg singled and Gee Walker advanced him to second while beating out a grounder. Detroit had two runners on base with Marv Owen batting. Then the trouble began. Walker got daring and stepped too far off first base, prompting catcher Rollie Hemsley to rifle the ball to first baseman Jack Burns. They had Walker trapped, so Greenberg headed toward third to take the pressure off Walker. Greenberg got caught in the rundown and the speedier Walker advanced to second. Moments later, Browns pitcher Jack Knott wheeled around and picked Walker off second base. Two sloppy base-running errors cost the team its best shot. The Tigers lost 4–3 in ten innings. New York regained first.

Walker's carelessness flabbergasted reporters. One called him "the chief squanderer" and singed him for "his characteristic crack-pottery" and for acting as foolishly "brave as the boy on the burning deck." Another criticized him as "dizzy."

Cochrane was livid. After the game he raged in the dugout. He carried his anger into the clubhouse and then sequestered himself in his hotel room that evening, not leaving until lunch the next day. He had worked so hard to tame Walker in spring training. And now this? Twice in one inning? Of a tied game? With first place on the line? Cochrane suspended Walker and ordered him out of uniform. Walker watched the next day's doubleheader from the stands in street clothes. Afterward, on Cochrane's command, he boarded a train back to Detroit as the team headed to Cleveland.

"All I wanted to do is to get that fellow out of my sight in a hurry," Cochrane fumed. "I'm through with that fellow. I've done everything I could to help him. Everybody has tried to help him. And then he goes and kicks away a ball game through reckless, stupid blundering. It would not be fair to the other players to keep a fellow of Walker's type around."

Cochrane wanted to send him to the minor leagues as punishment, but Browns manager Rogers Hornsby said he would claim Walker, which forced the Tigers to either give up on him entirely or take him back. They didn't decide instantly. Walker's wife, with their small sons, picked him up at the train station. He was in a somber mood. He headed home, changed into a dress shirt, and went quickly to the ballpark to meet with Frank Navin, where he apologized profusely and promised to be more cautious if given another chance. The decision would be Cochrane's, and he wouldn't make it until he came back to town, Navin said. Walker headed down to the field and worked out "like a freshman footballer anxious to get in shape for the opening of the season," wrote Tod Rockwell of the *Free Press*.

The Tigers returned home for a July 4 doubleheader. Thirty-eight thousand fans packed into and onto Navin Field. Among them, with a fedora tilted over his left eye, was Gee Walker, whose request to suit up had been rejected by Cochrane. "I guess I had it coming," Walker said. In the outfield a mass of fans stood in front of the fences and sometimes made way for the fielders when balls were hit in their direction. Police on horseback patrolled the grounds, pushing back the men in their straw hats and the children in their shorts as they encroached on the territory. Navin Field had not seen such a crowd in half a decade. It had been a long time since the Tigers found themselves in the heart of a pennant race. A mania was beginning to percolate throughout the city.

After the Independence Day doubleheader—one win, one loss— Cochrane brought the team together for a private clubhouse meeting. He put the decision in the players' hands: Give Gee Walker another chance or cut him loose? By secret ballot they voted him back onto the team.

Walker was made to apologize to his teammates, serve out a ten-day suspension, and pay a twenty-dollar fine. The experience deflated him. He was, one witness said, "thoroughly chastened," the "saddest man" in the dugout, and "fighting off a severe case of the blues."

The next day, an off day, saw Cochrane, Walker, and the rest of the team at the horse races at the Michigan State Fair Grounds.

Perhaps Dayton Dean was there. He lived just blocks away.

The Little Stone Chapel

HEINRICH PICKERT TOOK OVER AS DETROIT POLICE COMMISSIONER IN April. A well-known character in city circles, he had served as commander of the Michigan National Guard, heading up parades on horseback in full regalia. When the cornerstone was laid for the Masonic Temple and President Warren Harding came to town, Col. Pickert, as he liked to be called, played a central role in organizing the stunning procession. He had also been the city's chief customs collector, appointed by President Hoover.

Born poor to German immigrants and raised in the Irish district of Corktown near the Tigers ballpark, Pickert provided reporters with good copy. He had color. He believed in astrology. He collected Oriental rugs. ("No one can tell what patience and what industry, what joy and sorrow, has gone into an old Oriental.") He had been awarded a Purple Heart in the Great War.

Col. Pickert had definite ideas about how his police officers should act. His first order as commissioner was to forbid officers from chewing gum. "Gum and police work don't go together," he said. "Imagine how a police officer looks walking down the street and in public places with his jaws working like a cow munching a cud." Col. Pickert didn't care much for tobacco chewing either, but he allowed it in moderation. He insisted on a more militaristic feel for his police force. He liked to be saluted fully, not halfheartedly, and the sight of officers with their feet on furniture or windowsills, or with their chairs tilted against walls, could set off a tirade. He called for clean white shirts to be worn without suspenders (unless covered by a coat). He also preferred that officers not have facial hair. His own face, clean-shaven, was topped by light-colored hair, cut starkly and parted crisply over his left eye.

Beyond his quirks and personality, Col. Pickert instituted a hard line against protesters, radicals, and labor organizers. Claims of police brutality rose under his administration, and the Special Investigations Division evolved into a Red Squad. He did not hide his feelings on these matters. Col. Pickert and his wife, Julie, spoke freely about their beliefs. They had met in their forties through patriotic organizations. Both were active in the American Legion. At the downtown Women's City Club, to which Julie belonged, Col. Pickert boasted that the police department kept lists of radicals and watched their activities "all the time." He accused Detroit public school educators of "teaching, living, talking, and breathing" communism. "The appalling thing is that the people in whom we put so much faith are forgetting their Americanism and teaching this rotten doctrine," he said. "If we allow these instructors to remain in our schools, pretty soon we will be on the downgrade." He worried about unions and labor troubles. "I wish we could have a showdown soon," he said.

The Black Legion was also ready for such a confrontation. By mid-1934 the legion had expanded in southeast Michigan to four regiments of 1,600 men in Detroit, one regiment in Highland Park, one in the downriver area south of the Ford Rouge plant, two farther south near Monroe, two north of Detroit in Pontiac, one or two in Flint, one in Saginaw, and possibly others. There were regiments in Ohio, Indiana, and Illinois as well. Not all were at capacity.

Legionnaires congregated in open fields and meeting halls. Smaller groups met in basements and darkened living rooms. Particularly in neighborhoods, frequent swarms of cars could pique curiosity. As the legion grew, the danger of being exposed swelled. With snoops and nosy neighbors a concern, the legion looked for more discreet meeting places. Fraternal halls, already hosting assemblies of men, offered the best camouflage. These ranged from the patriotic to the religious. Oddfellows, Maccabees, Pythians, Forresters, Woodmen, Veterans of Foreign Wars, American Legion, Masonic orders—the extensive lists of their meeting times and locations filled special weekly pages in the daily papers.

In the legion's third regiment, home to Dayton Dean, officers rented a vacant church, the Little Stone Chapel, figuring it would provide privacy. The chapel was situated on the northeast corner of Second and Ledyard. Built in the 1800s, it was a remnant from the days when the neighborhood sparkled as one of the city's most desirable, host to grand Victorian homes with brick turrets, bay windows, steep gabled roofs, and long porches with iron spindles. Its stone bell tower anchored the corner, adorned with a small sign that stuck from the surface like a starched flag. Two sides of the building featured round rose windows. The pews inside could seat more than five hundred people. But it wasn't the sanctuary or nave that interested the legionnaires. They liked the intimate meeting rooms that were tucked in the basement and off the main hallways. It was there that they conspired and conjured mystery and extracted promises of devotion.

It also helped that just down the block stood the crowning glory of fraternal life in Detroit, the magnificent, massive, fourteen-story, Indiana-limestone, Gothic-inspired, awe-engendering, accolade-inducing Masonic Temple, the largest Knights' temple in North America. Constructed in the 1920s, it towered over Cass Park. With more than one million square feet of space, the temple offered a labyrinth of a thousand-plus rooms. The place was so large that a child who wandered in from the street once got lost for nine hours before a passerby heard her frantic cries.

Among the grandest rooms were a 5,000-seat theater, two ballrooms with capacities of 750 and 800, and a cathedral for 1,600. Amenities and flourishes abounded: a hotel, a gymnasium, bowling lanes, billiard tables, a barber shop, and a shoe-shine stand. Lodge rooms were done in Tudor, Egyptian, Corinthian, Byzantine, Greek Doric, Greek Ionic, Italian Renaissance, and Medieval Romanesque. The temple featured marble walls, intricate wood carvings, a terra-cotta fountain, ornamental beams, and brass, bronze, and copper details. All of these added to the ambience, making a spectacular spot for testimonial dinners and a place where the rich, the celebrated, and the powerful—men like Walter O. Briggs, Will Rogers, Thomas Edison, Ty Cobb, and Mickey Cochrane—found comfort and companionship. In the late 1920s, before the market crash,

55,000 men belonged, representing twenty-eight groups. (Cochrane, often assumed by fans and reporters to be a Catholic, was in fact a Protestant and a longtime Shriner.) The temple's presence on the same block meant Black Legion members needn't worry about their parked cars drawing attention on the streets around Cass Park. There were always cars.

The Masonic Temple was still gloriously new. But the Little Stone Chapel, like the Victorian homes in the neighborhood, had seen more prosperous days. Parts of the building were in poor shape. Legion members spent Sundays and weeknights improving the facility. Dayton Dean and his lighting department co-worker Harvey Davis were particularly devoted. They wrapped furnace pipes and painted walls with supplies stolen from their employer.

Davis and Dean made quite the pair visually. Davis weighed twenty to thirty pounds less than Dean, but stood four or five inches taller. Beside the chunky, thickheaded Dean, Davis looked awkward and slump-shouldered. People who met Davis described him as gawky and gangly and as possessing shifty, suspicious eyes. His dark arched brows and pronounced widow's peak—he flattened his hair with tonic—gave him the unsettling look of a horror-movie mortician from the silent era or a devious butler. The two men had known each other before joining the Black Legion.

Many others contributed to the chapel. The legionnaires brought their own lunches for weekend work days. Sometimes their wives served potluck suppers. On occasion they roasted a pig. The legion paid $200 per month in rent and asked members to contribute a dollar each month for the place. They sometimes struggled to come up with the money. To make their charade complete, the legionnaires solicited the services of a pastor. The Rev. Sam Jacob White led them on Sundays. Initially unaware of the legion, White thought he had stumbled upon a fervent, driven group of Protestants hungry for the word of God and desperately in need of spiritual leadership. It surprised him when interested visitors would inquire about joining the church only to be rejected for membership by Dean or Davis. That was unusual, he thought.

Dayton Dean wasn't a religious man but he considered himself moral. "I believe in doing what's right," he said. "I don't believe in attending church all the time. You can be as good out of church as in church. Right is right."

Dean's stature within the legion had rebounded since his failure to kill editor Art Kingsley. Back in the good graces of his higher-ups, he had been promoted to head a death squad. The new position quickly ballooned his ego, which affected his relationship with his common-law wife Margaret O'Rourke. "Nothing could stop him after that," she said. "He was wild with power and importance and wouldn't listen to anything I said." The two weren't getting along. They fought. He slapped her. They and the kids would eat dinner in silence, then he'd run off to the chapel, the Blinking Eye beer garden, or some legionnaire's house. When the society added a women's group to spy on neighbors and report what had been heard in grocery stores and at card parties, O'Rourke got a night job so she could limit her involvement.

One evening, Dean and other legion members assembled in his and O'Rourke's house. She overheard them plotting a murder. When she confronted Dean later, he downplayed the talk. Another time, while drunk, he hinted that the legion had poisoned a man. When she raised issues, he told her to mind her own business. She began to fear him. Dean acted as if he had immunity from the law. Maybe it was because he had seen police officers at legion gatherings and heard Major-General Bert Effinger talk about how the legion had members at the highest levels of law enforcement.

———

Police headquarters sat about a mile and a quarter from the Little Stone Chapel. Cops got entangled the same way everyone else did, through friends, co-workers, and acquaintances. Patrolman George Pratt, still dealing with the lingering effects of having been trampled by a runaway horse in the mid-1920s, became ensnared through a close pal. A Marine veteran with five kids, Pratt introduced another department employee, Paul Jentsch, who was sworn in with nearly a hundred men in Highland Park. At his ceremony he recognized Detroit sergeant Ernest Lindemeyer, director of the police band. Accident investigator Robert Kingston, married with two children, had nearly a decade on the force when he joined. He thought he was going to a meeting to "discuss voting for the right man and keeping colored children out of our schools." Kingston tricked other cops into joining. He told patrolman William Chegwidden that they were going to "meet a bunch of American fellows who stood for clean things." Kingston also introduced his uncle Paul Dotten, a police electrician. Patrolman Alfred Roughley, who would be discovered dead in 1936, had also invited him. Dotten reported being inducted by a hooded and "very strenuous speaker" who "would have put fear in any man." Sixteen-year patrolman Lloyd Modglin also had been deceived by a fellow officer, but once inducted at gunpoint at the Little Stone Chapel, he came to appreciate what he learned about the group. Sure he was against communism. And no, he didn't think Negro and white children should attend school together. A former Klansman, he also didn't care much for Jews or Catholics.

Modglin invited another cop, Harlow Evans, out for a beer after work one evening. Instead he took him to the chapel. They went through a side door, down a darkened staircase, and into a room dimly lit in red light like a photo lab. A troop of hooded men encircled Evans and other recruits. Under threat of death Evans took the Black Oath. He found the ordeal childish but given the weaponry present didn't want to risk his life. Even a child with a gun can be dangerous, he thought. Legionnaires gave him the bullet and issued the usual warnings.

Outside afterward Evans chided Modglin and tossed the cartridge. He told Modglin he was done. But strangers soon appeared on his porch demanding that he appear at meetings. They told him that whipping squads were often sent for errant members. Evans wouldn't be bullied. He told them to leave. They returned another evening. Evans again ordered them off his porch, vowing "somebody might get hurt" if they refused. Evans considered going to Col. Pickert or the famous radio priest Father Charles Coughlin. "But I was afraid they would consider the whole thing ridiculous and laugh in my face," he said.

<hr/>

Col. Pickert's first months in the police commissioner's office saw his force mostly dealing with typical big-city troubles: missing persons, purse-snatchings, house burglaries, simple assaults, and river suicides. Traffic deaths—nearly one hundred by early April—kept morgues and funeral homes busy. There were numerous ways to be extinguished in or by "a machine" as Detroiters demonstrated in the span of one week: rollerskating in the street, pulling into the path of a freight train, alighting from a trolley, stepping from behind an automobile, or speeding on ice. Just crossing a road on foot could be deadly. The city was infected with hit-and-run drivers. They killed nine people in that time and injured eighty-four others. Among the dead was Ralph Wilson, a black man who was struck and left to die at Livernois and Fort Streets, a route driven regularly by the corpse-like Harvey Davis, who lived nearby. Likely just a coincidence.

The use of deadly force by police was not uncommon. During Prohibition the police presence in Detroit ballooned. It remained large afterward. The force had 3,500 officers, most with little training. On average their bullets were killing one person a month. In March a fourteen-year-old who had stolen an accordion and two watches was chased for a block by an off-duty officer who shot and fatally injured the boy. The officer's defense was that the youth had taunted him, saying, "You'll never get me." The incident merited only a few small stories. The shooting fell into a gray area. The police manual allowed officers who had witnessed serious crimes to fire at escaping suspects. But an officer should not "shoot at a person who is running away to avoid arrest for a trivial offense." An accordion was no trifling matter evidently.

Of more interest was the pursuit of John Dillinger, who had escaped prison. After one of his cohorts died in a shootout in Port Huron, word spread that Dillinger was in the region. At Detroit's Woodmere Cemetery near Baby Creek Park, visitors heard a shot fired, which led to rumors that Dillinger was on the grounds, hiding among the tombstones. Visitors fled the cemetery as police swarmed it. They found nothing. In nearby Dearborn one of Henry Ford's employees said he had seen a man resembling the mobster on Ford's wooded estate. More than fifty officers, including a mounted division, responded. Again, nothing.

Weeks into Col. Pickert's tenure, police raided what they called a "voodoo school." The University of Islam children's school was located in the heart of the city's black district along Hastings Street, a half mile from the Brewster Center where Joe Louis trained. The school was siphoning hundreds of black children from public schools. White officials were alarmed that some were taking Muslim names. Police arrested nineteen instructors and confiscated their learning materials. They feared that "many of the teachings would frighten and disturb the Negroes of Detroit." The school was believed to be run from another state by Wallace Fard, who had been ordered to leave the city two years earlier. Fard was the founder of the Nation of Islam.

Two days after the raid, hundreds of blacks marched toward police headquarters in protest. A handful of officers tried to stop them but the encounter escalated to violence. Police retreated to the steps of the headquarters until reinforcements arrived, some on horseback. Col. Pickert joined the effort. The riot was quelled after an hour. Thirteen police officers were injured and forty-one blacks were arrested. Most of the rioters escaped into the black neighborhoods. Such civil unrest was the sort of thing that infuriated Col. Pickert and legionnaires like Dean and Davis.

The Superstitious Schoolboy and His Gal

At his locker in the visitors' clubhouse at Comiskey Park, Schoolboy Rowe looked over his collection of good-luck charms. Some of the tokens, like his magical US Eagle ten-dollar gold coin, had been with him for years. Others had joined the mystical entourage recently. He possessed enchanted copper pieces from Belgium and the Netherlands, a fortunate black penny from Canada, and a chipped but still powerful jade elephant from the Orient. Rowe carried them all throughout the season and lavished attention on them before every pitching performance.

Rowe was not an anomaly in baseball. Almost everybody in the sport had superstitious beliefs. Many heeded the sacredness of the diamond's chalk lines, and plenty declined to wash a T-shirt or socks after a brilliant performance. Teammate Billy Rogell stepped on third base when going onto the field and religiously tightened his shoelaces and straightened the elastic bands on his uniform legs while in the on-deck circle. Rogell also knew that Sportsman's Park in St. Louis was jinxed, at least for him. He and his fellow Tigers infielders, upon realizing that their spectacular play might be attributed to the warm-up ball they used before games, wouldn't go anywhere without Black Betsy. Flea Clifton, the reserve fielder who had played only twice in June and July, shepherded the ball from town to town. When the team lost, he gave Betsy a bath in iodine to remove any hexes. Owner Frank Navin, with his affections for card playing and horse racing, also believed in omens, harbingers, and preventative routines. Following the rotten 1933 season, he had moved from his favorite seat along the right field foul line to a luckier one nearer home plate. He insisted on being in that seat for the start of every home game.

But few abided superstitions as much as Schoolboy. In his mind his methods worked. After the Saturday afternoon on Chicago's South Side when he had picked up his glove with his left hand—never the right!—who could dispute him? Rowe had pitched a complete game, winning 11–1 and allowing a mere three hits. It was his ninth straight victory. Schoolboy Is Invincible, said one headline. The next day he finished a game in relief and hit a home run for the win, his tenth straight. It marked Rowe's sixth appearance in ten games. Cochrane was using him as a starter, a reliever, and a pinch hitter, his batting average second highest on the club. Cochrane deployed him three days later to prevent a loss after Red Phillips loaded the bases with one out in the last inning in Cleveland. (Rowe struck out both batters.) Two days on, he pitched Detroit to another victory, not yielding a hit until the seventh inning.

"Young Master Rowe can't pitch nine full innings one day and do relief hurling the next much longer," warned Paul Gallico of the *New York Daily News*. He chided the Tigers for scheduling a scrimmage on their day off. It was one of three exhibitions that summer against the National League's St. Louis Cardinals. American League teams played National League teams only in scrimmages or during the World Series. Though nothing was at stake in those St. Louis games, the Tigers would lose all three.

Against the Browns on August 7 at Navin Field, Rowe headed out to the mound in search of his twelfth straight win. He didn't feel right. His warm-up pitches lacked punch. Harlond Clift, the first batter, drove a ball to the wall for a double. On the second pitch to the second batter, Rowe stumbled off the mound and grabbed his right side. Greenberg, Gehringer, Cochrane, Rogell, and Owen closed in around him, fearing he had reinjured his arm. He was rushed into the clubhouse and onto the massage table of Denny Carroll. As the game continued, coaches Perkins and Baker, scout Wish Egan, and Navin's nephew Charles, the team secretary, hovered nearby. They watched Carroll in a sleeveless white T-shirt probe the star pitcher's bare back and arms. If Rowe were seriously hurt, the Tigers might just have witnessed their downfall. A crucial series with the Yankees was a week away.

Within days, recovered from the muscle strain, Rowe resumed his streak against Cleveland. He pitched eleven innings, breaking the 5–5 tie himself with a long sacrifice that brought home Greenberg. The next Tuesday in New York, he threw a four-hit, complete-game victory. The Bronx stadium was packed. Then, on Friday, August 17, nearly 80,000 people jammed into the park again to watch as he held the Yankees to three hits. His complete-game shutout put Detroit five and a half games ahead of New York. "Rowe pitched one of the greatest games I ever saw," said Cochrane.

Rowe's incredible run—fourteen straight and counting—overshadowed other fine performances. He wasn't winning on his own. The team had taken fifteen of its last seventeen games. Rowe was 18–4, but Tommy Bridges was 15–6 and Elden Auker was 10–4, and seven everyday players were hitting above .300, among them a league leader, Charlie Gehringer. (Henry Ford presented him with a V-8 convertible coupe as a thank-you.) But the nation's attention had turned fully to Schoolboy Rowe. Photographers and reporters hounded him. Here was another story to uplift the masses, whether in the Dust Bowl or the silted cities. Rowe needed to win his next two games to tie the American League record for most consecutive victories.

At Boston's Fenway Park more than 46,000 people turned out for a Sunday doubleheader, hoping Rowe would pitch. He didn't. The Tigers won anyway. Afterward Cochrane and the boys boarded three boats and headed toward Graves Light for an overnight fishing trip. They spent their off day, Monday, on Massachusetts Bay to escape fans, journalists, and the building pressure. On Tuesday Rowe pitched another complete game, beating the Red Sox 8–4. It was his fifteenth straight win.

Back to Washington the team went. It was hot. Because the hotel did not have air-conditioned rooms, players were given private rooms. Rowe and Pete Fox had their own rooms on the first and second nights. But after the Tigers lost both of those games, Rowe became suspicious. Perhaps the change in routine had thrown off a winning pattern. He didn't like what it meant for him and the record. The next night Rowe showed up at Fox's door and asked if he could stay with him. When he explained why, Fox agreed.

On Saturday Rowe, pitching on a sprained ankle, went for his sixteenth consecutive win. The Tigers looked deflated and Rowe didn't feel his usual self. They wasted several scoring chances. The streak was in danger of ending. The Tigers were behind 2–1 entering the last inning when Hank Greenberg launched a solo home run to tie the game. Marv Owen and Fox followed with singles, and Rowe got one too, bringing in the winning run. The victory tied the record. With one more win he would break it. The opportunity would come in Philadelphia.

The story of the polite twenty-four-year-old sensation had spread across the nation. Rowe seemed to have come out of nowhere and risen rapidly to proportions matching his size. Here might be the start of a living folk hero, a fresh figure from El Dorado, emerging just as the old glowing light that was Babe Ruth faced the dimming days of his luminous career. They described Rowe as "Frank Merriwell in the flesh," a bow to the fictional hero of dime novels, comic strips, and radio serials who excelled at all the sports he tried. They floated new nicknames for Schoolboy: "Man Mountain from Arkansas," "The Pygmy from El Dorado," etc. The newspaper verse-makers wrote odes to him. One began, "Today they're pitching Schoolboy Rowe, I shut my eyes and see; immortal stars of long ago, in days that used to be . . ." After reminiscing for many stanzas about dozens of pitchers of yore, like Cy Young and Christy Mathewson, author Harry Bannister concluded, "The vision fades, the past stays dead, the Schoolboy flings one through; I know that in the years ahead, he'll be immortal, too."

In Philadelphia chaos engulfed the elegant nineteen-story Bellevue-Stratford Hotel. Reporters, well-wishers, agents from vaudeville, programmers of radio, and purveyors of profit schemes waited in the lobby to speak with Rowe. They phoned his room. They pestered him in the restaurant. They knocked on his door at all hours. They filled his mailbox with pleas and offers. Pete Fox tried to guard his roommate's time, but Rowe accommodated all news requests, answering the same questions repeatedly in private interviews, telling his life story over and over again. He was, said Cy Peterman of the *Philadelphia Inquirer*, "handsome in the athletic way, neither taciturn and inarticulate, like Lefty Grove, nor voluble, like a good many lesser lights in the game . . . what I would call a right agreeable lad." With good cheer Rowe also obliged the photographers, sunnily executing their goofy requests. One cameraman said he "has practically a fool-proof face."

The Tigers were in Philadelphia for four days, four nights, and four games. With all the interruptions and commotion, Rowe slept only a few hours most nights. The pressure felt almost unbearable. "He's becoming nervous," Fox said. Teammates innocently added to the stress by heaping absurd expectations upon him. Marv Owen looked beyond the American League record toward the major league best. "He will break Rube Marquard's record of nineteen straight," he said. "Mark my words." Pitcher Vic Sorrell guessed: "Rowe probably will not be beaten for the rest of the year." But it wasn't just Rowe bearing it. Fox would take ill the next day and miss several games. Cochrane, his catcher and manager, felt it too.

The return to Philadelphia, where he had spent nine years, saw Cochrane reconnecting with friends. In a private room at a little dance club, with the sound of a piano seeping through the walls, Cochrane shared dinner with coach Perkins, former teammate Bing Miller, and several other men. Jimmy Powers of the *New York Daily News* joined them. With the Tigers five games ahead of New York, the conversation turned to a cataloguing of teams that had blown their pennant chances during the final weeks of a season. Cochrane endured it silently and then left the table abruptly. When he returned, his eyes were wet and red. He swiped at his tears. "The man had been crying," Powers said. The guy next to Cochrane laid an arm over Cochrane's shoulders and consoled him. "Aww, you can't miss, kid. Quit worrying about it."

The Bellevue-Stratford presented Rowe with his own room the night before the big game. He declined, of course, choosing to stay with Fox, who traveled with a radio and liked to play it loud before bed. The phone interrupted their sleep late into the night until Fox left it off the receiver. The next morning, the streets around Shibe Park throbbed with fans. Connie Mack had not seen such a turnout since the World Series three years earlier. More than 33,000 people packed into the stadium for the midweek doubleheader. Thousands were turned away. Many found spots atop nearby buildings. Others occupied Lehigh, Twentieth, Twenty-First, and Somerset Streets. Unrecognized in the stands in street clothes, Schoolboy Rowe watched his Tigers crush the Athletics 12–7 in the first game before heading into the locker room. He changed for the game and paid homage to his coins and jade elephant. Rowe was haggard. He had lost a few pounds. On the field coach Perkins caught his warm-up sessions.

"How's he look?" Cochrane asked.

"Pretty awful," said Perkins. "But what can you do? There's a crowd here to see him, and, anyway, maybe he will find himself as he goes along."

Rowe's arm felt dead. Cochrane realized it as soon as the game began. Rowe had nothing on his fastball.

Back in Detroit, sound trucks stationed in busy sections downtown broadcast play-by-play recreations over loudspeakers. The game account blended with sounds of horns and shifting gears, the usual commotion of a busy city. Crowds ballooned to 4,000 around the Christopher Columbus statue on the grassy median of Washington Boulevard near Grand Circus Park. Lawyers, doctors, office workers, teens, and homeless men listened.

Cochrane visited Rowe at the mound in the fifth inning after Philadelphia went ahead by three.

"You need some help, don't you?" Cochrane asked.

Rowe admitted as much, but Cochrane left him in.

"This is your ball game today," he said. "Get to it."

But he couldn't. More runs scored and Rowe's hope of immortality evaporated. There was second-guessing among those listening in Detroit: Cochrane should have let him pitch the first game; he should have held him back until Boston. Midway through the seventh inning, Cochrane finally removed Rowe. Philadelphia fans showed their appreciation to the pitcher with a rousing ovation. The Tigers lost 13–5. The streak had ended.

Cochrane, his teammates, and newspaper observers mostly blamed the defeat on the stress of the spectacle, the swarms of people hounding Rowe, and his lack of sleep. Rowe took the defeat in stride. "I guess it was just not my day," he said. He also wondered whether a hex had played a part, noting "too many colored people . . . brought various objects into the park . . . to conjure up a jinx." Black Betsy got painted again with iodine.

—◆—

William Mollenhauer had a dose of bad luck too. A federal forestry worker (and a former musicians' union officer), Mollenhauer was outspoken and principled. After offering his Oakland County farm as security in a court case against an auto union striker, he had been warned he would face retaliation. It came on the evening of August 20. While he was in Detroit, the Black Legion sent its arson squad to Mollenhauer's farm. Neighbors noticed the fire at eleven o'clock that night and rushed to extinguish the flames. They called the police but couldn't get any lawmen to come to their aid. Armed with shotguns, neighbors guarded Mollenhauer's property until dawn. When two deputies finally arrived to investigate days later, they treated Mollenhauer as the criminal. One of the deputies was a legion member who would run for county sheriff. The other would eventually become chief of police for General Motors Truck Corporation. Searching Mollenhauer's home, they smashed furniture and confiscated clothes, legally owned guns, and a keepsake samurai sword. Before an insurance adjuster could get prints from a broken window, the farm was torched again on August 30, the evening after Rowe's defeat.

—◆—

Fans mobbed Schoolboy Rowe in a coffee shop at Union Station. The poor man couldn't go anywhere without attracting a crowd, not even to get a cup of joe and a fry cake. Given his height, he couldn't hide easily. He almost always stood above the throng, which now included dewy-eyed high school girls smitten by his fame, his sturdy athletic build, and his shiny, slicked-back hair. They came just halfway to his chest and he floated above the sea of them, a steady buoy atop dreamy water. Of course Rowe drew other fans: squawky teenage boys, old women in their Sunday hats, and grizzled baseball veterans. And there were reporters and photographers too. They followed him whenever he left the hotel.

It was eight o'clock on a Thursday morning and Rowe was awaiting the train carrying his beloved, Edna Mary Skinner. They had been sweethearts since eighth grade in El Dorado. In high school, as he tore up the sports leagues, she wore his varsity sweater. They had always been together, and once the Tigers' season ended, they planned to marry. "I've been knowing Edna ever since we were kids," he said.

Every Tigers devotee knew of Edna. She had catapulted into the public eye just after Rowe's pitching streak broke in Philadelphia. The rest of the team had headed to Cleveland, but Rowe went to New York. The next night at seven o'clock, he made his national radio debut on singer Rudy Vallee's popular NBC hour. Vallee sang his usual opening lines: *"My time is your time. Your time is my time."* In stylish spats Rowe sang with Dot, Kay, and Em, a Texas female trio barely out of high school. He chatted with the crooner Vallee and predicted the Tigers would win the World Series in four games. There was a skit about "Anglo-American hillbillies" and one about Napoleon and Josephine. As the segment ended, Rowe spoke the words that would follow him to his dying days, "Hello, Ma. Hello, Edna. How'm I doing?" It was scripted, not impromptu. Those weren't his words. He never called his mother "Ma." Rowe was merely reading. Soon the "Hello, Ma" portion of the line fell from the public consciousness. Wherever he went, admirers called out Edna's name. Opponents mocked his words while he pitched. When he gave up a hit or a home run or walked a batter, some boisterous player in the other dugout would squeal sarcastically, "How'm I doing, Edna, honey?" It made him cringe.

But when Edna stepped off the train that morning, Rowe carried her into his arms. They kissed and she wept. It had been too long. Spectators called out their best wishes and congratulated them on their upcoming nuptials. A fan handed her a bouquet of dahlias. With reporters and station agents clearing a path, Rowe swept her toward his sedan and drove to the Leland, where she would share a room with his mother, who would arrive in a day or two. Hours later at Navin Field, Edna glowed like the sun, turning heads and drawing stares in her bright yellow dress and matching hat. People greeted her as she passed. She was tired from the journey but watched Schoolboy pitch a nine-inning shutout. He occasionally looked her way and grinned.

Reporters dropped by to chat. She was leery because a writer in Kansas had published a story that parodied her, making her sound like an uneducated hick and inaccurately stating that her father was dead. It didn't help that papers were misidentifying her. She straightened that matter quickly. "My name is Edna Mary Skinner, and not Edna Mae," she said. "I don't like the name 'Mae' or 'May,' anyway. My mother's name was Mary and there are about fifteen other Marys in the Skinner family." Photographers who had already captured poses at the hotel took more pictures of her at Navin Field. The Tigers' two broadcasters, WWJ's Ty Tyson and WXYZ's Harry Heilmann, both interviewed her.

Edna and Schoolboy's love story was sweet, true, and endearing. He did indeed cherish his Edna. Dailies carried updates on her activities and much of the nation followed their romance. It was a pleasant antidote to a year of violent confrontations involving Teamsters in Minneapolis, longshoremen in California, and factory workers in Toledo and elsewhere. It was a joyful diversion from the still high, though improving, unemployment rates and from housing foreclosures, food lines, and the congregations of desperate men in big cities. The country remained in a funk economically and emotionally, but the tale of Edna and Schoolboy's long courtship brightened the world a tad, imbuing the Tigers' pennant chase with the glitter of a hundred Valentines.

In September Edna's picture would appear on the front page of the Detroit papers more often than that of any player. One hired her to write a column. Dining establishments added "Schoolboy" sodas and "Edna, Honey" sundaes to their menus. Henry Ford invited them to tour the Rouge plant and Greenfield Village and to have lunch with him. Rowe talked openly about moving back to El Dorado in October after they married. "I know everybody in the town back there, and it's nice to walk down the street and say howdy-do to the folks," he said. "It's more friendly like." The city had fallen in love with Edna and Schoolboy. Even those men in the Black Legion could lustily applaud Schoolboy and his gal. That wasn't the case for Hank Greenberg.

Happy Rosh Hashanah, Hank

As he entered the clubhouse on the morning of September 10, Hank Greenberg did not know whether he should play. It was Rosh Hashanah, a high holy day and the start of the Jewish New Year when observers typically do not work, instead spending time in prayer and reflection. Greenberg had grown up in a religious household, and though not overly spiritual himself, he felt torn. The Jewish community in Detroit had welcomed him. He had worshipped with his local friends at their synagogues and he did not want to disappoint them. He didn't want to disappoint his parents either. He also didn't want to let his teammates down. The Tigers stood four games in front of the Yankees thanks to Greenberg. His hot swing had powered the team's fortunes. In games during which he hit a home run, the Tigers were 17–3. In each of the last six contests, Greenberg had brought in at least one run, sometimes two. He was driving the team's offense, all of which meant that he faced a difficult decision. His teammates wanted him to play. So did Navin, Cochrane, Navin's nephew Charles, and scout Wish Egan, all of whom gently encouraged him to suit up—all the while telling him the final decision was his.

The debate had become public. The day before Rosh Hashanah, perhaps hoping to influence the first baseman, the *Free Press* had run a headline proclaiming "Happy New Year, Hank" in Hebrew. Reporters solicited the views of rabbis. Joseph Thumim of the Orthodox Temple Beth Abraham gave his blessing. "You tell Henry Greenberg that he can play ball today and Saturday with a clear conscience," he advised the *News*. "The Talmud gives him ample right." On page one of the *Detroit Times*, Rabbi Leo Franklin, a onetime friend of Henry Ford and longtime head of Temple Beth El, left the decision to Greenberg, giving him support either way: "In a game such as this, Mr. Greenberg, who is a conscientious Jew, must decide whether he ought to play or not. From the standpoint of orthodox Judaism, the fact that ball playing is his means of livelihood would argue against his participation in the game today. On the other hand it might be argued quite consistently that his taking part in the game would mean something, not only to himself, but to his fellow players and in fact at this time to the community of Detroit."

In the clubhouse surrounded by teammates, Greenberg put on his uniform. He played and made the difference, scoring all of Detroit's runs by hitting two home runs, one to tie, the other to win (in the ninth inning no less). The latter ball left the park and landed on Cherry Street beyond the left-center wall. The Tigers beat Boston 2–1, increasing their grip on first. On the ride home in his sporty roadster, Greenberg confessed his doubts to third baseman Marv Owen. "I hope I did the right thing," he said. "Maybe I shouldn't have played. It's a sacred day. . . . It's on my conscience."

"I wish I had a couple of home runs on my conscience," Owen responded.

The decision to play brightened Greenberg's already shining star. The papers praised him on the front page. The *News* showed an embarrassed Greenberg, wet, smiling, and bare-chested beneath a shower spigot in the locker room. The story said he had "celebrated Rosh Hashana . . . with two over-the-fence home runs." His performance was evidence of his fulfilling "a civic duty." Harry Salsinger anointed Greenberg "a truly great competitor" and "a very fine chap." And *The Sporting News* acknowledged him with "Oi, Oi, Oh, Boy!"

The clamor over Greenberg felt double-edged. In one sense Greenberg served as a counter to common, offensive stereotypes of Jews as short and wispy. He had fans of all denominations. Many Protestants and Catholics, as well as Jews, were cheering his at-bats. His prominence couldn't help but soften vulgar caricatures. And to youngsters of his own faith, Greenberg certainly served as a role model and an inspiration. But the new year's greeting in Hebrew and the talk of Greenberg honoring his faith and his people—coming from gentiles in the press—bordered on condescending and manipulative. It felt forced, as if trying to cloak the region's virulent antisemitism.

Since his first days on a professional ball field, Greenberg had endured anti-Jewish remarks from fans, opponents, and teammates. In the minor leagues while playing for Beaumont, Texas, he got the feeling that he was the first Jew many fans and most of his teammates had encountered. "They seemed surprised I didn't have horns and a long beard," he said. Kike, hook-nose, hymie, sheeny, mockie, pants-presser, Christ killer—he heard them all. Coming from opponents on other teams, he viewed the insults as much a matter of psychological warfare as prejudice (though probably both). To some degree no one was spared the heckling. Italians were Dagos and WOPs, Germans were Krauts, Catholics were "knee-benders" and "cross-backs," and on and on. The slurs shadowed Greenberg into the major leagues. "My religion was seen as an appropriate topic for ridicule," he said.

Beyond the ballpark one needn't look far for signs of intolerance. It came in all shades. Several Tigers pitchers—Tommy Bridges, Elden Auker, Elon Hogsett, Vic Sorrell—thought nothing of living in the four-story Tanton Apartments on West Chicago Avenue, with neighbors named Palmer, Morrison, Kuenzel, Emery, Morris, Donnelly, Johnson, Jensen, Weaver, Hays, Peters, Longyear, Murray, Ewing, and Russell. "There was a sign there that read 'Restricted,'" Auker noted later. "I didn't know what it meant." No Greenbergs or Goldsteins allowed.

In the suburb of Royal Oak Father Charles Coughlin fanned anti-Jewish bigotry through his radio broadcasts to tens of millions. Henry Ford had long ago established his reputation as antisemitic. Detroit's more than 50,000 Jews saw Ford as an enemy not an ally. But Ford liked Hank Greenberg. He described him—with no substantiation other than his personal opinion—as "mixed." In cases where he liked individual Jews, Ford rationalized his feelings by claiming "he's not all Jewish."

And then there was the Black Legion, plotting privately and festering with resentment. Major-General Bert Effinger had some ideas of what could be done about the Jews. He sometimes showed visitors a small box with a tube that he said contained hydrocyanic gas, supposedly prepared at the Edgewood, Maryland, military arsenal. He envisioned releasing the gas in the country's largest synagogues during the Jewish holiday season. For these purposes he compiled a list of synagogues.

Regardless, Hank Greenberg's reputation rose like a lotus lantern. On September 14 he lofted a game-saving home run. He had tied the score, broken a tie, or brought in the winning run in twenty-nine of Detroit's ninety victories. In just his second season, he was already being mentioned as one of the Big Four with established long-ball hitters Ruth, Gehrig, and Foxx.

With Yom Kippur, the holiest Jewish holiday, approaching, Greenberg faced another decision. He wouldn't let his conscience be troubled again. He announced days ahead that he would not be playing. "This time it's different... I've made up my mind this time," he said. "This is a serious business with me." He added that he hoped the game would be canceled for rain. It wasn't and the Tigers lost without him. Greenberg spent some of the day at temple. It would be the only game he missed all season.

<hr />

When the Yankees returned to town, Babe Ruth conceded the pennant race from the ambassador's suite of the Book-Cadillac. The Yankees weren't mathematically eliminated but Ruth said it would take a miracle to prevail. Tiger mania gripped the region. Ticket sales were on pace to break all Navin Field records and demand for World Series tickets was unquenchable. Workers were hurriedly constructing temporary bleachers for 17,000 people in left and center fields, installing them over the grass in one direction and over Cherry Street in the other. The bleachers would reduce the outfield's dimensions by twenty feet, to 319 feet along the left field line. "I wish I had 100,000 seats for every game," said Frank Navin.

So much fan mail flooded into the offices that Navin assigned a secretary to assist Cochrane with answering his letters. Songs and poems were being composed and everybody associated with the club was receiving his time in the spotlight. Batboy Whitey Willis, the envy of all kids, showed photographers he could palm seven baseballs at once (just like Marv Owen), and younger clubhouse assistant Joe Roggin (he preferred not to be called by his actual name, Roginski, because of anti-Polish bias) revealed how during the game he took all of the Tigers' suits to a dry cleaner to be pressed and returned before the men had showered. Fans learned how Joseph Patrick Donoghue changed the numbers on the outfield scoreboard and how trainer Denny Carroll resuscitated the careers of a half-dozen players.

Representatives of outstate cities came to present floral bouquets, silver platters, ten-foot telegrams, and fishing rods and reels to favorite players. Five hundred Flint Elks marched onto the diamond to honor Billy Rogell. Every team member, including number-five outfielder Frank Doljack, had his supporters. (Local Yugoslavians from the Serbian Hall in his case.) Wattie Watkins, who had managed Michigan's 1887 championship baseball team, showed up to shake Cochrane's hand. "They're the best of them all," he said of the 1934 team. Harold Parker, a fifteen-year-old from Mason, was brought to the park to meet Cochrane. In July he had lost his left leg in an accident, ending his baseball dreams. "Keep your chin up, lad," Cochrane told him. "Remember, there's a lot more to life than just baseball. So keep your chin up."

Merchants lavished gifts on the players, everything from new suits and shoes to automobiles. The players' windfall was a contrast to the reality of average fans. The economy was improving, but one-third of Detroiters still qualified for assistance. And joblessness touched most families. For ordinary folks, nightclub dinners and flashy clothes were the stuff of whimsical dreams. On some days even the twelve-cent-a-pound cost of hamburger meat was a luxury.

Advertisements and endorsement deals abounded for the players. In one campaign Cochrane, Greenberg, Rowe, and several others highlighted the benefits of smoking Camel cigarettes. Everyone on the team appeared in an ad for Grunow radios (and received one in return). The same for Bulova watches. Jo-Jo White was shown being measured for an Alpacuna overcoat by tailor Harry Suffrin. Gehringer parlayed his success into a Standard Service Station on Cass Avenue. (Gehringer used to work for Hudson's Department Store in the off season but seeing that others needed jobs desperately, he declined the position.) Hudson's now promoted its wide selection of Tigers sweatshirts, sweaters, polo shirts, and jackets for boys of all ages. Even Cochrane's children participated in the hype. Little Joan and Gordon Jr. got their picture taken with comic sensation and duck puppeteer Joe Penner, who had almost everyone quacking his radio catch line: "Wanna buy a duck?"

———

Henry Ford went to his first major league game on September 17. He sat in a box near the Tigers dugout with his son Edsel, Edsel's wife, Eleanor, and their youngest children, William Clay, nine, and Josephine, eleven. (Thirty years later William Clay Ford would own the Detroit Lions.) Edsel had recently secured a $100,000, first-of-its-kind deal for Ford to be the exclusive sponsor of the radio broadcast of the World Series. At the park Frank Navin made a point of visiting the Fords. "I hope you win that pennant, Mr. Navin," Henry said. Cochrane came by as well. The Fords liked Cochrane. In August they had hired him to do a radio series of seven baseball broadcasts over CBS stations.

The stadium was packed with 34,000 people, incredible for a Monday. The rival Yankees were in town for four games. Detroit had just swept Washington, putting them five and a half games ahead of New York. All box, grandstand, and bleacher seats were sold, so fans stood on the grass, roped into overflow areas in the outfield and foul territory. Police on horses enforced the boundary. The potential for injury concerned Henry Ford.

"You don't think they will get hurt out there by a batted ball?" he asked.

"I certainly hope not," Cochrane said. "I imagine very few balls are going to get past those fielders."

The Tigers defeated the Yankees 3–0, with Greenberg driving in a run. As Ford left the park, he stopped to sign a scorecard. Instantly, dozens more fans surrounded him. Tigers officials whisked him away.

———

Frank Navin refused to get his hopes too high. Cochrane had so excited him that Navin didn't miss the start of any home game. When his Tigers took to the rails, if he didn't accompany them, he kept tabs by reading ticker-tape updates. A machine in his office provided them. Ever the cautious poker player, Navin didn't chance a jinx by dreaming out loud of a world championship. He wouldn't make predictions. "So many things can happen that it would be folly to say we will win the pennant, although the boys are right up there now and look good," he said. "You never know when a pitcher's arm may go wrong or when injuries will wreck a ball club. All we can do is wait and hope for the best."

Detroit was baseball crazy. Having weathered the worst of the Great Depression, city residents invested their hearts in the Tigers. Everyone talked about the ball club, especially Cochrane. Even before his team had clinched the pennant, he predicted a World Series win—the first in Detroit history. It would be the crowning achievement of Navin's distinguished career. It didn't seem a stretch. The Tigers owned baseball's best record. "I've been on four championship clubs but never have I been so confident of winning the world championship as right now," Cochrane said.

In the final week of the regular season, Detroit celebrated its team. Nearly every day in late September, Cochrane appeared at a luncheon, a dinner, or both. They were often in his honor. He ate with Navin's Rotary Club members one afternoon—"If we don't win the pennant, look for me at the bottom of Lake Erie," he said—then partied at a last-minute supper with one hundred admirers on Monday, September 24, at the English Grill. Golfer Walter Hagen spoke at the gathering, which Ford's Harry Bennett had organized. On Thursday Cochrane and Greenberg addressed a thousand fans for the Community Fund Exposition, a charity dear to Clara Ford, Henry's wife. That night the Tigers and their dates danced heartily with nearly four hundred celebrants at a ball staged by the Civic Pride Association. Greenberg, Gehringer, and Goslin—nicknamed the G-Men by one news reporter—were all bachelors with a preference for blondes, one observer noted. Gee Walker demonstrated the most daring moves. But the biggest burst of applause erupted when Edna and Schoolboy took the floor. Days later, Cochrane was before a luncheon of police lieutenants and sergeants. They bestowed upon him an ebony nightstick. In the evening at the exclusive Detroit Athletic Club, Edsel Ford and his peers made Cochrane an honorary member.

The most elaborate pre-series celebration, a testimonial dinner, occurred on Saturday, September 29, when a thousand admirers packed into the Statler Hotel. Cochrane and the Tigers sat at a long head table with owners Frank Navin and Walter O. Briggs, Mayor Frank Couzens, and Governor William Comstock. Even Whitey Willis, "the world's best batboy," had a seat. The team had literally brought the city together. The biggest names in Detroit business mingled with ordinary fans who had paid seven dollars apiece to attend. As a show of appreciation, $3,000 of the proceeds would go to buy diamond rings for all team members. In addition every Tiger would be receiving thirty gifts donated by merchants: shoes, ties, suits, clocks, radios, and more.

Guests dined on filet mignon and hashed creamed potatoes—no bacon-grease sandwiches here. William Finzel's Orchestra and "singing milkman" Harry A. McDonald, president of a creamery company (and future chairman of the Securities and Exchange Commission), provided the musical entertainment. They performed the old standard "Take Me Out to the Ball Game," as well as newer regional tunes: "The Tiger Team Song" (. . . *With Mickey riled, the Tigers wild are pretty hard to tame; Mister Navin, flags are waving, one for every name* . . .), "Tigers on Parade" (. . . *Mickey's aces have sure gone places, around those bases on parade* . . .), and "Fight With the Fighting Tigers" (. . . *Fight till the battle's over and the Giants put to rout* . . .).

The last lyric was now suspect. In the National League the Giants had been in first place from July 1 through the last week of September. Sports fans had assumed they would be facing the Tigers in the championship. New York mayor Fiorello La Guardia was looking forward to seeing a World Series game or two—and perhaps Schoolboy Rowe—at the Giants' Polo Grounds in Upper Manhattan. "Yes, sir, you've got a great pitcher in the Schoolboy," he told a Detroiter. Cochrane had been anticipating a New York match-up and felt the Tigers would do well. "I'm going to make a prediction," he had said a week ago. "We're going to win the World Series. I have every respect for the Giants, but I have a feeling that we're going to take them."

Except it turned out that the Tigers wouldn't be playing the Giants. In St. Louis the Cardinals had been rampaging. They had won thirteen of their last fifteen games while the Giants had lost their last five. Two days before the end of the regular season—the very day of the testimonial dinner—the Cardinals overtook the Giants and won the pennant. Navin's Tigers would be facing a wild, streaking St. Louis team, the Gashouse Gang, so nicknamed for the scrappy folks who lived on the poor side of town. The Dean brothers were coming to Detroit with Leo Durocher, Ducky Medwick, and Pepper Martin.

Oh, Those Dean Boys

Dizzy and Paul Dean stretched out across a bed in the Book-Cadillac Hotel, a mile down Michigan Avenue from Navin Field. They were partially dressed and puffing on cigars. It had been a good year so far, especially for Dizzy. Just twenty-four years old, he had won thirty games, something only two other pitchers had done since 1920. Paul, two years younger and a rookie, had won nineteen. They were baseball's newest famous siblings, overshadowing the Waner brothers, "Big Poison" and "Little Poison." Dizzy and Daffy, as some reporters insisted on calling Paul, were stars on the St. Louis team that would be facing the Tigers in the World Series.

The Book-Cadillac, standing thirty-three stories tall with 1,200 rooms, served as the unofficial Detroit headquarters for the series. It was where the Cardinals and many Tigers stayed, along with umpires, league officials, and celebrities like Mae West and Will Rogers. It was where saxophonist and bandleader Ozzie Nelson and singer Harriet Hilliard took up residency for an eight-day gig at the Mayfair lounge. It was where in a few days umpire Bill Klem would shove his way through a crowded lobby and profanely castigate outfielder Goose Goslin for some past indiscretion. The press room was at the Book-Cadillac, equipped with twenty Western Union circuits for relaying game stories. (Officials installed another ninety circuits at the ballpark.)

Hundreds of reporters, photographers, and cameramen had come to town. About a dozen of them gathered in Dizzy Dean's room, sitting on chairs or the floor or leaning against the wall, occupying whatever spot they could find. Dizzy, as usual, did the talking. "I know just what you want me to say. You want me to pop off a lot of bragging about how me and Paul are gonna knock the Tigers off like a bunch of semi-pros. Well, I ain't gonna say it. I ain't gonna brag. All I'm gonna say is that I aim to plow that ball through there and Paul there is gonna fog 'em through. Ain't that right, Paul?"

"You're telling the genuine truth, Diz."

Dizzy Dean was, in fact, a master at bragging and he didn't mind popping off. He did it all the time, delivering gutsy challenges in his jolly, aw-shucks, homespun persona that left his targets more confused, unsettled, and baffled than angry. Otherwise they might have round-housed him.

When St. Louis manager Frankie Frisch looked around Detroit, he "never saw a city wilder," he said. Part of it could be traced to the Tigers' twenty-five-year absence from the playoffs—and part to its painful, ongoing climb out of the Depression. The city hungered for something to celebrate and the Tigers had provided it all summer. "Detroit is as crazy about the Tigers as a lovesick schoolboy is about his teacher," wrote Bill Corum, *New York Evening Journal* columnist.

Hundreds of fans had spent the night outside the ballpark, warming by hobo fires, waiting for 17,000 bleacher tickets to be put on sale. In the early morning hours, police on horses had to repel twenty young men who formed a wedge and tried to ram their way to the front of the line. At nine o'clock when the bleacher gates opened, early arrivers rushed to claim their bench seats. The temporary bleachers were massive. They ran two hundred feet in a straight line from foul territory in left field to dead center and stretched upward fifty-five rows. The layout, open to the skies, resembled an immense, horizontal cookie tray tilted sideways. For the enemy outfielder in left, it would be an intimidating place to be, separated from a potentially angry horde by a flimsy-looking stretch of fence. It was more than three hours before game time and the bleacher fans, mostly men in hats and coats, sat biding their time. Odds were that at least a few Black Legion members, maybe dozens, were among them. They were fans too. They followed the team like everyone else in Detroit, even with the Jewish Greenberg and the Catholic Gehringer in starring roles. An on-field band of trumpets, trombones, and a sousaphone roused the fans to their feet, helping them pass the time with cheers and songs.

All across the city people had adopted the "Tiger Rag," a Dixieland tune, as the team's theme. *Hold that Tiger, hold that Tiger*, they sang.

Frisch started Dizzy Dean in the opener. Cochrane, concerned about his young team's lack of championship experience, decided against Schoolboy Rowe and went with thirty-five-year-old Alvin "General" Crowder, who had been acquired in August from the Senators and gone 5–1 while wearing the Old English D. Crowder had pitched for Washington in the 1933 World Series. He had enjoyed a long career and could handle pressure, Cochrane believed.

It was chilly on Wednesday, October 3. Well-to-do fans in the box seats wore furs and wool overcoats. Henry and Edsel Ford chatted with Will Rogers, who had earlier visited the Tigers clubhouse. ("All the boys flocked around him," said Cochrane. Rogers said that he had bet money on Detroit. Consequently the Tigers felt as if he had adopted them.) Edna Mary Skinner, Schoolboy's girl, shared a laugh with rubber-lipped comedian Joe E. Brown, dapper in his wide-lapelled houndstooth coat. Big-screen gangster George Raft, who had starred with James Cagney and Carole Lombard, sat two rows over. Edna met Raft, as well as Mrs. Babe Ruth. The Babe himself lumbered by on the field, draped in brown-mustard camel hair, as Judge Kenesaw Mountain Landis, at sixty-seven still the ruler of baseball, settled into the front row, tufts of his Mark Twain hair escaping from beneath his hat. Everywhere one looked, there was a recognizable face: Walter Chrysler, Grantland Rice, Westbrook Pegler, old Senator Couzens, and his son the mayor.

Crowder pitched well initially. The long-sleeved T-shirt under his uniform kept his pitching arm warm and concealed a wartime tattoo of a naked woman. But the Tigers behind him proved jittery. The best infield in baseball made five errors in the first three innings, giving St. Louis a 3–0 lead. The Cardinals' advantage grew to 8–1 after sixth innings. Though the Tigers added a couple of runs, they were outmatched by Dizzy Dean. Afterward Dean said as much: "I think the Tigers are not as good a ball team as I figured them out to be. . . . I would be tickled to death to pitch tomorrow's game, too, and could probably shut those Tigers out."

That was just Dizzy being Dizzy. There was no way Frisch would start him two days in a row. Before Thursday's game, the second, Dean posed with a sousaphone and then watched his teammates take on Schoolboy Rowe before a record Detroit crowd of 43,451. Somewhere in the skies above was national columnist Henry McLemore aboard the Goodyear blimp, approaching from the south, passing the Rouge complex. "Henry Ford's big plant slipped by," he reported. "The skyscrapers popped up out of the mist, and there, looking for all the world like a fancy cardboard toy, was Navin Field."

Rowe surrendered two runs early, and it appeared going into the ninth that his team would lose 2–1. But after Pete Fox opened with a single and Rowe moved him to second on a bunt, Gee Walker, batting for Jo-Jo White, singled him home to tie the game. The stands exploded. It was a blizzard above the bleachers. Scorecards, napkins, and shreds of newspaper floated on the wind. In the twelfth, with Rowe still in the game, Charlie Gehringer scored the winning run on Goose Goslin's single. The crowd went wild again. Among the cheering throng were radio priest Father Charles Coughlin and Col. Heinrich Pickert, the police commissioner. The series was even.

Later that night, after Dean and the Cardinals slipped out of town, 3,000 fans jammed into the Fort Street Union Station for a friendly sendoff for the Tigers. Moving through a gauntlet of policemen, the players were patted, praised, and applauded. Fans cheered wobbly Frank Navin, as well as Gehringer, Greenberg, and Cochrane—the whole lot. But the appearance of Schoolboy and Edna brought "a yell that nearly stopped the tower clock," said one observer.

So many Detroiters were making the trip to St. Louis that six separate engines were deployed. In all sixty Pullman cars would be chugging along the Wabash Railway toward Sportsman's Park. It would be an overnight trip with a game to follow the next day. The World Series was scheduled to take place on consecutive days—no rest between contests—in two cities. Games one and two were in Detroit, three through five would be in St. Louis, and, if necessary, six and seven back in Michigan.

Sportsman's Park held fewer fans than Navin Field, but when filled it brought a more lucrative gate because more of its seats were reserved and, thus, more expensive. At Navin Field with the temporary bleachers, almost half of the spectators paid the lowest World Series ticket price: a dollar, plus ten cents tax. Not so at the Missouri park. Thirty-eight thousand fans in St. Louis would bring in more money than 44,000 in Detroit.

The stadium was festive for the St. Louis opener. Red, white, and blue bunting hung along the second deck, and a marching band outfitted in Cardinal Red paraded on the field. The concourses were loud with the churning voices of spectators and the calls of vendors selling sodas, hot dogs, coffee, tiny Dizzy Dean straw hats, and live chameleons. The main scoreboard stood in left field behind the bleachers. Along the outfield walls in fair territory were banner ads for Camel cigarettes, the *Globe-Democrat* newspaper, and Enders Speed Razor—"swift and smooth."

Shortstop Billy Rogell arrived at the ballpark in pain. He had been playing on a broken ankle for several weeks since suffering the injury in September. Rogell had decided to forgo a cast because he didn't want to sit out the World Series and risk losing his job. But on this morning he hurt badly. He mentioned it in the locker room but his teammates reacted quickly and fiercely. Rogell asked Cochrane to put someone else in the game but he refused. They couldn't afford to risk it. Trainer Denny Carroll taped Rogell's ankle so thickly that Rogell could barely bend it, and still his teammates treated him like the goat.

Hank Greenberg was also having troubles, but his were with his bat. In the first game Greenberg had stranded Cochrane and Gehringer by striking out to end an inning. In the second game he had halted three rallies. It wasn't the performance anyone expected. Now Greenberg would be playing before his parents, who had come from the Bronx to St. Louis to watch their famous son. Their presence did not alter the outcome. In game three, Greenberg was impotent, flying out in the first with Gehringer on base and striking out in the third with Cochrane and Gehringer waiting to score. Dizzy's brother Paul won 4–1.

In the clubhouse the next day, Cochrane unleashed his fury and gave his Tigers "a tongue lashing" before the game. He told them to bear down and rise to the occasion. Frustrated by his power-hitting first baseman's inability to connect in pressure situations, he dropped Greenberg to number six in the batting order and elevated Goslin and Rogell. All three responded. Greenberg got four hits, Goslin scored twice, and Rogell drove home four runs. The fourth inning saw Dizzy Dean enter the game as a pinch runner. On a ground ball to Gehringer, Dean charged toward second base, hoping to break up a double play. Gehringer tossed to Rogell at second. Rogell fired the ball toward first but it struck Dean in the skull. The ball ricocheted off Dean's helmetless head and veered into shallow right field. Dean dropped like an anchor, falling to the ground beyond second base. He was unconscious. The stadium went silent. Rogell stood over Dean to see if he was okay as Dean's teammates rushed the field. It looked as if he might have been killed. But after a few minutes, Dean recovered slightly. He was carried off the diamond in the arms of his comrades and rushed to a hospital for x-rays.

The next day Dean reappeared at the park ready to pitch. His entrance helped ease the criticism being lobbed at manager Frisch by those who wondered what the hell he was thinking in putting his best pitcher in to run. Before the game Rogell delivered a military helmet to Dean as a joke. Dean absolved him of any blame. They posed for photos, arms around one another, and then went about playing the game. It was a subdued, low-scoring affair, with the Tigers prevailing. The win gave Detroit a 3–2 lead in the series. Frank Navin watched from his box seat, the anticipation building in his roiling belly. The team needed one more win to capture the world championship.

On the train ride back to Detroit, the Tigers swelled with confidence. They expected to prevail and to enjoy the big payoff that would follow. Everything favored them. They had momentum—two straight wins. They would be playing at home before their own fans. They would be pitching their ace, Schoolboy Rowe. They had just defeated Dizzy Dean, so he wouldn't be a factor. They would be among friends and family. Rogell, Walker, Sorrell, and Marberry could see their kids, Gehringer his mother, and Flea Clifton his beloved Doberman pinscher.

⌁

TIGERS INSIST IT'S IN THE BAG, said the *Detroit News*. Bud Shaver, the *Times* columnist who had earlier described St. Louis as the better team, apologized in print: "We now cheerfully eat those words. There isn't any better ball club than the Tigers, not in this year 1934." Coach Cy Perkins flat-out predicted a triumph: "I don't care who pitches for the Cardinals," he said. "Rowe will beat them." Tommy Bridges buffed the varnish off the barrel of a bat, making it easier for his teammates to sign it—a memento from the day they would make history. On cigarette stands the latest issue of *News-Week* endorsed their expectations. Cochrane peered from its cover, his hands framing his mouth megaphone-style, as if yelling directions to his soldiers. MICKEY THE MANAGER, it proclaimed.

Fans anticipated a championship celebration. The mood around town was jubilant. Tickets were going for several times face value. The biggest crowd yet would pack into Navin Field. Judges canceled their afternoon sessions. School principals set up radios so children could listen to the game in their gymnasiums. "We thought Detroit was a madhouse as we played the first two games of the series," Frisch, the St. Louis manager, said later. "But . . . the excitement was ten times greater [for game six]. Crowds milled in front of our hotel as we arrived and police had to push back the mobs so we could make our way from taxicabs to the hotel entrance. The horn-blowing was deafening."

But at the ballpark signs were surfacing that perhaps the baseball gods would once again deprive Frank Navin. Something was amiss. The omens ranged from the relatively minor—Greenberg's severe headache, Frank Doljack's breaking of Goslin's favorite bat—to the significant— Cochrane's bandaged legs and hobbled gait after two spiking incidents. Most worrisome, though, was Schoolboy Rowe's pitching hand. The star pitcher had already been to Providence Hospital that morning to have his swollen hand x-rayed. It showed no broken bones, but he was hurting. He cringed when comedian Joe E. Brown greeted him with a handshake. Rowe insisted on pitching and Cochrane agreed. He wanted—needed— Rowe to take the mound. Rowe's explanation as to how he had injured his hand struck listeners as unconvincing. He said someone had slammed it in a hotel door. An elevator, he said one time. The revolving door, another. For much of the week, a Detroit detective had been accompanying Rowe because he had received threats. One had been handed to his sister by a boy in the hotel lobby. The threat was not the work of a child. Don't win or else, it said. After the game speculation would turn to gamblers. What Happened to Rowe's Hand? a banner headline would ask from atop page one of a daily.

The Tigers fell behind early. Rowe lacked his usual spark. His fastball was slower, the break of his curve softer. His hand was definitely injured. That afternoon the bench jockeys turned even more brutal with Rowe, Cochrane, and Greenberg the favored targets. When Rowe gave up a hit or run, players in the Cardinals dugout would ask profanely how Edna thought he was doing now. When Cochrane came to the plate, they would mimic the morning headlines that painted him a hero and a warrior for playing injured. With Greenberg they focused on his poor series and his Jewish roots. The Cardinals' own Frisch found the heckling "unparalleled" in all his years in baseball.

The Tigers began a rally in the sixth inning. Jo-Jo White walked and Cochrane singled him to third. White scored when Gehringer reached first on an error. No one was out when Goslin bunted. The throw went to third, where umpire Brick Owens, who was facing third baseman Pepper Martin's back, called Cochrane out. No Tiger fan in the park agreed, and neither did the photos in the late-edition papers. They had been robbed. The Tigers scored two runs but would have added more if not for the bad call, Cochrane said. The umpire—not Rowe or any of the Detroit players—would be blamed for the defeat. On a later play Cochrane tore a ligament and suffered a deep gash above his knee. He limped severely for the remainder of the game. The Tigers lost. In the clubhouse the frustrated manager flew into a fury, flinging his mask and shin guards against a trunk before heading to the hospital, where he would stay the night. A seventh game would be played, but by most accounts the series had been decided. The Tigers were deflated. They had wasted their prime chance.

Billy Evans called his old pal Frank Navin that evening. Evans, a baseball executive and former umpire, tried to lift Navin's spirits. He noted that on the bright side playing a seventh game would bring Navin $50,000 more in ticket sales. "To hell with $50,000," Navin responded. "I'd give $50,000 and five times that much to have won today. I've been waiting thirty-five years to see Detroit win a world's championship and here we have one within our grasp, and that umpire blows it for us."

His sentiment mirrored the dour feeling at the next day's contest. Forty thousand tickets were sold, yet seats were empty. In the vast ocean of temporary bleachers, wide gaps existed. It was game seven of the World Series for God's sake. Normally it would be a prized ticket, but scalpers couldn't dump their inventory even below cost. What a difference one miserable day could make. Yesterday, 20,000 more tickets could have been sold. Today, not so.

Pitchers Dizzy Dean and Elden Auker faced one another in the deciding game. Auker threw submarine style, and his blend of underhand and sidearm kept the Cardinals scoreless for two innings. But whatever smoldering hopes Detroiters harbored that afternoon died in the third inning. Auker surrendered in quick succession a double, a single, a walk, and a bases-clearing double. Cochrane called upon Schoolboy Rowe. After getting one out, he allowed two hits. Two more runs scored. Cochrane brought in Elon Hogsett and he permitted four straight batters to reach base. Two more runs. Tommy Bridges relieved him and he finally ended the inning. The seven-run deficit squeezed the last drop of optimism from the hometown crowd.

In the sixth inning fans' despair detonated when Ducky Medwick tripled and slid into third base with spikes high. Marv Owen leapt to avoid being slashed and landed on Medwick, who then kicked Owen. Benches emptied and words flew. The Cardinals scored twice more, increasing their lead to nine. When Medwick headed out to his position in left field, he faced a furious army of fans, who bolted to their feet and rained fruit, bottles, vegetables, cups, and pretty much anything unbolted at Medwick. The torrent stopped the game. "I watched the crowd and Medwick and the pelting missiles through my field glasses," reported Paul Gallico of New York, "and it was a terrifying sight. Every face in the crowd, women and men, was distorted with rage. Mouths were torn wide open, eyes glistened and shone in the sun. All fists were clenched. Medwick stood grinning with his hands on his hips, just out of range of the bottles."

After workers cleared the garbage, Medwick tried to return to his position. The bombardment resumed. Where were they finding all this food? As it turned out, concessions owner Charlie Jacobs had spotted an opportunity and sent two dozen vendors to the bleachers with tossable treats. Three hundred pies disappeared within minutes. The grass had to be swept three times. Chants rose for Medwick to be removed. To prevent the first forfeiture of a World Series game, Commissioner Landis, sitting field-side, ejected Medwick. The game resumed; St. Louis had prevailed.

Syndicated columnist Westbrook Pegler reported: "Those coarse and vulgar Cardinals of St. Louis finally won the World Series in a contest fraught with vulgarity, personal rudeness, and swaggering contempt. They beat the Tigers, 11–0, and dragged the proud spectacle down from its wonted high plane to the level of a contest played with dice up an alley." Cardinals fans undoubtedly felt different.

A vast contingent of police officers assured that Medwick and his teammates got from Navin Field to the Book-Cadillac to the train station safely. "I never knew a city to take a World Series defeat so bitterly," said Frisch, the manager.

So as not to have the whole season tainted by the disgraceful last twenty-four hours, the local papers focused on the high points of the campaign. In a page-one editorial, the *News* implored city residents to see the Tigers as an example: "If the spirit engendered in Detroit by a winning ball team were applied to the business of life, if it were expressed in all we do on our own behalf and that of the community, if it gave us half the confidence in ourselves that we have reposed these last few months in a ball team that decided it could not be whipped, there would need be no misgiving about the future of Detroit."

Free Press editorial director Malcolm Bingay, writing in character as cantankerous Iffy the Dopester, addressed Cochrane: "There are no regrets in the hearts of real sportsmen, Mickey. You fought the fight; you did your damnedest. You gave a tired and jaded old town the thrill it needed, the call to battle and high courage. . . . We'll be with you when the robins nest again, Mickey, me boy. And O what a team we'll have next year!"

Two days after the World Series, Schoolboy Rowe married Edna Mary Skinner in a private ceremony at the Leland Hotel.

The Attorney down the Street

MAURICE AND JANE SUGAR LIVED ON SECOND AVENUE IN THE WIN-chester Apartments, one of several three- and four-story dark-brick residential buildings that faced Cass Park. Developed in the 1800s, the park occupied a full block amid the homes of some of the city's most prominent early families. It featured a statue of Robert Burns, a water fountain at its center, and crisscrossing paths lined with benches that provided a lovely vantage point to witness the changing of seasons. In spring the park burst with budding trees and flowers. In summer it provided a shady haven of green. In fall it burned with autumnal color. In winter it looked pristine beneath the snow. By the 1930s many of the old-money mansions had disappeared. In their place had risen two major buildings: the wondrous Masonic Temple and the world head-quarters of the S. S. Kresge dime store empire. The Sugars' apartment complex sat in the middle of the Second Avenue block, flanked on one end by the splendid temple and on the other by the Black Legion's fatigued Little Stone Chapel.

Maurice Sugar had grown up on Michigan's Upper Peninsula in the tiny lumbering town of Brimley, where his Jewish family—the only one in town—operated a small store. They moved to Detroit before Maurice began high school. At the 2,200-student Central High, Sugar ran for student government and lost. (Fellow students told his gentile campaign manager that they liked Sugar and would have voted for him if not for his religion.) He was a studious young man who read literature, fiddled with music, and played quarterback on the school's reserve team.

Sugar went to the University of Michigan to study law. At a gathering of socialists in Ann Arbor, he met Jane Mayer. She was on her way to becoming a physical education teacher. Their lifetimes of political activism flowered on campus. Two years after they married, he ran and lost as a socialist for Wayne County district attorney. During the Great War he spoke against the Conscription Act and refused as a pacifist to register for military service. The government prosecuted him. After his appeals had been exhausted, he spent ten months in jail. His sentence began weeks after the war ended. Sugar was disbarred because of the conviction. But he regained his law license. The experience emboldened him. He consulted with Clarence Darrow in the defense of Ossian Sweet, a black dentist who had moved into a white neighborhood and used weapons to defend his house from an angry mob. In 1932 Sugar represented families of the young men shot and killed in the Ford Hunger March. Afterward he traveled to Soviet Russia. Impressed by what he saw, he toured the United States and lectured at Friends of the Soviet Union events.

Maurice and Jane were now in their forties and they remained politically absorbed. They still had their sturdy physiques and their most distinctive physical features: he his dark-browed, deep-set eyes; she her short-cropped red hair. Though Maurice often wore a serious courtroom business suit accented with a pipe clenched between his teeth, he loved to be less formal and spend time in the outdoors. He had learned to hunt and fish at a young age, and with Jane he enjoyed canoeing and tent camping up north. They had no children. Their work and activities consumed them.

Sugar's practice revolved mostly around labor law. He fought for strikers, defending in 1933 those who had picketed at one of Walter O. Briggs's plants, and he regularly represented black Detroiters. Earlier in the year, as the Tigers were pursuing the pennant, Sugar had drawn headlines as the defense attorney in an incendiary assault case against car washer James Victory, who was accused of slashing and robbing a white woman in an alley. Sugar contended that Victory, who had a tight alibi, was being framed by police. He told the all-white jury: "There are a thousand times more illegal arrests by police than legal ones. . . . You know that. You know it if you read the newspapers at all. And it's pretty tough on the colored people. The police don't treat them very gently. They treat them even worse than they do whites." His words amounted to an attack on the integrity of Col. Pickert and his police force. Sugar won a not-guilty verdict and soon the Detroit and Wayne County Federation of Labor formally called upon him to run for judge. In December 1934 he launched his candidacy.

Sugar had always loved music, dating to his boyhood when his mother enrolled him in piano lessons. Though of middling talent, he plugged along, carrying his interest into adulthood, where he found a way to combine it with his activism. At the height of the Depression, he penned "The Soup Song," which would become a union hall standard. (*I'm spending my nights at the flophouse, I'm spending my days on the street* . . .) Encouraged by its success, he wrote a musical response in 1932 to an official, G. Hall Roosevelt (Eleanor's brother), who said a worker could eat adequately on $1.75 a week. One stanza declared: *To hell with your plan of starving a la Roosevelt, to hell with you and your dollar seventy-five. We're strong enough to fight to keep from starving, and you will learn that we are still alive.* Sugar took pride in his songs. He had fun composing them. He felt a good song could build unity within a movement.

The prospects of an election campaign must have filled Sugar with high spirits, for on the last day of 1934—New Year's Eve—he wrote a new piece called "Be a Man": *There's a cry that starts them shaking as they sit upon their thrones. . . . There's a cry that serves them notice that they can't do as they like. It's the workers' call to action, it's the workers' call to strike!*

Black Legion leaders knew of Maurice Sugar. They realized that one of the city's best-known radicals and most prominent leftist attorneys lived in their midst. Sugar took on the kinds of cases that irritated, exasperated, and angered legionnaires. Every few months, he seemed to do something that thrust himself into the spotlight on the side of someone whose rights had been violated. Sugar staged rallies and fought passionately. While doing so, he made enemies of powerful men like Col. Pickert and Harry Bennett, Henry Ford's confidant.

Radio magnate George Richards put together a business group in the spring of 1934 and bought the Portsmouth football team for $15,000, moving it north to Michigan. Known in Ohio as the Spartans, the team had struggled financially through the Depression, so much so that star Earl "Dutch" Clark had sat out the 1933 season because he needed to earn more money doing something else. "We'd get 5,000 people out to watch the practices because they were free. . . . But we'd only get about 2,000 out for the games. . . . They couldn't afford it," said Clark.

Richards changed the team name to the Lions, figuring it would fit nicely with the popular Tigers. When they debuted in the fall of 1934, wearing silver leather helmets and Honolulu blue uniforms, they weren't the city's first professional football team. Others had tried and failed. Richards, who had helped introduce Father Coughlin to America, figured that as owner of WJR he would be able to give the Lions a boost through radio promotion. (Even Coughlin would hype the team in his broadcasts.)

Professional football existed in the shadow of college football. Army, Navy, Notre Dame, and numerous other colleges regularly outdrew pro teams. Though the sport was beginning to make headway in New York and Chicago, it struggled elsewhere. Fans weren't sold on it. They quibbled over whether the professional teams could even beat the best college teams. The Lions played their home games at the University of Detroit Stadium along McNichols Road, blocks from where Mickey Cochrane lived and near the border of Highland Park, where the Black Legion thrived. The stadium could seat 24,000. The Lions needed 8,000 to 10,000 fans per game to break even. Each game cost about $8,000, with $4,000 going to the visiting team and $2,300 toward team payroll. The remainder covered everything from referees to promotion.

A former All-American at Colorado College, Dutch Clark came out of retirement at age twenty-seven to become the Lions quarterback. Coach George "Potsy" Clark, no relation, described his running style as "like a rabbit in brush . . . no set plan, no definite direction." In 1934 Dutch Clark became the subject of *News* photographer William Kuenzel's iconic profile of an American football player. It later ran in *Life* magazine. Thousands requested prints, including Cochrane and Harry Bennett.

In their first nine games, the Lions kept their opponents from scoring any points. Every victory was a shutout. During that spell the team drew between 4,800 and 18,000 spectators each Sunday. Their only home sellout came on Thursday, November 29, Thanksgiving Day, when the Lions turned thousands away. Football teams had a long tradition of playing on Thanksgiving. But the Lions' game against George Halas's Chicago Bears helped turn a sporadic practice into an annual ritual. Richards arranged for the game to be broadcast nationally over a vast network of NBC stations. The celebrated Graham McNamee was at the microphone. In the final minutes of the game the undefeated Bears, led by Bronko Nagurski, came from behind to take a 19–16 lead. Dutch Clark drove the Lions back down the field. From the sixteen-yard line on the last play of the game, Clark passed toward receiver Glenn Presnell. The aging Red Grange, playing in his final season, deflected Clark's pass. The game ended. Disappointed Lions fans battered Grange. His teammates rescued him as beer bottles rained upon them.

After the 1934 World Series, the Tigers scattered across the country. Cochrane, Gehringer, and Rogell lived in the Detroit area year-round. Those who didn't returned to their hometowns. Newlywed Schoolboy Rowe went back to Arkansas with Edna, Tommy Bridges to Tennessee, Elden Auker to Kansas, Marv Owen to California, Pete Fox to Indiana, Gee Walker to Mississippi, Jo-Jo White to Georgia, Goose Goslin to his New Jersey farm, and Flea Clifton to the Kentucky-Ohio border area. Vic Sorrell and Ray Hayworth headed to North Carolina to hunt deer together. Most of the men had come from humble backgrounds and the reality of life in their native states—the sight of struggling neighbors and shuttered storefronts—must have reminded them just how fortunate they were. Across the country headlines confirmed that for the average family troubles persisted.

DEMOCRATIC GOVERNOR SAYS NO ONE WILL STARVE IF HE IS GOVERNOR
3,000,000 RELIEF JOBS URGED ON U.S.
U.S. EMPLOYEES START CAMPAIGN FOR MORE THAN ROOSEVELT PROMISES
OUTSIDERS WARNED AGAINST JOB SEEKING
AUTO WORKERS PROTEST CUTS

Immediately following the World Series, Dizzy and Paul Dean headed out on a barnstorming baseball tour, raking in thousands through exhibitions. They followed it with a vaudeville tour, a lucrative reward for the two of them having won all four St. Louis games—and for Dizzy being one of the most colorful characters on the planet. Opening night was at the Roxy Theatre on Broadway, and Hank Greenberg went to the show. Dean might have been unaware of his presence when he asked from the stage, "Is Greenberg in the house?" Rightly suspecting a setup for a joke, Greenberg didn't answer.

"If he is," Dean continued, "I wish he'd come up here on the stage. I'd like to strike him out again." The jab got some laughs, as well as some boos from Greenberg's friends. It must have stung Greenberg, who was unhappy with his own series performance, fanning nine times (five against Dean) and faltering in crucial, high-pressure moments. Greenberg intended to ensure such a dismal performance would never haunt him again.

The most profitable spoils went to the triumphant Cardinals. But the Tigers also enjoyed their success. Cochrane, voted the league's Most Valuable Player, took a long vacation to Hawaii and then drove back to Michigan from California in his flashy new Ford Lincoln, accompanied by his wife Mary and his best friend Cy Perkins. Rogell made extra cash by taking his own barnstorming team to small towns in Michigan and Ontario and, later in winter, by coaching hockey at Assumption College. Gehringer got the sweetest prize: Connie Mack selected him to join Babe Ruth, Lou Gehrig, and others on a tour of Japan and to play scrimmages against an all-star team from Nippon. The Japanese athletes impressed Gehringer, but sleeping on floor mats didn't. While in the Pacific, Gehringer heard rumors from the wife of a teammate that he was being traded to Cleveland to become the Indians' player-manager. A soft-spoken man with no desire to lead others, Gehringer rightly dismissed the talk.

During their winter planning sessions, Navin and Cochrane discussed the possibility of luring all-star outfielder and Cochrane pal Al Simmons from the White Sox, but the price forbid it. Though the Tigers' outfield rated as average, Navin and Cochrane decided not to hazard a trade or disrupt the chemistry of their team (unless they could get a good deal for rambunctious Gee Walker). They hoped to add a lefty from their troop of pitching recruits and they reasoned that their young players had gained a year of valuable experience and would be better for it. Among their other decisions was that Flea Clifton would be sent to the minors. Clifton had spent the year with the team but appeared in only sixteen games. He needed more playing time, they felt. They planned to option him to the Pacific Coast League's Hollywood team. When Clifton got word in northern Kentucky, where he had bought a farm with his playoff money, he leapt into his car and raced to Navin Field uninvited. Clifton shocked Frank Navin by showing up at the headquarters. Impressed by his persistence, Navin made time to talk with him.

Navin knew his players, and he undoubtedly knew Clifton's story. Since boyhood Clifton had wanted to play for the Tigers because of Ty Cobb, his baseball god. Clifton had read Cobb's biography and patterned himself after him. He was scrappy because of Cobb. He didn't take guff from anybody because of Cobb. He worked hard, he led a clean life, and he adopted a never-say-die attitude, all because of Cobb. Cobb's message resonated with Clifton, particularly during his teen years when he became orphaned and homeless. "He turned out to be my guiding light," he said. Clifton's father had died in the Great War. His mother remarried. After she was strangled by a drunken acquaintance, Clifton's stepfather booted him from the house. Clifton lived behind a garage in Ludlow, Kentucky, pilfering milk bottles from nearby porches. He managed to stay in high school, and though he had scholarship offers for football, he pursued baseball—because of Cobb. He had even turned down better money with other teams so he could play in Detroit.

"Let me go to camp," he pleaded with Navin. "You never can tell. One of those other infielders may not be up to form and I will have a chance to take his job. I don't want to be fiddling around in Hollywood and missing opportunities in Detroit." Navin couldn't help but be impressed by Clifton's fighting spirit. Cochrane appreciated the same quality about him. Navin relented. Clifton would be allowed to go to Lakeland with the team, but beyond that Navin was making no promises.

On the poor side of town, Margaret O'Rourke, Dayton Dean's wife, went to the police after one of her teenage daughters complained that Dean had taken indecent liberties with her. Black Legionnaires worried that an investigation of Dean would bring unwanted attention. They pressured Margaret to drop the charges. If she did so, they said they would punish Dean themselves. If she refused, they said they would kill her. She didn't prosecute and the legionnaires followed through on their promise. At an outdoor meeting deep in the winter woods, Dean was court-martialed. A hood was placed over his head, his hands were cuffed, and fifteen legionnaires each took a turn lashing his bare back with a blacksnake whip. "I gritted my teeth and didn't say a word," Dean would remember.

The legion concerned itself with a broad range of matters, from the petty and personal to the shockingly grandiose. But its aim was scattered, like buckshot, and its principles, such as they were, got applied arbitrarily. On one end of the spectrum were issues related to unseemly or immoral behavior (as judged through the lens of whoever happened to be in charge locally). These might include living out of wedlock or marrying a Catholic woman. Most often the targets in such cases were fellow legionnaires or their family members. At the other end of the spectrum were outrageous plots, several of which would surface early in 1935.

Mickey Cochrane was becoming good friends with the fearsome Harry Bennett, who ran the innocently named Ford Service Department, a private force of spies, guards, and detectives that permeated the gargantuan Rouge plant and tried to keep Ford workers from unionizing. Depending on one's perspective, the Rouge plant was either a shining example of American innovation or proof of capitalism's dehumanization of workers. By any measure it was large and important. One *New Republic* writer termed it "Fordissimus." The complex offered stunning images: the smokestacks, the factory lines, the workers. When Diego Rivera did his Industry murals, he focused on the Rouge. The plant also enticed the lens of photographer Margaret Bourke-White. National writers almost always described the Rouge when profiling Detroit. One writer proclaimed upon beholding the masses coming and going: "At last I had witnessed the god in the machine."

Bennett reigned over the Rouge. His service department was responsible for "upholding a rule of terror and repression," according to the National Labor Relations Board. Bennett served as its powerful and much-feared leader. Frank Murphy, who as mayor had battled with Bennett, described him as an "inhuman brute." Bennett had been at the heart of the 1932 Hunger March, which left several dead, and he would be instrumental in one of labor's pivotal moments, the violent Battle of the Overpass.

A former Navy man, Bennett endeared himself to Henry Ford by fulfilling his darker commands. The two men talked or met daily. Bennett became Ford's prime confidant. In Bennett's estimation he was closer to Henry than Henry was to his own son, Edsel. Ford appeared to enjoy the mystery and shadowy intrigue that followed Bennett. Despite having little knowledge of cars, Bennett was the company's most powerful non-family figure. "I am Mr. Ford's personal man," he said simply.

Though five-foot-six, Bennett made an intimidating impression. A former boxer, he retained his wiry physique and always looked ready to pounce. His reddish hair and blue eyes added to his air, as did his memorable bow ties, which he preferred because in a fight one might be strangled with his own necktie. Bennett carried a gun and was not shy about flashing it. He regularly took target practice with an air pistol in his basement office, which was protected by his men. The place had a "pool hall clientele, the air thick with menace," wrote author Robert Lacey. It was "right beside the garage, so that his visitors could be driven straight in to see him without anyone being aware of their identity."

Bennett hired an assortment of semi-known tough guys, like boxer Kid McCoy, who had served time for manslaughter, and Eddie "Knuckles" Cicotte, a former pitcher who had become entangled in the Black Sox gambling scandal of 1919. Bennett's service department was peppered with convicts released from prison into his care, an arrangement helped along by Bennett's position on the state parole board. Bennett also had relationships with mobsters, in part to deter the kidnapping of Ford's grandchildren. Bennett's enemies branded his servicemen violent thugs. He denied it. "They're a lot of tough bastards but every goddamn one of them's a gentleman," he said.

Bennett was an adventurer. He liked boats, he flew an airplane, and he most enjoyed the company of his celebrity sports friends. He took them on his Ford yacht, gave them lucrative Ford jobs if needed, and entertained them at his castle-like home outside Ann Arbor. Henry Ford had helped him design and pay for the sanctuary, which sat along the Huron River on a 155-acre parcel. The house was a fortress and featured modest turrets, two-foot thick walls, secret rooms, hidden escape tunnels, and a steep, pitch-dark, seventy-foot staircase with asymmetrical steps to frustrate would-be pursuers. It also had a movie theater, a Roman bath, and living quarters for his pet tigers and lions. Armed guards sometimes patrolled the roof.

Bennett and Cochrane had much in common. Both flew planes, were former boxers, played musical instruments, and prided themselves on being vigorously masculine men. They were also loyal to friends, not easily frightened, and strongly conservative politically. (Most of the Cochrane men were; in 1964, Mickey's brother Archie would chair the Montana presidential campaign of his Staunton Military School roommate Barry Goldwater.) In the years ahead Bennett, active in Republican circles, would persuade some of his athletic pals to run for office. He would get two football coaches elected: Harry Kipke to the University of Michigan board and Gus Dorais to Detroit City Council. And in 1940 he would nearly convince Cochrane to run for sheriff of Wayne County. By then Cochrane would be a manufacturer's representative for Dryden Rubber, selling to Ford and other companies and making more money than he had in baseball. The Cochranes and Bennetts would become so close that Cochrane's children would call Bennett "Uncle Harry." The families would even have homes next to one another on Grosse Ile, south of Detroit.

But that was years off. In 1934 the men were just drawing close. Given Bennett's reputation and his association with questionable characters, not everyone thought it wise of Cochrane to be buddies with him. Malcolm Bingay, as Iffy the Dopester, was apparently among them. Without naming Bennett, he warned in print that Cochrane was surrounding himself with admiring "yes" men whose advice wasn't always solid. He implied that some were disreputable. Who knew what kind of influence Bennett might have on Cochrane?

PART II:
GRAND PLANS

1935

A New Year

The optimism of a new year smiled upon Detroit. Col. Pickert felt so terrific about the dawn of 1935 that he didn't make any resolutions. "My life is just about perfect. In fact, I might say exemplary," he told a reporter. Crime had dropped in 1934. The department's numbers were almost too good to believe. Detroit saw only sixty killings, inspectors said. Half amounted to justifiable homicide, and ten of those were by police officers. All but six had been solved, according to John Navarre, head of the homicide division. Deaths classified as suicides had fallen too. There were 209. Further, of the 936 men reported missing, all but seven had been located, police noted. Given such statistics, how could the police commissioner's spirits not be high?

Maurice Sugar was hopeful about his judicial campaign. He focused on labor and liberty issues. He supported improved working conditions and the right to organize. He opposed fascism, the spy system in factories, and discrimination against Negroes and the foreign-born. Labor unions would soon begin aligning behind Sugar. So would ethnic organizations like the Ukrainian American Club and the Polish American Political Club. Sugar would earn an acquittal for two black men, Charles Lee and Monroe Brown, who had already been held ninety days for, in his view, being unemployed—officially for having "no home, no job, and no visible means of support." The case would help him land the endorsement of black ministers and leaders, including Dr. Ossian Sweet. Sugar's candidacy would grow rapidly.

Joe Louis also had much to anticipate. If all went well, the year might bring big money and a shot at the heavyweight title. After turning pro in July, Louis had averaged two fights a month and won all twelve.

On Wednesday, January 2, 1935, he appeared at the Naval Academy in Detroit for the first round of the Golden Gloves competition. Organizers wanted to honor their best-known alumnus. Louis accepted a trophy from the Briggs company, for whom he had once worked. Mickey Cochrane was on hand for the matches. When fans spotted him in the crowd, they began chanting, "We want Mickey! We want Mickey!" Cochrane climbed into the ring to acknowledge the cheers of 3,000 fight fans. Jovial heavyweight champ Max Baer served as master of ceremonies. He told reporters beforehand that Louis would lose his Friday bout to the experienced Patsy Perroni. But he was wrong. Louis defeated him and a week later scored a technical knockout over Hans Birkie. Months earlier, writers had begun referring to Louis as "The Brown Bomber." Despite Louis's victories, his black managers could not break him into the New York market, which was controlled by Madison Square Garden. An official said Louis needed to take on a white manager and be willing to throw some matches.

Cochrane and Navin, of course, had grand expectations for the new year, though Navin hedged his words. "A lot of baseball men are predicting trouble for the Tigers next season on the supposition that we will be hit hard by the injury jinx," he said. "They don't believe we can go through another season with our regular lineup intact as we did in 1934. They may be right. However, any team that wins a pennant must get the breaks. We ought to get them again next season if the law of averages still is in operation."

Life wasn't just about baseball, not even for Cochrane. Everyday affairs still needed to be addressed. In January he went to the Wayne County clerk's office to get license plates for his vehicles. While there, he requested a permit for a concealed weapon. All applications needed the backing of two local figures. Longtime scout Wish Egan endorsed Cochrane's request, and so did Ford strongman Harry Bennett. It was approved while he waited.

Mr. Hoover, Investigate

WILLIAM GUTHRIE SHOWED UP AT THE LITTLE STONE CHAPEL FOR what he thought was a card party. Lured into the basement, he quickly found himself ringed by hooded legionnaires who placed a rope around his neck and forced him to take the oath beside the American flag. For weeks afterward Guthrie succeeded in avoiding the legion. He stopped going to meetings until two men arrived at his large house on Hendrie Street and commanded he come with them. They drove to a gathering in a field, where legionnaires told him he would have to evict his German-speaking mother-in-law and fire his Catholic maid. Guthrie protested that his wife's mother was sickly. He refused to expel her. His decision led the legion to court-martial him. They handcuffed him to a tree and whipped him. Bloody wounds snaked across his back. At home he acted angry with his wife so she would keep her distance and not discover the beating. He slept in the basement. The legionnaires persisted about the mother and the maid until Guthrie fired the housekeeper and forced his mother-in-law out of her sickbed. He told his stunned wife that they could no longer afford to keep her.

For his livelihood Guthrie offered massages, therapeutic baths, and foot care in his basement. Though he had no medical degree, he didn't discourage anyone who assumed otherwise. Visitors called him Doc. When legion state commander Arthur Lupp discovered Doc's house—an impressive two-story structure with a gabled roof, wraparound porch, and wide exterior staircase—he commandeered use of it. The fact that the Hendrie neighborhood, a mix of industrial and residential, had large parking lots added to its appeal. Plus the legion would be able to cram a hundred men into Guthrie's basement. It would be one more place to rotate gatherings. When Lupp further discovered that Guthrie was storing a friend's printing press, he insisted it be used for legion business. They printed membership cards with it. An unwilling participant in the early days, Guthrie became so involved in the Black Legion that one could no longer tell whether he had come to believe fully in what it stood for or whether he had resigned himself out of fear.

Hoods, robes, and guns. Midnight initiations. Red lights in dark rooms. The Black Oath with its death pledge. Floggings, night rides, and porch visits. Police officers and public officials. Friends in high places. Co-workers, bosses, and jobs. Weekend musters. All of these things, the whole accumulation of them, combined to prey on the minds of members, whether truly devoted, reluctant, or errant. At every initiation recruits heard that the only ex-members were dead ones. Beatings and killings—real or faked?—marked inductions.

Early in Dayton Dean's tenure, he saw a man hanged. Or believed he had. Peg-Leg White was there. It was nighttime and they were in a wooded area in Macomb County, just outside the Detroit city limits. A car ferrying a screaming, terrified man pulled into the meeting and drove past a throng of recruits and members. "A man carrying a red lantern was standing in the roadway leading to the woods," Dean said. "The men in the car with him pulled him out and hanged him to a tree. After a while they cut him down and put the body in the car along with some shovels. They said they were going to bury him in a ditch in the woods." Dean never forgot it. He believed his life hung on his success as a legionnaire.

On the west side of the state, at a convention of milk and dairy inspectors, Arthur Lupp spotted Charles McCutcheon, a bacteriologist for the Detroit health department. Lupp was a dairy inspector with the agency. McCutcheon had been trying to avoid Lupp and everyone else associated with the Black Legion for more than a year, ever since he had been invited to a political meeting and found himself in a dark basement, lit only by the beam of a flashlight trained on a pistol that was aimed at him. Petrified, McCutcheon had taken the oath and then tried to break free. He ended up going to a few other meetings after being visited at his home by enforcers. At one he saw an inductee faint with fear. When leaders insisted he bring friends into the organization, McCutcheon told them he had no friends. In the ten months since, he had been ducking the group by not going out at night. Now the state commander stood before him.

Lupp asked McCutcheon if it would be possible "to inject typhoid germs into bottles of milk." The inquiry staggered him. Typhoid was deadly and highly contagious. He told Lupp it was a foolish thing to ponder. Typhoid would spread "like wildfire." In the coming weeks Lupp posed more questions to McCutcheon: Could the germ be produced in large quantities? Could it be put into milk bottles? Would the germs flourish in cottage cheese? Could typhoid be spread by jabbing an infected needle into an unsuspecting person on the street or in a theater? It became clear to McCutcheon that Lupp's intended targets were "class enemies"—Jews, blacks, and Catholics. Lupp hoped to direct his efforts at entire neighborhoods. A registered pharmacist, McCutcheon had no intention of creating typhoid germs. He wanted to tell someone about Lupp's reprehensible plan. But who? He knew the legion's reach. He fretted over his predicament. He feared that Lupp would retaliate against his wife and young son.

Typhoid continued to intrigue Lupp. He visited "Doc" Guthrie at his home and inquired about his basement. It was warm and humid—ideal for breeding germs, Lupp noted. The comment baffled Guthrie until Lupp laid out his plan. He wanted to spread typhoid in targeted neighborhoods. Astounded, Guthrie said he would have no part of it. He told him it was Frankenstein-like. "It might wipe out the whole city," Guthrie said. Realizing the gravity of the plot, Guthrie said he would tell police. Lupp reminded him that the Black Legion had spies in every police department and that they would frame Guthrie if he said anything.

Lupp was also curious as to whether Guthrie had the ability to make bombs. He brought him sketches of prototypes: one for a pocked grenade that would explode into shrapnel, one for a tube packed with dynamite, and one shaped like a cigarette that could be tossed into vehicles. He also asked what he knew about stench bombs and whether cyanide gas could be blown successfully through the keyhole of a synagogue door.

As the Black Legion spread, Major-General Bert Effinger must have wondered how to keep so many men motivated and in line. The legion had been targeting individuals, primarily union organizers, political enemies, and wayward members. But Effinger needed a more substantial project, something national in scope, to keep the men engaged.

Effinger didn't like the changes being speedily implemented by President Roosevelt. He talked often about how much better the nation would be without Roosevelt. At a gathering in January, Effinger mentioned for the first time his plans to overthrow the US government. "They did it in Russia with 30,000 men and we are stronger than that here in the United States and are better equipped," he said. He set the date for September 16, 1936.

—⁓—

Before 1,900 people at the glorious Wilson Theater—an ornate testament to the wealth of capitalistic automotive pioneer John Dodge and the generosity of his widow, Matilda—Maurice Sugar took the stage prior to British communist Evelyn John Strachey, the featured speaker. Sugar blasted publisher William Randolph Hearst, calling him "the greatest menace to the American people." He also castigated the Detroit Board of Education for denying his own application to speak at Northern High School. But the audience members had come to see Strachey, not Sugar, and they cheered when he brought him to the stage.

Strachey, an eloquent and passionate proponent of Marxism, was facing deportation for his stormy lectures calling for political change in the United States. "This capitalist system must be in a precarious position indeed if it can't afford a discussion of its difficulties," he said. Author of *The Coming Struggle for Power*, Strachey criticized Father Charles Coughlin and Senator Huey Long of Louisiana. "There is nothing Coughlin or Long has said that was nearly so radical as what Hitler or Mussolini said. Goodness knows it isn't hard to find things wrong with the capitalist system. But they hope by reckless demagoguery to switch off the masses—and they are an immense danger."

Of course he wasn't alone in targeting Coughlin and Long. On the very same day as Strachey's talk, Orthodox Jewish leader Rabbi William Margolis called Coughlin "an alleged man of God . . . a false prophet" and his church, The Shrine of the Little Flower, "a tower of shame, for across its altar lies the trammeled figure of the priesthood." In *The Nation*, just on newsstands, writer Raymond Gram Swing labeled Coughlin a fascist and leader of a movement "of passion and prejudice." At the Cass Theater and then later in a Book-Cadillac banquet room, social commentator Alexander Woollcott, radio's Town Crier and a member of New York's literary Algonquin Round Table, spoke of the power of the new medium and the "toxic twaddle of the Gentleman from Louisiana," Huey Long. He defended free speech and public discourse and said America could withstand "the huffing and puffing of such a big, bad wolf as Evelyn John St. Loe Strachey."

Activists on the same side didn't always see things the same way. At the Wilson Theater, after Strachey had spoken and while he was offstage gathering a breath before returning to answer questions, Maurice Sugar took to the podium again and invited attendees to drop coins into pass-ing trays to support Strachey's legal fight against deportation. Strachey's family was affluent and he didn't need the money. Furious, he rushed onstage, waving his arms.

"I have authorized no one to collect funds for me," he said.

The stunned crowd quieted momentarily before Sugar filled the void: "Well, if Mr. Strachey needs no collection for fighting his deportation, there is a need, and an urgent need, for one to fight fascism in Detroit." The contributions continued, but backstage Strachey chided Sugar, tell-ing him the basket passing was "an utterly stupid thing to do."

The night prior, as Strachey spoke in Ann Arbor, the Bullet Club—another name for the Black Legion—met behind curtained windows on the third floor of a Pontiac hall. Recently ousted police chief George Eckhardt had been making noise at civic hearings about a secret society that had infiltrated local politics. The club was presumably plotting its response. A snooping *Free Press* reporter watched as fifty men entered the building. He followed an elderly man up the stairs. A guard turned away the journalist, telling him it was a private meeting. The reporter described the attendees as "working men." He noted, "Public officials, lawyers, police officers, and others who direct the club's activities . . . seek to prevent their identity becoming known by never appearing at general membership meetings." Weeks later, a story about a police hearing mentioned the Bullet Club again. "The club has operated under various names—the Night Riders, Searchlight Club, and Black Legion, among others." It was likely the first mention in print of the Black Legion, but the attention was fleeting. The club name receded back into darkness. Reporters had no idea what they had almost stumbled upon.

In Lima, Ohio, home to Major-General Bert Effinger, a prominent businessman telephoned postal inspector J. F. Cordrey and asked to speak in confidence. He said he had learned about an organization from one of his employees, a young man who had been a member and felt his life was "in more or less constant jeopardy" after leaving the group. It was called the Black Legion.

Cordrey launched an investigation. What he found troubled him. He believed the legion was fomenting revolution against the Roosevelt administration. He highlighted what he had discovered in a three-page letter to his boss. He outlined the organization's structure, naming Dr. Shepard in Bellaire, Ohio, as its head and Effinger as director of operations east of the Mississippi. Cordrey told of the robes, the Black Oath, and the armed inductions. He blamed Effinger for the destruction of the Lima movie house that had been showing *White Angel*, a film that presented Catholics favorably. He reported that Lima's chief of police and other officers belonged, as did the vast majority of local Federal Emergency Relief Administration employees, including Effinger's son, Guy, who worked as a timekeeper.

The postal inspector named several leaders, identified their local meeting places—primarily a farm and the Ford Dance Hall on Findlay Road—and revealed that members pledged to lie in court rather than testify against their brothers. "If they resign or abandon the organization," he noted, "their only escape from punishment is suicide or to leave the country." He related that Effinger had bragged that sixty-two legionnaires worked for the Department of Justice and other federal bureaus. Cordrey's report moved quickly through the chain of command, from Lima to the Cincinnati inspector to the chief postal inspector to the attorney general's office in Washington.

The report arrived on the desk of John Edgar Hoover, director of the Federal Bureau of Investigation. Hoover, his bureau, and the G-Men had ascended to heroic prominence. They had successfully executed a war on crime, depleting through arrests and shootouts a roster of bank-robbing, ransom-demanding, headline-hogging public enemies. On September 22, 1933, the G-Men had captured Machine Gun Kelly in Memphis. Eight months later, they had killed Clyde Barrow and Bonnie Parker in Louisiana. John Dillinger fell that July in Chicago, followed by Pretty Boy Floyd in October and Baby Face Nelson in November. Now Hoover was reading a cover memo from Attorney General William Stanley's office wondering about Cordrey's report related to Justice Department employees. Hoover wasn't inclined to investigate. In a note at the bottom of the memo, he directed an assistant to return the letter to Stanley "and state there is no indication that any members of the bureau belong and consequently no action needed here."

Hoover might have thought he was done. But his curt response irked Stanley, who promptly offered a terse reply of his own. "In view of the fact that it is alleged that sixty-two employees of this department are members of this organization, I wish that you would conduct an investigation with a view to ascertaining who they are."

On the night of March 29, 1935, Joe Louis defeated Natie Brown at Olympia, raising his professional record to 17–0. Afterward he and his local team celebrated at the Frog Club on Madison, working out an agreement with white New York promoter Mike Jacobs that would soon bring Louis into the lucrative Big Apple market and, they hoped, lead to a heavyweight title shot. Louis already had a group of black advisors in place, and they would remain with him. Detroit bookmaker John Roxborough, who had been managing Louis informally, had earlier signed Louis to be co-managed by Julian Black and trained by Jack Blackburn, both of Chicago. But they needed Jacobs and his cohorts to go further in a boxing world that, following the reign of controversial Jack Johnson, was reluctant to give another black fighter a significant opportunity. Jacobs also had Hearst's national sportswriters in his pocket.

A mile and a half away at the Little Stone Chapel, Dayton Dean was getting his next assignment. Among those present were Lupp, Col. Roy Hepner, Wolverine Republican League president Leslie Black (a clerk to Judge Eugene Sharp), and the inelegant Harvey Davis. The plan called for two groups to head out the next night, one to torch a communist camp beyond the city limits and another to disrupt a campaign appearance by Maurice Sugar. Dean wanted to be with the arsonists but got assigned to the Sugar event.

Woodward Avenue divided the city's east and west sides. It began downtown near the riverfront at Jefferson and cut diagonally through the city, past the 1871 former city hall, past the crisp towering J. L. Hudson Department Store building, and beside Grand Circus Park and the Fox Theatre. The legion's stone chapel was a few blocks off Woodward, which continued past the Maccabees Building (home to WYXZ and the popular *Lone Ranger* radio show) through the cultural center, with the main branch of the library on one side and the arts institute on the other. Woodward skirted within a block of the General Motors headquarters in the New Center area. It edged alongside the ritzy Boston-Edison neighborhood where Henry Ford once lived and where many titans of industry and society remained, including Frank Navin and Walter O. Briggs. Woodward sliced through the incorporated city of Highland Park—carved right out of the center of Detroit—before reemerging near Palmer Park. Miles north beyond the city limit, still along Woodward, stood Father Coughlin's Shrine of the Little Flower.

Northern High School sat at about the midpoint of the ten-mile stretch of Woodward from the waterfront to Eight Mile Road. It was three blocks from the city's largest synagogue, Beth Temple El. The night after Dayton Dean received his assignment, attorney Maurice Sugar's supporters gathered at Northern High for a rally. It was three days before the election. Detroit school officials had tried earlier to block the meeting. Citing Sugar's leftist leanings, the school system had rejected his petition to use the building. Sugar sued, noting that other candidates had been provided access. A court agreed and ordered that Sugar be allowed to hold his gathering.

On Saturday night, as hundreds were arriving at the auditorium, Dayton Dean and Leslie Black headed to the site. They stopped to buy an ax and a ladder. Black despised Sugar, in part because of the Victory case. He had talked at legion meetings about wanting to lynch both Sugar and Victory. But tonight his mission with Dean was to cut power to the high school during Sugar's rally, thus throwing the hall into darkness and allowing legion members inside to hurl stench bombs—lightbulbs filled with chemicals—and rain fake campaign literature upon the attendees. Dean tried to break into the basement of the school, thinking he could punch out the custodian and disrupt power from inside. Alas the basement door was locked. Black started to shimmy up an outside electric pole but didn't get far before growing exhausted. Dean tried next and climbed high enough to chop at the wires with an ax. Sparks flashed as Dean scurried back down. Confident he had done the job, he approached the school on foot only to discover that the lights were still on. He had cut the wrong wires, dimming a nearby safety zone.

This failure was not lost on state commander Lupp. Upon returning from the successful camp-burning mission, he chided Dean for having failed him yet again. Without cover of darkness, legion members inside the auditorium did not throw their smoke bombs. They did, however, leave behind hundreds of flyers in support of "comrade Sugar." The pamphlets, attributed falsely to the "Communist Party of America," had been printed by the legion. They urged rebellion. "Throw out the bosses and kill the aggressors of the common people," they stated. "Negroes, rise against your white oppressors. . . . Tear down this damnable form of government." The literature drew coverage in the press, with school and police authorities contending erroneously that the flyers had been created by powers aligned with Sugar. Actually, legionnaire Leslie Black had ordered them.

Sugar's allies reassembled the next day. An automobile parade, begun at four distant points in the city, converged into a massive procession toward Arena Gardens, a 3,000-seat place also along Woodward that often hosted wrestling matches. The crowd's size convinced Sugar's supporters that with a strong election-day turnout he might win one of nine seats on the judicial bench. The backing of several black ministerial associations would not hurt. In his limited newspaper advertising, Sugar highlighted only one of the many endorsements he had received. "Clarence Darrow urges election of Maurice Sugar," the copy proclaimed. The ad featuring Darrow, renowned for the Scopes "Monkey" Trial, ran in the *Detroit News*, the only of three major dailies offering anything resembling fair coverage. The sharply pro-business *Free Press* mostly ignored Sugar, and William Randolph Hearst's *Times* editorialized against him—twice in a week.

On election day Sugar drew 63,000 votes but fell short of capturing a court seat. The defeat did not extinguish his desire to be elected to public office. He decided to pursue a spot on the Detroit City Council. News quickly reached the Black Legion and Dayton Dean soon received a new assignment: Murder Maurice Sugar.

Harry's Caravan

In the Tigers' Lakeland, Florida, clubhouse at Henley Field, two veteran pitchers were talking, maybe Carl Fischer and Elon Hogsett or Vic Sorrell and Fred Marberry or some others altogether different.

"How many pitchers we going to carry this year?" asked one.

"I read in the paper where we was going to carry nine."

"Yeah, nine. And they got fourteen working out down here. . . . That means about five of us is going to get the air. I suppose they'll be keeping a couple of them young hams so they can get experience and letting a couple of real pitchers go."

"Club does that sometimes."

"Yeah, and what does it get them?"

"I'll say it gets them a lot of grief. And then some."

Harry Salsinger, "The Umpire," didn't identify the men, but he captured their conversation in his sports column. He wanted to give his readers a sense of what young players encounter when they come to camp dreaming of landing a job, which inevitably means displacing another player. "The men who have established themselves in the major leagues, consciously or unconsciously, unite against a newcomer," said Salsinger. "They have a common bond this time of year."

One look around the locker room revealed the Tigers to be a youthful team. By mid-March only four men—bespectacled Vic Sorrell, veteran starters Fred Marberry and General Crowder, and Goose Goslin—were thirty-two or older, though Cochrane and Gehringer were rapidly approaching the milestone. Almost all of the rest were in their twenties. Eleven rookies had been invited to camp, five of them pitchers. Of those Steve Larkin was the only one with major league experience.

He had pitched six innings over two games in 1934. "Whistling" Jake Wade, Clyde Hatter, Joe Sullivan, and Mike Cesnovar had yet to rise above the minors, but all held hopes. So did outfielders Hugh Shelley and Chet Morgan, infielder Salty Parker, Rose Bowl football star Dixie Howell (who had no set position), and catchers Frankie Reiber, with a sixteen-game tenure over two seasons, and Birdie Tebbetts.

The Tigers had been high on Tebbetts since his high school days. He felt an allegiance to the team because Navin had occasionally sent money to Tebbetts's widowed mother, who was bringing up three children. The team also supported his education at Providence College and saved his life by getting him medical treatment when he came down with a serious infection. If he failed at baseball, Tebbetts planned to become an attorney.

Every pitcher tells a story, and Elon Hogsett's involved his bad teeth and his nickname. His choppers had pained him so severely last season that the club ordered him to get "a flock" of infected teeth removed over the winter. His mouth was feeling better now, though his nickname, Chief, always aggravated him. (It would for the remainder of his career.) A man of few words, Hogsett told anyone who asked that he had but drops of Indian blood coursing through his veins. He was one-thirty-second Cherokee, he protested, yet writers insisted on calling him Chief. A relief pitcher, he didn't mind so much that fans responded with Indian war calls when he entered a game, but he preferred to be called Elon.

Not everyone liked one another. Pete Fox refused to talk to Goose Goslin after a smarting remark about his intelligence. They wouldn't speak for the entire 1935 season. Fox, described by baseball writer Fred Lieb as "a grim little fellow, game as a pebble," had his supporters, among them Hank Greenberg and roomie Schoolboy Rowe. Goslin preferred Gee Walker and Jo-Jo White, southern boys who called one another "nigger."

The Lakeland locker room was lively and warm. It had been improved over the winter. A coal-burning stove now stood in the middle of trainer Denny Carroll's room, with showers off to the side. Carroll kept it toasty to prevent chills. Massage tables, draped in white linen, set on each side of the stove. The room smelled of ointments and medications, a potpourri of alcohol and arnica, wintergreen and witch hazel.

Spittoons were scattered about the clubhouse, and each player had a cage to call his own with two sets of uniforms hanging inside. Players usually brought their own shoes, but this year Cochrane had purchased everyone a pair. While in one of his angry moods during a losing streak last season, he had told the screwball bastards that if they won the goddamn pennant, he'd buy them all a pair of fucking shoes. "That's a bet, Mike," Greenberg had said. Cochrane made good on the pledge. Doing so nourished team camaraderie.

Cochrane's confidence no longer drew bewildering looks from his men. When he forecast a pennant and a world championship this time, his players bought into the likelihood of it. His self-assuredness was as infectious as Heinie Schuble's smile. Schoolboy Rowe predicted he would win twenty-five games. (He was tempted to go with thirty but didn't want anyone thinking he was popping off like Dizzy Dean.) Greenberg announced he was setting his sights on the home run title, even though he had hit twenty-three fewer than leader Lou Gehrig in 1934. His hopes were bolstered by word that Navin had removed the twenty-foot screen from atop the left field fence. It had been erected originally, opponents believed, to thwart visiting sluggers like Jimmie Foxx. The screen had more than doubled the height of the wall, turning home runs into two-base hits. Need proof? Greenberg pointed out that he had led the majors with sixty-three of those buggers. But now, with Navin Field home to one of the game's most powerful hitters, the screen was coming down. And Greenberg was salivating.

He desperately wanted a taste of fame, like Rowe got with his win streak. "That's the thing that makes stars," he said. "Sixteen victories are pretty nice even if they are not won in a row. But because the Schoolboy won his in one-two-three order he became famous. . . . I am a first baseman. I can distinguish myself in three ways. I can become a superb fielder. I can lead the league in batting. Or I can lead it in hitting home runs." The first two were unlikely, he said. "Why shouldn't I go after the slugging championship? With that screen out of the way, the park is almost made to order for me."

One longtime observer noted: "The big dream lures him."

Gee Walker's spring dream was more modest. He wanted to start. He wanted to be the main guy in right field. During the World Series he had gotten only three at-bats because Cochrane favored Jo-Jo White and Pete Fox. Rumors of trades swirled around Walker like Kansas twisters. Prognosticators pointed to the team's underwhelming outfield—who was there beyond Goose Goslin?—as Detroit's drawback. Walker, whose pay had been cut by almost half, yearned to prove them wrong. Almost everyone could see his potential: The boy could hit. But his weaknesses surfaced as persistently as a cork bobber. More important, they frustrated the hell out of Cochrane, who was touting Chet Morgan as his possible right fielder.

"Gerald Walker remains . . . one of the puzzles of baseball," said Salsinger, the baseball sage. "Walker, a most likeable man and one of the most aggressive of players, has never learned to control himself on the field and to harness his ability. He should be one of the headliners of baseball, and he would be if he bridled his temper and concentrated on the game."

On this point Charles Ward, Salsinger's competitor at the *Free Press*, agreed. Ward had all sorts of splendid nicknames for players, but he fashioned nothing endearing for the popular Walker. He referred to him bluntly as "The Mississippi Hard Head." Walker's prime flaw was that he could be distracted easily. Opponents could pick him off by heckling him. So they did. During the World Series, after Walker had tied the score by driving in a run in the ninth inning, the entire Cardinals bench began yelling at him. Walker was twenty feet off first base when he engaged in the argument, screaming taunts back as the pitcher threw the ball to the first baseman, who tagged him out. The Cardinals howled with laughter. What Walker needed was to show the same attentiveness in baseball as he showed when playing the Ballyhoo and Wiffleboard games in hotel lobbies.

Throughout winter and into spring, Cochrane consistently forecast great things for his Tigers, provided they stayed healthy. "We didn't win the World Series," he told one gathering of fans. "But things will be different. . . . I think we will repeat [by capturing the league pennant] and win the series, as well." Weeks later he told his team, "We'll win again unless something serious happens." He also informed Grantland Rice that the Tigers would be back in the World Series. Rice agreed, but many observers didn't, thinking that the Tigers had gotten lucky in 1934. A pre-season poll of baseball writers showed Cleveland the favorite. New York, others said. Frank Navin, who wanted a World Series ring more than anyone, hid his thoughts behind a wall of jinx-driven caution. He admitted the Tigers had a good team. However, he noted, "Luck is a big thing in baseball. We had some last year."

One man who had no qualms about speaking his mind was Dizzy Dean, still puffed and prideful over his and his brother Paul's victories. In Bradenton, Florida, before taking on the Tigers in a spring scrimmage, Dean said the best Detroit could hope for was third place. He projected Cleveland in first and Boston or New York in second. The Indians, he explained, have "Hal Trosky, who is a much better hitter than Hank Greenberg."

All fall and winter Greenberg had been aching to pay back Dean. Because they competed in different leagues, the only opportunities arose in exhibitions and the World Series. One spring game Greenberg came to the plate with the bases loaded. He had "blood in his eye." He worked the count full before blistering a Dean pitch to deep center. It cleared the bases and gave Detroit the lead. The Tigers went on to beat the Dean brothers 13–8. It was an inconsequential game but it felt good.

Bad feelings flowed between the Tigers and the Cardinals. When a photographer tried to get Joe "Ducky" Medwick and Marv Owen to shake hands and to show that all had been forgiven after the World Series spiking incident, Medwick refused. "To hell with Owen," he said. "I tried to shake hands with him in the [1934] series and he refused. I don't want to shake hands with him now."

—— ——

Joe Louis's handlers carefully sculpted the fighter's public image, coaching him continually on what was prohibited. The idea was to make him acceptable to white America. Among the don'ts: gloating, showing too much emotion, going out on the town alone, and being photographed with white women. He was to lead a clean lifestyle in the ring and out. In April there were staged photos of Joe Louis at training camp reading his Bible. The effort worked. One observer said that Louis "is the kind of man who would make the customers forget the antics of Jack Johnson. . . . Louis is a quiet, easy going Negro who goes about his own business until he gets in the ring." Trainer Jack "Chappie" Blackburn had lived through Johnson's tumultuous tenure as champion. "If you really ain't gonna be another Jack Johnson, you've got some hope," he told Louis. "White man hasn't forgotten that fool nigger with his white women, acting like he owned the world." While Louis wasn't wild or out of control, he also wasn't the muted, sexless black man his managers hoped to see portrayed in the press. He liked flashy clothes and sporty cars. He liked clubs and parties, and he certainly enjoyed sex.

The Detroit Lions were looking for ways to improve on their 1934 performance, so they tried to recruit a few college football stars for their 1935 season. Among them was the man voted Most Valuable Player of the Michigan Wolverines, senior Gerald "Jerry" Ford. Following the Michigan season but before graduation, Ford traveled to San Francisco and played in the Shrine East-West charity game, where he impressed scouts. Afterward, on the long train ride back to Michigan, two teams, the Packers and the Lions, tried to sign him to professional contracts. The Lions offered more money: $200 per game, $2,800 for the season. But law school was calling him, so he went to Yale to coach football there, biding his time until he would be accepted.

Some of Mickey Cochrane's pals drove down to Cincinnati on Saturday, April 13, to see the Tigers in one of their final exhibitions before the regular season. The Tigers were scheduled to play the Reds at Crosley Field, but cold weather canceled the game. Cochrane held practice anyway, mostly hitting and fielding, perhaps to keep his guys fresh or maybe to give his chums something to see for their 260-mile journey.

Harry Bennett led the visiting party of ten men, including figures from sports, the armed services, and the auto industry: Wolverine coach Harry Kipke, Ford executive Russell Gnau, Ford attorney Lou Colombo, animal trainer Allen King, former UM athlete and auto-parts manufacturer Doug Roby, future four-star general Emmett "Rosie" O'Donnell, and two intimidating former athletes whom Bennett had brought into Ford, ex-boxer Elmer Hogan and former football player Stan Fay, a UM teammate of Gerald Ford. Most of the men had crewed on Bennett's steel power cruiser, *The Margaret II*. Cochrane chatted with them and joked with the animal trainer, asking him not to tame his Tigers. "We want them all wild except the pitchers when the season opens," he said.

Bennett had recently been dealing with some unpleasant attention at the Rouge plant, where a camshaft worker had died from eating poisoned food. Louis Sherry, twenty-five, had fallen over dead during his lunch break after biting into a sandwich powdered with cyanide, a substance used at the factory. Bennett said that he and his staff, working with the county prosecutor's office, interviewed 140 employees. Though Bennett initially insisted the sandwich wasn't sold in the plant, a coroner's jury determined that Sherry bought it from lunch wagon number five.

More than a year later, after Dayton Dean's wife suggested that the Black Legion might have been involved in Sherry's death, Bennett would respond forcefully: "We believe a satisfactory explanation of Sherry's death was discovered at the time, although there was not sufficient evidence to justify an arrest. The investigation has not been dropped but there is no reason whatever to believe that Sherry was a victim of the Black Legion or any other gang." At the same time physician Dr. Nathan Bicknell would send a letter to Congressman John Lesinski Sr. urging a national investigation into the legion. "I would like to know . . . if Harry Bennett, chief Ford stool pigeon, is not behind the scenes." Lesinski would forward the letter to J. Edgar Hoover. What Bicknell wouldn't say was that he was a member of the jury that had investigated Sherry's death but couldn't determine what had happened.

Might Bennett have been in the Black Legion? Bennett showed a willingness to align himself with individuals and organizations that could help him. The legion, with its strong anti-union stance, qualified. By one member's estimate some Ford departments were comprised mostly of legion members. The secret society also had a separate "businessman's regiment" with a more dignified initiation ceremony for men like Bennett. At the very least it seems improbable that Bennett, whose spies knew everything happening on the factory floor, did not know and approve of the legion.

The visit with Cochrane must have been a welcome diversion for Bennett. The Tigers had taken shape over the past days. Almost all of the questions had been answered. Football star Dixie Howell turned out to be an unspectacular player who desperately needed time in the minors—even before a line drive struck his cheekbone and put him in the hospital. Flea Clifton, twenty pounds meatier than the previous season, won a backup spot, thus avoiding a trip to Hollywood. And Gee Walker fulfilled his dream, for the moment anyway, by being anointed the right fielder. His new stature led to an unusual editorial. It appeared in the front section of one daily beside opinion pieces about the Nazis and the National Recovery Administration. It said, "Navin Field fans are ever ready to forgive Gerald Walker his lapses and will be amiably disposed to his latest restoration to grace. . . . [But] two hours a day is not too much to have to focus one's interest on a job. In the name of the baseball-loving population of Detroit, we urge the young man to turn a deaf ear to repartee from the sidelines and try to concentrate on the matter in hand, namely the bringing of a second pennant to Detroit."

Back in his office in Detroit, Frank Navin flustered writer W. W. Edgar by not out-and-out predicting a pennant. Navin said he expected six of eight American League clubs to be competitive and that the Tigers would be in the hunt. "A lot of things can happen in baseball between April and October," he said. "If we only knew what was in store in the way of luck and the form of the players, it would be much simpler to forecast."

Navin looked jowlier than usual. Red blotches tinted his cheeks.

"Then you think the Tigers have a good chance of repeating?" Edgar asked.

"As I said, we should be right up in the fight all the way, unless something unexpected happens." Navin sounded evasive, but perhaps he was just being honest.

The Tigers started the season by losing nine of their first eleven games. Cochrane was furious.

The Radio Priest

FATHER CHARLES COUGHLIN FINALLY TOOK THE PLATFORM AFTER eleven o'clock on the night of Wednesday, April 24, 1935. The 15,300 men and women who had jammed into Olympia Arena, hundreds without seats, exploded in a feverish frenzy. Finally the man they most wanted to hear—the famed radio priest from Royal Oak, whose over-the-air sermons drew ten million to thirty million listeners weekly—approached the microphone.

Two and a half hours had passed since the addresses had begun. Eleven men had already spoken, including farm and labor leaders, senators, representatives, and a rabbi. The priest's devoted followers had reason to be weary after so many talks, but they greeted the white-collared Coughlin exuberantly. All night they had cheered the mere mention of his name. The event, with socialists and communists protesting outside, was the first mass public gathering of Coughlin's National Union for Social Justice. The audience consisted mostly of working class people "from the more humble walks of life." Coughlin's message—anti-communist, anti-banker, share-the-wealth—appealed to a wide swath of struggling Americans, not merely Catholics.

Of Irish ancestry by way of Canada, Coughlin had a voice that writer Wallace Stegner described as "of such mellow richness, such manly, heartwarming, confidential intimacy, such emotional and ingratiating charm, that anyone turning past it almost had to hear it again." Over the years his radio sermons had shifted from religious lessons about charity to increasingly fiery political diatribes. As his listenership increased, so did his boldness. In 1932 he had endorsed Franklin Roosevelt. Now he was accusing him of being in cahoots with Wall Street. Roosevelt had not gone far enough in helping the poor, he felt. Coughlin's intensifying attacks got him lumped with Senator Huey Long of Louisiana. Both were seen by Roosevelt's supporters as a threat to FDR and by many others as either dangerous demagogues or national saviors.

Six weeks earlier in a long radio denunciation, General Hugh Johnson, a former Roosevelt appointee and 1933 *Time* magazine Man of the Year, had condemned Coughlin and Long as "two pied pipers" riling the "lunatic fringes."

"It is not," Johnson said, "exaggeration to say that, through the doorway of his priestly office, covered in his designs by the sanctity of the robe he wears, Father Coughlin, by the cheap strategy of appealing to the envy of those who have nothing for those who have something, has become the active political head of an active political party. . . . We can neither respect nor revere what appears to be a priest in holy orders entering our homes with the open sesame of his high calling and there, in the name of Jesus Christ, demanding that we ditch the President for Huey Long, bastardize our American system, and destroy the government of our country."

Johnson coyly fanned anti-Catholic bigotry under the guise of doing the opposite. He said he rejected the "ridiculous rumor . . . that Father Coughlin is the agent of the Pope in trying to upset this Protestant country in the interests of the Church in Rome. Nothing could be more absurd, and yet it is perfectly plain that either the Church or Father Coughlin should promptly sever his revolutionary political activities from his priestly office."

Coughlin's rebuttal had been equally harsh. He described Johnson as a "comic-opera, cream-puff general" and "a political corpse whose ghost has returned to haunt us." Johnson responded by labeling Coughlin and Long "political termites."

Coughlin was too powerful to ignore. The fear that he would align with Long and create a third party coursed through political circles. Coughlin commanded a motivated audience. His broadcasts elicited literally tons of letters, 80,000 on an average week and up to one million on occasion. He received more mail than anyone in the country. A post office had been erected in Royal Oak to handle the influx. Coughlin's own office staff exceeded one hundred employees. Many of the letters they handled included donations. The money was funding construction of Coughlin's new, larger limestone church, Shrine of the Little Flower. Already erected on the site was the seven-story art deco Charity Crucifixion Tower. It featured a twenty-eight-foot relief of Christ on the cross, and it glowed at night within a confluence of floodlight beams.

When Coughlin began his National Union for Social Justice, he outlined sixteen principles. Among them were that every citizen willing to work receive "a just, living, annual wage," that the Federal Reserve be abolished, and that farmers be ensured a "fair profit." It was a remedy cheered by his backers.

Coughlin was one of the most famous men in America. Everybody knew of him, including the Black Legion. Early on Dayton Dean began going to meetings of Coughlin's National Union. Dean was sent as a spy, but he found Coughlin's words, spoken in his rolling, booming voice, alluring. Dean felt that Coughlin, religion aside, supported working men like himself. One night at a local church meeting, Coughlin startled Dean during his talk. "There are men in this audience tonight who would like to get rid of me," he said. Coughlin looked at Dean. Their eyes connected. "But I'm not afraid. I'm going to speak the truth." Dean told his wife that he thought Coughlin was addressing him directly.

When he spoke, Coughlin held his notes in his left hand and waved and jerked his right arm as if angrily conducting Stravinsky's *The Rite of Spring*. His hand was balled into a fist. He hammered his pulpit with it. His head bobbed as he made his points. At Olympia, sweat streaming down his face, Coughlin proclaimed that he would organize auto workers into one bargaining unit. "For years the laboring man has endeavored to obtain a just and living wage in Michigan, and for forty years he has failed to organize his bargaining power. . . . The du Ponts and General Motors and Ford, Packard, and Chrysler—I am not afraid of them," Coughlin said.

Indeed in 1930, appearing before a congressional committee, Coughlin had predicted that within three years there would be a communist revolution in America—and that Henry Ford would be to blame because he had falsely advertised the need for new workers. "As a result of that statement, many more than the 30,000 flocked to Detroit. . . . [But] there were no jobs for them and the only redress was to have the fire hose turned on them," Coughlin testified. Such treatment had driven the men toward the communist party, he said. The discord between Coughlin and Ford would not last. Three years later Coughlin reached out to Ford, bidding him Easter greetings. He also mailed him a copy of his book, *The New Deal in Money.*

Earlier in the evening at Olympia, Rabbi Ferdinand M. Isserman of St. Louis had addressed the crowd. Isserman had visited Nazi Germany in 1933 and warned of what was transpiring there. His presence at the Coughlin event was in support of social justice, but it played as a response to critics of the priest. Isserman gently nudged Coughlin, encouraging his union to be "animated not with malice but mercy, not with hate but with love, not with frenzy but with reason." Coughlin lately had been drawing fire for statements seen as anti-Jewish. Beginning in mid-1937, Coughlin would veer harshly into the world of antisemitism, becoming a dark, unambiguous presence. But his words in 1935 were more shaded. He talked of international bankers and money changers. He referenced "Jewish gold" and chastised various figures whose names—Morgenthau, Warburg, Rothschild, Kuhn, Loeb—left little doubt to their roots. His gauzy attacks prompted New York rabbi Stephen Wise to appeal publicly to Coughlin to choose words that would not "feed and fan flames of anti-Jewish feeling." Wise based his mild reproach on the premise that Coughlin's offenses had been unintentional.

Others thought not. In Los Angeles, speaking to a thousand people at a B'nai B'rith meeting, entertainer Eddie Cantor described Coughlin as lacking "an atom of sincerity in his entire system." He added, "Free speech is a wonderful thing, but through the radio we are permitting many like him to address millions. We are living in precarious times. You know the situation in Europe, as far as our Jews are concerned, but I doubt if any of you know how close to the same situation we are here in America. We must recognize the facts. We must stand united."

In 1935 Henry Ford was still the Detroit region's most prominent antisemite. Ford's prejudices were no secret. He was "bigoted about Jews, and just as much so about Roman Catholics," Harry Bennett would say later. Over the decades Ford had built a notorious reputation and his long record spoke louder than the apologies engineered by underlings. He had published the weekly *Dearborn Independent*, which regularly castigated Jews. Typical was this banner headline from May 22, 1920: THE INTERNATIONAL JEW—THE WORLD'S PROBLEM. Venomous stories from the *Independent* were gathered into a book, *The International Jew*, which was translated into sixteen languages and distributed worldwide. Among its admirers was Adolf Hitler, whose waiting room had a table featuring multiple copies of the release. In 1938 Ford and Coughlin would become allies in their dislike of Jews, discussing such issues during regular lunch meetings.

Standing in their brown robes, the Capuchin friars of St. Bonaventure Monastery were among the more noticeable attendees at Olympia. Coughlin was friends with several of them, especially Father Solanus Casey, a gray-bearded and bespectacled man two decades older than he. Aside from their faith and their Irish ancestry, Coughlin and Casey shared a joyous love for baseball and the Tigers. Coughlin had played with the St. Basil College team in Waco, Texas, while a young faculty member at the seminary. In one game St. Basil upset Baylor, a Baptist university, with Tris Speaker reportedly in uniform under an alias. The Catholic vs. Baptist confrontation ended violently with Coughlin suffering "the worst physical beating of my life. But it was worth it," he said. "We showed them that Catholics could beat Baptists."

In Michigan in the 1920s, Coughlin was assigned to start a parish in Royal Oak near a Klan stronghold. After he built the church, the Klan torched a cross outside the chapel. As he was growing his community, Coughlin became friends with Wish Egan, one of the Tigers' Catholic scouts. He asked for Egan's help with a fund-raiser, and one day when the Yankees were in town Babe Ruth and teammate Joe Dugan, as well as Tiger Harry Heilmann, convened at the church doors. They collected donations from the throngs who had heard they would be there. "No change today!" Ruth called out. "No change today!"

Solanus Casey wasn't a promoter. He was quiet and reserved. Born Bernard Casey in rural Wisconsin, Barney was one of sixteen children. Their large family had a baseball team, the Casey All-Brothers Nine, for which Barney served as catcher. Though older than his seminary classmates, Casey continued to catch, stubbornly refusing a mask, content to protect himself with a blessing. Like Coughlin, Casey ended up in Detroit in the 1920s. Late in the decade, after the market crashed, poverty and hunger overwhelmed the city. The Capuchins never turned away those in need of a meal. But as the crowds grew, their informal feeding of the poor became unsustainable. So the Capuchins, with Casey playing a key role, founded a soup kitchen. During the dire days of the Depression, the kitchen served up to 2,000 people per day.

Casey, who did not go to college, admired Coughlin and fell into the political sway of his better-educated friend. He came to agree with Coughlin's opposition to Roosevelt, describing the president in a letter to his sister as "simply of the bankers" and noting that "my enthusiasm for him is almost—or fast becoming—ancient history." In one letter he referred to Coughlin as a "prophet." Biographer Michael Crosby said that in political matters Casey had a "gullibility [that] . . . was able to be exploited. . . . While Solanus might have intuitions about matters of the Lord, they were not always paralleled in his social analysis." But matters of politics rarely entered into his official role.

As the monastery porter, Father Casey was becoming known throughout Detroit. Numerous Catholics, as well as an occasional Protestant or Jew, came to meet with him at his desk, which sat to the right of the door, plainly in public view. A conviction was strengthening among believers that his intercession and prayers could bring relief and healing. Those who consulted him ranged from the meek to the powerful, including a Detroit mayor, Frank Murphy, and a governor, Alex Groesbeck. Father Casey's growing popularity and unhurried manners meant his waiting room was often filled with visitors who might be in line for two or three hours. One who came in 1935 was eighty-nine-year-old French Canadian brother André Bessette, a future saint. He had traveled from Montreal. Each knelt before the other to receive a blessing.

After his Olympia appearance, Coughlin held rallies of the National Union in Cleveland, where 25,000 turned out, and in New York at a packed Madison Square Garden. He railed against Roosevelt, whose mere name elicited boos. He also tore into the "kept press" for siding with financiers and suppressing "the voice of the people." Such raucous displays upset some Catholic leaders. "All these disturbing voices . . . the shouting, yelling, and screaming are so unbecoming," said Boston cardinal William O'Connell. "They are hysterical. And no priest of God, no teacher of the Christian Church, ever permits himself to be hysterical."

The Killing of Silas Coleman

FOR SOME TIME HARVEY DAVIS HAD BEEN WONDERING WHAT IT WOULD feel like to kill a black man. Promoted over co-worker Dayton Dean to colonel of the third regiment, Davis intended to find out. He hated blacks. He opposed any movement toward integration. He did not want blacks in his neighborhood and he did not want black children in his children's schools. He preferred blacks not be in his world at all.

As a teenager in Kentucky, Davis had had small run-ins with the law. He spent a month in a reformatory after tricking a dim farmer out of six dollars in 1913. (He used the money for a picnic of sodas and candy for friends.) In 1917 he stole a horse from a black livery worker. Just adolescent skylarking, he explained.

Eighteen years on, Davis had a wife, Ruth, and four daughters, from three months to fourteen years old. He and Ruth hoped to move to a bigger home, where his mother could have her own room, but illnesses and unexpected bills disrupted their plans. When they could get away, they liked to spend weekends at a multicolor shingled cottage along Rush Lake near Pinckney. A friend owned the place but allowed Davis frequent use of his cabin.

For some men the Black Legion's appeal centered on politics. They hoped to elect like-minded, fiercely anti-communist candidates and to crush their enemies. For others the legion's hatred of Jews and Catholics provided the attraction. For Davis it was mostly about race. Davis had gotten a taste of blood in February 1935 when he, Dean, and Charles Rouse went to Ecorse in search of a political opponent. Failing to find him, Davis decided to target one of the man's black supporters, Clarence

Oliver. They intended to kill Oliver but couldn't locate him either. Davis wasn't ready to leave though.

"I want to shoot a nigger," he said. They drove up and down nearby streets, seeking a black man, any black man. It was winter and dark already. Edward Armour was returning home from his job at Ford. Rouse stopped the car. From down the street Armour saw the headlights dim. As he neared the vehicle, he could see the silhouettes of three men.

Davis called to Armour from the car.

"Hey, Sid," he said. "Hey, Sid."

Armour ignored him and kept walking. Davis and Dean leapt from the car as Armour ran toward his home. On the porch Armour banged on the door and waited for Louise, his wife, to let him inside. Davis took aim and shot. The bullet went through Armour's metal lunch box and into his side near his spine.

"Let's get the hell out of here," Davis said. The men drove off as Armour's wife called for help. The shooting put Armour in the hospital for months. Police had no suspects and Armour could offer little in the way of a description. One was short and one was tall, he told police.

On another night Dean and Davis drove slowly through a downriver neighborhood with thirteen sticks of dynamite and a starter cap in their vehicle. Dean worried that the explosives could go off at any time. Davis wanted to bomb a black man's home, but he insisted that it be occupied. They surveyed several residences, checked for cars, and peered into windows. They found one potential target, but couldn't be sure that anyone was there. Davis told Dean, "Well, I don't see no use wasting all this dynamite on this shack 'less the nigger's inside."

Poor blacks made safe targets. More often than not, they faced the wrath, not the assistance, of law enforcement. Police forces were almost entirely white and in the Detroit area notoriously brutal toward blacks. Complaints of violence abounded but drew minimal press coverage. The stories that appeared in the dailies usually justified and rationalized police aggression rather than condemned it.

In Highland Park in early April, police fired at an unarmed homeless man, Frank Massie, at one-thirty in the afternoon. Massie was naked and reportedly accosting schoolchildren when police arrived and chased him into an alley. They shot Massie in the back, claiming that he had earlier grabbed a child and begun to twist his neck. *Highland Parker* editor Art Kingsley doubted the police. Under the headline POLICE OFFICER'S SHOOTING OF CRAZED NEGRO CALLS FOR INVESTIGATION, Kingsley questioned the need to gun down a fleeing, unarmed man. "Shooting a human being to death—black or white—is not a trivial matter," he said. "It is not a thing to be lightly dismissed as merely 'a regrettable occurrence.' Likewise, when a policeman uses his revolver and especially with fatal effect, all the circumstances deserve to be thoroughly investigated, without delay."

One May afternoon Davis and Dean were working at the Mistersky Power Station, a six-story coal-burning plant not far from the pre–Civil War Fort Wayne, when Davis asked him if he could "get hold of a colored guy." Davis said he was planning a weekend party at the place near Rush Lake and wanted to provide his guests "a little excitement." It didn't matter which black man; any would do. They were just going to shoot him for amusement. Dean said that he didn't know any candidates but that Charles Rouse might.

Rouse owed Silas Coleman eighteen dollars for carrying bricks. Rouse had hired him off the street so there was no paper trail. He was an ideal candidate, Rouse thought. Coleman, forty-two, had been working sporadically through the winter and spring. He had come into a bit of money recently, probably from illicit activity. (He had earlier served time for breaking and entering.) With the windfall Coleman had bought three new suits. He felt optimistic. His job prospects had brightened recently. A Great War veteran, Coleman possessed a letter from an American Legion post commander recommending him to Donald Marshall, one of the supervisors who hired blacks at Ford Motor Company. It was a form letter from a man who didn't know him, but Coleman hoped it would work magic. He kept the letter in his jacket pocket.

<hr>

Jesse Owens, already a collegiate track star, had sports fans speculating about how well he might do at the Big Ten Western Conference championship. Maybe a world record? Or two? Owens, a sophomore at Ohio State University, had been amazing track enthusiasts with his performances. Expectations were high. In March he had set the world indoor record in the sixty-yard dash, defeating defending champion Willis Ward of the University of Michigan. Owens was looking forward to the outdoor championships in Ann Arbor. But not everyone was. "A guy can't get a word in edgewise what with the shine-boys, locker-room attendants, and janitors proudly relating the feats of strength and skill and speed performed by their 'cullud' brethren," wrote Braven Dyer of the *Los Angeles Times*. "My favorite bootblack can rattle off more of Jesse Owens's records than I can, and that's supposed to be my business."

Six days before the big event, Owens injured his back roughhousing with friends after a flag football game in Columbus. Throughout the week his coach, trainer, and teammates worked on him, applying heat and massaging his muscles, trying to get him ready for the big day. When Saturday, May 25, arrived—a pleasant sunny afternoon in Ann Arbor—Owens was unsure whether he would be able to compete.

Twelve thousand people came to Ferry Field, former home of the Wolverines football team. Among the horde of students was Gerald Ford, Michigan's star center. He came not only to root for his college, but also for Willis Ward, one of his closest friends. Ward, like Owens and Joe Louis, was Alabama-born. He played football at Michigan, contributing to its national championships in 1932 and 1933, as well as its dismal 1–7 1934 season. Ward was also black, a fact that had prompted a visiting Georgia Tech team to vow not to play if Ward took the field. Ford and other teammates threatened to quit if Ward was not allowed to play, but Ward intervened and encouraged them to compete.

Minutes before the track championship, Owens told his coach he wanted to try his first event, the 100-yard dash. At three-fifteen he won the race, tying the world record at 9.4 seconds. Seven minutes later in the long jump, he topped Ward and others by leaping more than twenty-six feet and eight inches, another world record. By four o'clock, he had set two more records, in the 220-yard sprint and the 220-yard low hurdles. Even Michigan fans cheered wildly for Owens. Though injured, he delivered a performance for the ages. On sports pages through the country his feat overshadowed not only the local ball teams—the Tigers won their sixth in seven tries—but also Babe Ruth's final three career home runs, delivered in one game.

Meanwhile the still-undefeated Joe Louis was in New York, training for his biggest match yet, a June Yankee Stadium bout against former champion Primo Carnera, whose punches had once killed a man. Louis and Owens, the brightest black athletes in the country, had yet to meet. But soon the twenty-one-year-olds would become friends. Between them it seemed as if black Americans were making significant strides. But hours after Owens's glory, just miles up the road, came a sickening reminder of the depth and persistence of racial hatred.

——

Charles Rouse told Silas Coleman that he was going to Pinckney to get money owed him by a contractor. Coleman would get his eighteen dollars if he came along. He agreed. Rouse and Dean picked him up at nine-thirty that night at Grand River and Schoolcraft Roads. Coleman was not physically daunting. Just over five feet tall, he walked with a limp. He was wearing a white linen cap and looking forward to partying with his landlady in the evening. He had bought a couple cases of beer for the occasion. Coleman and his wife, Eulah, hadn't lived together in several years, but they remained married and in contact. They had a young son named Donald.

The drive to Pinckney took more than an hour. The village, situated in a region marked with lakes, offered a quick getaway for folks looking to fish or swim. The weekend tourism trade fueled part of its economy, which hadn't heard much good news since Henry Ford purchased the old mill pond in the 1920s. As part of his Village Industries program, he had talked of building a small factory there. But it had never happened.

Pinckney was three and a half miles northeast of Hell, a community known mostly for its name. On the other side of Pinckney was Rush Lake, where legionnaires Harvey Davis, James Roy Lorance, John Bannerman, and Ervin Lee were drinking beer and whiskey with their wives at a table behind the cottage. It was nearing eleven o'clock and the kids were in bed when Dean and Rouse pulled up with Silas Coleman in the backseat.

Dean went around back and after greeting the clan asked to speak with Davis inside the house. He told him they had lured Coleman there in search of a contractor. Davis said to tell Coleman the contractor was fishing on the old mill pond and that they would all drive out there to find the man. When they went back outside to the drinking table, Davis announced, "Get your guns, you fellows, we're going to have some fun. . . . We got a Negro that beat a white boy. . . . We're going to take him for a one-way ride."

Davis rode in the lead car. They headed past St. Mary's Cemetery along Mower Road, beneath the tall trees that lined both sides and created a leafy tunnel. Davis directed his crew to Nash Bridge, a low, primitive, wood-plank structure that allowed unpaved Cedar Lake Road to cross Honey Creek. They stopped on the bridge, a familiar spot to locals. A year earlier, a man's twisted body had turned up nearby; Steve Lazlo's skull had been crushed by a vehicle (driven over him, it would turn out, by an angry stepson). Decades before, twenty-four-year-old Carrie Gardner, a teacher, had jumped from the bridge and drowned herself after her father forbid her from seeing her boyfriend.

A half-moon hung in the sky, highlighting the shadowy terrain, glimmering on open water. The pond, three hundred yards wide, stretched over a mile. It was dark and ominous and thick with cattails, brush, and lily pads. Some nights, fishermen would be on the water around midnight, trying to land catfish in the reeds. Lucius Doyle did a good business renting boats to them. Gawky Harvey Davis had been a regular customer for four years, arriving at eleven o'clock or so with his friends, even when it rained. Doyle would usually be in bed when they returned.

Silas Coleman was out of the car. He edged toward the water, scanning the horizon for the nonexistent contractor. The nighttime sounds of nature—croaking frogs, chirping crickets—scored the scene.

"Don't see any boat fishing out there," Coleman said.

Davis pulled his .38 first and walked toward Coleman. All but Lorance followed. Coleman looked shocked but got out no words before Davis shot him in the stomach. He tried to speak, then turned and ran—"like a deer," one said.

"Don't let that nigger get away," Davis yelled.

Coleman managed to run two hundred feet with legionnaires chasing and firing at him. Dayton Dean didn't get off a shot. His .45 jammed with his homemade lead-jacket bullets. Coleman leapt into the swamp and the barrage continued. Teenager Joan Spears, returning from a late movie, heard the shots. So did fisherman Harold Hinchey.

When Coleman collapsed into the water, Davis, Dean, and their cohorts headed back to the cottage where they had beers and shots of whiskey. Davis warned the men to keep their mouths shut "or it will be too bad for you." Davis told them that Coleman had likely fallen into the pond's sinkhole, which he approximated at twenty by thirty feet and two hundred feet deep. The hole, he said, held many bodies.

The next morning, a man discovered Coleman dead near the bridge, leaning against a post six feet from shore. He had been shot multiple times—in the head, chest, and neck. Local blacks were asked to identify him, but no one knew him. Police theorized Coleman had been killed by other blacks. They showed little interest in investigating. On Monday Dayton Dean spotted a small news story about Coleman's death. The *Detroit Free Press* described the shooting in three sentences, noting that "the bullet-riddled body of a Negro about forty was found lying on the edge of a pond"—and that police had no leads. The death was bigger news in the village of Pinckney, where the editor of the *Dispatch* complained, "The crime of murder is no novelty in Detroit and it is hard to get the officers there greatly interested, especially when the victim is a friendless Negro with a police record."

Worries

Schoolboy Rowe wasn't himself. He had become sulky and withdrawn, even anxious. He was rejecting all requests for public appearances, which was unlike him. Some teammates attributed his mood to poor pitching. He is "worried about his failure," one theorized. Rowe certainly wasn't throwing well. As of June 10, he had won three games and lost five. The outings in which he had been sharp could be counted, with a digit to spare, on the pitching hand of "Three Finger" Brown. In four of ten starts Rowe had bombed, surrendering six, seven, or nine earned runs. The previous year he had done that only twice in thirty-five starts. Cochrane labored to find ways "to bolster his morale." Despite his teammates' beliefs, it wasn't weak pitching that consumed Rowe. It was his wife Edna. She was expecting a child and having trouble with the pregnancy. Her doctor worried that her weak heart might not be strong enough for delivery. Rowe was fretting over her health, but apparently keeping his concerns to himself.

With their star pitcher floundering, the Tigers stumbled from fourth to fifth to sixth place in a league they had planned to dominate. The team as a whole was failing. Cochrane ripped his men for not trying hard enough, for not bearing down. Within the first two months he benched Goose Goslin, Marv Owen, Jo-Jo White, Pete Fox, and himself (not all at once). He scrambled the batting order repeatedly. He gave Flea Clifton and Heinie Schuble a shot at ousting Owen at third base. He dropped Elden Auker from the rotation and then reinserted him. He talked trades with other managers, sent Chet Morgan to the minors (forever) after he flubbed a catch, released five-year veteran Carl Fischer, retired loveable old Fred Marberry (who would soon become an umpire), and added Hubby Walker, Gee's brother, to the roster.

"We've got to do something," Cochrane said.

Not everyone was performing poorly. Little Tommy Bridges—"the human slingshot from sunny Tennessee" or whatever else the ink rogues were calling him at the moment—strung together eight wins, including two shutouts. For a few weeks Gee Walker kept company with the league's leading batters while smartly focusing on the game instead of his hecklers. But the two men who most helped Detroit avoid the abyss played next to one another, Charlie Gehringer and Hank Greenberg. Gehringer was averaging a hit at least every three at-bats and Greenberg was battling for the home run title—and grating on opponents.

Those who studied him described Greenberg as thoughtful, usually in combination with another adjective: "thoughtful and observant" or "thoughtful, wide-awake." He continually sought explanations, answers, and advice, hunting ways to improve. "Hank puts more thought, effort, and determination into his bid for baseball success than perhaps any other ball player," noted one spectator. Greenberg's quest led him to use a larger baseball mitt, which brought protests from managers who thought the webbing was too big. They also objected to his preference for black licorice over chewing tobacco, contending that he spit the licorice juice into his mitt to discolor the baseball. As his power surged, Greenberg found himself targeted more often by opponents. Within a month's time he nearly squared off against three players, all of whom had gotten rude with their words.

Greenberg and Gehringer alone could take their club only so far. The Tigers needed their distracted pitching ace to return to form. Someone surely noticed that Edna was carrying a child. Or did they? Edna had stopped coming to the park. The Rowes lived in the Seward Hotel, not far from Henry Ford Hospital. Almost all of the other Tigers lived elsewhere in Detroit. They may not have known the source of Rowe's anguish.

Joe Louis watched films of Primo Carnera and spotted several weaknesses. Carnera had never been a fabulous boxer. He had benefited from matches rumored to be fixed by mob supporters. But at six-foot-six and 265 pounds, he was a huge, lumbering man who could be dangerous if he connected with one of his over-the-top, ax-like chops. Most clear-eyed observers expected a lopsided Louis victory. "I don't think Carnera can fight a lick, never could," wrote New York's Paul Gallico, who within a few years would give up sportswriting for fiction (and, in time, write *The Poseidon Adventure*). "I think that Joe Louis is the most vicious and damaging young man who has been turned loose to commit public assault and battery in many a year." Against Louis, Carnera would hold substantial advantages in weight (sixty-five pounds) and arm reach (four inches). But Louis possessed youth, speed, and power. Louis noticed on film that when Carnera jabbed he left himself open. "When he does that to me, I'll be right in there with a left hook, just like this," said Louis, demonstrating for reporters.

The Carnera fight was crucial because it would be the first time Louis faced a former heavyweight champion. Some of his earlier opponents had been contenders. But Carnera had actually held the title, and the glory that went with it, for almost a year before Max Baer dethroned him in June 1934. It would also be Louis's first New York appearance.

The buildup began six weeks before the bout. In mid-May Louis headed to his training camp. When he arrived at Grand Central Station in New York, an army of black, red-capped porters hoisted him onto their shoulders and carried him into the terminal. Louis had become a hero to blacks. "I started noticing some things I thought was strange," he said. "A lot of black people would come to me and want to kiss me, pump my hand. . . . Now they started saying things like, 'Joe, you're our savior' and 'Show them whites!' and sometimes they'd just shout, 'Brown Bomber, Brown Bomber!'"

Before heading to camp, Louis stayed in a Harlem apartment. He could see Yankee Stadium from the window. Louis appeared in skits at the Harlem Opera House and frolicked with Harlem chorus girls. He also enjoyed the company of seventeen-year-old singer Lena Horne before departing. At Pompton Lakes Louis sparred daily with three or four boxers. All were six-foot-five or taller and had previously faced Carnera. They emulated Carnera's style in the ring. On some days a thousand fans turned up to watch Louis train. Even Jack Johnson showed up. The match was expected to be one of several warm-ups to a fight with Baer.

But when Jimmy "Cinderella Man" Braddock upset Baer on June 13, Louis's path was altered.

Before the Carnera match Louis bought his mother a new house in Detroit. He also arranged for her and three of his sisters to be driven to New York to see the fight. His sister Eulalia looked forward to going to the Cotton Club. "I hope Joe can take us around to some of the nightclubs. That is, after he wins," she said. His mom planned to watch the match from the second deck of Yankee Stadium.

The day before the big night, rumors spread that gangsters were plotting to abduct Louis. As a safeguard, Louis's team added more security and police increased their presence in Harlem, where the fighter was staying. Worries of race riots also drove concerns. A significant police presence was planned at the ballpark. On the day of the event, Grantland Rice reminded his readers, "It was twenty-five years ago when Jack Johnson knocked out Jim Jeffries . . ." Johnson's victory over the white Jeffries had set off racial violence across the country.

Louis was the first black man allowed to be a true contender in years. Excitement was high in black America. "He sure is a wonderful man," said singer Ethel Waters. "I'm going to say a prayer for him." Harlem prepared for a celebration. Outside the Savoy Ballroom a "MEET JOE LOUIS" banner declared that win or lose he would be appearing there after the fight. Across the nation radio dials turned to the broadcast of the bout. In Detroit a visitor could walk through almost any neighborhood and hear the blow-by-blow account wafting on the air. The fight went six rounds, just twenty minutes, before the big man fell. As the referee stopped the match, police flooded into the ring. "Joe just whipped him badly," recalled Jerry Ford, who was listening at the University of Michigan. In Black Bottom and Paradise Valley, also known as Detroit's Harlem, "There was so much noise along St. Antoine Street and along E. Adams Avenue . . . that the Negro hero must have heard it in New York City," reported one paper. "He won! He won! He won!" yelled a woman running along Hastings Street.

On a Tuesday morning in June, Edna Rowe gave birth to a four-pound son, Lynwood Jr. Both she and the baby—though a little underweight—

were in good health. Schoolboy, flowers in hand, went to visit. He was overjoyed and relieved when he saw them. He had feared the worst. Finally he revealed what he had been going through. "I've been in a nightmare," he said. "I didn't know what I was doing half the time. I'd be trying to pitch to a batter and right in the middle of a pitch I'd think of Edna. Lots of times, I'd forget I was even pitching."

The day after his son's birth, Rowe threw a three-hitter and defeated the Boston Red Sox. Afterward, as Rowe stood shirtless and sweaty and gulped a soda, visitors congratulated him. What a way to celebrate his son's birth! Wolverine coach Harry Kipke chatted with him at his locker as Cochrane entertained Harry Bennett and two Ford co-workers. Rowe won his next two games. He restricted Philadelphia to six hits and shut out New York. Schoolboy appeared to be back. When he won his eighth game, the Tigers moved into second place, a game behind the Yankees. The narrowing race prompted Grantland Rice to pen this ditty:

> Look out, Yanks, there's a bengal loose.
> Look out, Yanks, for the coming thrill!
> There's the snarl of the jungle on the winds
> With fang and claw all set for the kill.
>
> Cochrane, Gehringer, Schoolboy Rowe,
> Bridges and Greenberg—pipe the din.
> Look out, Yanks, there's a Tiger loose
> With the snarl of the jungle rolling in.

Joe Louis and manager John Roxborough arrived in Detroit on the morning of Monday, July 1, days ahead of schedule. The early arrival disrupted Mayor Frank Couzens's plans for a big to-do on July 4. The mayor had wanted to be at the train station with a welcoming party. He would be facing reelection in the fall and being photographed in the presence of Louis could help his standing with black voters. A twelve-man committee was formed to put together the event. It included newsmen, Lions owner George Richards, and police chief Col. Pickert. Organizers envisioned banners, a huge crowd, and festive music. But Louis frowned on such a gala. "I don't want no celebration," he said. "Wait till I do something, like winning the title."

Louis visited his mom, his sisters, and a few friends before going to Navin Field to watch the Tigers. It was Ladies Day and the grandstands were filled with women, some checking out the young boxer in the snazzy white double-breasted suit coat with patterned, open-neck silk shirt and matching pocket square. In front of the dugout, Louis traded fake punches with Greenberg for the photographers. Louis pretended to land a blow on Greenberg's stomach. Both grinned. Louis loved baseball and followed the Tigers daily. He still played pickup games on city sandlots with his buddies. Given a choice he might have preferred a career in baseball over boxing (not that his talent was equal in the sports).

Detroit had hosted Negro league teams over the years and Louis would soon be asked to financially back another one. (His manager would deter him.) The major leagues remained all white. The color barrier wouldn't come down for another dozen years. But that didn't keep Louis from rooting for the Tigers. He listened to games on the radio, saw them in person when time allowed, and read about his team every morning at breakfast. He even defied his managers by playing scrimmage games between boxing matches. In the summer he would launch a barnstorming softball team, the Brown Bombers, as a way of helping his unemployed friends. Louis was the gate attraction and played first when his schedule permitted.

On Tuesday, before flying to Chicago to announce his next opponent, King Levinsky, Louis relented to demands for a quick meet-and-greet with politicians. As he walked through city hall, black admirers fell in line with him. They paraded with Louis through the corridors toward the mayor's office, the entourage growing into a crowd as he went. "All I can say is I'm glad to be home," Louis offered. The visit was brief, but he shook hands with Mayor Couzens and the wide-bottomed police commissioner, Col. Pickert.

A few weeks later Pickert showed up in the Tigers dugout.

"Hi there, fellows," he said. The players did not recognize him and assumed Pickert to be a cop assigned to guard them. They should have known by his glistening buttons and shoes and his polished gun belt that he was no ordinary flatfoot. As it would turn out, he didn't recognize them either.

Greenberg came into the dugout.

"Hello, Schoolboy," Pickert said. "How are you feeling today?"

As the tallest Tigers, Greenberg and Rowe often got mistaken by casual fans. Frequently, they didn't bother to correct the error.

"Sign this, will you, Rowe?" asked the commissioner. He held out an autograph book. Greenberg obliged and mimicked Rowe's signature. If precise, he would have put "Schoolboy" between quote marks, as Lynwood always did.

With the third-ever All-Star Game approaching, speculation turned to which players would make the team. In the first two years fans had voted for their favorites, with managers disregarding many of their selections. This year fans had no say. In the American League the eight managers cast ballots. They favored several veterans—Lou Gehrig, Al Simmons, Joe Cronin—whose performances so far were lacking. The managers omitted Hank Greenberg, the league leader in home runs and runs batted in. Greenberg did not receive any first-place votes, not even one from his boss, Cochrane, who said he didn't want to be accused of favoring too many of his own players. (Cochrane, Rowe, Gehringer, and Tommy Bridges had all been selected from Detroit.)

Responding to the snub, Greenberg chose his words delicately at first: "I guess they take experience into consideration when picking the team, and Gehrig has more than I." Typical of his personality, Greenberg was soon engaging in a lawyerly conversation with reporters and teammates. He liked to debate and to argue and, of course, to be right. (Who didn't?) He asked questions until the person answering arrived at the same conclusion.

"How many runs batted in have I got?"

"How many does Gehrig have?"

The All-Star choices were announced two weeks before the contest. In the thirteen games that followed, Greenberg drove in twenty-one runs and hit five homers, a performance that underlined his omission. Fans castigated the managers for excluding Greenberg. The condemnations were so loud that league president William Harridge had to respond. Harridge said he also would like to see Greenberg (and a few other players) on the team. "But there are limitations which must be considered," he noted.

The dispute irritated writer Harry Salsinger, who sounded more like a frustrated parent than "The Umpire" of his column heading. "The only solution is to cancel the game and end the bickering and quarreling," he wrote.

Greenberg and several pals, including his gentile blond love interest, Helen Young, drove with him to Cleveland to watch the game. A front-page headline soured the trip for Greenberg. HANK MARRIED? TIGER AND BLOND DON SAGE GRINS, it read. The rumor was false. They hadn't—and wouldn't—wed. The report angered Greenberg. "You can light your cigar on the adjectives he used," said one witness to Greenberg's reading the article. The American League won the game without him, which in the eyes of the managers justified their selections.

— ⁓ —

In mid-August Will Rogers was flying in Alaska with friend and fellow Oklahoman Wiley Post, a one-eyed pilot and globe-trotting adventurer. They were heading to Siberia. Rogers filed news reports along the way, composing them on his typewriter aboard Post's red monoplane.

"Was you ever driving around in a car and not knowing or caring where you went?" he wrote on August 12 in his homespun voice. "Well, that's what Wiley and I are doing." A day later he described Alaska as a wonderful country. "If they can just keep from being taken over by the U.S., they got a great future," he offered. The next day he reported seeing Mount McKinley, "the most beautiful sight I ever saw." In one dispatch he told of Eskimos who "were thicker than rich men at a 'Save the Constitution' convention." In another he said Alaska's governor was a fine chap—"a Democrat, but a gentleman."

On August 15, battling low visibility and bad weather, Post spotted a small lagoon through a break in the clouds and landed his pontoon-equipped plane near a camp of Eskimos. He asked directions to the town of Barrow and learned it was just ten minutes away. After a short break Post and Rogers took off. The plane climbed and banked sharply toward Barrow when the engine suddenly sputtered and then exploded. The Eskimos watched as the flight crashed into the lagoon, killing both men instantly.

When news reached the states, radio airwaves filled with urgent bulletins of the tragedy. Presses thundered out special editions. On the streets newsboys parroted the front-page banner headlines of Will Rogers's death. "He loved and was loved by the American people," said President Franklin Roosevelt.

Bill "Bojangles" Robinson, preparing for his appearance at the Detroit Police Field Day, learned of his friend's death. They had known each other for thirty-five years, back to their early days in vaudeville when Rogers did rope tricks and Robinson danced with a partner. They had recently finished filming *In Old Kentucky*, which would be Rogers's last movie release. Robinson said Rogers had told him of his adventure plans. "We all tried to get him not to go, but he loved to travel," he said.

Robinson showed up at the office of the *Detroit Free Press* accompanied by Olympic gold medalist Eddie Tolan, one of several black athletes he mentored. Another was Joe Louis. "There isn't a man in the world who can lick little Joe," Robinson, fifty-seven, had noted days earlier. The press quizzed every black celebrity who came to town about Louis—and every famous baseball fan about the Tigers. Robinson qualified as both. He reaffirmed his support for the Yankees. "But if the Yankees can't win," he said, "I'd sure like to see Mr. Cochrane win again."

Cochrane and the Tigers had gotten to know Will Rogers during the 1934 World Series. Like almost everyone else, they liked him. Cochrane considered Rogers a friend. "It seems that a member of our club has been killed," he said. At home plate before the game, rather than discuss ground rules, the umpire and coaches all lamented the loss of Rogers. In the locker room it was no different. Rogers had pledged to return for the 1935 World Series. "I guess when your number comes up, there ain't anything you can do about it," said Flea Clifton.

Experience did not keep Mickey Cochrane from worrying. He stayed up late worrying. His usual diversions of books and music—he liked to check out bands at clubs and prided himself on being able to identify groups by their sound—no longer relaxed him. He awoke in the middle of the night worrying. He worried about actual problems and potential ones. By mid-August he had lots to worry him. Legitimate concerns.

The troubles started on a Sunday when Tony Piet of the White Sox slid into Charlie Gehringer and injured Gehringer's right knee. The Tigers had Monday off. But Gehringer, who had not missed a game in three years, could not play on Tuesday or Wednesday. Cochrane used his hobbled star as a pinch hitter on Thursday and Friday. Meanwhile his substitute, Flea Clifton, plunged into a 0–13 hitless spell. Cochrane and Greenberg weren't connecting either. Cochrane's average fell twenty points. Around the same time Greenberg went nine days without a home run. And pitcher Tommy Bridges took a line drive to his leg.

In the locker room before his team would lose to Washington, Cochrane worried that the whole season might fall apart: "These things like injuries come in bunches, and I almost get the jitters when I get to wondering where they will strike next. For two years we've been going along great. Maybe it was luck or something, I don't know. But it looks as though they're catching up with us now."

The Tigers remained in first. Cochrane simply feared it could all slip away. He also worried that his players were growing complacent. When they let an 8–4 lead turn into a loss, Cochrane had seen enough. Prior to the next day's game he calmly cleared the clubhouse of everyone but the team. Behind closed doors he thundered and fumed and called out numerous men, telling them they were wasting games. The fire in his voice made the paint "curl up and crackle," one scribe reported after talking covertly with his ball-playing sources. When he was done, most players looked beaten and refused to talk. Not General Crowder, the oldest Tiger at thirty-six. "I just love to hear Mike cuss," he said. "Brother, we just heard something classical. It will do us a lot of good. See if it don't."

Unwanted Attention

A YELLOW, BROWN, AND GRAY-BLUE HAZE—THE COLORS OF AN OLD bruise—tinted the sky over Ecorse, Michigan, on some days, staining the air with a sulfuric, metallic, petroleum stench. It could be like that in River Rouge, Lincoln Park, and other downriver communities too. The dirty factories bordering the rivers and rail lines tinged the entire region. Their massive iron, steel, and concrete structures, discolored by residue from smokestacks, swallowed wide swaths of terrain, creating a grim, forbidding landscape.

With just 13,000 residents and less than three square miles of land, Ecorse looked trivial on a map, especially when compared to Detroit, the behemoth a few miles upriver. But Ecorse's significance dwarfed its size. It was home to Great Lakes Steel, an employer of 8,000 men. Those who worked for years by the flames, corralling the red-hot rolls of steel with tongs, wore their work on their faces, especially the cheek nearest to the heat. "You'd see men walking down the street, one side of their face would be sweating, and the other side not," said a resident. "All the pores had been baked closed on the one side of their face. That side would be red and the other side would be white. . . . You knew where he worked."

Because of Great Lakes Steel, the village carried weight in the coarse, turbulent world of 1930s industrial politics. Crime and corruption had long been part of Ecorse's composition. During Prohibition its proximity to Canada across the river made it a favorite outpost for rum-running gangs. The islands arrayed off its shore offered cover for bootleggers. Now with Prohibition over, gambling flourished more than ever. Federal agents had recently seized 20,000 counterfeit five-dollar bills at a garage being used for gaming. Prostitution remained wide open as well. But something else was going on. Newspaper editor William Mellus detected "an undercurrent" but couldn't identify it. In Ecorse and the other downriver communities he covered he heard rumors of a secret organization and spotted gatherings of men that left him uneasy.

Bill Voisine had been the mayor of Ecorse since 1933. The son of a barge captain, he had parlayed his popularity as co-owner of an auto-sales agency into a council position and then the village's top office. He had been elected by cobbling together a coalition of blacks, pro-union workers, foreign-born citizens, and white Catholics like himself. Voisine, an extrovert, peddled jobs and favors to followers. His contacts helped him place residents at the steel plant and in other industries. Along the way he made enemies, including the Black Legion. The nearby *Wyandotte Herald* described him as "a stormy petrel in Ecorse politics."

The village's population was varied. Clubs that operated there testified to the kaleidoscopic nature of the town. Each southern state seemed to be represented. Natives of West Virginia, Ohio, Kentucky, and Tennessee had their own meeting places. Likewise for the Poles, Hungarians, Romanians, and Germans. Blacks had their own hangouts too. The politics could be volatile. Voisine clashed repeatedly with council members. In September 1934 four of them tried to illegally remove him from office. That action followed months of thunderous public meetings. In the middle of the night after one of them, bricks crashed through the front windows of three of his opponents' homes. Months earlier James Bailey, one of his black supporters, had died in a suspicious fire at his small house. It occurred the night before an election, hours after Bailey had appeared at a Voisine rally. Voisine suspected the fire was political but couldn't prove it. Two and a half years later he would accuse the Black Legion. No one would ever be charged.

Jesse J. Pettijohn despised Voisine. Pettijohn served on the city council in 1934 and 1935 and operated a grocery store. During a graft hearing he and Voisine exchanged slanderous, curse-filled accusations about bribes, payoffs, and gambling houses. Pettijohn was part of a faction aligned against the mayor. He also belonged to the Black Legion. At a July 1935 outdoor meeting, legion members lamented that they had no strong candidate to challenge Voisine in the coming year's election. They didn't know anyone who could defeat him.

"Why not get rid of him?" somebody asked.

"Catch him at home and bomb him," another suggested.

It sounded like a good idea to gangly Harvey Davis.

Just after midnight on Wednesday, August 7, Mayor Voisine returned home from an American Legion carnival and settled into his chair in the front room to read the newspaper and unwind before bed. The papers were filled with previews of Joe Louis's fight with King Levinsky. Reporters talked about Levinsky's secret punch and how it might fool Louis. (Tomorrow radios throughout the region would be tuned to the broadcast of Louis knocking out his opponent in two minutes and twenty-one seconds, regardless of Levinsky's sly punch.) Voisine's thirteen-year-old son Bobby was in his room with a pal who was spending the night. Voisine's wife was in the back of the house. The mayor heard an old car turn onto his street and stop near his house at 21 Knox. Footsteps tapped quietly on the walkway. Voisine figured it was a neighbor who lived in the garage apartment behind him. Outside Harvey Davis was lighting a bundle of dynamite and placing it on the porch.

When Voisine heard the car race off, he began to wonder more about the commotion. Too late. The dynamite exploded. The blast rocked the neighborhood. It blew in Voisine's windows, shredded his front door, and threw him, his wife, and the boys onto the floor. The bomb left a large hole on his concrete porch. It also cracked windows on two blocks, including those of the police commissioner, B. F. Loveland, who had been at the same party. The blast awoke everyone in the vicinity but didn't injure anyone. Voisine was shaken but refused to acknowledge his fear. "So far as I know, I haven't an enemy in the world," he said. "I always try to be nice to people."

Albert Bates, a retired police detective, worked at Ford as a transportation superintendent. Days after the Voisine bombing a man showed up at his home. Bates remembered him vaguely. They had worked together briefly on a railroad gang. The man asked to speak privately with him. Bates stepped outside to the curb. The man inquired about Bates's plans for Saturday night.

"We are having a little party and I'd like for you to come to it."

"Who is giving it?" Bates asked.

"Do you mean you don't know?"

The man threw out a few names of others who would be there. Harvey Davis? Lowell Rushing? Bates didn't recognize them.

The visitor pulled a bullet cartridge from his pocket and flipped it in the air a few times.

Bates was confused.

"Don't you know what this means?" the visitor asked.

Bates thought the man might be a cop.

He thanked him for the invitation but told him he wouldn't likely be at the party. Bates's wife, viewing the bullet routine as a threat, urged him to inform police. He refused. On Saturday he attended a ball game. The Tigers beat the Chicago White Sox 4–0 that day. It was their eighth straight win; little Tommy Bridges pitched a three-hit shutout. Bates's wife worried for his safety. She told her son Edward about his father being pressured to attend a mysterious meeting. Edward didn't like it either. It sounded like an act of intimidation, so he enlisted two police officers to check out the gathering at Baby Creek Park near Ford's Rouge complex.

By the time Bates returned home, his son was there, urging him to go to the park, where police had stopped more than fifteen vehicles. When they arrived, Bates spotted the former co-worker. He was talking to the graceless Harvey Davis and baby-faced Lowell Rushing. At just twenty-three years old, Rushing was a handsome, clean-shaven young man who had become one of Davis's sidekicks.

Automobiles had flooded into the park, lining Vernor and Woodmere Streets. The two officers identified themselves and questioned Davis, who claimed it was just a picnic. (Police theorized later that the legion was preparing a death march with Bates as the victim.) Finding Davis's answers unsatisfactory, police arrested him and several others. They found a pistol on Rushing and discovered a revolver hidden under a seat in their car, which also held a suitcase with rope and five black-and-red robes all emblazoned with skulls and crossbones. The vehicle also contained racist literature.

Police knew they had stumbled upon something, but they had no sense of its size or the gravity of their discovery. Neither did the judge, a brother of future Supreme Court justice Frank Murphy. Months later he dismissed all charges because of illegal search and seizure, a decision that—given different suspects and circumstances—would have inflamed the Black Legion. Reports of the arrests merited only a few paragraphs on the inside pages of the Detroit papers. Spooky Hoods Found in Auto, stated one.

Lavon Kuney didn't like what he was hearing. Thomas Heinrich, sitting before him, was telling the Lenawee County prosecutor of his dodgy induction into an organization called the Black Legion. It had occurred six weeks earlier and Heinrich had refused to attend any more meetings. Now he was being ordered to appear at an August 19 gathering at a local farm. The meeting was to be outside Adrian, a county seat halfway between the legion strongholds of Toledo, Ohio, and Jackson, Michigan, and about seventy miles southwest of Detroit.

Kuney called the Michigan State Police for assistance. He told them that for several months a secret society had been convening from sundown to midnight outside the college town. On the night of the meeting two state troopers patrolled the area but couldn't find anything suspicious. They kept looking for signs of an open-air assembly. Around midnight they noticed a vehicle emerging from the farm. And then another. They recorded plate numbers and trailed a car from Detroit. They pulled the automobile over. Inside were Roy Hepner, Elsworth Shinaberry, and Andrew Martin, all in their forties. Martin had been unemployed for seven years, but the other two worked in the auto industry, Shinaberry at Ford and Hepner at Graham-Paige. One of the intriguing things about the legion was how many of its members held jobs within auto factories. Unemployment appeared less of a problem for legionnaires than for others.

In the car police discovered a .38 Colt revolver, a 6121 German Luger automatic pistol with attached dagger and scabbard, three hooded black gowns, and information about the size of platoons and companies. There was also an address book that listed Harvey Davis of 775 Ferdinand Street, the same Davis who had been arrested the week prior in Detroit. Hepner, Shinaberry, and Martin protested that the weapons, carried in a suitcase, weren't theirs. They said higher officials they did not know had given them the guns. All three were arrested for carrying concealed weapons. The next day the FBI was brought into the case.

Three men appeared in Adrian on behalf of the accused. One was Leslie Black, a court clerk from Detroit. Another was Harry Z. Marx, whose law office was on the twenty-first floor of one of the city's most prestigious buildings, the Union-Guardian. The third man, whom an FBI agent described as "very stout" and from Lima, Ohio, identified himself as "one of the highest officers of the Black Legion." It was Bert Effinger. All three appealed to Prosecutor Kuney to release the suspects, contending that the guns were merely ceremonial, used as part of a harmless initiation. Kuney refused. The suspects were arraigned. But within ten days a local judge dismissed the case, saying police had exceeded their authority by searching the vehicle.

The Black Legion had spies who infiltrated unions and political organizations. They attended those groups' events and planning sessions. They ingratiated themselves with their unwary enemies. Others spied on the legion. For Fred Gulley it started innocently enough. A Great Lakes Steel worker in his twenties, he agreed to go to a stag party barbeque with a friend. Of course there was no barbeque, and Gulley took the Black Oath at gunpoint. Newly married, he tired of the group's shenanigans after a month. He disliked the legion and tried to extricate himself. But he had heard of what happened to those who left. He confessed his predicament to his friend, Mayor Voisine, whom he had known for years. Voisine convinced him to stay in the legion as his spy. Gulley agreed. Gulley's wife, Mary, was rewarded with a secretarial position at the village office.

One night at a beer garden in Ecorse, Gulley got into an argument with other legionnaires about Voisine. Yes, Voisine was a Catholic but he had done some good things, Gulley said. He defended the mayor, saying he intended to vote for him. One of them remarked, "Bill won't be in office after tonight. We got two cars following him to Detroit now." Gulley objected and threatened to go to police. "It looks as if two people will have to be killed: you and Voisine," someone said. Gulley agreed to keep quiet but informed Voisine as soon as he could.

The legion's campaign against Voisine was in its early stages. Harvey Davis hoped to enlist Dayton Dean in the effort. But Dean was still looking for the right moment to take down attorney Maurice Sugar. It wasn't as easy as he had thought. Sugar, who was still running for city council, had testified at a raucous statehouse hearing against a bill designed to quell union activities. The hearing turned loud and accusatory with former governor Wilber Brucker, business interests, and the American Legion on one side and labor and left-wing forces on the other.

"There is room for only one 'ism' in America," said Lester Moody, Michigan commander of the American Legion. "That is Americanism. There is no room for pacifism, Hitlerism, fascism, syndicalism, Orientalism, or communism." Jesuit Joseph Luther, dean of men at the Catholic University of Detroit, backed the bill too. "This insidious propaganda of communism wants religion abolished," he said. "The issue is clear. God, religion, morality, and Americanism on one side. Soviet Russia on the other."

Sugar spoke against the legislation, dismissing it as "an effort of the great barons of labor to stop talk about conditions when corporate profits have gone up" while workers' living standards have declined. "Thomas Jefferson and Abraham Lincoln, by their words, could be convicted of a felony under the terms of the bill," he said. Sugar blasted another speaker, Harry A. Jung, founder of the American Vigilante Intelligence Federation, as "a fascist and anti-labor body." Jung was known in anti-communist circles. In April 1933 Father Coughlin had sent Henry Ford a letter of introduction on behalf of Jung. "To my mind he is the best advised man in America on radicalism," Coughlin wrote. "I feel that he would have information that he could give you that would be very hard to get from any other source."

Weeks after Maurice Sugar's committee appearance, he and his wife Jane got a new neighbor. Recently separated from his common-law wife, the man moved into unit four at Winchester Apartments, down the street from the Little Stone Chapel. In his wallet he kept a newspaper photo of Sugar. Every day Sugar walked past the new tenant's unit, unknowingly breezing by the door of Dayton Dean, the man assigned to kill him.

Zero Hour

What did Frank Navin think? Were his Tigers a lock to win a pennant? He chased that black cat. "No, no, no!" he stammered to a reporter.

Navin veered off into a tale about a Cleveland team—it was Cleveland, wasn't it?—back in 1905 (or was it 1906?) when the Indians held a ten-game lead and felt so confident that the players went to a jeweler and bought diamond rings in anticipation of their championship. "The team went east and came back in second place," Navin said. Navin's Tigers would soon be heading to Philadelphia, Washington, Boston, and New York for fifteen games. Navin wasn't about to jinx his team. He didn't want his squad returning in second place.

The Tigers had built an eight-and-a-half game lead over the Yankees by Monday, August 26. Though five weeks remained in the season, opponents were conceding that Detroit would be winning another title. "The only way for the Tigers to lose the pennant is for all of them to drop dead," said Boston manager Joe Cronin. Connie Mack, speaking before an audience of five hundred at St. Juliana in Detroit, went so far as to forecast a world championship. "Great as your team is today, it is only on its way up," he said. "Your team is great because of Mickey Cochrane. He never could lose." Demoralized by his dismal crowds in Philadelphia, Mack looked at Navin Field with wonder. "It's a lovely sight, you know, to see all those thousands of men and women climbing the ramps. I could just stand . . . and watch them and never get tired."

In the National League Dizzy and Paul Dean pitched back-to-back wins in a Sunday doubleheader, putting the Cardinals in first. The photo of them side by side kissing a baseball ran in papers across the country. The mere sight of the Deans annoyed the Tigers. "Those guys make me sick," said one.

—⁃—

While in Washington, D.C., Mickey Cochrane and the team's G-Men— Gehringer, Greenberg, and Goslin—met the nation's top G-Man, J. Edgar Hoover. *Free Press* editorial director Malcolm Bingay, a figure known in power circles, arranged the introduction. Hoover led the players on a tour of the bureau's headquarters. They saw the gymnasium and the fingerprinting division. Hoover shared with them the evidence used against Richard Hauptmann, the convicted killer of the Lindbergh baby. They learned about eavesdropping equipment.

"Listen, Mr. Hoover," Greenberg said. "Can't we get one of those machines for use during the World Series?" Greenberg said he wanted to plant one in their opponents' dugout. The mood was breezy. Hoover joked that Gehringer would make a good gangster. Gehringer probably didn't mention that in 1931 while in Chicago he and several Tigers had visited Al Capone, a baseball fan, at his Lexington Hotel office.

At FBI headquarters the Tigers took target practice with Hoover. Cochrane handled the machine gun best, Goslin the pistol. The facilities impressed all of the men. "After getting an eyeful of the machinery they have for catching up with crooks, I can scarcely recommend a life of crime," said Cochrane.

—⁃—

The day before Silas Coleman died the FBI had filed its first report on the Black Legion. It came from the Cleveland office and it identified Dr. Shepard as the legion founder and Effinger as its most prominent leader. It listed forty-five Lima, Ohio, members by name, among them the city's police chief, and it put area membership at 3,000. The report included a copy of the oath and detailed the initiation ceremony. It conveyed that legion members took gun practice in Bowling Green and noted that Effinger had obtained dynamite. It also mentioned numerous rumors, everything from crimes (like the torching of two local roadhouses) to the existence of a hit list and the purported membership of a Cincinnati FBI agent. The report also hinted at a strong Detroit contingent that possibly controlled a machine gun company and a battalion in the National Guard. It also noted that "General Upps" (a misspelling of Arthur Lupp's name) and "Ike White" were central figures. White, the agent added mistakenly, had "lost his leg in a gun battle with the Purple Gang." Agent C. E. Smith produced the fourteen-page, single-spaced account, relying on interviews with postal inspector J. F. Cordrey and several former Black Legion members in Lima. The agent chose not to interrogate the one man whose name appeared throughout the document: Major-General Bert Effinger.

Cordrey, however, had recently been to Effinger's house. He had interviewed him in his office. This was the same basement office in which Effinger reportedly kept a large yellow map that pinpointed the country's secret fortifications. Cordrey found himself the target of one of Effinger's attempts at intimidation. As they talked, Effinger received a call, reportedly from his own son, who ordered that Cordrey not "leave the house for a half hour." Effinger relayed the message, hoping to rattle the inspector. Cordrey told him he would go whenever he wanted.

In a follow-up letter weeks later, Effinger accused six men of being associated with "the only registered communist in Allen County, Ohio." Cordrey wasn't fooled. He recognized four of the names. They were Effinger enemies. One was an employment officer who had investigated the group. Three were former legion members who had grown concerned that the organization was becoming revolutionary. They had been asked to commit crimes and refused. Two had worked to expose it. After leaving the legion, all had faced threats. On a winter evening one man found fifty carloads of legionnaires occupying the streets around his house. For protection he enlisted armed friends to stay with him. The man warned Effinger that should he or any of his friends be killed Effinger would be the next to die.

The postal inspector had been watching Effinger's mail and logging return addresses. Effinger had recently received letters from throughout Ohio, Indiana, Louisiana, and Michigan. FBI agents in other jurisdictions followed up on the leads. In Detroit an agent went to one of the addresses, 15877 Indiana Avenue. It was "a modern two-family dwelling," he observed. He asked a local postmaster to find out who resided there. Two men lived in the house, a Catholic in the lower flat and a

Sweden-born, naturalized American citizen in the upper—or so the officer reported. This information was wrong. The agent or postmaster had gone to the wrong address, had been misled, or had supplied erroneous information. The brick home at 15877 Indiana housed state commander Arthur Lupp and his wife.

Hoover and the FBI were receiving other urgent notices about the group. A letter arrived mentioning the activities of a secret society in Indiana. The letter came from a police official with the Baltimore and Ohio Railroad Company. He alerted Hoover that the terrorist organization met every Thursday night across the street from the Majestic Theatre in Fort Wayne. One meeting of two hundred men featured a speaker from Michigan who told them to arm themselves and be prepared to assemble with weapons and ammunition when commanded to do so. In such an event the order would be preceded by the code word "Lixto" ("Luxor" or "Sixto" at some meetings) and followed by a location where the group would mass. "This man derided both political parties, all fraternal organizations, and all churches," the report said. Oh and he had a peg leg. The railroad executive identified the group as the Black Legion. "I assume that it is of interstate character," he wrote Hoover, "and I thought you might be interested in its activities." The author said he would help the FBI infiltrate the group if so desired.

The "Lixto" order was surfacing at many legion gatherings, most often related to what was being called "zero hour"—September 16, 1936. Officers were vague about what would happen on that day except that all legionnaires would respond armed and ready to fight—or else. "If you don't go, you will be taken care of when we get back," one officer said. Members were told to expect shooting, killing, and bombings.

———

Cochrane's worries increased as Friday the Thirteenth neared. There were omens for those looking. In Philadelphia Schoolboy Rowe and Elden Auker stepped into a hotel elevator after dinner. The operator closed the gate. As the car was rising, its cable broke. The car began to plummet. It jolted the players as it plunged. Rowe heard it pass through two "safety dogs," iron teeth designed to stop a runaway car, before it caught a third.

They expected it to fall again but it didn't. Rowe and Auker crawled out of the elevator. "I like to died," said Rowe.

Two nights later on the train to Washington, Billy Rogell got hit in the eye, reportedly with a cube of sugar. It was supposedly thrown in the dining car by one of his teammates, whom no one would identify. Cochrane fumed. Rogell went hitless the next day and sat out the two games that followed. The Tigers lost two of three. Back in Detroit thirty men walked off the job while installing temporary World Series bleachers at the ballpark. Workers picketed the use of nonunion employees. Then came the assassination of Senator Huey Long, who had recently announced his support of the Tigers. It didn't make the week feel any more charmed.

Cochrane could not sleep. He spent his early morning hours gazing at the sky from his hotel window, pondering what might go wrong next. "Sleeping powders—they're only a joke," he said. The following day the team began a five-game stand in New York. The Tigers' lead over the Yankees had dropped from ten games to seven and a half. If the Yankees swept them, they could turn the final two weeks of the season into a race.

Joe Louis, who had been training at Pompton Lakes in New Jersey, made the thirty-mile trip to Yankee Stadium—where he would soon fight—to see his Tigers. Louis had pummeled King Levinsky at Comiskey Park in Chicago. He was so dominant that the referee stopped the fight in the first round. Still undefeated, Louis was preparing for his biggest bout, against Max Baer, the former champ. He was standing beside the Yankees dugout when Cochrane approached at the request of cameramen. Given the size of Detroit's lead, most fans felt the Tigers had a lock on the title. Louis was among them. He offered his compliments to Cochrane.

"But we haven't won it yet," Cochrane retorted.

"It's as good as won," Louis said. "Nobody can beat us now."

Greenberg, playing in his hometown, noted that Louis's presence always seemed to jinx him. "In fact, every time Joe comes to one of our games, I have a tough time getting the ball out of the infield," he said. "Still, I shouldn't squawk. I don't believe he has seen us lose yet. He's luck for the team but not much luck for me."

The Tigers took three of five games in New York, dropped three of four in Boston, and headed back to Detroit for a Saturday doubleheader against the St. Louis Browns, where they clinched their second straight league crown.

—◆—

Detroit fans had not grown complacent. They remained exuberant. The winning of the league title brought 100,000 fans downtown on September 21. They crushed onto Woodward Avenue, halting traffic in front of the Hudson's Department Store. Patriotic bunting lined the street. Fifteen times, once every minute leading up to noon, a celebratory explosion echoed through the downtown area, reverberating off the brick buildings. A deafening cheer rose from the streets when Mickey Cochrane appeared with his darling five-year-old daughter Joan, bow in hair, on a balcony above the gathered masses. Baseball Commissioner Landis and Tigers broadcaster Ty Tyson joined the Cochranes on the platform as little Joan pushed a button, symbolically releasing a sixty by ninety foot banner. It unfurled down the building's exterior. It featured a colossal illustration of a tiger and the words "Champions—Detroit Is Proud of You." The crowd cheered. Perhaps caught in the moment, Cochrane discarded caution and proclaimed that the Tigers would win the World Series. The fans responded deliriously.

In the evening after they had officially secured the pennant, Cochrane rose before a thousand men at a banquet honoring Tigers owners Frank Navin and Walter O. Briggs. Business leaders dominated the audience, everyone from the head of Chrysler to the chair of the board of commerce. "These Tigers are not my champions," said Cochrane, downplaying his own contribution. Looking at Navin—whom the papers had taken to calling "Uncle Frank"—and then Briggs, Cochrane credited them for making back-to-back pennants possible. "These two men," he said, "gave me the greatest break I ever had in my life, and I am glad to have the opportunity to thank them publicly for it."

They were heartfelt words, the kind usually said at eulogies. Navin even managed a slight, cherubic smile.

Louis vs. Baer

Most Detroit blacks lived in the areas of Black Bottom and Paradise Valley near downtown and east of Woodward. Though the name Black Bottom derived from its river-enriched soil, it had taken on a double meaning by the mid-1930s, becoming synonymous with the "colored" residents who lived there. The nature of Black Bottom varied by its overcrowded blocks, with some parts offering acceptable housing and others unfairly priced shacks. Hundreds of black-owned businesses operated in the two neighborhoods. The nightclubs of Paradise Valley drew such national acts as Louis Armstrong and Duke Ellington. When in town, Joe Louis visited many of the establishments, including the Frog Club, Club Plantation, and Club Three 666.

On Monday, September 9, weeks before Louis faced Max Baer, first lady Eleanor Roosevelt came to a section referred to as the East Side Slum Districts to announce construction of the Brewster Projects. Approximately 10,000 people, a majority black, greeted her. Roosevelt listened to a black youth choir and visited with the children. She waved a handkerchief to signal demolition of one symbolic dilapidated building and she addressed the audience. "Housing is one of the basic reasons for many of the social problems we have in rural communities as well as cities," she said. "Better housing makes for better living standards."

Louis was in New Jersey at the time. He had spent his adolescent years in Black Bottom. The old neighborhood around Catherine Street brimmed with stories about him. "We all knew him," said Rosa Lee Kirkman Wheeler, who lived a few streets over and used to go to Saturday movies with one of his sisters. A friend of hers had a crush on Louis when he was a teen. "He used to work on a wagon. . . . So we used to tease her because she liked this boy that rode on the coal wagon." One young man remembered working with Louis before school at the Eastern Market, where they removed apples and oranges from tissue paper and piled them high on carts. Louis's friend Fred Guinyard recalled peddling ice with him. They'd rent a horse and wagon for three bucks a day, buy hundred-pound blocks of ice, and go up and down the side streets selling chunks. Saturday was their big sales day "because they churned ice cream on Sunday."

As Louis's bout with Baer neared, life in Black Bottom increasingly revolved around the big event. The gambling rackets saw bets placed on Louis's lucky numbers: his current weight, the round at which he predicted victory, his growing number of knockouts. On St. Antoine Street fans gathered at a large bulletin board and debated the stories posted from the New York papers. Russ Cowans, a reporter for black newspapers, doubled as Louis's secretary and tutor. He wrote weekly letters from Pompton Lakes updating friend Doc Long about Louis's life and activities. Long posted the letters in the window of his pharmacy. Men grouped around them to read and discuss the news. Within days hundreds from Black Bottom would be boarding special fight trains to New York. Hundreds of others would be joining the cheaper automotive caravans.

At training camp reporters noticed that Louis had matured personally in his fourteen months as a professional. "What impressed this observer was the marked difference in Joe Louis's response to questions," said Harvey Woodruff of the *Chicago Daily Tribune*. His answers were no longer limited to a word or two. "Now, Louis of his own initiative adds whole sentences of explanation to some answer he has given, speaks freely of his coming bout with Baer, and in general shows the advancement in poise and manner which so often corners boxers as they rise from the humbler pugilistic ranks to public prominence."

Louis was asked repeatedly how he would fare against Baer. One day his Chicago-based trainer Jack Blackburn asked the question on behalf of the assembled reporters. Louis looked at Blackburn and laughed. "What am I going to do to Baer?" he said. "Just what my Tigers is going to do to your Cubs in the World Series—clean them up—and be sure you pay me the ten dollars you'll owe me when the series is over."

The world learned that Louis would be marrying stenographer Marva Trotter and moving to Chicago, her hometown and a city where he was spending a good deal of time. Both his trainer and co-manager lived in Chicago, and thirteen of his first twenty-one professional fights had been staged there. Trotter was already buying furniture for their apartment. The news brought a flood of letters to the Pompton Lakes training camp. The writers, mostly women, begged Louis to stay single. Others urged him to remain in Detroit with his family. The local Joe Louis Boosters Club, which planned celebrations and organized transportation to his far-off fights, even adopted a resolution imploring him to stay. Club president Edgar Pitts explained: "We aren't going to let Joe do it if we can help it. Joe is a Detroit boy and we aim to see that he stays a Detroit boy."

Louis was in love and talked considerably about Trotter, their wedding, and their future life together.

"When will you be married?" a writer asked.

"Probably a few days after the fight," said Louis. "We won't decide definitely until after she comes to New York. . . . Even if I knew, I'd rather not tell for we hope to have a quiet affair."

Members of the fan club in Detroit tried to get Louis to postpone the date, figuring it would distract him from the fight. Club officer Johnny Tears recalled how nervous he was before his own wedding and imagined Louis might be the same. "Maybe Joe shouldn't marry for a week after the fight," he said.

Louis and Trotter decided differently. On the day of the fight, Tuesday, September 24, two hours before the opening bell, they were wed in a New York apartment by Trotter's brother, a minister. Several friends and a few family members joined them. "Marva was too beautiful and sweet," said Louis. "She looked like something you'd see in a fairytale book." Immediately after, he left for Yankee Stadium.

The loss to Jim Braddock had humbled Max Baer. He no longer spouted off about how he would destroy Louis. He respected him. Leading up to the bout, Baer had limited his clowning and trained seriously. He had engaged sparring partners who had faced Louis and had consulted the advisors of Louis's previous victims. Baer knew that a second straight loss would severely limit his income, if not end his career. In the days before the match Baer had gone back and forth on his projections, sometimes mildly predicting victory, other times being ambiguous about the outcome. More than a few observers thought he was scared. Baer had, after all, seen the Brown Bomber demolish opponents.

At Yankee Stadium, hours before the encounter, Baer threatened to cancel if the boxing commissioner didn't waive the rules and allow extra padding in his gloves over his knuckles. "These are the gloves we'll use or there will be no fight," Baer said before storming off to his hotel with his entourage. Louis had come too far for the fight to be scrubbed. "Give Max anything he wants," his co-manager Julian Black told the commissioner. "We don't care." Later the open-air stadium filled with 84,000 paying customers and possibly an additional 9,000 others, including more than a thousand on-site police officers. Baer worried in his dressing room. He told ex-champ Jack Dempsey, who had been working with him, that his hand was injured. He didn't want to fight Louis. "He'll slaughter me," Baer said. Dempsey told him it didn't matter if both hands were broken. "You're not quitting now," Dempsey said.

The Louis-Baer event was huge, spectacularly so for a nontitle bout. The gate approached a million dollars. Around the ring, which had been erected near second base and was flooded in light, an army of celebrities congregated. There were major stars of sports, entertainment, and politics: former president Herbert Hoover; governors and mayors; Babe Ruth; Ernest Hemingway; reigning champion Braddock; actors James Cagney and Edward G. Robinson; ex-champs Gene Tunney, Jack Sharkey, Primo Carnera, and the blue-bereted, gold-toothed Jack Johnson; and so many more. Among them was Mickey Cochrane, a pair of binoculars around his neck. He had skipped a Tigers game and flown to New York.

At the fight's start, with the cold autumn air above the ring clouded with cigar and cigarette smoke, Louis looked across at Baer in dark trunks adorned with a white Star of David and saw a man "scared to death."

From the ring an announcer told the crowd, "Although Joe Louis is colored, he is a great fighter, in the class of Jack Johnson and the giants of the past. . . . American sportsmanship, without regard to race, creed or color, is the talk of the world. Behave like gentlemen, whoever wins." About a third of the audience was black. Seconds later Louis landed a left uppercut. He knew then he had control of the fight. Louis drew blood in the second round and nearly knocked out Baer in the third. The bell saved him. The men in his corner revived him enough to return. Louis finished him in the next round. Baer "fell like a marionette whose string had snapped," wrote Grantland Rice. He managed to get to one knee but no further. It was the first time he had been knocked out.

Black America celebrated. From Harlem to Paradise Valley blacks poured out of their homes and into the streets laughing, clapping, cheering, screaming, singing, drinking, blowing horns, clanging pots, and voicing unadulterated joy. "It was twice as noisy as the coming of New Years to Times Square—and twice as happy," said one observer. "He's the Brown Embalmer now," said a cabdriver.

In Chicago writer Richard Wright witnessed a bold torching of pride: "Something had popped loose, all right. And it had come from deep down. Out of the darkness it had leaped from its coil. And nobody could have said just what it was, and nobody wanted to say. Blacks and whites were afraid. But it was sweet fear, at least for the blacks. It was a mingling of fear and fulfillment. Something dreaded and yet wanted. A something had popped out of a dark hole, something with a hydra-like head, and it was darting forth its tongue." A similar scene played out in Detroit, where Louis's mother had listened to the fight on the radio.

The following weekend Louis was back in the city. On Sunday he and Marva went to Calvary Baptist Church where his family worshiped. Word had spread before and during the service. Two thousand five hundred Detroiters packed into the church. Another 5,000 gathered outside along Joseph Campau and Clinton Roads. The celebration was being piped outdoors. Louis was to speak about sons and mothers, but the mere sight of him at the front of the church caused such a blissful uproar that he couldn't get out a word. Parishioners crowded around Louis.

"Since President Lincoln freed the slaves," said visitor Sherman Walker, a pastor from Buffalo, "there hasn't been a one of the race made as much of his talents as Joe Louis. Yes, sir, he's a powerful man himself and for his people."

World Champions

On a chilly Wednesday, October 2, throngs of fans weaved across the brick pavement of Michigan Avenue between taxis and long lines of streetcars, pouring toward the turnstiles of Navin Field. The air felt of football, but this was the World Series, America's grandest sporting event. Jovial chaos reigned. Cops whistled, newsboys yelped, car horns blared, streetcars rattled, trucks rasped, mobs of people pushed. Officers on horseback guarded the perimeter of the park, trying to keep order, their shoed mounts clacking on the sidewalk. The police had vowed to come down on scalpers if they charged more than face value for tickets, and they were enforcing that dictum.

In the Tigers dressing room, Mickey Cochrane was growing frantic and angry. An hour before the one-thirty game time, with batting practice over, Schoolboy Rowe, his starting pitcher, had yet to arrive. Cochrane couldn't reach Rowe by phone. After last year's threats and the injured hand—and his knowledge that Rowe liked to sleep late (and that Edna was back in Arkansas with their son and, thus, not there to wake him)—Cochrane alternated between worry and irritation.

Rowe arrived at twelve-forty.

"Where've you been?" Cochrane demanded.

"I been at the hotel resting," Rowe said. "I didn't see any sense in coming out here early and wasting a lot of energy mingling with the mob. I did that last year and it didn't do me any good."

Cochrane accepted the explanation.

Gee Walker's boys, Jerry, four, and Mike, three, flitted about the clubhouse in matching blue overalls. The older boy said he wanted to be a cop, the other a fireman. As their dad took a pre-game shower, the boys haphazardly swung bats, hitting a visitor's shins. One spilled soda pop on golfer Walter Hagen's shoes.

Hank Greenberg appeared the most nervous of the players, certainly more anxious than Rowe. Greenberg had led the league in home runs and RBI and had just been named Most Valuable Player by *The Sporting News*. He wanted desperately to erase memories of his disappointing World Series showing against Dizzy Dean and the Cardinals.

Outside in the dugout, a white flower popping from his buttonhole, retired Babe Ruth called a batboy to his side and whispered a message. The teen darted into the training room and told Denny Carroll, the Miracle Man of Mustard Plasters, "The Babe wants his drink." Carroll laughed and mixed Ruth a bicarbonate soda for his stomach.

As the start time approached, fans jammed the aisles. In the outfield bleachers, for which only game-day tickets were sold, some men and women had been seated on benches for four hours—after having spent a night outside in line. Elsewhere celebrities and dignitaries from sports, politics, and entertainment occupied the best seats: the Fords, the Firestones, the Fishers, the Chryslers, the Gehrigs, Joe Louis, various mayors, a governor, actors George Raft and William Frawley, hockey and football players, myriad baseball figures of days past, Broadway composer George M. Cohan, Harry Bennett of Ford, and J. Edgar Hoover, among others. Hoover said he would be rooting for the American League team. "Knowing the Tigers personally makes me pull for them to win," he said.

The World Series qualified as a society event. Men were outfitted in suits, ties, and overcoats, their heads topped with fedoras, homburgs, and trilbies. Women wore satin and sable and collars of black Persian lamb with feathers and red ribbons and flourishes of flowers. One woman modeled an authentic tiger skin. Orchids as purple as a stormy night sky burst from Mrs. Navin's coat lapel.

Frank Navin, not one for glowing oratory, had already delivered his encouraging words to his ballplayers. He did it in the form of a note.

If you play the same confident brand of ball that you did to earn the American League pennant, you will have no trouble winning the World Series. Here's hoping.—Frank J. Navin

His letter lacked the fire of Knute Rockne or Cochrane, but his players knew him, knew his personality, and had seen subtle flashes of his heart when not in negotiations. They realized how much he longed for the elusive world championship and what it would mean to their veteran boss "Uncle Frank."

Cochrane expected his team to win. Most of America's baseball writers did not. By a narrow margin they forecast a Cubs victory. Chicago had momentum. Managed by Charlie Grimm, the Cubs had finished strongly, winning twenty-one of their final twenty-three games and leaping from third to first in the final month. Their amazing close—"Grimm's Fairy Tale"—shamed Detroit's dismal concluding week: one win, six losses. Still many who had seen the Tigers throughout the year believed they would prevail. Why? "Greenberg's bat," said Lou Gehrig. "I think he will hit at least two or three home runs." Jimmie Foxx agreed: "Greenberg will be a star."

Commissioner Kenesaw Mountain Landis set the tone before the first pitch, announcing over the public address system from his front-row seat a list of infractions that would not be tolerated. No one had forgotten the riot last year when Ducky Medwick was chased from the game in a shower of glass and apples. This time a massive screen had been erected in front of the 19,000 people sitting in the temporary bleachers. A fan would need an arm like a howitzer to hurl a missile over the barrier. The screen also meant that Greenberg would have to hit a ball higher and farther to get a home run.

Even before the game started, Chicago's brutal bench jockeys began launching verbal bombs at Greenberg. They believed that the 1934 Cardinals had needled him successfully, breaking his concentration and distracting him from the game. The Cardinals had told them so. Greenberg's position at first base put him near the Cubs' dugout and he discovered quickly that they "were a bunch of tough SOBs" and their attacks "especially vicious." They shouted "Jew this and Jew that," Greenberg said.

The Cubs scored twice in the first inning, taking a quick lead. Before Greenberg came to bat in the second, home plate umpire George Moriarty, himself a combative individual, strode to Chicago's bench and ordered Cubs players to tone down their profane, antisemitic taunts.

"Those ladies in the boxes shouldn't have their ears sullied," he reportedly said. The Cubs told him to mind his own business and began targeting him. It was part of their plan: hound one ump relentlessly. "The trick is to make the umpire believe that he is biased beyond recall," wrote Harry Salsinger. "Tell a stupid man that long enough and he begins to believe it and as a matter of self-defense will begin giving every break to the other side to prove he is really honest and fearless, as [Brick] Owens did last year." Although he had been an umpire for fifteen years, Moriarty, the Cubs felt, had an allegiance to Detroit after spending much of his playing career as the Tigers' third baseman during the era of Ty Cobb. He had also managed Detroit for two seasons.

But the Cubs harassed Greenberg most of all. Years later they would admit to targeting him for abuse. "Some of the words shouldn't be printed," said Phil Cavarretta, who was nineteen years old in 1935. It likely wouldn't have mattered in the first game because pitcher Lon Warneke threw superbly, defeating the Tigers and Rowe 3–0 before 47,000 people. Warneke, described by *Time* as a "hay-pitching, coon-hunting twenty-six-year-old," had pitched the best game of any Tiger opponent all season, according to Cochrane. One-fourth of the Tigers who made contact with the ball bounced it back to the pitcher. Greenberg went hitless, but so did the other men who also formed the heart of the order: Cochrane, Gehringer, and Goslin. With J. Edgar Hoover watching, the G-Men performed abysmally. In the locker room Charlie Grimm told his pitcher, "Boy, you certainly tied a knot in the old tiger's tail today. A great big goose-egg knot!"

———

Ernie Wettler, thirteen, stood along Trumbull Avenue in front of the Checker Cab company on Thursday, hoping he and his pals might stumble into free tickets for the second game. It was as frigid as a winter day but snowless. Hard winds swirled papers and dirt in the streets. Despite the cold, the scene hummed. A muted cheer rose from within the ballpark during batting practice. Wettler looked up as a ball zoomed over the right field wall, slapped the pavement, and careened into his nose. Blood gushed from his face. Police took the boy to the first aid area inside Navin

Field, where a doctor splinted his broken schnoz. For his troubles the Tigers found him a seat near the dugout, not far from Father Coughlin.

Starting pitcher Tommy Bridges was loosening his arm. Writers liked to latch on to the most dominant physical trait of a player and turn him into a caricature. With Cochrane it was the ears. With Tommy Bridges it was his size. At five-foot-ten Bridges wasn't the smallest guy on the team. But his 155 pounds, along with the larger physical stature of fellow pitchers Rowe and Auker, cast him in the role. Over the years he would be described by Damon Runyon as "frail looking," by Bill Corum as "Little Tennessee Tom," by Joe Williams as "not much bigger than a hickory bootjack," by Jack Cuddy of United Press as "skinny . . . slender, wiry," and by Red Smith as "about as big as thirty cents worth of liver." One columnist would offer that Bridges "doesn't look like he could break an overripe egg against a concrete wall." Bridges, the son of a doctor, had a spectacular curveball. Over the season he had been the team's best pitcher, winning twenty-one games and leading the staff in strikeouts, complete games, and fewest earned runs. In the first inning, after a lead-off walk, Bridges mowed down the Cubs.

Jo-Jo White opened the game for Detroit with a single. Cochrane drove him in on a double and came home on a hit by Gehringer, which brought Greenberg to the plate. The Chicago bench jockeys resumed their ranting. "We had Greenberg's goat, and Hank's play showed he was jittery," manager Grimm said. "We intended to keep up our jockeying." This time Greenberg won, launching a home run to deep left.

By the seventh the Tigers were ahead 7–3. Fans began leaving the park to escape the biting cold. The Tigers added another run, but the inning would be costly. Greenberg, trying to score on Pete Fox's single, injured his wrist sliding into catcher Gabby Hartnett. After the win, as Greenberg got his wrist checked, Cochrane smoked a cigarette and predicted a quick World Series victory. "I knew they couldn't keep us down forever," he said. The players rushed to pack their bags for the Tiger Special to Chicago, which would be departing soon.

In the physician's office Dr. W. E. Keane examined Greenberg's wrist. It didn't appear broken but he didn't like what he saw. Though in severe pain, Greenberg insisted he would be able to play on Friday. By his side was batboy Joey Roggin, Greenberg's pal and good-luck charm. When it had been revealed that the team wouldn't be paying for Roggin to go to Chicago, coaches and players pitched in to cover his costs. Roggin was thrilled. His mother bought him a suit for the trip. But he worried that he and Greenberg would miss the train. The ballplayer tried to calm his nerves.

"Never mind about the train, Joe. We'll be in Chicago at game time tomorrow if we have to walk."

"Maybe you'll get a rest anyway tomorrow, Hank," said the boy. "They say it's snowing in the south part of the state, and with more of the wind we had today, they may call the game off."

"I don't need a rest. I'll be okay, Joe."

They made their train. Joey filled up on ice cream, pie, and milk in the dining car.

During the series Spike Briggs, son of Tigers' co-owner Walter O. Briggs, approached Cochrane. "Mickey, my wife is pregnant," he said. "If this child turns out to be a boy and you win the World Series, I'll name him after you." Others had honored Cochrane in similar ways. Cochrane was unaware of most of his namesakes, including the tyke in Oklahoma who would soon be turning four, little Mickey Mantle.

Greenberg's wrist swelled to twice its normal size. It felt even worse the next day but he wanted to play. He pleaded his case at Wrigley Field. "You know what this means to me," he told Cochrane. "It's what I've played for all year, and I want to get in there and do my part." Greenberg's hand was soaking in a bucket of ice water. Cochrane sympathized but said the risk was too great.

"I'll be all right in twenty minutes," Greenberg told trainer Denny Carroll.

But he wouldn't.

The Tigers lacked a backup first baseman. Cochrane considered various options. He could play first himself and put Ray Hayworth behind the plate, but he preferred to call the pitches. He could put Gehringer at first and bring Flea Clifton into second, but in practice Gehringer had lacked confidence at the corner. He toyed with the idea of Gee Walker or Heinie Schuble starting there, but both seemed risky. Schoolboy Rowe, a good hitter, offered to play first, but Cochrane refused to endanger his pitcher.

Owner Frank Navin involved himself in the discussions. Though he rarely intervened in managerial decisions, he inserted himself into this one. He directed a reluctant Cochrane to move Marv Owen to first and to place Clifton—the guy who had talked himself out of a minor league trip to Hollywood—at third. Some of their teammates disliked the idea, feeling that it weakened the team's hitting. Goose Goslin questioned Navin privately.

"Did you order Owen shifted to first and Clifton to third?"

"I did, and that's what will be done," Navin said. "If you lose the series, I'll take the consequences and I alone."

Prior to the game a twenty-four-year-old broadcaster cornered Elden Auker for an interview. The kid had movie star looks and a warm, resonant voice. The Chicago Cubs had recently named him their official World Series announcer. His name was Ronald Reagan. That moment represented such a thrill for him that decades later as president of the United States he would occasionally reminisce fondly about it. Among the other 45,000 people in attendance was a teen from Georgia. The boy loved baseball, but his father could no longer take him to games since becoming paralyzed from the waist down. So a great-uncle in Chicago bought him tickets for all three local games. It was the first World Series that seventeen-year-old Ernie Harwell would see. Up in the press box, Graham McNamee had been replaced on the national radio broadcast by an up-and-coming Cincinnati Reds radio man named Red Barber. Thirteen years later Harwell would be working with Barber in the Brooklyn booth and Reagan would be the president of the Screen Actors Guild.

The Cubs took a 2–0 lead in the second inning and added another run in the fifth. But any decorum that existed began to evaporate in the sixth when Tiger coach Del Baker got ejected for arguing a play at third. A half-inning later Chicago manager Charlie Grimm charged out of the dugout to resume his series-long debate with George Moriarty. Grimm got tossed too. A few minutes passed before Cubs captain Woody English began hollering at Moriarty from the dugout steps. As Moriarty approached the Chicago bench, Cubs fans drenched him in boos. Moriarty, flaming the Cubs with the kind of expletives they had used on him, banished English from the game and then expelled the normally restrained Tuck Stainback.

National League president Ford Frick, seated nearby, overheard Moriarty. After the Tigers won 6–5 in eleven innings—with Rowe pitching the final four and Jo-Jo White driving home Marv Owen for the lead—Frick criticized Moriarty. He "used blasphemous language in talking to the Cubs." But, he added, "Unfortunately, there were a lot of words exchanged on both sides."

Verbal wars marred the series. Players and coaches castigated both umpires and opponents. Jewish umpire Dolly Stark said he had never been treated so terribly for so little money. (Stark would sit out the 1936 season over pay.) The ditty the Cubs directed at Flea Clifton would stay with him his whole life: "Pappy's in the poorhouse, sister's in jail; momma's on the front porch, pussy for sale." Perhaps they didn't know his parents were dead.

The Tigers were joyous afterward, predicting that they would finish off the Cubs quickly. Cigar and cigarette smoke filled the dressing room, which was crowded with visitors. Amid the joy Greenberg was glum. "It looks like they don't need me," he said.

Detroit won the next game. General Crowder pitched the full nine innings. He also scored one run and drove home another. Flea Clifton also scored. Chicago fell 2–1. The victory gave Detroit a 3–1 advantage in the series. Frank Navin's Tigers needed one more win. Their boosters were already looking forward to the grand celebration they would have on the train ride back to Detroit when they won on Sunday. But Uncle Frank was having none of it. "I'll wait until the numbers go up on the scoreboard," he said. "I've waited almost thirty years for a championship, and I guess a few more hours won't hurt."

Chicago prevailed in Game Five on Sunday, forcing the series back to Navin Field. On the train home Goose Goslin was in the dining car with Ty Tyson and General Crowder, slicing a Bermuda onion for his salad. Goslin predicted that he would be the ninth-inning hero in Monday's game. They thought he was joking and laughed. Four thousand fans were waiting when the Tigers arrived at Michigan Central. It was late and the players tried to push quickly through the hordes of supporters shouting congratulations and encouragement. "The crowd oozed confidence," said one witness. "You could tell by their greeting the peanut was in the bag."

Throughout the series each Tigers victory had been marked by celebrations, wild parties, and noise-making into the early morning hours. Already newspaper confetti, ticker tape, and shredded city directories had snowed upon the streets. What would happen when the Tigers finally won? Or worse, if they didn't? A city election was scheduled for Tuesday, the day after the game. Officials reminded the public that because of primary voting, liquor consumption would be prohibited after midnight on Monday and until eight o'clock on Tuesday night when the polls closed. No drunken voting, in other words.

At the ballpark concessions chief Charlie Jacobs had ordered 40,000 hot dogs, truckloads more of beer, and thousands of pies in case another Medwick-type protest sprouted in the stands. A thrown pie, after all, could make its way partly through a mesh screen. With the Tigers on the verge of winning, the papers brought Dizzy and Paul Dean, last year's nemeses, gratingly back into the news. The Deans announced that they didn't care who prevailed. The game meant nothing to them. In Detroit it meant the world.

Charlie Gehringer had so far hit brilliantly, played sharp defense, and scored more runs than anyone else. Writers and fellow players singled him out for praise as the top contributor. "That guy is as game as they come," said Fred Lindstrom of the opposing Cubs. Babe Ruth added, "He's the best ball player all around." When asked to comment, Gehringer deflected the spotlight and spoke of how the team missed Greenberg.

Though it was Yom Kippur, Greenberg intended to play. Trainer Denny Carroll thought it unlikely, but he worked Greenberg's wrist, treating it alternately with heat and ice and massaging it with ointment.

Greenberg flinched. Carroll tried to lighten the mood with some teasing, telling him that he was not only one of the biggest men on the team but also the biggest baby.

"Go away, Doc, you old quack," said Greenberg, finding a smile.

"Shut up, Hank, you big baby."

And so it went as Carroll wrapped his arm tightly and thickly in tape. "That's the best I can do for you, son," he said. "I hope you can make it."

Greenberg tried to swing a bat. He had Joey Roggin toss him a few balls, lightly at first, then with speed. The pain jolted him each time. His arm throbbed. Greenberg finally conceded that he would be unable to take the field. A day later his wrist would be x-rayed again and several small fractures would be revealed. A physician would set his arm in plaster.

With the Cubs pitching lefty Larry French, Cochrane juggled his lineup slightly. He elevated Flea Clifton into the lead-off position and replaced Jo-Jo White with Gee Walker. It was the first and only time Walker would start a World Series game. During the last contest in Chicago Walker's young sons had been listening to the game on the radio in Detroit when they heard Ty Tyson announce that a Tiger player had been picked off third base. "Was that my daddy?" one of the boys had asked. (It wasn't; it was Pete Fox.)

On Monday in the first inning, before the largest gathering ever at Navin Field, Fox drove a double to left, bringing Mickey Cochrane home for the first run. The stands awoke. But the Cubs responded in the third when Billy Jurges scored on Billy Herman's single. In the fourth Gee Walker singled and moved his way around the bases one at a time on Rogell's single and Owen's sacrifice bunt. Careful not to take too big a lead or to be distracted by the bench jockeys, Walker concentrated on the game. When pitcher Tommy Bridges grounded to third, Walker scored. A half-inning later, Bridges allowed a single to French and a home run to Herman, giving Chicago a 3–2 lead. Detroit tied the game when Owen drove in Rogell from second.

The score remained even into the ninth inning.

Stan Hack, leading off for Chicago, blistered a pitch to deep center field. By the time Walker retrieved it and hurled it back to the infield, Hack was on third base with no one out. The long hit deflated the hometown crowd. Bridges had not been his usual crisp self. He had already given up twelve hits and now the Cubs were on the cusp of taking the lead. Then they would need only three outs to force a seventh game—as St. Louis had done one year ago.

But Little Tommy Bridges bore down and struck out Jurges on three straight strikes. He then got French to ground out back to the mound. Hack remained on third base. Augie Galan, who had managed only four hits the whole series, came to bat. Bridges pitched him outside and Galan, reaching across the plate, popped an easy fly to Goslin to end the inning. It was, in the estimation of Cochrane and almost every other veteran observer, the most exemplary, high-pressure World Series pitching performance ever.

During the pandemonium Bridges went into the tunnel beyond the dugout and smoked a cigarette to calm his nerves. He was on his haunches puffing away when Mickey Cochrane singled through the right side of the infield. Cheers rose from the stands. Bridges could hear the commotion above him. He wanted to go into the dugout to see what had happened, but he didn't want to risk a jinx. So he lingered in the tunnel, still in a crouch as Gehringer blazed a grounder to first. It wasn't fielded smoothly and Cochrane moved into scoring position. He was there when Goose Goslin strode to the batter's box with two outs. Usually Goslin talked to the pitcher or catcher. This time he didn't.

The crowd began its usual collegiate-style chant. "Yeaaaaa, Goose!" The cadence rose on the first word and fell on the second. "Yeaaaaa, Goose!" All season fans in the bleachers had been welcoming Goslin to the field with "Yeaaaaa, Goose!" After fouling off the first pitch, Goslin looped the second one into right field. It got beyond Chuck Klein. Center fielder Frank Demaree relayed it toward home.

The throw was late.

Cochrane scored. Detroit won.

The Tigers charged off the field to escape the fans who were flowing over the fences and hurling scorecards, hats, and seat cushions onto the field. Police stood at home plate and the pitcher's mound, which last year had been excavated by souvenir hunters. They guarded the dugouts, atop which stood six or seven fans who soon began calling for Goslin. "We want Goose! We want Goose!" It was just after three-thirty in the afternoon and word was spreading like a gas fire across the city. The Tigers had won their first world championship.

In the clubhouse Cochrane clenched Goslin and kissed him on the cheek. Schoolboy Rowe hoisted Bridges onto his shoulder. Players shouted and embraced, broke out sodas, and lit cigars and cigarettes. Each man was $6,544 richer. Cochrane spoke of Bridges as if he were an Arthurian knight. He had "the heart of a lion." He was "150 pounds of grit and courage." He "never flinched." He was brave and gallant and "he threw the six greatest curves I ever caught." Bridges shook Cochrane's hand. "Mike, I owe it all to you. You kept me going in there."

Uncle Frank Navin fought his way through the aisles, past the pawing hands of the crowd, and into the dressing room. He went from cage to cage shaking players' hands, thanking and congratulating them, and whispering promises of bonus checks. He found Gehringer, Owen, and others naked in the showers and walked onto the steamy tile to grip their soapy hands. Navin posed with Bridges and Goslin and kissed their foreheads. A smile splintered his usually impassive face. This was his moment too. "Without question, I am the most pleased man in America," he said. "I'm almost speechless with pride. . . . I am a sober man. But I have an almost irresistible inclination to get intoxicated tonight."

If he partook, he wasn't alone. All night thousands flowed into the downtown area to revel in the glory. Nearly a half million people joined the carnival, blocking avenues, clogging sidewalks, packing beer gardens, halting streetcars and automobiles, singing and drinking, blowing horns, and banging trash cans. They partied outside the hotels near Washington Boulevard and Grand Circus Park. From the high floors they dropped streamers and, sometimes, bags of water on the celebrants below. In spots the rowdier elements broke store windows, set fires, and tried to tip trolleys. The city had not seen anything comparable. It dwarfed even the merriment of Armistice Day in 1918.

Some ballplayers, like Elden Auker, accepted invitations from friends to dine in fine fashion (at the Detroit Athletic Club, in his case). Others, including Gee Walker, hung out in their apartments with friends and family. Tommy Bridges, feeling the pains of a stress headache, went to bed early. Schoolboy Rowe, seeking an escape from visitors, went to a movie—maybe a *Midsummer Night's Dream* with James Cagney or *The Return of Peter Grimm* with Lionel Barrymore—hoping to sleep unnoticed in the dark theater. The World Series finale and the merriment it inspired generated an estimated 800,000 words from the more than three hundred journalists in town. Much of it, in Detroit especially, bordered on the elegiac and sounded as if written for the ages.

"The Leaning Tower can now crumble and find its level with the Pisan plain," wrote Grantland Rice. "The Hanging Gardens can grow up in weeds.... The Detroit Tigers at last are baseball champions of the world."

Offered Sam Greene of the *Detroit News*: "We graybeards of the years to come will be telling our children and our children's children how poetic justice once descended on Navin Field as the long October shadows fell softly across its broad green carpet, how it fell over the slender shoulders of Tommy Bridges like a mantle, and how it draped itself about the broad proportions of the Goose and Mickey Cochrane, two battle-scarred heroes of many a World Series contest."

On its front page the *Free Press* editorialized about what it all meant: "It was Detroit's salute to America.... Detroit celebrated because it had won the world championship. It celebrated because it was the city that had led the nation back to recovery. It celebrated because it was the city that wouldn't stay licked; the city that couldn't be licked. It was Detroit the unconquerable, ready to tell the world when the moment arrived. The moment had arrived, and the world was told."

For owner Frank Navin it was the fulfillment of his dream. "I can now die in peace," he said.

Amid the Joy, Punishment

THE BLACK LEGIONNAIRES WERE BASEBALL FANS LIKE THE REST OF Detroit. One legion crew even waited until the contest had ended on Saturday before heading out on its mission. A half-hour after the Game Four victory Fred Gulley appeared at Robert Penland's door on Auburn Street in Ecorse. They lived about a mile apart, southeast of the Ford Rouge plant. It was five-thirty. Penland had just sat down to dinner with his wife, Mamie.

"Your foreman wants to see you out in the car," said Gulley, motioning toward the street. Penland repaired massive cranes at Great Lakes Steel. He thought nothing of being called for emergencies at odd times. He headed outside in shirtsleeves. It felt cold for early October. The air smelled slightly putrid from the nearby industrial plants. When Penland looked in the car, he realized the visit had nothing to do with his job. Two Black Legion members, Thomas Cox and Earl Angstadt, occupied the front seats. Angstadt, who had done time in Ohio for stealing a car, lived in Ecorse; Cox lived in Detroit. "I know what you want," Penland said. "If you come back after dinner, I'll go with you."

Gulley ordered him into the car. He pressed a gun against Penland, who reluctantly climbed into the backseat. The four headed out to a field a good hour's drive away. Penland was cold. One man loaned him a coat and another turned on the heater. They offered him a few grapes and invited him to light a cigarette. Maybe their mood had been lightened by the Tigers' win, or maybe they realized they were all in a similar bind— sworn legion members who no longer wished to belong but feared the repercussions of quitting. Gulley had nothing against Penland, but he had heard that legion members who didn't follow orders paid with their lives. He had been instructed to bring Penland to stand trial for missing meetings and had resigned himself to the task. En route, they talked about baseball much of the time.

By the time they arrived, two dozen members had gathered at the site off Lahser Road in Oakland County. They drove up to the outer guards and provided the proper passwords. A quarter-mile farther was the inner circle where hooded men awaited. Formally charged, Penland offered his best defense: Family illnesses had kept him from attending meetings. He promised he would do better. Stripped of his shirt, Penland was tied to a tree and lashed with a whip. Gulley, the spy, turned away. He knew a worse punishment might find him if legionnaires discovered he was Mayor Bill Voisine's pigeon.

Penland returned home at eleven-thirty. He refused to tell his pregnant wife where he had been. Some wives, unaware of their husbands' legion activities, viewed their late hours as evidence of romantic affairs. Sworn to secrecy and wanting to protect their spouses, many of the men wouldn't reveal the actual reasons they didn't return until after midnight.

Frances Wellman, Rudyard Kipling Wellman's wife, suspected her husband of being unfaithful. He owned a service station at Kercheval and Springle Streets, blocks south from where Peg-Leg White had once lived. Wellman had narrow eyes and a pencil-thin moustache, which drew attention to his crooked, gapped teeth when he smiled. Wellman could be brutal to his five-foot-two wife. He had been known to blacken her eyes, and she feared he would do worse if he discovered that she had been searching his pockets. She knew about his involvement in a secret society. A member of an intelligence squad, he bragged about being a big shot in the organization. Occasionally, she pawed through his coats, writing down the names of various members, including prominent ones. Regardless, she imagined that given such frequent nighttime absences, he must be having an affair. The Wellmans lived less than a mile from the border of affluent Grosse Pointe and she suspected a dalliance with a wealthy woman. She had even had him followed by a private investigator.

Floggings like the one Penland endured were not uncommon. If you missed meetings, you might be whipped. If you questioned the legion's actions, you might be whipped. If you spoke of the group to nonmembers, you might be whipped. Legion leaders preferred to deliver floggings before an audience, making examples of errant members. Rather than one man dispensing the punishment, many shared the responsibility, one lash delivered by each of seven, eight, twelve, or thirteen members. The beatings left victims with painful cuts, slashes, and blood blisters and they terrified those who witnessed them.

The family of Thomas Ness noticed that he had changed suddenly in the spring. Though he didn't share the reason, Ness had seen his good friend, a fellow Irish immigrant, beaten bloody by the legion, to which both hesitantly belonged. Ness would only acknowledge that he had beheld "a terrible, shameful sight." The stress weighed on him. Within a few months he collapsed and died while marching in an Orangeman's parade in Windsor, Ontario. After seeing whatever he had seen, he was never the same, his family said.

In the autumn of 1935 Harley Smith's family in the village of Norvell, not far from Jackson State Prison, watched in horror as men shoved Smith into a car and drove off. An unemployed farmer and a father of five children under the age of twelve, Smith had been roped into joining the legion by a friend. He had taken the oath with a gun pointed at his chest. He went to one other meeting and then quit attending. His truancy brought the legion to his door. Awakened from his sleep, Smith was drawn outside. When his wife saw him forced into a vehicle, she charged after the men, screaming for her husband. She loaded the kids into the family car and drove into town, telling a deputy that her husband had been abducted. The deputy said that without more information he couldn't do anything. Smith was driven blindfolded to a farmhouse that belonged to Dite Hawley, a guard at Jackson Prison. A hooded legion jury convicted Smith and ordered six lashes. Smith recognized the voice of the man who pronounced his guilt. It was Ray Ernest, a prison employee who had successfully enrolled many of the 380 guards at the state institution. Ernest, who had a sub-machine gun secreted away in his home, frequently testified to his willingness to "die for the Red, White, and Blue on any or all occasions."

Stripped from the waist up, Smith endured his stinging punishment. The tongues of the whip were studded with brass. Blindfolded again, he was returned home, writhing in pain. He told his wife what had happened but insisted she not go to the police. He feared the legion would kill him.

Denver Carter, thirty-nine years old and a friend of Smith, was another man beaten by the Jackson-area legion. He died of a heart attack months after the assault. His wife blamed the lingering impact of the attack. Authorities disagreed, saying that his heart trouble was unrelated. A similar fate would befall Paul Every, forty-one years old, another prison guard. Ernest and company flogged him for poor attendance. Already sickly with diabetes, Every saw his health immediately decline. He never recovered, dying two months on, according to his wife and son. And then there were the disappearances, suspicious deaths, and suspected suicides of Black Legion members and their enemies. Three weeks after the World Series, patrolman Alfred Roughley, who had brought several of his Detroit co-workers into the legion, turned up dead in his car, an apparent victim of carbon monoxide poisoning. Police ruled it a suicide.

Not long after, streetcar conductor Alexander Murdy, forty-seven years old, got up from his living room chair and walked out of his house. It was a mid-January evening and he didn't say a word to his wife or his two teenage children. He grabbed some coins and left. His family assumed he was going for cigarettes. Murdy had joined the Black Legion two and a half years earlier and even introduced several co-workers into the organization, but after being whipped harshly for not attending meetings, he grew reluctant to leave his house at night. Murdy had a decent job and had been talking of buying a new car. He was also looking forward to traveling to Ireland to see his mother. But he did not return that night or the next or ever again.

The Pastor Who Said No

THE OCTOBER PRIMARY SHOWED ATTORNEY MAURICE SUGAR TO BE A
serious Detroit council contender. With nine seats in play, Sugar finished
tenth, making him one of eighteen candidates to advance to the November election. His goal appearing within reach, Sugar wrote an optimistic
song titled "We're Moving to the City Hall." (*When we get wise and
organize to battle for our rights, they set their sneaking stools and spies to get
the guy that fights.*)

But forces were mobilizing against Sugar. As the general election
neared he was receiving more death threats. Black Legion officers suggested that Dayton Dean bomb Sugar's apartment, but Dean refused.
Despite all his depraved actions, the legionnaire drew a few moral lines.
He worried about collateral damage. More than a hundred people lived
in the building and Dean feared that a bomb would kill children and
innocent bystanders. He had two kids of his own and he loved them. He
also preferred not to shoot Sugar in public. The idea was to escape, not
leave a trail of witnesses. He needed to choose his moment carefully, he
told his legion bosses.

Masquerading as prospective clients, Sugar's enemies tried repeatedly
to lure him from his law office. Forceful and confident, Sugar couldn't be
scared easily. His labor battles had hardened him. Still he took precautions. He refused to meet any unknown clients outside his office in the
Barlum Tower. From his window Sugar could see into the rooms of a
neighboring hotel. He figured the occupants could see him as well. Concerned that one of his enemies would have a clear shot, Sugar moved to
a less prominent office.

Sugar advertised on the radio to spread his campaign message. He bought ten minutes of time during the WEXL Polish Hour. "The automobile manufacturers of this city are making tremendous profits," he said. "In 1933 General Motors' profits were $84 million. In 1934 their profits were $95 million. And already for the first nine months of 1935, their profits have risen to the tremendous total of $114 million. . . . While the working people are in poverty and suffering, big business is making greater and greater profits." On the more substantial WJR station he blasted officials who denigrated those seeking relief. "I say that the unemployed of this city are entitled to relief—adequate relief—and not as an act of charity, either. And they're entitled to get relief without standing in line for six or seven hours, too."

Sugar's big publicity coup came when he debated Upton Sinclair, author of *The Jungle* and numerous other works, who a year earlier had finished second in the California governor's race. A longtime socialist, Sinclair had switched to the Democratic party for that election, advocating for his End Poverty in California (EPIC) platform. On a Sunday afternoon, two days before the Detroit election, Sinclair appeared in the city for a debate with Sugar: "America's Way Out—EPIC or Labor Party?"

Six thousand people, most aligned with Sugar, labor, or leftist parties, packed the Naval Armory along Jefferson Avenue. Two thousand people couldn't get through the doors. The audience booed Sinclair repeatedly. They booed when he blamed the communists for abetting the rise of Hitler in Germany. They booed when he endorsed Roosevelt for reelection, saying that the only other choice would be a "reactionary Republican." They booed when he said that those who "denounce and ridicule procedure under our Constitution, as has been done in this hall today, and . . . breathe violence and threats" were opening the door for fascism.

The audience cheered when Sugar rebutted him. "Upton Sinclair still loves Roosevelt," Sugar said. He continued by parodying a popular folk song. *"Oh, Frankie and Uppie were lovers,"* he sang. The audience roared. "Mr. Sinclair, you lovely man, you have been seduced by the demagogy of the New Deal and Roosevelt, the demagogue whose demagogy has not been matched in decades."

Sinclair chided Sugar and the gathered masses. "I'm sorry for the state of the brains of some of you people who cheer my opponent," he said. "If and when Mr. Sugar polls 879,000 votes in Michigan, as I did in California, I'll grant him the right to criticize working within Constitutional frameworks and in a Democratic fashion."

Among the audience were spies—opponents of Sugar, likely Black Legion members. They left behind a new batch of fake campaign literature. "Vote for Comrade Sugar who . . . will aid in making the revolution. . . . Comrade Sugar has come out definitely against the church. . . . Down with religion. . . . There is no god."

Using the flyer as justification, Col. Heinrich Pickert's Detroit police raided communist party headquarters on Fourteenth Street the next morning. The building was a few doors from *The Daily Worker*. Police arrested several party officials. They told journalists that they had found the (counterfeited) pro-Sugar literature at the office. One paper included a story in that day's pre-election issue. Seize Sugar Literature, read the headline. "On the walls were pictures of Lenin, Trotsky, Tom Mooney, and Sugar," said the story. "Other placards bore the slogan, 'Every factory a fortress of communism.'" Sugar protested, "It's a last-minute move on the part of interests that want to defeat me." On election day the papers noted that Sugar had been absolved. "There was nothing of an incriminating nature," one story stated. But the damage had already been done. Sugar lost the election by 12,000 votes, finishing tenth. The top nine vote getters won council seats.

The Black Legion's interest in Sugar waned but didn't expire after the election. Dayton Dean, who had been dividing time between the state headquarters and two legion regiments, got transferred full-time into Harvey Davis's command. One night in a nearby meeting hall, Davis asked Dean if he'd like to make an easy hundred or two hundred bucks by killing Ecorse mayor Bill Voisine. Dean said he would. He didn't feel it was actually a question, but a directive with financial benefits.

The bombing of Mayor Bill Voisine's Ecorse home and the burning of the communist camp in Farmington Hills were not anomalies. The Black

Legion had an arson squad and it used gas and kerosene-like naphtha to torch buildings. The legion also deployed dynamite and black-powder explosives. Dean himself had hurled bombs at a house of prostitution and at "black and tan" clubs where the races mixed.

Suspected communists provided a favorite target. In Berkley, Michigan, near Father Coughlin's Shrine of the Little Flower, the legion set a fire that destroyed a picture frame store where radicals met. In Detroit the Modern Book Shop along Woodward, with its selection of revolutionary literature, endured a daytime back-door bombing that damaged stock, busted windows, and terrified children at the dance school next door. Eight months after a communist party office was hit, a second office, near Belle Isle, was bombed. The reaction of the police reinforced Col. Pickert's reputation. Police pulled party members' names from the carnage and investigated those individuals. One communist fumed, "One of our party sections is bombed in the dark of the night and the Detroit Police instead of hunting for the outrageous perpetrators of this crime are endeavoring to prosecute the victims." In Highland Park, blocks from the home of a legion officer, Hazelwood Cleaners, a workers' center, bore the impact of heavy explosives, which also blew out the windows of neighborhood homes. In Warren a Ukrainian Education Center was bombed, and in Royal Oak, a socialist hall. The legion also opposed a strike at Motor Products Company, damaging a UAW local and the homes of five picketing workers.

When he resided near the State Fair Grounds, Dayton Dean had gotten to know his neighbors. He was in charge of recruiting a northern section of the city. He took particular interest in John George Quindt Jr., a nineteen-year-old who lived a block over. Dean entertained the young man with self-aggrandizing stories of his days in the Navy: how he had fired shots during the race riot in Washington and how he had crewed for President Woodrow Wilson aboard the *Mayflower*, which had seen action in the Spanish-American War before becoming a presidential yacht.

One evening Dean convinced Quindt to go with him to the meeting of a patriotic organization. In a house in Highland Park Quindt took the

Black Oath at gunpoint. The experience frightened him. Quindt wasn't new to guns. His father had been taking him on hunting trips since he was a boy. He could handle a shotgun and both he and his dad had belonged to a shooting club before his father started the Wayne County Rifle and Pistol Club. It was Quindt's father-son shooting trips and the rifle club that interested Dean most.

The Rifle and Pistol Club met on Mondays for target practice at Eppinger Sporting Goods in Cadillac Square. The store was a few doors from Sugar's office in the Barlum Tower. It had a gun range on the fourth floor. Many clubs used it. Dean joined the rifle club. He was followed by state commander Arthur Lupp, Col. Wilbur Robinson, and a few dozen other legionnaires. The older Quindt, a Russian immigrant, must have wondered about his good fortune. How were all these men hearing of his club? His son had not told him about being forced into the Black Legion or about Dean hounding him to attend meetings. Junior kept the pledge of secrecy and went to occasional gatherings, including a major barbeque in the Irish Hills region where four hundred legionnaires watched one hundred men be inducted. "If you'd ever been to a meeting and seen all the guns, you'd understand why everyone who was forced into the outfit was terrified," Junior said.

Was it possible to refuse the Black Legion? Some men heard word of the secret society and successfully dodged membership by repeatedly declining invitations from persistent friends. Some even faced down the legion. In Vassar, where Dayton Dean was born and still visited family, a meat cutter at Economy Market spurned two local men who approached him several times. When they threatened him, asking what he would do if a gang of armed men showed up at his house and forced him to join, he fought back. "I told them that I had a gun in the house and that at least six of them would have to be carried out," he said.

In June 1934 legion members had organized a patriotic gathering at the VFW hall in Sandusky, a town in the thumb of Michigan. Without revealing their identity, the recruiters invited VFW and American Legion members to attend a meeting. Organizers envisioned forming a new unit of men with military experience. Sixteen ex-servicemen showed up. The armed legionnaires began their usual procedure, adding the names of the prospects to the fake insurance cards. But before they got far the Sandusky men began peppering them with questions. They refused to accept the vague platitudes about Americanism and pushed for answers. Unimpressed, they demanded their cards be returned. This time the Black Legion relented. No Black Oaths were sworn. The legion left town.

The Rev. Ralph C. Montague, a minister at the Baptist church in Rives Junction, a dozen miles north of Jackson Prison, had been asked repeatedly by a parishioner's husband to attend a meeting of good Americans. Montague, forty-five years old, had served in France with the 328th Field Artillery Battalion in the Great War. He loved his country and considered himself a patriot. After repeatedly declining, he relented and out of kindness and curiosity accompanied the man on a fifty-minute drive to a field near Norvell. It was nighttime and dozens of cars were parked there. When Montague spotted men in black robes, he was amused at first. Tomfoolery, he thought.

Montague had studied at Michigan State College before the war and at Moody Bible Institute in Chicago for two years afterward. Described as "outspoken" and "square-jawed," Montague wasn't anyone's dupe. From where he stood in the field he couldn't clearly hear the speech being delivered. But he could tell that the man delivering it was angry.

Finding himself in a line with fourteen other recruits, Montague listened as the robed men asked their usual questions. Their demeanor and their guns temporarily filled him with fear and he responded by answering "yes" to their questions. Yes, he was willing to kill if ordered to do so. When they began reciting the oath, Montague hesitated. He kept quiet as others repeated the words. A legionnaire noticed his unmoving lips and questioned his defiance. Montague felt emboldened and spoke his mind. He told them the ceremony was "despicable and un-American." He told them they ought to be ashamed. When one legionnaire argued with him, Montague, a minister since 1928, accused him of misquoting the Bible. He told the crowd that the ceremony was un-Christian. One man argued that legion members were God-fearing men. Several shouted threats. A salesman from Jackson pointed a gun at Montague.

"String him up," someone hollered.

Another peppered him with profanities.

"Don't swear at me," Montague said. "I'm a minister of the gospel."

"You know too much about our organization now," a leader replied. "You've got to join."

He wouldn't, Montague said. "I've taught the gospel of God, and if you're going to kill me, I'm prepared to die," he said.

Perplexed by his defiance, Black Legion leaders talked privately about what to do with him. Finally he was loaded into a car and driven away. They released him unharmed.

The other recruits didn't immediately know what had become of him.

Uncle Frank

On the crisp morning of Wednesday, November 13, Frank and Grace Navin headed out to the Detroit Riding and Hunt Club, as they had been doing for thirteen years. Both had been horse lovers before they met. Their mutual passion was one thing they found attractive in each other. In her earlier days Grace, thirteen years his junior, had been a competitive rider, participating sidesaddle in dressage and jumping exhibitions. They still frequented horse events and owned a small horse farm in Kentucky. The Navins typically rode at the Detroit grounds three times weekly, though Frank had not been there since late October. He had once served as president and director of the club, located about six and a half miles from their home. The facility's paths wound through a wooded and pastoral landscape in northwest Detroit along Seven Mile near Wyoming and Meyer Roads. The rustic landscape had seen development in recent years. The new campus of the University of Detroit Jesuit High School, with its red clay mission roof and imposing, four-story front, had risen nearby.

At the stables Grace mounted her horse and set off on a mile-long trek. Frank liked to ride by himself. He preferred a leisurely pace and enjoyed solitude. Feeling tight and tired, he asked groom Elie Lukin to boost him on to Masquerader, his favorite of the two horses he kept there. He had been riding Masquerader for a decade. The horse had a gentle demeanor, but its unusual gait made for a bumpy ride that Navin appreciated as "good for my liver." He had difficulty getting on the horse that morning.

Navin looked like a proper squire of a certain age: tan breeches tucked inside brown boots, black coat accented with red scarf, and atop his head a black derby similar to the one he popularized in the Cobb era, when Michigan gentlemen began emulating his look at his ballpark. Alone on the trails, Navin could contemplate life.

Perhaps he remembered the World Series triumph over the Cubs and the multiple tributes that followed. The night after the victory, Navin and every Tiger but sickly Joe Sullivan had attended a glamorous testimonial in the majestic, chandeliered ballroom of the Book-Cadillac. Navin's and Cochrane's admirers, among them Harry Bennett, put on the affair. More than eight hundred political, business, and sports leaders, along with ordinary fans, came out to honor the team. They cheered wildly as each member shared a few words. It was a warm, sentimental night, with several acknowledgments of Navin. "I'll never forget our dressing room after the series was over," said Jo-Jo White. "You should have seen Mr. Navin grab Goose Goslin and kiss him twice." Even umpire George Moriarty spoke glowingly. He was given a flashy suitcase with no qualms about a conflict of interest. Batboy Joey Roggin got in a few words too, describing himself as "the luckiest and happiest boy in the world."

Atop his horse Navin might have chuckled about the various opportunities the championship had brought his players. How Goslin had guest starred on Rudy Vallee's show with Edward G. Robinson, how he had appeared before sold-out crowds at the Fox Theatre with broadcaster Ty Tyson, and how he had allowed a sculptor to mold a living mask over his face. Or maybe Navin pondered how Gehringer, Bridges, and Schoolboy had gone barnstorming together. Or how all the guys had received endorsement money from Camel cigarettes. Or how even Mrs. Billy Rogell had benefited, being pictured in an ad for Wonder Bread.

Or perhaps he fretted over financing of the construction project taking place at his ballpark, where larger stands would be erected in right and center fields. Or maybe he wondered about his nephew Charles, the team secretary, who was so exhausted after the stressful season that he had taken refuge at the Battle Creek Sanitarium.

Or possibly he was recalling another tribute dinner, this one also chaired by Harry Bennett and held last week at the English Grill, where Navin jokingly expressed his worry that Cochrane might not sign a contract to continue as manager because of the toll the job took on his nerves.

Or conceivably he was thinking over Cochrane's request that the team get Al Simmons from the White Sox, another expensive gamble. Or recalling that he needed to deliver on his promise of a horse for Cochrane after having persuaded him to take up riding.

Whatever was on his mind, somewhere along the bridal trail that November morning, Frank Navin suffered a heart attack, fell from his mount, and gasped his final breath. Ten or fifteen minutes later, Grace Navin saw Masquerader canter toward the stables, the saddle empty. She went for help. The search party found Navin crumpled along the path near a bush, not breathing. They tried to resuscitate him. Harry Link, his longtime chauffeur, went for the car. They rushed Navin to the nearest hospital, Detroit Osteopathic in Highland Park. Grace knew her husband was gone. She didn't bother with the hospital. A friend drove her home. In Highland Park physicians tried to breathe life back into Frank Navin. But they could not. Uncle Frank was dead.

Come to Detroit, Lindbergh

DETROIT LIONS COACH POTSY CLARK TALKED BOLDLY FOR A MAN whose football team was at the bottom of the division and had won only five of its nine contests. "We've lost our last game this season," he said, "and if we get a break, the national professional football championship will be decided in Detroit in December." The Lions had three games remaining, two against the Chicago Bears and one against the Brooklyn Dodgers. To make it to the title game they could not afford to be defeated, and they needed the teams ahead of them—the Packers, Bears, and Cardinals—to each lose at least once. Fans could be forgiven if they had doubts, but the success of the Tigers and Joe Louis had filled them with optimism. Anything seemed possible.

Detroit was already promoting its standing in the sports world. By mid-October local headlines described the city as being home to the "kings of athletics." There were the Tigers and Joe Louis of course. But in trying to make the case the *News* dug deep for other evidence, extending its search back several years, proudly embracing boat racer Gar Wood, doubles tennis champions Esther Politzer and Constance O'Donovan, gold-medal sprinter Eddie Tolan, Olympic diver Dick Degener, racehorse Axucar, golfer Walter Hagen, and assorted other conquerors in boating, bowling, billiards, swimming, fencing, racing, weight lifting, and even checkers (all hail Newell W. Banks). And don't forget the Dixie Oils softball team—national champs too. All these winners helped keep spirits high in a Detroit that, though recovering, was still Depression-battered.

In their November 24 game the Lions built a 13–0 lead against the Bears at Wrigley Field. But Chicago fought back to tie the game. The Lions scored again and the Bears answered again. The resulting 20–20 tie dimmed the Lions' hopes, but didn't extinguish them. Ties did not count in the standings. Green Bay remained in first, with the other three teams in second.

On Thanksgiving 1935 a throng of 20,000 fans watched from the University of Detroit bleachers as Dutch Clark propelled his team to a 14–2 win over the Bears. Instead of throwing passes, he caught them this time. Clark, playing the role of receiver, scored both touchdowns and kicked both extra points. He now had two nicknames: Dutch and The Old Master, which worked well together. The Bears were eliminated from the race. Elsewhere the Packers lost, elevating the Lions' chances. Three days later the Lions crushed the Brooklyn Dodgers 28–0. When the Packers fell and the Bears beat the Cardinals, the Lions advanced to the national title game.

Even before Frank Navin's burial, speculation turned to the future of the Detroit Tigers. What would happen to the team? Who would run it? Who could possibly replace Frank Navin? The man had been glorified over the past fifteen months as "a genius of baseball." Tributes flooded in from across the country. A giant of the sport had died, one of the game's leaders.

Navin's nephew Charles seemed a possible choice as president. Mickey Cochrane was too. Billy Evans, Cleveland's general manager, was mentioned as well. Initial press coverage sounded oblivious to the fact that part owner Walter O. Briggs, the automotive titan, would play a huge role in making the decision. It was no secret that Briggs also owned the team, but he was often in the background and the fifty-fifty nature of his stake failed to make print in the immediate aftermath of the Navin tragedy. Longtime journalists and Navin confidants Harry "The Umpire" Salsinger and Malcolm "Iffy the Dopester" Bingay appeared unaware that Navin and Briggs had an agreement: Whoever died first would purchase the other's stock. Or if they knew, they had agreed not to report it.

Though six years younger than Navin, Briggs had significant health problems that kept him from coming north for his business partner's funeral. He stayed in warm Miami Beach, where he spent most of his time when the baseball season ended. "Our business association always had been a fine one, and our friendship was one that has endured through the years," he said. "His death is a great personal loss to me, and I feel it keenly."

Briggs had been looking forward to stepping out of Navin's shadow and leading the Detroit Tigers. Now he would have his chance. He wasted no time. Within a day of Navin's death Briggs sent a representative with a check to Mrs. Navin. She accepted the offer, which exceeded one million dollars.

Navin and Briggs differed greatly. Financially they had lived in separate worlds. Navin had had money, but nothing on the level of Briggs's fortune. Briggs owned multiple manufacturing plants, supplying auto bodies and interiors to the major automakers. He employed thousands and cleared millions most years. He owned three mansions, one in the Boston-Edison neighborhood of Detroit with eleven bedrooms and nine fireplaces. It was blocks from Navin's comparatively modest home. Another, a converted hunting lodge, sat on 165 acres in Bloomfield Hills amid lush gardens and a beautiful lake. The third was in Miami Beach, the nicest of all, with five hundred feet of ocean frontage and a 235-foot yacht.

Briggs was tough and hard-edged in a way Navin had never been. Almost all of Navin's experience had been in baseball. Briggs, however, had built an empire in the rough world of industry and he did not shirk from confrontation or controversy. He had weathered employee strikes and a 1927 factory fire that killed twenty-one workers, prompting claims that he had ignored worker safety issues. If the ballplayers thought Navin had been a difficult negotiator, they would face in Briggs someone who could be much fiercer if he chose.

Briggs summoned Mickey Cochrane and Charles Navin to Miami Beach. He named Cochrane vice president, putting him in charge of players and acquisitions and giving him a role in contract negotiations. He promoted Charles Navin to secretary, treasurer, and business manager, and named his own son, "Spike" Briggs, as Navin's assistant. Walter O. Briggs himself took the title of president.

For two years observers had been remarking about Cochrane's moods and nerves. He flew into furies. He cried. He sulked. There was a reason some called him Black Mike and it had more to do with his disposition than his Irish roots.

Columnist Harry Salsinger's descriptions of Cochrane had evolved over time as he got to know him better. Early in Cochrane's Detroit tenure, Salsinger portrayed him as "unorthodox . . . moved by impulse . . . turbulent . . . passionately excited." Then he characterized him as "highly emotional and extremely aggressive." In the final days of the 1934 pennant race, Salsinger noted that Cochrane was "unlike any other man who ever managed . . . the most emotional player in baseball" and, still later, the kind of person sometimes "moved to bitter resentment."

Sam Greene of the *Detroit News* couched Cochrane's temperament in lighter terms, describing him as "not exactly in the mood to drag out his saxophone and strike up a merry tune" and as "speaking in mournful tones." So did John Kieran of the *New York Times*: "When everything is rosy and treasure trove is being dumped into his lap, the Man in the Iron Mask says: 'Boys, it will probably rain paving blocks on our heads in no time.'"

How would Cochrane carry the additional burdens of vice president?

Iffy the Dopester, Malcolm Bingay, raised the issue. "He is taciturn, surly, sullen, or boyishly happy as befits his mood and, like a boy, he makes no effort to hide his feelings," he wrote after Cochrane had been promoted. But, Bingay noted, with Navin gone a calming influence had disappeared. Cochrane possessed "elements of greatness," Bingay wrote. "It may be that responsibility, complete charge, will mature him. . . . There is going to be more than baseball to interest Old Iffy next summer. There is going to be an interesting study in human nature."

In early December former heavyweight champ Max Schmeling of Germany turned up at Pompton Lakes to watch Joe Louis train. The undefeated Louis was a worldwide sensation, the "uncrowned champion" of boxing. He was preparing for a December 13 match against Paulino Uzcudun of Spain. Jimmy "Cinderella Man" Braddock remained champion. Louis, at 22–0, ranked as the top contender. Schmeling was behind him.

Schmeling studied the Detroit boxer as he punished a series of sparring partners. He claimed to be unimpressed, but he was just playing mind games with Louis. Schmeling said he worried that Uzcudun or Charley Retzlaff, Louis's January opponent, might land a lucky punch, floor Louis, and derail their plans for the summer bout to determine who would face Braddock. Paul Gallico asked Schmeling what Hitler would do if "Massa Joe" defeated him. Schmeling laughed and said Hitler had greater concerns.

On Friday, December 13, Louis knocked out Uzcudun in the fourth round before 19,900 fans at Madison Square Garden. Schmeling was in the crowd. Afterward Uzcudun said, "Nobody can hit like Louis, and nobody can lick him. That goes for Max Schmeling, too. I know. I fought both." Meanwhile boxing legend Jack Dempsey was looking to train a man who could take on Louis. "There isn't a fighter in the game right now who can lay a glove on Joe, so I'm going out and find me a white hope to develop," he said. "Do you know how long Max Schmeling will last with Joe? . . . Less than one round."

Four days before the football championship between the Lions and the defending title-holding New York Giants, tickets went on sale at three locations: the cigar counter at the Book-Cadillac Hotel, the University of Detroit Stadium, and Watkins Cigar Store in the Fisher Building. They went quickly, but the game did not sell out. For the first time the Lions sequestered themselves for practices, holding sessions in secret at the State Fair Grounds. The title game would mark the return of Harry Newman, the onetime star quarterback of the Michigan Wolverines. Prior to Hank Greenberg, Newman had been the state's best-known Jewish athlete. He now played in New York's backfield.

On Sunday it snowed, sleeted, and rained at the football stadium, making the field a muddy, slippery mess. The poor weather held down attendance, listed at 12,000 in one account and 17,000 in another. Before the game one Lions team owner announced that a bonus of fifty-five dollars would be paid to any Lion who blocked a kick. (Three would.) Fans endured a cold, wet two hours in the open-air bleachers.

The lighter, younger, quicker Detroit team scored minutes into the game when Art Gutowsky spun into the end zone untouched. The game was lopsided, more so on the field than in the score. The Lions won 26–7. "New York was no match," said Salsinger. The victory, following the Tigers' title and the announcement by the Associated Press that Joe Louis was Outstanding Athlete of 1935, added to the city's momentum. Organizers of the annual Goodfellows Christmas newspaper sale capitalized on the attention, bringing together Cochrane, Louis, and Lions coach Potsy Clark to sell papers to benefit poor children.

"Detroit is a City of Champions," trumpeted a *Free Press* editorial. "And so are we all proud to be citizens of a city that has so justly vindicated its name of Detroit the Dynamic." The only thing that could make it better would be for the hockey team to win.

Frank Navin's gift to Mickey Cochrane of a cow pony arrived weeks after his death. It came from Beaumont, Texas, where the Tigers had a minor league team. His name was Texas Ranger. In autumn Cochrane had been hunting on horseback in Wyoming and had discovered he enjoyed riding. Convinced Cochrane needed a horse, Navin had vowed to buy him one. In Michigan, before the baseball season, Cochrane put on his jodhpurs and rode Texas Ranger daily. He boarded the animal at Detroit Riding and Hunt Club, traversing the same trails where his friend, boss, and mentor had died.

The outdoors appealed to Cochrane. He liked wide-open spaces. He and his wife bought a 224-acre farm on a lake in Commerce Township, thirty miles from their city home. He hoped it would be a refuge during the hot, hectic days of the baseball season. He would need one.

Cochrane was intent on acquiring his friend and former Philadelphia teammate Al Simmons from the White Sox, who were managed by another of his Philadelphia teammates, Jimmy Dykes. Cochrane and Simmons were pals. They were so close that after the 1934 World Series Mickey and Mary, along with Cy Perkins, went with Al and his new wife on a meandering cross-country drive from Arkansas to Los Angeles and then by boat to Hawaii for a belated honeymoon. Cochrane evidently doubted the stories coming out of Chicago about Simmons being a bad influence on other players. But Dykes would be happy to be rid of him, recalling how Simmons had demoralized the younger men as the team departed on a road trip while in first place. "When we got on the train," Dykes recalled, "Al came into the dining car, looked around, and with a broad grin said to those kids, 'Well, we're going east in first place, but we'll be coming home in last.' Wasn't that a hell of a thing for an old timer to tell a bunch of kids?"

Simmons was born Aloysius Szymanski. If, as was sometimes reported, he changed his name to cover his Polish ancestry, like little Joey Roginski, he failed at it, for references to Simmons often described him as a Pole, usually prefaced by a modifier: the Milwaukee Pole, the grinning Pole, the swaggering Pole, or whatever other descriptor flashed in a writer's mind. In his prime Simmons rated with the best hitters in baseball. For eleven straight seasons he had driven in at least one hundred runs. Twice he had won the batting title. Four times he had been a top-five vote getter in Most Valuable Player balloting. Since the advent of the All-Star Game he had been selected every year. But last year with Chicago his production had plummeted. Cochrane hoped his chum would show a bit of his former brilliance. Simmons would be turning thirty-four soon and his best days were likely behind him.

The Tigers' purchase of Simmons, rumored for a year, materialized in late 1935. Walter O. Briggs spent $75,000 to get him. Though the club cut his salary from $25,000 to $15,000, Simmons would still make more than almost anyone else on the team, save for Cochrane and the unsigned Hank Greenberg. He would make more than Charlie Gehringer, and more than Pete Fox and Gee Walker combined. Cochrane felt Simmons would strengthen the club in its pursuit of a third straight pennant. Other teams had bolstered their rosters. The Red Sox had added Jimmie Foxx. The Yankees had promoted a phenom named Joe DiMaggio. Simmons was Detroit's answer.

But his signing stirred dissension. Many Tigers expected to be rewarded handsomely for their championship season. What if their pay didn't rise to the levels they anticipated? What if the team claimed poverty after shelling out big money for Simmons? What of the three outfielders—Fox, Walker, and Jo-Jo White—who had played significant roles and who would be losing playing time? And what about Simmons's close relationship with Cochrane? How would all of this work?

In late December Charles Lindbergh and his family left New York in secret, sailing to England under aliases because he felt unsafe in America. Col. Pickert weighed in on this bit of international news. "Had I known he was moving to England," Pickert said, "I'd have asked him to come to Detroit. Hoodlums and their ilk will not be permitted to operate here and they know it."

Not two weeks earlier Rudolph Anderson had turned up dead. Anderson had worked at the Mistersky power plant with Dayton Dean and Harvey Davis. The plant was where Davis had put in motion the joy killing of Silas Coleman. Anderson was discovered outside his car, a bullet through his heart, a rifle and a spent shell at his side. His body was found along the edge of Baby Creek Park, where police had disrupted plans for the Albert Bates death parade. Col. Pickert's detectives ruled Anderson's death a suicide.

The Black Legion was getting braver and brasher. Police had twice arrested legionnaires with robes and guns in August 1935. Both times the charges had disappeared. Such developments reinforced members' beliefs that the legion had well-placed friends. Maybe talk of a September 16 government takeover was more than bluster.

PART III:
JOY AND TERROR

1936

The 1920s saw Detroit's skyline explode with new buildings. By the 1930s the city was America's fourth largest.

WALTER P. REUTHER LIBRARY, WAYNE STATE UNIVERSITY

In the 1930s the majority of black Detroiters, like these children, lived in the east-side Black Bottom or Paradise Valley neighborhoods.

EDWARD STANTON

Before the 1934 World Series, Babe Ruth greets the managers and their star pitchers: Dizzy Dean and Frankie Frisch of the Cardinals and Mickey Cochrane and Schoolboy Rowe of the Tigers.

WALTER P. REUTHER LIBRARY, WAYNE STATE UNIVERSITY

Comic Will Rogers visits Henry and Edsel Ford before the start of a 1934 World Series game.

WALTER P. REUTHER LIBRARY, WAYNE STATE UNIVERSITY

Joe Louis (center without a cap) started a barnstorming softball team that carried his name. He populated it with talented friends, many of whom were otherwise unemployed, and he played with them when his boxing schedule allowed.

WALTER P. REUTHER LIBRARY, WAYNE STATE UNIVERSITY

Tigers batboy Joey Roginski, who called himself Joey Roggin because of anti-Polish sentiment, became Hank Greenberg's good-luck charm in the mid-1930s.

WALTER P. REUTHER LIBRARY, WAYNE STATE UNIVERSITY

Hank Greenberg and Joe Louis joke around before a 1935 Tigers game. Louis, a devoted baseball fan, was a frequent presence at Navin Field.

WALTER P. REUTHER LIBRARY, WAYNE STATE UNIVERSITY

At spring training in Florida, Mickey Cochrane shares a laugh in the dugout.

At the 1935 World Series, club owner Frank Navin talks with baseball commissioner Judge Kenesaw Mountain Landis.

Recovering from a nervous breakdown, Mickey Cochrane films the Wyoming landscape beside his friend Emmett "Rosie" O'Donnell, a future four-star general.
FROM THE AUTHOR'S PRIVATE COLLECTION

Harry Bennett, Henry Ford's right-hand man and infamous enforcer, became close friends with Tigers manager Mickey Cochrane.
WALTER P. REUTHER LIBRARY, WAYNE STATE UNIVERSITY

Football star Dutch Clark led the Detroit Lions to their first-ever championship in 1935.
WALTER P. REUTHER LIBRARY, WAYNE STATE UNIVERSITY

Police officers model confiscated Black Legion robes and weapons.
WALTER P. REUTHER LIBRARY, WAYNE STATE UNIVERSITY

As major-general of the Black Legion, Bert Effinger, an electrician, led the secret society from his home in Lima, Ohio.
FROM THE AUTHOR'S PRIVATE COLLECTION

Leftist attorney Maurice Sugar, a candidate for judge and city council, became a target of the Black Legion after representing blacks and pro-union activists in several high-profile cases.
WALTER P. REUTHER LIBRARY, WAYNE STATE UNIVERSITY

Captain Ira Marmon of the Michigan State Police tried for years to get the FBI to investigate the Black Legion.
PHOTO COURTESY OF MARMON FAMILY

Father Charles Coughlin attracted a massive weekly radio audience that varied
from an estimated ten to thirty million people.

Dayton Dean (left) and Harvey Davis (second from left) with two other defendants.

The Black Legion murder trials drew international press coverage.
WALTER P. REUTHER LIBRARY, WAYNE STATE UNIVERSITY

Gunman Dayton Dean, the prosecution's top witness, takes the stand in one of the 1936 Black Legion trials.
WALTER P. REUTHER LIBRARY, WAYNE STATE UNIVERSITY

Case Closed

As the Ecorse, Michigan, elections approached, the Black Legion stepped up activities against Mayor Voisine. The odd couple of Dayton Dean and Harvey Davis went to Hartridge's Beer Garden one night to meet with township clerk Jesse Pettijohn. A group of fifteen to twenty legion members gathered at the bar. They pushed together several tables. Dean had agreed to kill Voisine, but the specifics hadn't been fleshed out. The general plan called for Dean to shoot Voisine and for legionnaires to block streets and traffic, allowing him to escape after the assassination. Downstairs in the men's room Davis was chatting with Pettijohn. Both stopped talking when Dean appeared in the doorway. Pettijohn had never met him. Davis introduced Dean as "the one that is here to do the job." Dean asked if Voisine had been located. He hadn't. This news allowed Dean to play the tough guy.

"I did not come here to fool," he said. "All these men are in town here. I have orders to kill Voisine. It has got to be carried out. I do not want to be coming down here and putting ourselves on the spot . . . all the time. You are the man that wants him killed. He is your man, and it is up to you to find him. And we will do the job down here." Pettijohn went upstairs and made phone calls trying to get a bead on Voisine. The plot didn't come together that night.

On another evening Davis and two legionnaires accompanied Dean to a village council meeting. They pointed out Voisine. Clarence Oliver, one of his black supporters, gave the mayor a glowing endorsement that night. Afterward the legionnaires fired a bullet into Oliver's home. Davis thought Dean should bomb the mayor in a public place. Dean rejected that scheme, fearing he would be caught or injure himself.

Shooting was the way to go, they agreed. They hoped racketeers would be blamed for Voisine's murder.

Whenever Dean went to Ecorse he was accompanied by at least one and often two or three other legionnaires. They tried Hartridge's Beer Garden several times. They tried the Rumanian Hall, also known as the Seventh Street Hall. They tried Bill Boyne's place close to the ship-building yards. They could never locate Voisine. Nearer to the election Pettijohn, Davis, and a third man, whose wife was working as a nurse in the Voisine home, showed up at Dean's house. By this point Dean, permanently separated from his wife, was staying with his mother and stepfather at their place on Twenty-Third Street. Dean's two children lived with them. Dean came out to the car and was told this would be the night. Voisine would be at a budget meeting. Later Dean and company headed to Ecorse again. They stopped at Pettijohn's grocery. Dean met with him in a small back room where he learned the budget meeting had been canceled. It was almost as if Voisine knew ahead of time when Dean was coming to town. Possibly Voisine's spy was tipping him off. They drove past Voisine's house repeatedly. Dean got out with his guns once and knocked on the door. No answer. He looked in the windows but Voisine wasn't home.

On March 9, 1936, Voisine was reelected mayor, defeating a local high school civics teacher by one vote. Dean had failed yet again, though this one couldn't be laid entirely on him. Dean had so far been assigned to kill newspaper publisher Art Kingsley, attorney Maurice Sugar, and Mayor Bill Voisine. Not one of them was dead. He also hadn't managed a shot the night Harvey Davis and his posse hunted down Silas Coleman at the Ford Mill Pond. Dean was either an inept assassin or a reluctant one.

During the Voisine chase Dayton Dean had come to realize that he knew too much. He also was beginning to feel like a dupe. He recognized that orders always came from legion higher-ups, who usually commanded, but did not carry out, the crimes. Leaders made sure to involve several underlings in each assignment. It gave them something to hold over the men.

——

"I can promise you that your prints won't be checked against those of criminals," said agent H. H. Reinecke, head of the FBI's Detroit office. Reinecke was speaking to the Exchange Club on March 16 in the Book-Cadillac Hotel. He wanted to add members' prints to the FBI's collection of more than five million, strictly for noncriminal identification purposes. He said they could come in handy if a law-abiding citizen were killed without identification or stricken with amnesia.

——

It was just after six o'clock in the morning on St. Patrick's Day, Tuesday, March 17. Sexton William Currier was readying the Shrine of the Little Flower for the six-thirty mass. He stoked the furnace and prepared the altar. Nearby two nuns knelt in prayer. Father Cyril Keating and Perrin Schwartz, editor of *Social Justice*, the official publication of Father Coughlin's National Union, had arrived when a passing motorist noticed flames darting from the shingles of the wooden church. The driver rushed into the sanctuary and alerted the parishioners. The sexton headed to the roof with an extinguisher. The fire department was called.

As wind gusts spread the flames, the nuns, priest, and arriving parishioners rescued what they could from the burning church: vestments, the tabernacle, equipment from the radio room, and statues of Mother Mary, St. Jude, St. Christopher, and St. Therese de Lisieux, the Little Flower in whose honor the church had been built in 1926. Soon Coughlin came from his home. "The entire church was a fiery furnace," he said. He watched from across the street, his parents at his side. Within an hour "the building which I loved more than all the other buildings in the world" had been reduced to ashes.

Early in the decade, as Coughlin's radio show was making him one of the most famous men in America, the church had become a tourist attraction. On any Sunday cars from faraway states lined the roadways. People made pilgrimages to the shrine. Three years ago the church had been moved back from its original location to make room for the

Crucifixion Tower and the grand new church, which was now nearing completion. The plan was to keep "our little shingle church," as Coughlin called it, on the site as a treasured landmark.

A fire official said he believed the blaze was electrical in nature. He said it had started between the ceiling and the roof. Coughlin had his doubts. He had been targeted before. Three years prior, in the pre-dawn hours of a March 1933 morning, someone had tossed a black-powder bomb into the basement of his Royal Oak home. It was not unfathomable that someone would set his church afire. "I do not know what caused the fire," Coughlin wrote in the church bulletin, the *Shrine Herald*. "Perhaps there was defective wiring. Perhaps there was not. It is not my purpose to indulge in rash judgments." Coughlin was still unaware of the Black Legion.

— ◆ —

Mickey Cochrane struggled as Tigers vice president. Among his headaches was Iffy the Dopester. When Malcolm Bingay, one of city's best-known journalists, began writing The Dopester column for the *Free Press*, he envisioned a fun little read—and an answer to Harry "The Umpire" Salsinger, his former protégé, at the market-dominating *News*. Salsinger "was writing his head off, giving the folks what they wanted," said Bingay. "He was running us bowlegged and I had nobody to match him." Bingay had tried to lure a crusty sportswriter out of retirement but had failed. Bingay had once been a baseball beat man, so he turned to himself. In his early days Bingay was the *News'* wunderkind sports editor. Now he ran the enemy *Free Press*—the whole thing—just down West Lafayette Boulevard. He already authored the daily "Good Morning" column, which appeared on the editorial page. He hadn't wanted his byline over another column, so he adopted The Dopester alias and wrote history-tinged, inside-the-game pieces.

Over the summer of 1934 the column evolved. Disguising his identity he became Iffy the Dopester, a character depicted in a line drawing as a curmudgeonly, bearded, bespectacled elder. The column's flavor shifted too. Iffy's personality grew larger on the page. His prose became more whimsical, seasoned with words that harkened to another era. He called his readers "my hearties" and he gave players contorted, archaic-sounding nicknames: "Mickey the Mike," "Homer Hank the Big Greenberg Boy," "Peter Pan of the Ozarks" for Schoolboy Rowe, and "The Silent Knight" for Gehringer. By 1935 Iffy had become a craze, with Iffy clubs, Iffy buttons, Iffy contests, Iffy drinks, Iffy books, and pica poles of letters to Iffy. Most of Detroit didn't realize Iffy was the alter ego of Bingay, who peppered his stories with Latin phrases, Greek philosophers, and Roman warriors. Iffy described himself as the team's vicarious manager. Occasionally he made pointed comments, but usually in a lighthearted way. The column qualified as pure fan fodder, a love letter, with memories and easygoing advice swirled into the mix.

That changed in the spring of 1936. The team's treatment of Hank Greenberg served as the catalyst. Greenberg and the Tigers couldn't agree on the size of his pay raise. Coming off one of the biggest run-producing seasons in baseball history, he became the Tigers' first major holdout since Ty Cobb. The contract dispute played out in the papers, with Greenberg staying in New York and missing most of spring training as Cochrane played hardball, trying to convince the world through intermediaries that he didn't need Greenberg. It was as if Cochrane were adopting the forceful industrial ways of boss Walter O. Briggs and friend Harry Bennett. Stories began appearing that rookie Rudy York would be replacing Greenberg, which even York didn't believe. "We won't do so badly with York in there at first," Cochrane said. Hoping to turn fan sentiment against Greenberg, the Tigers planted a false story that he wanted $40,000, which would have made him the best paid player in the game—at age twenty-five. Then Cochrane forecast that Al Simmons would be replacing Greenberg in the number-four spot.

Greenberg downplayed the negotiations at first because the Tigers had advised him to do so. But when Cochrane leaked stories to undermine him with fans, Greenberg spoke up, denying he had asked for $40,000, saying he was standing on principle, and noting that he thought he deserved a larger raise. "I can't see why the Tigers aren't willing to gamble a few thousand dollars on me when they invested $250,000 in new bleachers and $75,000 [on Al Simmons] to strengthen the team," he said.

Bingay had known Frank Navin for decades and could count on him for insights and to act as a go-between when reporters had trouble dealing with Cochrane, who could be brusque and played favorites. With Briggs as president and Cochrane as vice president, the dynamics had changed—and so did Iffy. His columns turned harshly critical of the new leaders. The tone of his pieces felt out of character with Iffy's playful, grandfatherly image. While he chastised Briggs as "Sir Walter," he excused him as being sickly and out of touch. More often he took aim at Cochrane. As the Greenberg divisions deepened, Iffy's words intensified.

On March 15 he wrote: "Mickey's weakness is that he loves his friends, blindly, and resents criticism. Therefore, he is surrounded by more yes-men than a Hollywood producer. . . . The very spirit that makes him one of the great ballplayers of all time precludes his unbending gracefully."

On March 22: "If Frank Navin had lived, Hank would have been signed. . . . There is only one man in the world who drove home 170 runs last year and that one feller is pouting Hank, the Big Greenberg boy. . . . A large dose of diplomacy is needed to remove from the colon of the patient a 'go-to-hell' attitude, implanted by 'the club.'"

On March 23: "The club is a vast impersonal organization these days—something like the Chinese Empire. Once it was a personality—a baldish feller named Frank Navin. He did every thing but take the tickets and cut the grass."

On March 26: "Mr. Briggs has only owned the ball club six months and there are a lot of things he has to learn; one of them is that newly appointed executives who play favorites, carry chips on their shoulders, and use 'go-to-hell' as diplomatic technique don't get to first base in the League of Life."

On March 27: "This public-be-damned gag went out of fashion a generation ago. That is one thing Mr. Cochrane has not learned yet as vice president. . . . A little tact, a little diplomacy, a little understanding of the amenities of life, a little more maturity—and Hank would have been in the fold from the start."

Bingay, a Pulitzer finalist who had been active in a national effort to improve journalistic integrity, saved some of his strongest Iffy words for the boys who covered the team. They should "keep the public informed," he said. "They are supposed to be working for the newspapers and not for the ball club. . . . I do not see why vast newspaper properties, valued at many millions of dollars, should be used by sportswriters to win arguments for club owners in a duel of wits with hired hands over how much cash they should grab. . . . I want them to tell me what they know—not what the baseball management thinks we ought to be told."

The regular season had not yet started and Cochrane had enough pressures to overwhelm any mortal. He carried the weight of a star player, a championship manager, and now a novice vice president. He was dealing with locker room dissension over Simmons, Greenberg, money, and playing time. His team was hitting a dismal .226 in spring with the start of the season days away. Rowe and Crowder were having arm troubles, Gehringer's back hurt, Goslin's neck too, and Cochrane's eyes weren't focusing properly. "All is not peace and contentment in the Tiger camp," noted one reporter. "The boys are mumbling and muttering among themselves."

Located on the Canadian side of the Detroit River, Fighting Island could be seen from the shore of Ecorse and its southern neighbor, Wyandotte. It had witnessed much history. Native peoples had settled it. The French followed. Back in 1848 thirty-nine-year-old Congressman Abraham Lincoln was aboard a steamer that ran aground in mud off the island. Since 1918 the 1,500 acres had been owned by Michigan Alkali. The company stored industrial waste there, mostly by-products from production of soda ash used for manufacturing glass and cleaning products. Several buildings, including a watchman's shed, shared the island with assorted wildlife and three massive settling beds that consumed most of the land and gave it the look of a "white, desolate moonscape." One of many islands in the river, Fighting Island was uninhabited. But sportsmen, including Black Legion members, fished around it, keeping their boats at some of the dozens of docks in Ecorse and Wyandotte.

Roy Pidcock—no one called him Rector Brutus Pidcock, his birth name—worked at Great Lakes Steel and lived on Sixth Street in Wyandotte, nine blocks from the Detroit River. He and his common-law wife

Nellie, a Catholic, had two children of their own, a daughter and a son, both under age seven. She also had four children from a first marriage that had ended in divorce. With eight of them under one roof, it could be crowded in their small frame house. But their lives had been mostly fun and carefree until recently.

Pidcock's closest friend, Howard Mackey, had known him for years. They worked together and lived a half-mile apart. Mackey had stayed with the Pidcocks for two years. Months back he had shared New Year's dinner with them. By April Pidcock was acting oddly. Mackey had never seen him so restless, agitated, and fearful. One evening Mackey showed up at Pidcock's house to find strangers in his kitchen. They were arguing with him about Nellie's reputation as she waited in the basement. Nellie had a history beyond her failed marriage. But Pidcock had a secret of his own. Unbeknown to her, he had been deceived into joining the legion and now his fellow members were telling him that he had to leave her. Their lifestyle was immoral, they said. She was a divorced Catholic, they were unwed, and he was the father of two of her children. It wasn't the first time they had warned him.

Not long after, Pidcock disappeared for two days. When he returned, his back bore the scored marks of a vicious beating. Nellie questioned him repeatedly. At first he lied, saying he had been injured at the steel plant by a loose chain. She didn't believe him. She persisted, but he refused to reveal what had really happened. "I can't tell you about it," he said. "I'd be killed if I did." The flogging left him a miserable, changed man.

Pidcock bordered on frantic and paranoid in the coming weeks. He refused to tell Mackey the source of his angst, saying only that "they" were going to take him and maybe his wife. He would not explain further. He would not identify his tormenters. Mackey accompanied Pidcock as they went to the homes of three married friends, all Protestant couples. Pidcock begged them to write letters attesting to his and Nellie's good character. He didn't say who would be reading these references. Presumably he hoped to persuade fellow legionnaires. In addition, though he had never shown interest in religion, Pidcock asked Mackey to take him to a Baptist church. There he prayed quietly. Maybe for a different ending to his story.

FBI agent N. E. Manson pulled up to Bert Effinger's home at 1114 Harrison Avenue in Lima, Ohio. Manson had come down from Cleveland. This moment had been a long time coming. For more than a year the FBI had been getting tips and reports related to Effinger and his Black Legion. But the bureau had never talked to him. Director J. Edgar Hoover had shown little interest in pursuing the matter. Months had passed since agents in Detroit, Cleveland, or Cincinnati had issued any reports. There had been the case in Adrian in August 1935, but it was dismissed. On Halloween Hoover had received a tip claiming that a Toledo police sergeant belonged to a clandestine organization and was selling guns to members. Hoover offered a set reply: The bureau lacked jurisdiction.

In March J. P. MacFarland, the agent in charge of the Cleveland office, asked Hoover for permission to interview Effinger. MacFarland wanted to pressure Effinger for a list of members to finally and authoritatively determine whether any Department of Justice employees belonged. He wanted to put the matter to rest. Hoover signed off on the interview, noting that he hoped the "investigation may be brought to a logical conclusion at an early date."

Manson found Effinger's small bungalow in "a good section of town." The interior, like Mrs. Effinger, was "refined," he noted. Effinger himself made a far less favorable impression. He was a "loud and braggart type of individual," Manson said. "Effinger talked at great length, rambling from one subject to another, but he continually stressed the fact that he loved the U.S. and the republic for which it stands, that the Constitution must be upheld at all costs, and that there are enough red-blooded Americans trying to wake up the dormant citizens and politicians to realize that Russian communism was making great inroads in the United States."

Effinger admitted to being ultraconservative and described himself as a "constructive radical, in contrast to a destructive radical." He said that his politics had put him at odds with other electricians and had cost him his job. He lectured the agent about the destructiveness of communism and said the country was being "undermined and broken down until there is no respect for the law." He quoted from the Second

Amendment—"the right of the people to keep and bear arms shall not be infringed"—and said it meant that sometimes patriots must "take the law into their own hands . . . to cope with situations that the local enforcers have failed to handle."

When Manson asked Effinger whether he belonged to the Black Legion, Effinger denied it. He admitted to being a past KKK member. How did he explain complaints to the FBI identifying him as chief of the secret society? He blamed local communists. "Dirty rats," he said. How did he account for the rumored plots to bomb bars, movie theaters, and a post office? Communists again. "Effinger then made the bold statement that if any such bombings or destruction did take place, the situation would be well taken care of by the time that the Department of Justice would get to know about it," Manson reported.

The agent asked whether Effinger possessed a map showing the country's secret fortifications. Effinger said he did not have such a map, but if he learned of someone who did, he would report the person because "the very possession of such a map is a penitentiary offense." He also denied that he had ever attended meetings of the legion and said he had not been in Adrian related to the Black Legion case. He emphasized that he was not familiar with the organization.

Agent Manson interviewed others in Lima but discovered nothing new. He concluded that the legion was a political organization and that it "has now quieted down," adding, "This case, therefore, is being closed." On April 22 J. Edgar Hoover confirmed that judgment in a confidential memo to the attorney general's office. Manson's FBI report, he said, "completes the investigation."

Ten days later word came down from Harvey Davis that the legion needed to take a baseball-obsessed laborer, Charles Poole, on a one-way ride for allegedly beating his wife. Davis and Dean discussed what they would do with his body. They considered the sinkhole in Pinckney.

On the evening of May 2, Davis, Dean, Lowell Rushing, and two other legionnaires arrived at Poole's Detroit house. Dean and Rushing went to the door. Poole's pregnant wife Rebecca answered. She knew

Rushing. He was the brother-in-law of her sister. They had gone to elementary school together in Tennessee. She knew that Lowell, like a slew of other men, had a crush on her. She told them Poole was upstairs with their one-year-old daughter, Mary Lou. Poole loved caring for his child. He enjoyed playing with her, even changed her cotton diapers without a fuss. Mary Lou adored him. Poole liked to tease his wife that he was Mary Lou's favorite.

Dean and Rushing waited across the street in a restaurant. Poole eventually emerged from the house with his daughter in his arms. As he walked past the restaurant's windows, Rushing pointed him out to Dean. He wanted Dean to force Poole into the car right then but Dean refused. Not while he held the baby, he said. They left without talking to Poole.

City of Champions

CANADIAN-BORN PLAYERS DOMINATED THE DETROIT RED WINGS. OF the sixteen who would score a point during the 1935–36 hockey season, only one had been born elsewhere: Gord Pettinger, a native of the United Kingdom. The club was overwhelmingly Canadian, which was fitting. A substantial portion of its fan base came across the river from Windsor, Ontario.

Wings fans had a reputation for being among the better behaved in the National Hockey League. In Chicago fans tossed herrings on the ice; in Boston, an occasional monkey wrench. "If a player or an official can disregard taunts about his ancestry, his habits, his eyesight, or his honesty, he can get along well in Detroit," noted writer John E. McManis. Interaction between players and fans was not uncommon. In one Sunday game, as Wings star defenseman Ebbie Goodfellow headed to the penalty box for tripping, a longtime fan registered his disappointment.

"That wasn't necessary," the man hollered. "What kind of hockey is that?"

"Come down here and I'll show you," Goodfellow replied.

Goodfellow said later he felt bad about the exchange. "I shouldn't have noticed him but you know how it is." Goodfellow had been with the team since 1929. He had gone through its various incarnations. From 1926 to 1930 they were the Cougars. Then they became the Falcons. In 1932 new owner James Norris renamed them the Red Wings. Norris had once played for the championship Montreal Winged Wheelers of the late 1800s. They featured a white-on-blue emblem of a wheel with two wings. Norris adapted it for Detroit, paying homage to both his earlier team and the automobile capital of the world.

At the end of January, more than halfway through the season, the Wings were buried in last place. The poor showing dampened attendance. Some games were played before a few thousand fans. Olympia could accommodate more than 14,000 people if they stood and sat in the aisles.

The Wings' fortunes changed in February. They got hot and won ten of twelve games. The streak put them in contention for first place, which made coach Jack Adams—who had taken the Wings to the finals in 1934—hungry for another shot at a Stanley Cup.

At Madison Square Garden on March 12, Gord Pettinger missed two easy scoring opportunities and cost his team the game. Rangers goalie Andy Kerr fooled Pettinger both times. The defeat reduced the Wings' first-place lead to one point. It was their fourth straight loss. The next morning, on the train from New York City to Montreal, coach Adams laid into his players. He threatened to demote some men and to rearrange scoring lines. "I couldn't sleep last night in New York, fellows," he explained to reporters. "I walked the floor all night. I finally got dressed and walked and walked and walked around the block. It's awful to have a club like this that you know can play hockey and then it loses four straight."

With a tie in Montreal, the Wings increased their lead to two points. Adams was still bothered. On the ride to Detroit, he singled out Bucko McDonald, a hard-hitting defenseman with a serious appetite for steak. Adams felt McDonald's eating habits were slowing him and he ordered him to either eat normally or exercise more: ten miles on a stationary bike or additional skating every day.

"You can eat yourself out of the National Hockey League," Adams warned.

"But I gotta eat, Jack," replied McDonald, who at twenty-one years old was the youngest regular on the team—and the weightiest, listed at 205 pounds (and five-foot-ten).

"Well, what will you do to keep down that bulging stomach?"

McDonald vowed to skate two extra hours daily.

The Wings lost that evening at Olympia, but retained their lead. They clinched the division title four days later before raucous hometown fans, defeating their rival Blackhawks. In the dressing room John Carmi-chael of the *Chicago Daily News* congratulated Adams: "Jack, you've got a great team here and the boys played liked champions. It looks as though they'll do their part to give Detroit a cleanup. You've got the Tigers, the Detroit Lions, Joe Louis . . . Go to it, old boy."

The pressure was mounting on the Wings to continue the city's winning ways. SPIRIT OF REAL CHAMPIONS—THE RED WINGS HAVE IT WHEN THE PRESSURE IS HARDEST, offered one hopeful headline. Papers filled with optimistic stories. Wings players were pictured with their families: Larry Aurie and his wife sipping tea from delicate china, Ebbie Goodfellow and the missus playing cribbage, the Lewises with toddler Jerry, Mr. and Mrs. Doug Young with their boys, Doug Jr. and Bobbie. "Emulating the example of the Tigers on the diamond and the Lions on the gridiron, the Wings met the demands of competition when the chips were down," said a writer reviewing the regular season.

The playoffs began on March 24 with the winners of the American and Canadian divisions—the Red Wings and defending champion Montreal Maroons—facing off for the right to advance to the Stanley Cup. Meanwhile the two teams in second and the two in third played each other. The winner of those series would battle for the right to play Detroit or Montreal. This quirky system, designed to keep more fans interested, meant that one of the game's division champions would not emerge from the first round.

In Montreal, before the series opened, Adams issued special playoff rules for his men: Be in bed by midnight, eat breakfast by ten and follow it with a walk, eat dinner by three, walk again, take a nap, head to the Forum afterward, and be ready to "play like hell." Above all else do not go to the movie theater on game day. "Shows make the players loggy and, besides, they still retain the flicker in their eyes for several hours after leaving a motion-picture house," he said. Adams also called out Bucko McDonald again. "Remember, Bucko. One steak and no more on Tuesday afternoon."

Goalie Normie Smith, who often wore a ball cap when he played, was thought to be the weakest of the Red Wings starters—"just an earnest, everyday workman," in his coach's words. But in the first game he did the unthinkable. The game began at eight-thirty and went scoreless through regulation play. It continued into six overtime periods, concluding around two-thirty in the morning. Excluding breaks, the teams played for 176 minutes with Smith in the net for every one. Playing without a mask, as was typical, Smith stopped all ninety-two Montreal shots, occasionally executing acrobatic moves. He set an NHL record. Wings rookie Mud Bruneteau scored the winning goal. It was the longest game in league history. By the end all the players were exhausted. But the Detroiters could at least take consolation in their triumph.

"My boys are just like kids because they won," said Adams. "I know how terribly the Maroons must feel after playing as brilliantly and as courageously as they did—only to lose. I know how we would have felt." Montreal coach Tommy Gorman added: "It was a crime for either team to lose." The victory demoralized the Maroons and rallied the Wings, who swept the series. Smith allowed one goal in three games. The Wings carried the momentum into the Stanley Cup series against the Toronto Maple Leafs.

Approaching age forty-one, Maple Leafs goalie George Hainsworth was the oldest man on the ice. A popular figure in Montreal and Toronto, where he starred on championship teams, Hainsworth had already had a brilliant, Hall of Fame career. In his best season, 1928–29, he won twenty-two games by shutout, a milestone. But here in the second game of the Stanley Cup finals he looked almost feeble.

The Red Wings scored their first goal less than two minutes into the game. The second came minutes later. Two more followed before the first period ended. The onslaught continued in the final periods. The Red Wings added five more goals. Hainsworth, wrote reporter Doc Holst, "stood there a helpless little old man with a broom trying to sweep away the action." Detroit won 9–4 and took a 2–0 series lead. In Toronto officials considered replacing Hainsworth. But a group of fans appealed to General Manager Conn Smythe to stick with him. "We'd rather lose with the old guy in there than see him benched in the midst of the play-off," said the spokesman.

Coach Dick Irvin went with Hainsworth and he rebounded in game three. Toronto prevailed 4–3 at Maple Leaf Gardens. In the fourth contest, the Leafs scored first, but Ebbie Goodfellow and Marty Barry answered in the second, putting Detroit ahead. Pete Kelly gave the Wings a 3–1 advantage in the third. The Leafs quickly closed it to 3–2 and spent the final moments firing shots at Normie Smith. He stopped all of them, bringing Detroit its first Stanley Cup. The Red Wings achieved what the Tigers and Lions had done months earlier—winning the city's first world championships in their sports. Detroit could truly claim to be the City of Champions. Congratulatory telegrams flooded into Toronto. Champagne flowed in owner James Norris's hotel suite. "Go to it, boys," said Adams. "It's our night."

Two thousand fans cheered the Wings when they arrived at Michigan Central on Easter Sunday. They crowded the platforms and clogged the lobby. Women came bearing bouquets. Fathers held children atop their shoulders. The sound was deafening. Outside a long line of private cars awaited the heroes, ready to sweep each one home. "Upon what meat does our city feed but that it has grown so great?" asked writer Harry LeDuc. The city was heralded for its "unduplicated distinction of supremacy in all major sports." It was "The Sports Capital of the World." WHOLE NATION CHEERS CITY'S CHAMPIONS, noted one headline. "It is swell to be home in the City of Champions," wrote columnist Bud Shaver. "A citizen of Rome, howling for Caesar when Julius was fighting at his best weight, couldn't feel a fiercer pride in his hometown." The momentum beat like a heart. In an editorial the *Detroit News* urged, "Keep it up, Tigers." Around the corner Hearst's *Times* was planning a big celebration, a Champions Day Dinner.

Two days after winning the Stanley Cup several Red Wings drove to Cleveland to see the Tigers open their season against the Indians. An alliance existed between the Tigers, Lions, Red Wings, and Joe Louis. Detroit's champions—uncrowned in Louis's case—all went to one another's games and matches, the Wings and Tigers especially. Jack Adams was probably the most visible of anyone, showing up regularly throughout the town. It was good public relations and a way to enhance fans' sense of camaraderie, but it also reflected a sincere mutual appreciation. Adams made a point of seeing every major league baseball team—American and National—at least once each season. Tigers Billy Rogell and Charlie Gehringer, who spent their winters in Michigan, loved hockey and frequented games at Olympia. Through mid-January Gehringer had been to twenty-two of twenty-three home games.

"I've been watching hockey for nine years, but I've seen only one play-off game," he said. It was one of his regrets. Spring training pulled him away before the post-season began. Gehringer played hockey throughout the winter at his cottage on Cooley Lake. Adams supplied him with hockey equipment. (Gehringer gave him baseball bats in return.)

Ebbie Goodfellow, Herbie Lewis, Scott Bowman, Johnny Sorrell, and Adams were among the Wings who drove to Cleveland. (Harry Bennett was there as well, with Ford cohorts Russell Gnau and boxer Kid McCoy.) Most of the Wings predicted the Tigers would have another grand season. "Providing Charlie Gehringer or Billy Rogell or some other key man isn't injured," added Lewis.

In Cleveland (and at ballparks throughout the league) the flag flew at half-staff in honor of Frank Navin. And who happened to be throwing out the ceremonial first pitch at League Park? Joe Louis. He tossed the ball to radio jokester Jack Benny. It was just one of many honors that had come to Louis in the past year. He had been on Rudy Vallee's show. He had met President Roosevelt. He had cavorted with anyone he cared to meet. He went nowhere without drawing crowds. Louis was one of the best-known people in America, certainly the most famous black man. One Sunday morning he and his brother Deleon Barrow traveled to a park in Trenton, south of Detroit. Louis joined a pickup softball team and played an inning before other folks began to recognize him. Soon they were yelling to people on the Detroit River and Lake Erie. Word spread quicker than the Spanish Flu of 1918. "Good God," said Deleon Barrow, "we had to get all the police out there in Trenton to get us out of there. . . . There seemed to be thousands of people surrounding us."

In the Cleveland game Cochrane vibrated with energy. He wanted to set a good tone for the season. No complacency was allowed. When Earl

Averill popped a foul in the seventh, Cochrane went full force after it, hurdling over the rolled tarpaulin along the third base line. He flung himself headfirst into the stands, emerging with the ball and the out. The Tigers won 3–0. Gehringer got three hits, Greenberg—his contract settled—drove in two runs, and Schoolboy Rowe pitched a four-hit shutout. One game into the season and all was well so far as the public could tell.

Henry Ford would not be attending the Champions Day Dinner. He and Clara had been out late Friday night dancing at an old-fashioned ball at Washington and Jefferson University in Pennsylvania. When he returned on Saturday, reporters besieged him.

Who will you be supporting in the fall presidential race?

"I don't care who is elected president."

What about Roosevelt's taxes on business?

"Too many businessmen and industrialists are lazy," he said. "And I mean mentally, too. They won't think."

What about the eleven million who are unemployed?

"A lot of them don't want to work. . . . They're going to have to work all the harder for the loafing they're doing now. . . . They'll pay later."

Ford had nothing to say about the city's sports teams. He was only a casual fan.

On Saturday, Champions Day, bad weather canceled the Tigers' game. They had played their home opener on Friday at the expanded Navin Field. The new right field stands were filled and the ballpark workers wore fresh outfits. Two hundred ushers were in French blue and navy blue uniforms. Food vendors donned antiseptic white. Cigarette girls, caps strapped to their heads like hurdy-gurdy monkeys, wore satin jackets. They glided through the aisles as snow flurries fell, shivering while selling tobacco and gum. Owner Walter O. Briggs, still in Florida, missed the game, but 32,000 fans came out. Among them was Grace Navin in a heavy hat and fur coat, her colors appropriately dark and dignified for one in mourning. Mary Cochrane, Mickey's wife, sat beside her. Not far away were Harry Bennett and Harry Kipke in fedoras and overcoats. Bennett looked like a movie gangster in a bow tie and flipped collar.

In the evening limos and taxis pulled up to the Masonic Temple for the Champions Day Dinner. Those who drove parked around Cass Park on Temple, Second, and Ledyard. Some would have walked past the legion's Little Stone Chapel and Maurice Sugar's Winchester Apartments. Hundreds flowed into the temple ballroom to honor their sports heroes. The big names were all there: Joe Louis, Mickey Cochrane and his Tigers, Jack Adams and his Wings, Potsy Clark with assorted Lions, Gar Wood, and so many others. The stars spoke briefly, thanking their fans and the city repeatedly. "I'm not a champion yet but I hope to be," said Louis. They ate, drank, and talked together. It was a glorious moment, the celebration of an unparalleled achievement, a snapshot in one city's history that would be forgotten by no one who attended. It was, said the *Times*, "the greatest gathering of champions."

If only the joy could have lasted.

Rumors

SUNDAY BROUGHT UNUSUAL WEATHER FOR MAY 10, UNLIKE ANYTHING the city had seen in decades so early in the month. The day started with sunshine and warm temperatures. In the morning residents poured onto Belle Isle, the glistening Detroit River gem designed by Frederick Law Olmsted. By afternoon, with the thermometer peaking at ninety degrees, an estimated 100,000 people had crowded onto the island. Scorching, sunny days always drew Detroiters to the park, but usually those days occurred in July and August. The island provided an escape from stifling factories, cramped neighborhoods, and overcrowded apartment complexes. Outdoor parks and air-conditioned movie theaters were practically the only two places where ordinary residents could find relief during extreme heat.

Detroit's version of Central Park, Belle Isle offered long shorelines that looked either toward the city's Jefferson Avenue to the north or toward Windsor, Ontario, a leg of Canada nestled—as visitors were often surprised to learn—beneath and to the south of Detroit. The island's nearly one thousand acres had lakes, lagoons, and canals filled with canoeists. There were swimming areas, fishing spots, winding walkways in the shade, and myriad attractions: a casino for parties, a zoo, a yacht club, a glossy, green-tiled aquarium, a glass-and-steel conservatory, a gazebo on a hill, a band shell, athletic fields, water fountains, riding stables, and monuments to generals, newsboys, and children's temperance. On Sunday cars clogged the four-lane, one-way road that circled the island. With masses of people flocking onto the picnic grounds, empty tables proved almost impossible to find. On blankets, in chairs, beneath hats, and under umbrellas, hordes of visitors tried to cool themselves by sipping from bottles of Goebel and Stroh's pulled from buckets of ice. For the kids there were Cokes, Faygo strawberry sodas, and ginger ales by Vernor's. Music wafted from portable phonographs. It was a hot yet beautiful day.

But as evening arrived, the sun vanished. Clouds rolled in and storms rumbled through Detroit. Thunder shook the city. Lightning pierced haunted skies. Winds snapped power lines. Somewhere out in the mess was Roy Pidcock, who had once again left home without a word. He had departed on Saturday. When he returned on Monday, he told his beloved Nellie that he had been in the woods for two nights. He looked it. Unshaven and filthy, his clothes dirty, he had little else to say except: "They are going to get me and you, too." But he wouldn't explain. He sat around all day and night in his underclothes. Nellie found a piece of maple bark in his pants on which he had written, "I love everybody."

On Monday evening Dayton Dean went to Eppinger Sporting Goods for target practice. All Black Legion members were required to own pistols, but not all carried them. As part of a legion Death Squad, Dean did. The Wayne County Rifle and Pistol Club, to which he belonged, had been chartered through the National Rifle Association as part of a federal program aimed at encouraging such clubs. After qualifying, the group had received four rifles and thousands of rounds of ammunition from the government. Club founder John George Quindt Sr., unaware that the Black Legion had infiltrated his group, was hoping that one or two of his shooters would develop into marksmen. Until they did, he wouldn't allow use of government rifles or ammunition. He didn't want the supplies wasted.

Dean, despite his boasts about his Navy skills, lacked deadeye accuracy. He carried two pistols, a .38 and a .45, but he wasn't an expert shot. He did practice though. A good soldier of the Black Legion never knew when he would be called into action or what the reason might be, the sins of an errant member or the overthrow of a dictatorial US government. September 16—the ill-defined day of reckoning that Major-General Effinger had been hazily promoting for months—was four months away.

The Wolverine Republican League convened at eight o'clock in the evening on Monday, May 11, in Findlater Temple. Two stories, boxish, and with a front entrance that opened between twenty-foot columns, the temple stood in southwest Detroit at Waterman and West Lafayette. Nearby was an industrial area that included factories for American Brass, Ternstedt Manufacturing, and Fisher Fleetwood. Fewer than two miles away was sinister-looking Zug Island, a desolate, uninhabitable black, white, and gray place where Great Lakes Steel operated blast furnaces.

The temple itself had been built in a neighborhood of pleasant homes. A red-bricked school sat across Waterman Street and a half-block of shops (a butcher, grocer, and barber) lay kitty-corner from the temple. Originally home to Masonic Lodge 475, the facility rented space to twenty organizations. The Wolverine Republicans met there, usually taking a small room in the basement. The league was a front for the secret society. Who, after all, would rent space to something called the Black Legion? Some legion members didn't recognize their organization by the name for which it would become known. Among members the Bullet Club, Black Knights, and United Brotherhood of America were as familiar as the Black Legion.

In April, when former governor Wilber M. Brucker had made his first public appearance after announcing he would be challenging Senator James Couzens in the October primary, he did it before the Wolverine Republican League in the temple's auditorium. The elder Couzens, the father of Detroit's mayor and a wealthy man from his early business days with Henry Ford, had sided with President Roosevelt on some issues, angering conservative members of his party. Brucker, a teetotaler, accused Roosevelt and Couzens of abandoning American principles and toying with socialism. "The sooner the New Deal is rooted out, root and branch, and dumped in the ash can of history, the better it will be for all," Brucker said. Common pleas court judge Eugene Sharp spoke at the event. As the speeches ended, a supporter called for the league to endorse Brucker then and there. The crowd thundered its support, casting their "ayes" with him.

League members viewed Brucker's appearance as a triumph. It generated press coverage and "put the Wolverine League out in front," wrote Secretary Floyd Nugent in an April 30 letter to members. Along the left edge the letter included a list of league officers. Many were in the Black Legion. Leslie Black, Judge Sharp's balding court clerk, served as president. He had been involved in the plots against attorney Maurice Sugar and *Highland Parker* publisher Art Kingsley. The cadaverous Harvey Davis, organizer of the Silas Coleman joy killing, was on the league's entertainment committee. Jesse Pettijohn, who had schemed to have Mayor Voisine of Ecorse assassinated, belonged to the membership committee, along with Roy Lorance and Ervin Lee, who had participated in the Coleman hunt. The membership chairman was Wilbur Robinson, a legion recruiter. There were others. The most intriguing name on the letterhead belonged to Harry Z. Marx, the delegate chairman. Marx was the attorney who had intervened in Adrian when State Police pulled over the car of legionnaires. An up-and-comer, Marx had credentials more sterling than most of the men featured on the stationery. He had a successful practice with an office in the Union-Guardian. A losing candidate in the same judicial election as Maurice Sugar, Marx also had connections. He had once chaired the American Legion's Americanism Committee. More crucial was that one of his friends and clients was Col. Heinrich Pickert, the police commissioner. Within the league Marx wasn't a mere figurehead. His law office doubled as the Wolverine League's address. On the night Brucker spoke, Marx had introduced him.

Nugent's letter urged members to come to the May 11 meeting and to bring their signed Wilber Brucker nominating petitions. Many who showed returned the next night, on Tuesday, May 12, to hear Russian-born Victor Nicholas Schultz address the crowd. Schultz lived nearby and worked in an auto factory as a mechanic. In his younger days he had battled Russian revolutionaries. He lectured that evening against communism, lamenting that his beautiful native land had been destroyed. He warned the nearly fifty men present that the same thing could happen in America.

When Schultz finished, another legionnaire, a candidate for the statehouse, delivered a political speech, and then Harvey Davis took center stage. There was a serious issue to be tackled, Davis said. A Catholic man, Charles Poole, had beaten and kicked his expectant Baptist wife,

Rebecca, so badly that she had to be hospitalized, Davis said. She was in Herman Kiefer Hospital at this very moment and her baby wouldn't be born alive, he added. Davis indicated that members Lowell Rushing, Rebecca's brother-in-law, and Herschel Gill, whose wife was her close friend, had told him of the abuse. They had heard of the mistreatment from Gill's sister-in-law, Ruby Lane, who had heard it from Rebecca Poole's sister, Marcia Rushing, a woman later described by a family member as a loud, dramatic, boozing gossip. There was one big problem with the story: It was untrue. Poole had not hit his wife. No beating had occurred. Rebecca was in the hospital because she had delivered their second daughter, Nancy.

Lowell Rushing disliked Charles Poole. Rushing and Poole, along with Gill and Harvey Davis, lived within a half-mile of one another, all within sight of the gleaming, six-year-old Ambassador Bridge that connected Detroit to Windsor. Rushing had despised Poole for as long as he had known him, since 1933, when Rebecca met him. She and Charles married seventeen months later. Maybe he loathed Poole for being a Catholic. Or maybe he felt Rebecca could do better. Rushing had grown up with Rebecca back in Danville, Tennessee, and he was closer to her age, twenty-one, than Charley, who was thirty-one. Poole had been mostly unemployed since losing his job around Christmas and was now working two days per week with the WPA. Over the years he had been a mechanic, a chef, and a shipman on the Great Lakes, but money always seemed tight. While Poole's religion and job prospects didn't endear him to Rushing, another factor played into his aversion. Its roots had been planted before Poole ever came on the scene. Some years back Rebecca had spent a summer in her sister Marcia's home. Marcia was married to Owen Rushing, Lowell's brother. Lowell had spent that same summer under the same roof and had become smitten with the pretty, kindly, ninety-pound Rebecca and her high-pitched, childlike voice.

The rumor of the beating had begun with Marcia, who had recently been sitting at the kitchen table in her home, talking about an argument between the Pooles. Rebecca, according to Marcia, was angry with Charles because he didn't have a job, wasn't hunting hard enough to find one, and seemed to enjoy spending time at their home as Rebecca worked hard for her measly wages. Ruby Lane overheard the rumor and shared it with Agnes Gill. Harvey Davis and Lowell Rushing were there when she repeated it. "If the organization is any good, it will take care of Poole," one of the men said.

One day, while Marcia Rushing was at a beer garden on Junction Avenue, John "Scotty" Bannerman, another legion colonel, tracked her down and asked if the story was true. Had her sister married a Catholic who beat her? Marcia didn't actually hate Charles Poole. She saw him regularly. She had gone with him on Sunday to visit his newborn. She even took care of his and Rebecca's other daughter while Rebecca was in the hospital. But she had been drinking and there was no going back on her whopper. She answered yes, adding for good measure, "I'd like to kill him myself." Her liquor-embellished story grew into the large tale that Col. Harvey Davis spread at the May 12 meeting, inflaming the men with colorful details, working them into a fervor. He asked finally, What should be done?

Davis already knew. Hours earlier he had laid the trap for Charles Poole. He went to Poole's rental and found him and best friend Gene Sherman painting and doing plumbing. Poole lived in a four-family flat. The landlord was allowing him to stay free of charge temporarily with the understanding that he would pay him back when he found a job. Davis told Poole that given his talents as a baseball player he could get him a position that would include playing for the Timken Axle team. This would be convenient. Timken was located blocks from Poole's place. Davis said he would send someone by later to take him to a team meeting to be measured for a uniform. It was not uncommon for some workers to be hired based on their ability to contribute on the athletic field in the competitive industrial leagues. Poole had talent at baseball. He was a catcher, like Cochrane.

The livid crowd inside Findlater Temple called for justice. They demanded a beating, a lynching, or a one-way ride for Charles Poole. Men volunteered. Col. Davis had already procured his gunmen, Ervin Lee and Dayton Dean. Others had done little with the Black Legion until then, like twenty-two-year-old Urban Lipps. He had come to Michigan from Mississippi a year earlier. Feeling lonesome, he had accepted an invitation to a party, hoping to meet friends and build a social life outside his job at Hudson Motor Company. Instead he was inducted into the legion. Robes, red lights, the Black Oath—the ritual petrified him. Over time and under pressure he returned for more meetings. One was a dance. Another was the current affair with the "white Russian" and Davis's story about poor Rebecca Poole. Lipps had taken a bus to be there. "A fellow hardly knows how he gets into these things," he would say. Davis enlisted him in the effort to lure Charles Poole out for a drive.

Poole loved that he had a new daughter. When he visited her in the hospital, he joked with Rebecca about the baby's black hair, darker than his own and unlike Mary Lou's bald head at birth. With his family expanding he worried more than usual about money. He chewed his fingernails to the quick. On Tuesday morning he had appeared at Marcia Rushing's house to see his one-year-old daughter. He shared his concerns and committed to finding a job. He had scraped together money for a pair of shoes for Mary Lou. He returned an hour later with a high chair.

That evening Poole must have thought his life was finally taking a turn for the better with the baseball team and the job possibility. He may have wondered, though, if he had heard Harvey Davis correctly, for he and two pals went to three beer gardens near Fort Street looking for his baseball ride. They started out at Hayes Chop House around the corner from his flat. Poole usually didn't drink but he had a beer to be social. They walked next to the Blue Ribbon Café, a mile up Fort. They proceeded to Joe's Pavilion, a dancing spot across the street from Ternstedt Manufacturing. At each place Poole let the bartender know where he could be found if someone came looking for a ballplayer. He wasn't taking chances with his wardrobe either. He looked smart dressed in a secondhand dark-brown suit, red tie, stylish pin-striped red-and-purple shirt, gray socks, and black Oxfords. He was sitting in Joe's Pavilion with friends Sherman and Ralph Hyatt when blond-haired Urban Lipps came in and walked up to their table.

Lipps looked at Sherman and asked if he was Poole.

"No. I'm not Poole," Sherman said, motioning to his friend.

"Are you going to the baseball party?" Lipps asked.

"Sure. Where is it going to be?"

"Out on the west side."

The combination of a job and a baseball position sounded so good that all three men wanted to go to the meeting. Lipps said there was room for only Charles Poole. They left the bar. Lipps led Poole to Ervin Lee's car. Poole slid into the backseat next to Dayton Dean.

Poole and Pidcock

A NIGHTTIME CONVOY OF FOUR CARS HEADED OUT OF DETROIT ALONG Fort Street. In the back of one vehicle between Dayton Dean and Urban Lipps sat the unsuspecting Charles Poole. He was excited to be going to a baseball meeting. Dean and Lipps kept up the charade by talking about the Tigers. Ever since the World Series, baseball had been a topic of choice around town. Earlier in the day the Tigers had shut out Boston. It was their second straight win. But they had been only average at best thus far. Dean said he didn't think the Tigers would win this year's pennant. Poole agreed. It certainly didn't look good.

Hank Greenberg, fielding a wild throw at first, had fractured his wrist when runner Jake Powell plowed into him. Though Greenberg expected to return in a month or two, he wouldn't. He would be gone for the season. Schoolboy Rowe lacked his usual pizzazz too. He had left the team for a week to be with his dying father. Over the winter, with his World Series winnings, he had bought his dad a restaurant to occupy his time, but it was for naught. In his first two starts of the season, Rowe had thrown complete-game shutouts. Upon returning from the funeral he had managed a combined two-and-a-third innings in his next two starts, surrendering twelve runs. Gehringer was also hurting and so was Pete Fox. Expensive Al Simmons was being described as "all washed up" and injuries were limiting Cochrane's availability. A wounded throwing thumb, a reoccurrence of his eye troubles, a foul ball against his instep— all seemed minor but they were accumulating and he was missing games. On top of everything else, batboy Joey Roggin got an infection after being stung on the eyelid. Said Gee Walker: "That's as far down the lineup as we can go, so maybe our bad luck is over." It wasn't. The Tigers fell into sixth place as the Yankees stormed to the top of division.

Two of the four cars made it over the Rouge River before the Fort Street drawbridge lifted. The others had no choice but to wait for a ship to pass. The river had long ago been widened and deepened to accommodate freighters carrying ore and other materials that Henry Ford needed for production at the Rouge complex. Sunset complete, the industrial skyline took on its eerie, ominous, menacing nighttime disposition. Floodlights—white, red, and amber—dotted land and sky, spreading orbs over looming cranes and smokestacks and throwing shadows across hard, hostile structures. Flames flared from narrow pipes and massive, forbidding buildings stood silhouetted against the sky. Ghostly clouds of illuminated smoke hovered around them.

When the bridge lowered eight to ten minutes later, the rear cars led by John Bannerman went to Wyandotte toward Roy Pidcock's house, where Cecil Pidcock had come up from Toledo to visit his brother. Roy's wife had told Cecil about his recent bizarre behavior, about his spending two nights outdoors and returning disheveled, paranoid, and emotionally broken. He had been acting queer, she said. The brothers exchanged small talk and then Cecil invited Roy for a drive, hoping to cheer him and to learn the source of his torment. They were gone for three hours.

Upon returning, Roy Pidcock stripped down and went to bed. He had a room to himself that night. Cecil told Nellie that he couldn't figure what was on Roy's mind and that he was heading home. As Cecil left for Toledo, Black Legion members watched from cars parked on the street.

Charles Poole noticed the moon. It shone large, a scuffed cue ball against a blue felt sky. Poole commented to Dean about it as they drove. They were heading to Dearborn, holding close to the Rouge River where possible. Poole talked about his wife and two daughters. Dean could tell Poole had high regard for them and he began feeling there was "something fishy" about Harvey Davis's tale of the beating. But he had his orders and he knew he could be killed for not obeying them. It was a long ride and it wasn't smooth. On a back road their car got stuck in mud. Davis's vehicle pushed it out.

After forty-five minutes they stopped along Gulley Road. A branch of the Rouge River cut through the countryside and into a golf course, the border of which lay three hundred yards away. Lipps and Poole stayed in the car near the one-lane bridge. Dean and Ervin Lee got out to confer with Davis and the other men. They waited awhile, supposedly for the vehicles that had gotten separated at the bridge. (The original plan evidently had been for the men in all four cars to witness Poole's punishment.) A bottle of liquor passed between them. Lee went back to the car and offered Lipps and Poole a drink. Poole declined.

"What is this going to be, a party out under the stars?" Poole asked.

Lee laughed and said yes.

Poole was growing concerned.

In Wyandotte the legionnaires either lured Roy Pidcock outside, perhaps vowing not to harm his wife if he came quietly, or they abducted him from his bed at gunpoint. Pidcock left barefoot and in his underwear, his pants and shoes still in the room. He scrawled a note under duress before departing. It read, "To all that know me, I love you all. Don't worry about me. I can't explain."

Fleeing on Sixth Street, the cars would have thumped over the four rail lines that separated Pidcock's neighborhood from Jefferson Avenue. The shoreline set just beyond. A motorboat waited there. Either before boarding or while on the boat, someone killed Pidcock. He was strangled with an electric cord. He might first have been hit on the head. They proceeded to Fighting Island and took him to an abandoned watchman's shed on the north end. Ash dust covered the floor. They hoisted Pidcock into the rafters. His body dangled from a wire, making it look as if he had killed himself.

On Gulley Road, Harvey Davis directed Dean to get Poole from the car. Dean pulled his guns—a .38 and a .45 he had bought for five bucks from state commander Arthur Lupp—and ordered Poole out of the car. Poole didn't fight. "OK," he said. Dean ushered him to a spot near a ditch and stood six feet from him. Lee was to Dean's left. Davis stayed behind both of them, armed with a revolver.

Poole said he hadn't done anything and asked why they had pulled guns.

"You're a dirty liar," Davis said. "You know what you've done and what you have been brought out here for. You know you beat up your wife—"

"Boys, there must be some mistake," he said. "I never—"

Davis swore at him. "You'll never live to do it again," he said.

Dean looked around. There wasn't much light and he couldn't see Poole's face. In the brief, quiet pause, Dean figured it was time. He fired at Poole. Lee shot too, but off to the side so as not to hit the man. Dean shot eight times from the hip, unloading with both hands. Lee used three bullets. Poole collapsed into the ditch. He had been struck six times. They waited to make certain he was dead. The pop of the gun awoke farmer Fred Shettleman. He reasoned that the sound must be a backfiring car. He fell asleep.

Davis scolded Dean for shooting too early; he had wanted to lecture Poole some more. Davis told the men to keep their mouths shut about the killing. They drove back to Fort Street and a few of them went to a German inn, where they sat amid the cigar and cigarette smoke in the tawny light of a half-curtained barroom and chatted over beers. Davis walked home. The fresh air might clear his mind.

A farm woman toting heads of cabbage discovered Poole's body before six o'clock the next morning. She noticed something in the ditch, approached, and screamed. A couple sleeping in a nearby car startled awake. They drove to a grocery store to call the police. Poole had no identification on him. The first officers to the scene thought the man might be handsome Harry Millman, a mobster affiliated with the Jewish Purple Gang. But Detroit homicide chief John Navarre, who had helped put some of the gang in prison, recognized on sight that it wasn't Millman. He thought the dead man might be a gangster involved in a $65,000 robbery of a Detroit bank. Witnesses said one of the gunmen had been biting his nails while holding a gun. Examining Poole, Navarre noticed his gnawed nails. But the other evidence didn't make sense. Fellow gangsters would have executed him cleanly with a shot to the head, not several shots delivered haphazardly to the torso. As newsmen snapped photos, police took Poole's fingerprints. Failing to find a local match, they wired them to the FBI in Washington, speculating that the victim might be a mobster.

Within four hours Director J. Edgar Hoover himself called Detroit's chief of detectives. The FBI had a match, he said. The prints belonged to Charles Poole, who a decade earlier had been arrested for hopping a train in Dodge City, Kansas. The victim was identified in the evening editions of the Detroit dailies. AGAIN THE G-MEN SCORE A TRIUMPH, heralded one headline. Reporters had no idea that the whole affair could have been prevented had the police or the FBI more diligently investigated myriad crimes and complaints.

Gulley Road in Dearborn was outside the city limits, but Poole lived in the city, so both Detroit police and the county sheriff's department investigated. Navarre assigned detectives Andrew Jackson "Jack" Harvill and Charles Meehan to work with Deputy Mickey Farrell, a colorful figure who had been a cop for two years. Farrell had grown up near the ballpark and worked there as a young man, even encountering Ty Cobb. Before joining the force he had been an amateur prizefighter, a taxi driver, and a barroom bouncer. Physically daunting, he played the bad cop well.

Interviews with Poole's widow, family, and neighbors turned up no motive. Poole didn't have money. He didn't gamble. He didn't step out on Rebecca. He didn't drink much. He had no known enemies and didn't associate with criminals. His life mainly revolved around family, friends, and baseball. Everyone seemed to like him. At the morgue Marcia and Owen Rushing confirmed that the bulleted body inside the refrigerated glass case was that of their brother-in-law. Poole's aunt identified him too, as did Mrs. Robert White, owner of the Junction Restaurant who once employed him.

"Poor Charlie," she remarked to Harvill. "To think that two of the boys who work for me was out with him the night before he died."

Harvill, a veteran of the Detroit force, had just gotten a break. He, Meehan, and Farrell interviewed Poole's friends Sherman and Hyatt. They learned of the baseball meeting and then fanned out to bars and restaurants along Fort Street. They came up with descriptions of three men who had been looking for Poole the night he disappeared: a thin, pasty man whom Sherman had let into Poole's flat; a short, solid, tough-looking chap who had asked a bartender if he had seen a ball-player named Poole; and a young, blond, athletic guy who had escorted him from the bar and into a waiting vehicle. But police had no plate numbers and no names. Though someone mentioned that "Tennessee Slim" fit the first description, the nickname wasn't distinctive enough to lead them to their man. And no one at Timken Axle knew of Poole or a baseball meeting.

Harvill and Meehan went to the funeral, as did Poole's friend Sherman. They hoped he might recognize the graceless man who had invited Charles to join the ball club. But he wasn't there. Harvill gave Sherman his business card and told him that if he ever spotted "Tennessee Slim" to give the card to a police officer and have the man arrested. At the funeral police noticed that Marcia Rushing, Agnes Gill, and Ruby Lane were strangely quiet. They appeared to be fearful. They wouldn't talk. Over the next days the leads withered to almost nothing.

On May 14, the day after the Poole discovery, an employee of Michigan Alkali found Roy Pidcock's strung-up, scarcely clothed body on Fighting Island. Canadian authorities investigated and quickly decided he had taken his own life.

Several clues, though, should have raised questions. How did Pidcock get to the island? There was no boat on the shore and his underclothes had not been wet. Why were his feet clean? Ash covered the floor but no traces of dust appeared on him. Whose fresh shoe prints showed in the ash? No shoes were discovered in the shed. What about the gash on his head? No autopsy was performed. Canadian police pointed to the note that had been left at his house, to his odd behavior, and to his previous disappearance as evidence of suicide.

Secrets

DETECTIVE JACK HARVILL WORRIED THAT HE HAD STRUCK A STONE wall. Rebecca Poole had no clue why her husband had been targeted. She couldn't imagine who would kill him. "Charles was good to me," she said. "We didn't have anything but I was happy and a man's got to be good to you if you're happy with him under the condition in which we had to live." Rebecca liked that her husband was kind, cared about their children, could fix anything, didn't drink to excess, and even helped with washing and ironing.

Police interviewed friends, family, and former co-workers, but their words led nowhere. If Poole had been found with a union application tucked under his head, as John Bielak had, or been linked to the communist party, as was George Marchuk, police would likely have attributed his death to radical elements and closed the case. If he had been black, like Silas Coleman, the investigation would probably have been abandoned at the first roadblock. Something about the Poole murder pricked Harvill. Maybe it was the sight of Poole's infant daughters or his hapless wife, or maybe it was that Poole was a fellow southerner, born in Owensboro, Kentucky.

Harvill was from Tennessee, at Tottys Bend, fewer than two hundred miles from Owensboro. He was one of twelve children. Soft-spoken and reserved, he had become a teacher near his hometown. When the Great War called, he went with the 83rd Division to France. Afterward he landed in booming Detroit and found work at Paige Motor Company, which had a plant not far from where Poole would live eighteen years later. At age twenty-four he had joined the Detroit Police force, walking a beat near the headquarters on Beaubien Street, a block from Monroe, where Greeks socialized, ate moussaka and pastitsio, and admired scantily clad belly dancers. Harvill and his wife, Hildegard, were gardeners. He grew flowers, she grew vegetables. They had no children. Now a homicide detective, he had spent his entire career based at the central station. The Poole case would be his most significant.

The break came almost a week after Poole's disappearance. Near Fort Street, Gene Sherman spotted the gangly man who had visited Poole's house. He handed Jack Harvill's business card to a police officer and the cop arrested Harvey Davis. At headquarters Harvill, Meehan, and Farrell told Davis that they knew about Poole and the baseball meeting. Davis blanched but offered little. He denied knowing Poole, but during a string of questions admitted being an acquaintance of Marcia Rushing. Harvill headed to the Rushing home. He told the Rushings that police had Harvey Davis in custody. The detective bluffed his way through the conversation, letting on that he knew more than he did. He hoped to scare her into talking. It worked. She revealed that they were terrified of the secret society.

"Nobody is going to harm you," Harvill said.

"You don't know these people," Marcia Rushing replied.

It was the first Harvill had heard of it, but he didn't let on. They said they had warned Owen's brother Lowell, who lived in their house, against joining the group. Who else did they know in the organization? Harvill asked. Marcia Rushing offered some names. Harvill arrested Lowell Rushing and police grabbed the other men and raided their houses. They discovered guns, ropes, whips, black robes, ammunition, and literature for the Wolverine Republican League. Harvill found the men—even those not directly involved in Poole's disappearance—unwilling to talk. The prospect of being punished by the society frightened them more than jail time. But as the circle of suspects widened, detectives drew out bits of information and began playing suspects off one another. Over the next twenty-four hours the vague skeleton of a sinister organization and the specifics of Charles Poole's murder took shape. The key moment came when Dayton Dean opened up. At first he supplied little. But as police charmed and coaxed him and patted him on the back he shared more.

Overnight the story of the terrorist cult exploded in banner headlines:

Poole a Victim of Black Legion
Sixteen Officers of . . . Secret Society Held in Poole
    Murder
Murder Unmasks Political Activity of Hooded Vigilantes

The revelations overwhelmed the city's other big news. For activists and progressives May 22 had begun with the focus on a different issue: the requested ouster of Police Commissioner Col. Heinrich Pickert. The Conference for the Protection of Civil Rights petitioned the mayor and city council for Col. Pickert's removal. They charged him with leading a brutal police regime that repeatedly infringed on the rights of citizens, especially blacks, Jews, and leftists. Speaking before the fiercely divided crowd of 1,200 people that had jammed into council chambers, attorney Maurice Sugar and others testified against Pickert, decrying what they called his ruthless tactics. During a Motor Products strike procession, Col. Pickert's police had overseen the gassing and clubbing of pro-union marchers, injuring dozens, Sugar said. In recent weeks police had shot three young men in separate incidents. In one case an officer had used a machine gun to halt a fleeing fourteen-year-old who had been seen fumbling with a lock at a service station.

Pickert had his supporters and they turned out in large numbers, bolstered by petitions with thousands of signatures. Sugar's allies contended that Harry Bennett's security forces had pressured Ford workers to sign the pro-Pickert petitions. Father Coughlin also sided with Pickert, writing in a letter, "In the interest of good law and order, the actions of communists must be handled and checked by a strong man such as Commissioner Pickert." In the end the mayor and council backed Pickert unanimously. Among the attorneys representing Pickert at the hearing was Harry Z. Marx of the Wolverine Republican League.

If not for the Black Legion, the Pickert story would have drawn major headlines. But the coverage of it stood no chance against the rattling disclosures of the Poole probe. Few people recognized that there might be a connection between the police commissioner and the terrorist group. But Dayton Dean and others knew. Dean had seen Pickert at legion meetings. Others, including Detroit detectives, had seen Pickert's signed membership card.

Around four o'clock on a Saturday morning after the Pickert hearing, Maurice Sugar awoke to the ring of his apartment bell. Someone was outside the building. Sugar responded through the speaking tube, asking what the person wanted. A man responded in a muddled voice. Sugar couldn't understand him. The man buzzed a second time. Again his words were distorted. On the third ring Sugar didn't answer. He looked down from the window of his sunroom and saw two men leaving the apartment. They wore vests over short-sleeve shirts. They headed to a car forty feet away and drove off.

Detectives Harvill, Meehan, and Farrell built up Dayton Dean and kept him supplied with the plump cigars that he so loved. Dean continued to talk. Police moved him to headquarters, separating him from the other suspects, holding him in a private, double-sized cell. The others were in the county facilities across the street. Police slipped him an occasional glass of beer and made sure he had cheese or butter for his bread. (He detested dry bread.) Dean liked the attention. "This was his moment of glory," detective Farrell figured. Police probably let Dean read the story in which Harvey Davis blamed him for Poole's murder, calling him a "big fool." Davis said that Dean had fired on his own, without orders, and that the legion had had no intention of killing Poole.

Dean talked some more.

Dean, Davis, Lee, and Lipps all confessed to involvement in the Poole plot. They also identified themselves as members of the Wolverine Republican League. President Leslie Black contended that the Republican group had nothing to do with the legion. "It looks like an underhanded way of giving the league a bad name," he said. "Somebody is trying to pull a fast one and discredit the party." Black was lying. A court clerk, he himself had been involved in several plots. Within days he would be forced to resign his court position.

Attorney Harry Z. Marx, a Wolverine director, denied the league was a front for the cult. Marx said he had never heard of the Black Legion. This rang false, though, because ten months earlier he had represented legion members charged in Adrian and Detroit. Those men had been found with guns and black robes in their cars and they had been identified publicly as being with the Black Legion. "I don't remember what my clients told me nor why they were carrying guns," he said. Marx suggested that communists were behind the claims of a link between the league and the legion. They might also have murdered Poole, he suggested. "I have never heard any hint that a terrorist group might exist within [the league's] ranks," he said. "Of course, it is possible that such a group might form unknown to myself or other members of the league."

This was untrue, said former Pontiac police chief George Eckhardt, who had been ousted by legion forces. "It isn't a small clique inside the club," he said. "The club is just a small group inside the legion. The order has its national headquarters in Lima, Ohio." Eckhardt urged authorities to expose the whole enterprise. "Some well-meaning but stupid men must suffer," he said, "but the potentialities of a gang of hooded cowards banded together under iron discipline are too serious to allow it to exist."

In Lima reporters converged on the home of Bert Effinger. They crowded onto his lawn, pounded on his door, and waited near his front steps. When Effinger appeared, he took a seat on his porch swing. He spat tobacco juice as he talked.

"What if I am the leader?" Effinger asked defiantly. In his next breath he nearly admitted as much, saying the organization had three million members. Later he revised the number upward to six million. "I want the statement refuted that we are interested in taking over the government," he added. "We are interested in either party as long as they use honorable efforts in accordance with the Constitution." He said the men charged with killing Poole didn't represent righteous legionnaires. "I hope those damn fools up in Detroit burn in the electric chair." (Not possible: Michigan had abolished the death penalty in 1846.)

On his three-acre farm in central Michigan, Peg-Leg White got las-soed outside by a reporter. White stood in front of a graying wood cart, his partial thumb hooked over the belt of his dungarees, a workman's cap pulled low over his forehead. Dandelions and clover flecked the ground around his wooden leg. White worried that the exposure might cost him his police pension. He said he didn't think he had ever joined the Black Legion and suggested that there must be another Peg-Leg White some-where out there. He admitted to once having been in the Ku Klux Klan. Reporter John Carlisle asked him about the murder of Hudson organizer John Bielak and about reports that he, White, was one of the legion's top organizers. "I'd be ashamed to admit I belonged to anything like that," he said. When pressed, he derided himself as "just one of those boobs who went for the Klan stuff." Shortly after the interview White fled town.

Over the weekend, as his name emerged in the probe, state com-mander Arthur Lupp disappeared for a day. His health department bosses went searching for him and his city-owned vehicle. But he couldn't be located. Late Monday afternoon he materialized with his attorney at Prosecutor Duncan McCrea's office. Lupp offered innocently that he had been on a brief vacation in Algonac, fifty miles northeast of Detroit. Homicide chief John Navarre and McCrea began to quiz Lupp, but he requested that newsmen be invited. He wanted to give a statement. Lupp loved to lecture on Americanism and he appreciated an attentive audience. McCrea obliged him.

The prosecutor's office filled quickly with reporters and photogra-phers. The Black Legion had the press in furious competition for scoops. No one wanted to miss this opportunity. Lupp evaded direct questions about the legion's size, activities, and membership. Instead he offered trite platitudes about patriotism. In a haughty tone he spoke of high princi-ples. His voice thundered. He punctuated his words with the gestures of a better orator. Several times he saluted McCrea's flag for the cameras.

"You men must remember," he said, "that during this Depression, there was this condition: Many men were depressed. They had no pur-pose in life. They were floundering around. This organization gave them an interest in life. It is not a fly-by-night organization. There are many good citizens supporting this movement. Every cross-section of the country belongs. Someone is getting it over to them that they owe a duty to their country. This organization is not a racket. It is not a money-making scheme."

A reporter interrupted, asking sarcastically, "What organization is this, anyway?"

"The Black Legion," he blustered. "It is all volunteer service. . . . These have been days of trouble and dissension. The organization has accomplished much. Many men in different walks of life have dedicated their lives to the service of their country and through it to remain forever true to the Red, White, and Blue." Lupp's own words seemed to satisfy him. A few reporters applauded him. He might not have recognized that they were mocking him for he continued for several more minutes until his voice grew hoarse.

"Where is your headquarters?" someone asked.

"Well," he began anew, "I might say it is wherever we hang our hats. It is a proposition of carrying a message of pledging our undying allegiance to the flag and to our country."

"Are members of the Black Legion allowed to withdraw from it?"

"When I pledge myself to the flag and to America it means to me that I personally mean it for the rest of my life. What good is a resolution if I pass it off? As a recruiting officer, it was my purpose to get men to realize that when they took the oath, they were pledging undying loyalty to American principles, that it means forever to keep that obligation."

"Why is it called the Black Legion?"

"I might say: Why is up, up?"

"How do you enforce discipline in the legion?"

"The same as in any other lodge. Understand, when we get a man who is an American and he pledges himself to support nothing but American principles, if he shirks his duty, some of the members call on him and straighten him out. They may say, 'Now, Bill, you better get back into this and put your shoulder to the wheel.'"

Lupp droned on and on, with McCrea and Navarre encouraging him. After Lupp chattered for almost fifteen minutes nonstop his attorney, Clyde Fulton, tried to silence him. Fulton had been a losing mayoral candidate in Highland Park, where publisher Kingsley had editorialized against him.

"Come on, I've got to get home," Fulton said.

Lupp hesitated.

"Hurry up. You've said enough," his frustrated attorney added.

As he led Lupp, still jabbering, from the room, Fulton whispered at him, "Oh, shut up."

Black Legion Hysteria

"Terrorists!" "Vigilantes!" "Masked army!" "Secret militia!" "Cult!" The fantastical story of the Black Legion spread quickly across the country. Star reporters—among them the celebrated James Kilgallen of International News Service, Will Lissner of the *New York Times*, Forrest Davis of Scripps-Howard's *New York World-Telegram*—converged on Detroit from New York, Chicago, and Washington. The preliminary hearing for the Poole murder had to be moved from a courtroom to the expansive supervisors' hall on the fourth floor of the County Building, a landmark with a 247-foot, bronze-tipped Beaux-Arts tower. More space was needed to accommodate the army of reporters, photographers, and movie camera operators. According to one observer, the nation hadn't seen anything similar since the trial of Richard Hauptmann, murderer of the Lindbergh baby.

Judge Ralph W. Liddy delayed the start of proceedings for an hour as cameramen got their shots. A mesh of cords and wires rippled across the floor. Newsreel cameras whirred as operators cranked film. Banks of bright Klieg lights heated the room. Bulbs flashed. Speed Graphics snapped. A few of the thirteen shackled prisoners shielded their faces with hands, kerchiefs, and straw hats. But they could no longer hide, hoods or not. Observed one national writer: "The row of manacled Black Knights, minus skull-and-crossbones regalia, seemed strikingly familiar . . . as if you had seen them somewhere else a little while before, perhaps in the bleachers at Navin Field." Witnesses, cops, attorneys, and family members of prisoners and victims alike felt the stare of lenses. Cameramen even staged shots, faking testimonial scenes. Some stood atop chairs and desks to get better sight lines. Telegraphers in an adjoining room relayed updates to New York editors, who sent them by transatlantic cable to London and Paris.

As she waited to be called as a preliminary witness, Marcia Rushing, Poole's sister-in-law, sat in her ruffled blouse and black hat chewing gum vigorously. Her husband, Owen, was beside her in the church-like pews. Nearby was his brother, Lowell Rushing, and fellow defendants Dayton Dean and Harvey Davis, all in their best coats. They wore poppies in honor of Memorial Day. Ida Knacker, Dean's mother, sat nearby. "My boy couldn't have done what they say," she said. "It's all a mistake." Curious spectators, awarded seats by well-connected friends, jammed the high-ceilinged room. Some sat on the sills of tall, arched windows.

Prosecutor Duncan McCrea was getting acclimated to the attention. It had become a necessity, really, not only because of the murder but also because Hearst's *Times* had uncovered his Black Legion membership card. At first McCrea had denied belonging. Then he offered an explanation: "I can't say that the signature . . . is not mine. It certainly looks like mine. It might be a tracing or I might have signed it. I don't know. I've often signed cards like that—lots of times, I suppose. You know, people ask me to sign cards for different organizations and I do. But I am not a member of the Black Legion. Emphatically, no!" McCrea described himself as a "joiner," which led the *Times* to give him that as a nickname, identifying him as Duncan "Joiner" McCrea in news stories. As if to prove he had no loyalties to the legion, McCrea went after the organization with a zealous fervor.

Earlier in a small side room he had enlisted the newsreel cameramen in a publicity stunt. Knowing how state commander Arthur Lupp loved to talk, he arranged for Lupp to be interviewed on film. Lupp's attorney thought he and McCrea would be posing for photos, as was tradition. But McCrea had other plans. Holding a typed script out of view of the cameras, he quizzed Lupp as the film rolled. McCrea's voice boomed. "Mr. Lupp, I understand that the Black Legion stands for pro-Americanism. Is that a fact?"

"Yes, it is."

"I understand that it is also opposed to Catholics, Jews, and Negroes. Is that a fact?"

"Well," Lupp began, "not the individuals, but the acts of any foreign group."

"Are not Catholics, Jews, and Negroes Americans?" McCrea asked. "And do they not likewise fight valiantly and most courageously to uphold American tradition?"

"As individuals, yes; but as organized groups, no. They are here in this country—"

McCrea cut him off.

"Then I want to say to your face, sir, that yours is the most despicable crew I have ever heard of and I am going to do my best to stamp it out as I would a pestilence."

"Can I add something to that?" Lupp asked.

"We've taken too much time already," said McCrea, rising to block the cameras and end the interview.

— —

A panic was sweeping over southeast Michigan. Investigations spread rapidly beyond the city and Wayne County into the suburban counties of Oakland and Macomb, to Jackson, near the state prison, and into Flint. Those identified but not yet charged tried to distance themselves from the widening inquiry. Each morning multiple revelations greeted residents, further unnerving an already anxious city. The papers carried fresh names, new crimes, and more horror stories daily. THE BLACK LEGION MAKES KLAN LOOK LIKE CREAM PUFF, proclaimed one headline. Each startling exposure made logical questions seem unanswerable. Who belongs? How many people? How high up does it go? What else have they done? Is my husband or son or father involved? Our neighbors? Are they coming for us? Where will this end?

"The Black Legion probably is the craziest and most dangerous mob ever formed in the United States," said detective John Hoffman. "We are fighting a low type of mentality, men easily incited by mob psychology, who have taken a silly pledge and gone through a crazy ritual apparently created by a fanatic who seeks power."

Other officials tried to calm fears. Michigan's governor vowed to eradicate the legion. So did thirty-four-year-old Mayor Frank Couzens.

"I have ordered the police commissioner to give me names of all city employees found in the Black Legion, the KKK, or any similar organization," he said. The city suspended staff members, streetcar conductors, lighting workers, health inspectors, and a few patrolmen.

As the stories of mayhem multiplied, legionnaires on the outside tried to enforce the brotherhood's vow of silence. They sent warnings and retaliated against those who talked. Dayton Dean's former common-law wife, Margaret, had been sharing legion secrets with cops and Hearst's *Times*. In a series of ghostwritten, bylined stories, she painted a frightening portrait of a petty and brutal organization. She also portrayed her ex-husband as obsessed with the legion and offered details to embarrass him. She noted that Dayton supported the death penalty. "Dayton always said it was a shame Michigan did not have the electric chair," she wrote. "He said it made for law and order." One afternoon, while greeting an old acquaintance with a handshake, she felt a bullet pressed into her palm. The man warned her to be quiet.

Dorothy Guthrie, the thirty-three-year-old wife of legion printer "Doc" Guthrie, was jumped when she returned to her apartment after walking her dog. Two men hiding behind the kitchen door knocked her unconscious and left her beaten, bound, and gagged. The injuries put her in the hospital. She had been talking to police and reporters about the legion's use of her previous home as a meeting place. She had also complained about being forced to join the women's auxiliary, which had been created by the men to quell complaints from wives who didn't know where their husbands were going every night. A stranger also gave her husband a bullet, adding, "You don't know anything."

There were numerous other efforts at intimidation. A state witness in a flogging case repelled a gang of men who tried to force their way into his home. He barricaded his house. Police responded by stationing a twenty-four-hour guard outside. On a different block the four-year-old nephew of a witness answered a knock at the door and then delivered to his uncle a bullet cartridge. The car speeding away had an Ohio license plate. Near Jackson a mob set fire to the farm, barn, and outbuildings of a prominent Catholic family following a meeting of legion members in the nearby woods. In fields and fireplaces throughout the state, members burned their robes. "It seems you can't tell where those Black Legion birds will show up next," said one woman after reporters revealed that several of her neighbors belonged. Their shades were shut and their doors unanswered.

Widow Rebecca Poole, often pictured with her fatherless daughters, peered regularly from the papers, her sorrowful portrait a reminder of the legion's savagery. "My life is ruined," she said. Her somber expression provided an uncomfortable contrast to those of legion members facing charges in her husband's death. A few smirked knowingly from the court bench. "Some of the defendants awaiting trial in Circuit Court even now are convinced that judges of that court are members of the legion," said homicide chief John Navarre. "They believe they will be tried before a Black Legion judge and that nothing will happen to them and that they have nothing to worry about."

Dayton Dean became the public face of the legion. He frequently grinned from pulpy newsprint, his hair looking as if he had just run greasy fingers through it. He flashed the broad, toothy, ebullient smile of a man who had won a life's supply of King Edward cigars.

Many former members rejoiced at the legion's apparent collapse. "Two years ago, I didn't have a gray hair in my head," said Clarence Frye. "Then I was forced to join the legion—and now look. Gray hairs all over. I've worried and worried. I feel 200 percent better since I told the prosecutor all I know, because my conscience is clear. . . . I dare say there are thousands who are the happiest people in the world because this thing is broken up." Added another former member who hadn't left his home at night in a year to avoid legionnaires: "I made up my mind they would have to take me out of here dead if they came for me." But for every slightly optimistic story, there were several dark ones. Dayton Dean continued to talk. He revealed the inner workings of the legion; the plots against publisher Kingsley, Mayor Voisine, and attorney Sugar; details of the Poole killing; and myriad other damning facts. More arrests followed and others talked too.

Prosecutor McCrea's top investigator, Harry Colburn, proclaimed that the legion intended to set up a dictatorship and overthrow the American government. The state attorney general estimated membership in Michigan at up to 20,000. Colburn said 135,000. Others said the numbers ran much higher, into the hundreds of thousands. (No one except politically motivated alarmists believed Effinger's figure of millions.) In Detroit the county clerk froze all applications for concealed guns and gave 2,700 permit holders five days to sign notarized affidavits swearing they were not legion members—or they would lose their permits. Elsewhere a Jackson prosecutor attributed his county's jump in gun permits to the legion's growth.

Condemnations came swiftly. At the Michigan convention of the Knights of Columbus, Bishop Michael Gallagher, head of the Detroit diocese and Coughlin's superior, alluded to the legion in his address. "We thought for years that things such as are happening here were impossible," he said. "You men of the Knights of Columbus must show yourselves capable of preserving the United States as a free country, with freedom for all the people." Methodist, Jewish, labor, and Negro organizations all condemned the legion. When a civil rights group convened a conference to combat legion activities, 3,000 people attended. Still, fears flourished and there was plenty of news to fuel them. Dayton Dean told detectives that if the men in the jail across the street told what they knew, "you'd be busy for a long time."

The 1930s saw gangsters celebrated as seldom before. Dillinger, Capone, Bonnie and Clyde—their names carried a romantic gleam. Even the dire activities of the Black Legion held intrigue. Radio-entranced children, neighborhood pranksters, and mean-spirited acquaintances all found inspiration in news of the hooded society.

Near Jackson Prison a driver discovered a typed note on his car: "Dear enemy. You are to die soon. The Black Legion." (A childish lark, police said.) In Mount Pleasant an elderly man came home to a message on his door. "Beware! Black Legion!" A bullet accompanied it. (Just a joke, a friend confessed.) An unmarried man in his twenties who was in a sexual relationship with a teenager got a warning signed "Black Legion." It ordered him to marry her or be killed. (Family members, police theorized.) Another note, also with a legion signature, directed a Flint foreman to get out of town or be taken on a one-way ride. (Disgruntled worker.) A distressed Detroit toolmaker reported a Black Legion bomb on his porch. (A ticking clock inside a cigar box.) Declaring themselves the Junior Black Legion, three boys on an Italian block kidnapped two youngsters, tied them up, and kept them in a barn for four hours, threatening to hang them. ("Aw, we wouldn't have dropped him," one protested. "We ain't that dumb.") In New York an unemployed Hungarian baker claiming legion affiliation demanded five hundred dollars in exchange for not abducting the target's daughter. In Chicago, Stanley Field— president of the Field Museum—received a bomb threat by phone from someone identifying himself as a legionnaire.

Actual killers tried to use the Black Legion to sidetrack investigators. In San Luis Obispo, California, the body of a twenty-eight-year-old felled by a shotgun blast lay near a note that said, "Think you know too much. The Black Legion." More significant historically was the murder of nightclub hostess Florence Castle in a Chicago hotel room. When her young son awoke to the sight of his mother being strangled by Robert Nixon, he asked what he was doing. Nixon said he was a doctor and that the boy's mother was sleeping. He told the boy he would write his name on the nightstand mirror. Nixon drew a skull and crossbones and scrawled "Black Legion Game" in lipstick. Nixon, a serial killer, would become the inspiration for Bigger Thomas in Richard Wright's 1940 classic novel *Native Son*.

"A veritable nationwide Black Legion hysteria seems to have developed," declared the *Toledo Blade*. In a syndicated editorial cartoon published across the country, Nelson Harding portrayed the Black Legion as the rattling tail on a snake of intolerance and terrorism. "There remains life in the menace, and it must not be permitted to revive and spread new terror," he wrote. Fellow Pulitzer winner Rollin Kirby depicted a parade of hooded legionnaires hoisting a US flag that proclaimed, "The Right to Murder." He titled the cartoon "Moronic Criminality."

Heywood Broun drew parallels between the legion and the rise of a fascist president in Sinclair Lewis's 1935 novel *It Can't Happen Here*. "Indeed, when I looked at a photograph of the black shirt leader I was inclined to say, 'You're not real; you're a character in a story. Sinclair

Lewis invented you.'" Syndicated columnist Frederic J. Haskin of the *Kansas City Star* proffered that the legion "springs from an inferiority complex." A legionnaire can "patronize entire communities because he knows the mumbo-jumbo of passwords and countersigns and, while cloaking his own real identity, can bring terror to persons who are not of the elect." The *Washington Post* editorialized against night riders who "stripped of their hoods reveal a characteristic low intelligence often verging on dementia." The *Washington Times* added: "Homicidal fanatics of the Black Legion type have no place in America." The *New York Herald-Tribune* described members as "a strange and particularly evil manifestation of the mob spirit." The *New York Daily Mirror* called the Black Legion "a new zoological specimen" dealing out "its own masked mockery of 'justice.'" The *Indianapolis News* wondered whether poor law enforcement—and maybe collusion between police and the legion—could be to blame for the organization's growth.

Time, Newsweek, New Republic, Liberty, and *Nation* magazines, among others, joined in the coverage. Retired Major George Fielding Eliot posited that the legion had higher, unnamed leaders than Bert Effinger. "Outside the grooves of his prejudices, his mind flounders badly. . . . He is but a tool," Eliot said. Pennsylvania Governor George Earle decried the legion as a product of "the diseased minds of fanatics and bigots." A Democrat, he blamed Republicans. "The responsibility for this shameless, un-American, barbaric organization rests directly upon the doorsteps of those powerful financial and industrial interests which control the Republican party today," he said. In Vatican City Cardinal Dennis Dougherty of Philadelphia, after meeting with Pope Pius, predicted the legion would "fall to pieces as soon as it is dragged out into the sun." In Boston a Harvard history professor dispelled the society's claim of ties to the tea party patriots of 1773. "Bosh!" said professor Albert Bushnell Hart.

Newspaper editorials focused on whether the FBI should—or could—investigate. Attorney General Homer S. Cummings and Director J. Edgar Hoover repeatedly rejected pleas for the bureau to get involved, contending no evidence had been presented of federal violations that would allow the G-Men to take the lead. Most newspaper editors who weighed in on the debate urged federal control. "There are indications that several Michigan office holders have not been above using the legion for political purposes," noted the *Boston Herald*. "They cannot be expected to aid in the exposure of it." The *New York Herald-Tribune*'s Dorothy Thompson, whose "On the Record" column appeared in 170 newspapers, challenged the FBI director: "J. Edgar Hoover says the federal government can do nothing. . . . What the federal government can do, however, under the law is to investigate! Let us at least find out how widespread, how numerous, are these murder bands."

The *Chicago Daily Times* offered, "If the state inquiry reveals kidnapping conspiracies, the G-Men ought to step into the picture at once." The *New York Post* called for a quick resolution: "The sooner this thing is dragged out into the open, the less harm it will be able to do." The UAW and the communist *Daily Worker* wanted a national probe. So did Hiram Evans, imperial wizard of the Ku Klux Klan, who condemned the legion's "lawlessness."

On the morning of May 29, a woman set off from Dumont, New Jersey, for Washington, 240 miles away. In the early afternoon she arrived at the Federal Bureau of Investigation and at the office of Assistant Director Edward Tamm. She was frantic. Tamm referred her to agent Richard Hood, a Pittsburgh law school grad with two years on the job. He tried to calm her. She insisted that the FBI must investigate the Black Legion. "I advised her," Hood reported, "that in the absence of a violation of federal law, this bureau was conducting no investigation. . . . She became hysterical." The woman asked Hood to call the White House. He refused. Hood tried to soothe her. He told her that she was "unduly alarmed" and should head home.

Worried residents flooded the FBI with letters and telegrams demanding a probe. They inundated Hoover's office. They reported suspicious activities, leveled charges against neighbors, and begged him to save the nation. "John Dillinger was a gentleman in comparison to this organization," wrote a man from Kansas City. A Detroit physician said that the legion's political strength would prevent an honest investigation locally. "Decent Michigan people would welcome action," he said. A California orange grower asked Hoover to "show these outlaws . . . that this is a free country run by constituted authorities under the flag of justice to all." From the Mt. Alverno Retreat in Warwick, New York, Father Columban F. Kelly gently nudged Hoover. "Certainly this organization is a far greater menace to our rights and security than the gangsters," he said.

One cable message cut through the clutter and found its way to Hoover's desk. A news editor at the *Flint Journal*, R. E. Roberts, wired the director in confidence: "Organization intends harm to President Roosevelt—planning armed march on Washington. Informant available. Believe 2,000 here." Tamm phoned W. H. Moran, chief of the Secret Service, with the tip, and Hoover followed up hours later, ensuring that the message had been received. The Secret Service investigated and deemed the legion dangerous but the threat on Roosevelt's life not currently credible.

Appeals for action also came from politicians. Prosecutor McCrea in Detroit asked for federal assistance repeatedly, as did a few Michigan congressmen and several nationally prominent progressive lawmakers, including Representative Sam Dickstein of New York and Senator Elmer Benson of Minnesota. Given evidence of the interstate nature of the Black Legion and rumors of a government takeover, Hoover and Attorney General Cummings could have made a case for federal involvement. Neither one did. President Roosevelt also kept silent publicly on the issue.

Why the disinterest at the federal level?

Doris Fleeson, a respected political reporter, offered one theory in her "Capital Stuff" column. She said it had to do with presidential politics. She hinted that Roosevelt's relationship with southern states-rights Democrats played into the no-federal-probe determination. Describing Attorney General Cummings as "a savvy Connecticut Yankee," she said, "he knows he's got a good thing in the G-Men. But he has been long in politics and he realizes it would take very little extra zeal on his part in the use of those same G-Men to bring some very vocal senators or congressmen bounding into the arena. . . . Hence his unwillingness to inject his men into the Black Legion situation until he is dead certain specific federal laws are being violated."

A news reporter asked the attorney general whether the FBI would investigate if it were shown that Roy Pidcock, discovered on Canada's Fighting Island, were a legion victim. In such a case a victim would have been taken across international lines. Cummings did not answer. But in Michigan a veteran State Police commander had been wondering the same thing.

Frenzied Nerves

MICKEY COCHRANE COULDN'T SLEEP. THE STRESS HAD BECOME UNBEARable. As Black Legion hysteria spread nationally with calls to expose everyone involved, Cochrane was falling apart. He was sleeping at most two hours per night. In Detroit he would sometimes head to the airport and go flying in the moonlit hours after midnight. He'd soar toward the heavens, trying to soothe his nerves. From the plane everything below seemed smaller and less significant. It didn't always work though.

The Tigers were in Philadelphia on Wednesday, June 3, when Cochrane went hitless in five at-bats in an 11–7 loss. That night he did not sleep at all. Not a single hour. Still, the next day he penciled himself into the lineup at Shibe Park. He had already batted twice when he came to the plate for his third appearance. It was only the third inning. The bases were filled. Cochrane connected and drove a ball deep to center field. It struck the scoreboard. Cochrane charged around the diamond as the ball ricocheted and fielders gave chase. He slammed second base and then third. Rogell, Owen, and Fox scored. Cochrane rounded third and committed to home. He raced toward the plate. The relay throw was coming in. It arrived too late. It was an inside-the-park, grand-slam home run. The adrenaline carried Cochrane to the dugout. But he was exhausted.

After the explosive ten-run inning, Cochrane started toward his position wearing his catcher's gear. Huge dark spots appeared in his eyes. Suddenly he felt on the verge of collapse. Cochrane turned back and went to the trainer's room. His heart was racing. The game went on without him as a doctor settled on a diagnosis: Mickey Cochrane, the game's most intense competitor, was on the threshold of a nervous breakdown. The doctor said Cochrane needed immediate rest, but Cochrane was not convinced. The next day he appeared at the ballpark in Washington, intending to play. But he suffered another spell and spent the game coaching along the first base line. He said he would be examined at Johns Hopkins but he waited. On June 6 he attempted once again to play, but a sense of vertigo overtook him. Frankie Reiber caught instead. On Sunday he sat as well.

The team traveled to Boston, nearer to his parents and his childhood home. The series was to begin on Monday. Cochrane consulted a physician at St. Elizabeth's, who confirmed the diagnosis—a nervous breakdown—and ordered isolation for ten days. Cochrane left the team and returned to Detroit. His wife and Russell Gnau, one of Harry Bennett's confidants at Ford, picked him up at the Windsor, Ontario, train station. They took him to Henry Ford Hospital. Doctors there prescribed complete rest. Only family would be allowed to visit. Newspapers and radios were banned from his room. He wouldn't be following the Tigers—or the Black Legion investigation. No one was allowed to talk baseball. Cochrane honored the prohibition for most of a week.

Dayton Dean and the Negro Reporter

DAYTON DEAN WAS STAMMERING. SEATED IN A FOURTH-FLOOR ROOM at police headquarters, Dean, a white racist dressed in white shirt and white pants, was being quizzed by Russell J. Cowans, a black reporter from a black newspaper. Several white journalists and white detective Jack Harvill were also in the room. Beyond race Cowans and Dean differed starkly. Dean had attended grade school. Cowans had a graduate degree in English from the University of Michigan. Dean had grown up in a small town, Cowans in a big city. Until his arrest Dean had worked as a laborer, wrapping asbestos on pipes. Cowans's fortunes were soaring. A sportswriter for the nation's top black newspaper, the *Chicago Defender*, he doubled as tutor and press agent for Joe Louis—a lucrative conflict of interest in an era before modern journalism ethics. Cowans belonged to Louis's inner circle. He was part of his entourage.

"What was the general attitude of the members of the Black Legion toward colored people?" Cowans asked Dean, who was puffing on a cigar. One could imagine Dean feeling unsettled by the smart, better dressed, and more successful Cowans.

"There were many members in the legion who had no hatred toward colored people," Dean said. "But they were overruled by those in high office, especially Davis."

"By Davis," said Cowans, "you mean Col. Harvey Davis?"

"Yes," Dean said. "Davis was bitter in his hatred of colored people. He wanted to kill every one he saw."

Partway through the interview, which would be published in black papers across the country, Cowans began addressing Dean by his last name. The tone shifted to a mix of aversion and condescension.

"Well now, Dean, just what plan did the Black Legion have which was to be used against the colored people?"

"They had planned to start by having the children separated in the schools."

"When was this to start?"

"It started about two years ago when literature was distributed in Ecorse and other downriver towns, urging the parents to fight for segregation in schools."

Dean said an attempt by black parents to get the district to hire black teachers provoked the action.

"Why did the legion want separate schools?"

"Well, you know," Dean said. "If the children mingle in school, it will not be long before there will be inter-marriages, and this would weaken both races. Inter-marriages are bad."

Cowans asked Dean whether he had ever worked with Negroes.

He had at a Ford factory.

"How were the colored people you worked with?"

"I found them fine fellows. In fact I don't have any hatred toward colored. I was just following the policy of the Black Legion."

Dean said if he could do it over again, he wouldn't join the legion.

"I was in and couldn't get out—" he said.

Cowans shifted to sports.

"What did the members of the Black Legion think about Joe Louis?"

A white reporter, perhaps trying to frame Dean's response, interjected: "They held him in high regard, didn't they?"

"Some of them did and some of them didn't," Dean said.

"What about the boys who are members of the American Olympic team?"

Jesse Owens, Ralph Metcalfe, and other blacks were expected to do well in Berlin. The games were to begin on August 1.

"They're doing fine work," Dean said. "I think a lot of them will win Olympic titles."

Earlier in the week Dean had disclosed another legion crime. He said the legion had killed Silas Coleman at the Ford Mill Pond in Pinckney—"just for the hell of it," in Prosecutor McCrea's words. Until Dean's confession, no one had connected Coleman's death to the legion. Dean named those who had participated.

When Cowans asked about the killing, Dean began to squirm. Perhaps he felt guilty. In the murder of Charles Poole, Dean could convince himself that he had been misled—that he thought he was exacting justice against a man whom he believed had beaten his wife and killed their soon-to-be-born child. With the plots against publisher Kingsley, Mayor Voisine, and attorney Sugar, Dean likewise could rationalize that they were engaged in political war and a battle over the soul of America. They were enemies getting what they deserved. But Coleman's case was different. Coleman had not done anything. His only crime was being black. He had been killed purely for entertainment. On some level Dean must have seen the distinction.

Cowans wondered what Silas Coleman said en route to his death. "He didn't know that he was going on a one-way ride," Dean explained. "He talked about two cases of beer that he had at home and how he was going to have a good time with his landlady."

Not everyone thought Dean was telling the truth when he linked the legion to Coleman's death. The prosecutor who oversaw the town of Pinckney expressed doubt. "I'm afraid Dean is confirming anything that is mentioned to him," said Stanley Berriman. "It doesn't look right to me. Coleman was last seen with a group of Negroes and shortly later was shot to death. Farmers heard the shot, but did not see the killing. Just where the Black Legion could figure in that is beyond me."

Soon, though, another suspect confirmed the legion's involvement. Dean was telling the truth, as usual. He shared one other sensational detail. Dean said several more bodies might have been thrown into a sinkhole at Ford Mill Pond.

The Captain

Soft-spoken Ira Holloway Marmon took up residence at the Leland Hotel after the Black Legion case broke. Marmon was a veteran law enforcement captain, chief of the investigative bureau of the Michigan State Police. The Leland served as his base when he came in from Lansing. Not yet a decade old, it remained a destination—"one of the world's foremost hotels," according to a boastful advertisement that heralded its "seven hundred large rooms with bath." Rising twenty-two stories, the Leland was topped with a forty-foot steel grid that held ten-foot block letters spelling out its name on two lines, "Detroit" over "Leland." At night the support grid disappeared in the darkness and the glowing words hovered above the rooftop. The sign was a prominent part of the skyline in the popular Washington Boulevard shopping district.

The hotel was conveniently located around the corner from the *Times*, a couple blocks from the *Free Press* and *News* on West Lafayette, and less than a mile from the Detroit Police, the courts, Navin Field, and the Masonic Temple (Marmon was a thirty-third degree Mason, the highest rank). Several ballplayers lived in the Leland, Hank Greenberg among them. Schoolboy Rowe had married his beloved Edna there. Plus the place had a good bar. What more could an officer want?

Marmon had joined the state agency in 1917 after the army rejected him because of his poor hearing. The state troopers had just organized and Marmon was among their first recruits. Early on he guarded Port Huron's tunnel and power plant after reports of a German terror plot originating from Canada. While working along the St. Clair River Marmon saved two men when their boat capsized on a stormy night. Two of their friends drowned. In Jackson he protected railroad war shipments. In Muskegon he spent five weeks at a manufacturing plant battling anti-war saboteurs. By 1920 he had become head of the state detective bureau. He led the probe of "King Ben" Purnell of the House of David, a religious colony, and commanded a liquor-related corruption investigation in Hamtramck that saw fifty-two people indicted. In 1927 Marmon began a three-year stint in Detroit as the leader of a Prohibition squad that chased rum-runners and battered down their doors. Like almost every lawman who worked the region in that era, he had stories about the Purple Gang, reputed to be involved in Chicago's St. Valentine's Day Massacre.

Marmon's biggest achievement may have been establishing the state's fingerprinting system. It began in a shoebox he stashed under his bed in the portable barracks. He also helped create the scientific lab and the photo and ballistics departments. Born in Arkansas and described as "quiet . . . unobtrusive . . . determined," he proudly wore the Michigan shield—two deer bucks and an eagle accenting the word *Tuebor* (I Will Defend). He also had the respect of men in other departments, like Deputy Farrell, who found him "wise and smart," a high compliment given the rivalries that could flare between agencies.

Marmon enjoyed being in Detroit. Though he missed his wife Lillian and his sons, Leon, fifteen, and Owen, thirteen—and certainly their dog, Sport (a German shepherd who had failed as a police canine)—he delighted in the time away from his mother-in-law, Frieda Spreksel, who lived with them in Okemos. Frieda rattled his nerves. In her mid-sixties she harbored fierce opinions and spouted them forcefully in German.

Several Black Legion investigations were underway, including Marmon's. Detroit detectives and Wayne County deputies took the lead on the Poole case. Prosecutor Duncan McCrea had an investigative crew, as did the state attorney general, whose assistant would be challenging McCrea in the coming election. "Big Jim" Chenot, a popular judge, had been appointed as his own one-man grand jury and a heap of local departments were looking into matters too. Various institutions, like the state prison and the streetcar department, had their own agents. Toss in the politics—McCrea being a Democrat; the governor, mayor, and attorney general being Republicans; and an election approaching—and you had a tangled mess of pressures, loyalties, and motivations. In addition Prosecutor McCrea and Police Commissioner Col. Heinrich Pickert disliked each other. They had a long-running feud. A year earlier Pickert had accused McCrea of failing to cooperate with police after McCrea had made similar charges against Pickert. In March McCrea had told a judge that he would not allow his prime witness in a case to be held in a police cell because he distrusted Pickert's department. It was just one of many run-ins between the two men.

Days into his investigation Captain Marmon had shocked almost everyone when he announced that the Black Legion might be responsible for fifty deaths in Michigan alone. Until that point law enforcement officials had implicated the secret society in only the Charles Poole killing. If they harbored other suspicions, they hadn't disclosed them to the press. But Marmon did. For starters he shared his belief that the hanging of Roy Pidcock and the shooting deaths of auto union organizers John Bielak and George Marchuk were done by the Black Legion.

The Pidcock probe took Marmon to Wyandotte, near Fighting Island, where he interviewed police, Michigan Alkali employees, and Pidcock's wife and friends. The next day Marmon pointed out the improbability of a man walking unseen in his underwear for three-quarters of a mile through Ecorse and then swimming undetected a half-mile to the island. Furthermore no one knew Pidcock to be a swimmer. Marmon noted that Pidcock's briefs showed no signs of having been wet and the soles of his feet were spotless, though ash powdered the floor of the shack where his body hung. Plus he had disappeared hours after Poole had been killed. And what about those cars that supposedly got separated at the drawbridge? Where did they really go? Marmon said he wanted to exhume Pidcock's body and have a proper autopsy.

Provincial Police had handled the case because Fighting Island lies on the Canadian side of the Detroit River. Inspector Phillip Walters defended his men against Marmon's insinuation that they had botched the case. Walters said no inquiry was held because it was an obvious case of suicide. "Pidcock had been out of work and was despondent," Walters said. "He first tried to commit suicide by jumping from a window of his home but was stopped by members of the family. Later, he got out of a locked room and, with only part of his clothing on, fled to the river and apparently swam to Fighting Island. A few hours later, his body was found. It was suicide and a verdict to that effect was returned."

Marmon relied on an informant who belonged to the Black Legion. He called the man X-9, a nickname filched from the comic strip "Secret Agent X-9," created by Dashiell Hammett. The source told Marmon that Bielak and Marchuk had been executed by the legion. Marmon wanted the cases reopened. At Detroit Police headquarters homicide chief John Navarre bristled at Marmon's suggestions. Of Bielak, whom Peg-Leg White had identified as a troublemaker to officials at the Hudson factory, Navarre said, "He had been a communist and had quit the party. We were convinced communists were responsible for his death. I don't know what information Captain Marmon has, but we have never learned anything to change our opinion."

Marmon's claim of fifty deaths couldn't have been timed any better. Days after he made the declaration a bloated body surfaced off Fighting Island. Members of the Coast Guard pulled it from the water. The man had been dead a long time. He carried no identification but wore a heavy coat, leading police to speculate he was a duck hunter. He wasn't. It was Alexander Murdy, who had walked out of his home in January and never returned. His son identified him at the morgue. Murdy had been a member of the legion, Marmon said. The captain challenged the coroner's verdict of suicide. Three days later Murdy's friend Steve Lada turned up in the same waters. Police said he had stabbed himself multiple times, including once in the heart. Marmon didn't buy it. Two other bodies turned up in the river around the same time, one near Belle Isle and one near the Ambassador Bridge.

During the first weeks of his probe, Marmon sent a daily memo to his boss, Commissioner Oscar Olander. "There have been several bodies recovered this past week from the river," he reported one afternoon. "The coroners say they are all suicides. I doubt them very much." Proclaiming a questionable death to be a suicide was an easy to way to reduce the number of unsolved murders. One former legion member recalled being at a house meeting in Highland Park where legion state commander Arthur Lupp appeared. "A lot of people are going to disappear," Lupp said.

"Some will commit suicide, some will be found in the river, some will be hold-up victims, and some will be found shot to death by 'gangsters.'"

From across the state Marmon fielded reports from other troopers. He couldn't help but notice the breadth of the legion. Marmon shuttled between Detroit and the downriver communities of Ecorse, Wyandotte, and Lincoln Park and then out to Pontiac, the county seat of Oakland. "It looks as if Oakland County is solid Black Legion," he reported to Olander, writing on Leland Hotel stationery. "I have talked to many out there, and if you ever saw fear, you should see some of these people. They tell me practically every one in office or power is a member." In another memo he told of a mass gathering outside of Oxford in 1934, where a village marshal learned of a beating being given to an errant member. The marshal wanted backup from county deputies before heading to the site, but they were unwilling to come, he said. A one-legged fellow was instrumental in the event, the marshal reported.

From northern Michigan Marmon learned that in 1934 trooper Irvine Wurm, twenty-two years old, was flagged down on a road near Traverse City, forced into a car, blindfolded, and taken to a legion initiation. His abductors didn't know he was a trooper. At the last minute, with guns trained on him and after multiple recruits had taken the pledge, Wurm gathered the courage to refuse the oath. Pretending to be a teacher, he said the vow would violate his job. Legionnaires yelled at him, lectured him, called him yellow, questioned his American citizenship, and generally gave him hell. They told him they would kill him if he talked. He hadn't until now.

X-9 continued to send Marmon reports. In one labeled "extra confidential," X-9 proposed trying to set up a meeting of all legion officers who were battalion majors or higher. He hoped to lure them with an agenda that would explore how to halt the police investigations, how to defeat Senator Couzens because his son, the mayor, was pledging to wipe legionnaires from the city payroll, and how to beat Frank Murphy, the former mayor who had come home from the Philippines to run for governor and was promising to round up all legionnaires. X-9 said he would issue the invitation in Major-General Bert Effinger's name. It's doubtful the meeting ever took place. Records indicate that X-9 issued only two more reports to Marmon. What became of him is not clear. Maybe he drifted back into normal society.

In his memos Marmon told Commissioner Olander of additional interviews he conducted related to the Bielak, Marchuk, and Pidcock cases. He was absolutely certain the legion had killed Roy Pidcock. Some other law enforcement individuals agreed with him. If in fact the legion murdered Pidcock, then what about Hazen Branch? He had died on January 25, months before Pidcock. According to Michigan State Police files, he supposedly knew of the legion's long-running plans to force Pidcock to dump his wife or be killed and he may have threatened to expose the group. Branch, age thirty-eight, died from an explosion while working at Wyandotte Oil and Fat Company, thawing pipes with an acetylene torch. Co-workers said the father of five was far too smart and cautious to be using the torch without having taken precautions. The resulting fire burned Branch severely. It melted his clothes to his skin. He died within hours. The death was ruled accidental, but friends and family viewed the circumstances as suspicious.

Captain Marmon's talk of multiple murders put pressure on officials to reexamine old cases. Some did so enthusiastically; some didn't. Marmon forced the issue. He listed other men whom he thought the legion might have murdered in Michigan: Charles Allran of Wyandotte, who was shot roadside the day after Alexander Murdy disappeared; Jerome Wolf, an oil prospector who socialized with legionnaires and who was beaten to death in the legion hotbed of Napoleon; Howard Curtis, a former steel plant investigator in Ohio, who was found dead near the GM Proving Grounds in Milford; Vernon Dodge, an ex-probate judge in Flint, whose hanging death was thought to be a suicide; R. T. Philip, a city railway inspector who worked with legionnaires and drowned in the Olympic-size pool at Rouge Park; Walter Fisher, who died in a May 1936 fire after reportedly placing his own head and shoulders into the fire of a furnace; Cornelius Vanderveen, who also died beside a furnace in his Grand Rapids home; and Oliver Hurkett, twenty-two years old, whose brother said he belonged to the legion and had been threatened with death. Hurkett died of carbon monoxide poisoning in his car after having been beaten.

During the Black Legion inquiry, Marmon displayed a willingness to be uncommonly open and uncharacteristically blunt. His candor irritated not only Detroit and Canadian command officers but one of his own higher-ups. State Attorney General Crowley complained about "a certain official, who should have known better" that has been saying the legion committed "dozens of murders." While not naming Marmon, Crowley criticized the person for creating unrealistic expectations with "exaggerated accounts" of crimes. Republican Crowley had established the one-man grand jury in Wayne County, blocking Democratic Prosecutor McCrea from the proceedings. Crowley felt that as a result of Marmon's statements if the investigative body didn't return "innumerable indictments the entire work of the grand jury would be discredited and those conducting the grand jury adjudged incapable and inefficient."

Or worse, part of a cover-up.

Wyoming

Mickey Cochrane looked bad. His dark eyes bulged. His shoulders sagged. His face harbored more creases than usual. "It is painful to watch the creeping shadows of a man's sunset," wrote Austen Lake in the *Boston Evening Transcript*.

Cochrane remained in the hospital as speculation swirled about the cause of his mental breakdown. At Hearst's *Times*, columnist Bud Shaver cited a list of reasons, ranging from Hank Greenberg to Al Simmons. "Cochrane has been doing a couple of men's jobs under exceptionally trying conditions and it backfired on him as it inevitably would," Shaver said. Harry Salsinger blamed Cochrane's condition on "a highly nervous temperament" and "terrific mental pressure." He also attributed it partly to Malcolm "Iffy the Dopester" Bingay without naming him. Salsinger wrote that Cochrane's mental state was "aggravated by a Detroit newspaper columnist who set out on a campaign of persecution . . . criticizing Cochrane for every real and imaginary act." Only Bingay qualified. From down the street came Iffy's response: Bunk. "It has been no fault of Mickey's, nor has it been the fault of anybody else," said Iffy.

Doctors eased Cochrane's restrictions on his eleventh day in the hospital. They allowed him to listen to the Tigers' game in his room. After the Yankees' phenomenal rookie Joe DiMaggio started a four-run rally in the first, Cochrane turned off the radio. He gave it another try later, but the Tigers lost their seventh straight. They had not won since Cochrane left the team. They had fallen twelve games out of first place. In the evening Cochrane, ever the boxing fan, tuned his radio to the same event that had much of the world listening, the heavyweight bout between Joe Louis and Max Schmeling.

———

Boxing writers predicted a rapid and resounding victory for Joe Louis. The question wasn't whether Louis would beat former champion Max Schmeling, but how quickly he would dispose of him. "Louis inside of five," offered Curly Grieve of the *San Francisco Examiner*. "Louis in three," said Nat Fleischer of *Ring* magazine. "Two rounds," said Gene Kessler of the *Chicago Times*. The consensus was that Schmeling was washed up—a "condemned man," in the words of W. W. Edgar of the *Free Press*. One of Louis's sparring partners added: "I think I can lick Max." Detroit prepared for a Joe Louis celebration like no other.

The first round passed at Yankee Stadium without a knockout by Louis. Then the second, then the third. In the fourth Schmeling connected with a flurry of punches that stunned Louis and dropped him to the canvas. The fight would go another eight rounds, but it had been decided then. Schmeling had injured Louis. In the twelfth he finally finished him. He knocked out Louis, delivering to him his first professional loss. The defeat was so unexpected, so shocking, so painful, that across the country nearly a dozen listeners reportedly collapsed and died of heart attacks.

———

Cochrane was discharged on Saturday, June 21. The next morning he boarded a *Detroit News* airplane with close friend Captain Emmett "Rosie" O'Donnell, an athletic chap who in the fall had helped coach the West Point football team. They flew to Billings, Montana, stopping in Minneapolis and Bismarck on the way. They drove the final 110 miles to Cody, Wyoming, where Cochrane was expected to continue his recuperation for two to three weeks. The plan: lots of rest, riding, fishing, shooting, maybe a little catch. He would have the company of O'Donnell and well-known guide Max Wilde. The secluded ranch, difficult to reach, sat in a valley amid mountain cliffs, canyons, and creeks. "It's the greatest place on earth," he said.

News reports and photos emerged occasionally from Wyoming, showing Cochrane on horseback or throwing a baseball. Often he was pictured wearing a cowboy hat with a kerchief tied around his neck. Last Roundup? asked one headline. The cutline speculated that Cochrane's playing days were done. Reports offered conflicting information as to who owned the place. It was either Wilde's cabin or Harry Bennett's. Either way Bennett had played a role in Cochrane's escape from the pressures of Detroit. Cochrane left behind his troubled team, as well as all the commotion about the Black Legion. He would remain in Wyoming until mid-July. His stay was extended twice. The Tigers played without him, managed by coach Del Baker.

Within two weeks' time Mickey Cochrane and Joe Louis—the two supermen most responsible for Detroit's sports ascendancy, for its anointing as the City of Champions—had been exposed as mortal.

The Cover-Up

Captain Ira Marmon hit obstacles wherever he turned. He tried to reopen old murder and suicide cases but found some police uncooperative. He wanted bodies exhumed but they weren't being exhumed. Without them the new autopsies he requested couldn't be conducted. Legion members not yet charged were pleading ignorance or maintaining their silence. Several cases—those of Bielak and Marchuk especially—pointed to Peg-Leg White, who had vanished shortly after the legion's unmasking.

Marmon's men searched across Michigan. The easy thing about looking for White was that people tended to remember a fellow with a wooden leg. One lead placed him on a fishing trip near West Branch in the center of the state. Troopers checked campgrounds and tourist spots and interviewed locals. Nothing. They followed rumors to his home in Lyons. Neighbors and the postman reported he hadn't been there. Two troopers spent a day watching a ranch elsewhere; another false tip. Police heard White was vacationing on land he owned up north. Again, no luck.

Captain Marmon and Prosecutor McCrea wanted to explore the secrets of the sinkholes at Ford Mill Pond, where Silas Coleman had died. They were told that dragging the pond would be futile due to thick vegetation and deep depths. They asked Ford Motor Company for permission to drain the marsh. It was denied. A company official directed onsite caretaker Lucius Doyle to "refuse anyone the right." Draining the pond would hurt fishing and hay crops, a spokesman said. Asked whether he thought the marsh was a graveyard, a police sergeant was unequivocal in his answer: "Absolutely, I do."

Major-General Bert Effinger was proving elusive. Lima police refused to execute a search warrant on his house. Two times during the summer Michigan detectives went south to Ohio seeking the legion leader. After finding Lima authorities again uncooperative, they asked the FBI for assistance. J. Edgar Hoover said the matter did not fall into his jurisdiction. When a grand jury finally indicted Effinger on charges of criminal syndicalism and possession of bombs, Michigan officials secured an extradition hearing in Columbus before Governor Martin L. Davey. The case was not going Effinger's way. During a recess he slipped out of the courthouse. Davey signed the extradition order, but Effinger was gone—a fugitive.

Captain Marmon hadn't become head of the Michigan State Police investigative bureau by needlessly provoking political leaders. He had nearly twenty years of experience in the field and had dealt extensively with both politicos and the press, so he knew what he was doing when he spoke publicly about his suspicions, about there being fifty legion murders, about reopening old cases, about incorrect assumptions by police. He didn't make his opinions known quietly behind the scenes. He hyped them. They were more difficult to ignore that way. The record does not indicate whether Marmon suspected a cover-up, but he certainly acted as if he did.

Others hinted at it. Senator Elmer Benson was among them. "No organization like the Black Legion of Detroit can operate for four or five years enrolling peace officers, prison guards and other men in public service unless the duly constituted authorities winked at their crimes or quietly acquiesced," he said.

The Black Legion became a partisan political fireball. When Democratic Prosecutor McCrea's membership card first appeared, Republican state officials quickly drew a hard line. State Attorney General David Crowley said that if McCrea took the legion oath he shouldn't be prosecutor. Governor Frank Fitzgerald expressed doubt that McCrea could continue "as a public servant sworn to uphold the law." Those condemnations from the top two state officials came within a day. Crowley also acknowledged rumors that two judges and a prominent politician were members. "I don't care who they are or how influential they may be. If they are allied with the legion, they'll be exposed," he said.

But soon he shaded his statements. After conferring with the governor, Crowley announced it wouldn't be enough for someone to have simply taken the Black Legion oath. "There probably would have to be an overt act on the part of a member," he said. In a short time Crowley had gone from saying Black Legion membership made one unfit for office to contending that membership didn't matter at all, just the crimes. This change did not go unnoticed. "The danger of uncovering ramifications of the legion in influential circles seems to have put a check upon the zeal that was at first manifest in the local investigation," reported *Christian Century*.

Crowley's assistant would be challenging McCrea in the fall election and he would have loved to drape McCrea in a legion cloak. But it became a dangerous tactic. Figures from his own party were more involved than McCrea had ever been. That became apparent when the Wolverine Republican League was revealed to be a front for the legion. Senate candidate Wilber Brucker had launched his campaign at one of its meetings. Attorney Harry Z. Marx and court clerk Leslie Black, both heavily involved, were Republicans. Former Highland Park mayor Markland, a legion member, had served on a key Republican party state committee. Further, the brother of the governor's chief of staff was a member. Perhaps the governor and attorney general had also heard about Col. Pickert.

Prosecutor McCrea wasn't about to allow himself to be the lone tainted public official. Two years earlier he had been at a large outdoor meeting where several legion-backed candidates spoke, all hoping for votes. Now he slyly flecked mud, saying that the suspects in custody were told by legion officers that high-ranking politicians would protect the organization. "They were told that I was a member of the Black Legion, that Sheriff Behrendt is a member, that Police Commissioner Pickert and other high police officials are members, and that Governor Fitzgerald, circuit and recorder's court judges, and others prominent in public life are members."

Without identifying anyone, police confirmed it. "We have had several big names linked with the legion, but are not announcing them without a thorough check," said inspector John Hoffman. Among the many legion membership cards, detectives uncovered one signed by their boss, Col. Heinrich Pickert. But investigators did not divulge the information. If Hoffman made it sound as if names might be forthcoming, he soon doused those prospects. Without offering any evidence, Hoffman judged the prominent men innocent. A few weeks later Col. Pickert announced the August 8 promotion of Hoffman to chief inspector of detectives and of Navarre to assistant deputy chief of detectives. Mickey Farrell worked at a different agency, but for his silence about Pickert's membership he secured a promotion for his brother, a Detroit cop.

◆

By the end of 1936, Black Legion members had been sentenced in several cases prosecuted by Duncan McCrea. Twelve were convicted of first-degree or second-degree murder in the death of Charles Poole. Three of those men, as well as two others, received life sentences for the killing of Silas Coleman. Convictions followed in the plots against publisher Art Kingsley, Mayor Bill Voisine, and attorney Maurice Sugar, as well as in the flogging of Robert Penland. All resulted from Dayton Dean's willingness to talk.

Another break in the case came in the winter when records surfaced showing that Peg-Leg White had traded in his vehicle to purchase a new car in Cumberland, Maryland. White had taken an alias, I. M. Stull. On December 16 police arrested him in Oldtown, an unincorporated village in northern Maryland. He had been living in a storage building. He was sick in bed waiting for a doctor when a detective arrived. White's wife and four-year-old boy were with him. White had pneumonia. He was hospitalized and too ill to be interviewed, doctors said. Officers guarded his room. As a precaution, they confiscated his leg. The only statement he made was given to an Allegany County constable. White said he hadn't communicated with Bert Effinger in seven months, not since Poole had died. "He said the orders for the death of Mr. Poole were not given by him," wrote Constable R. Bucy. "He said the orders were given by a man higher than himself and that Mr. Effinger was not to be trusted." White died on Sunday, December 20.

That left Effinger. James Blissell, editor of the *Lima News*, informed J. Edgar Hoover that the "same large grocery orders are being delivered" to Bert Effinger's house in Lima, though Effinger, "a prodigious eater," was supposedly not there. Hoover offered his usual response: The bureau has no authority in this matter. An investigator for the Michigan attorney general also asked the FBI to help apprehend Effinger. The attorney general feared that an attempt to remove him from Lima would result in bloodshed. Same answer. When Captain Marmon's men visited Lima again, they heard rumors that Effinger wouldn't be back until the trials in Michigan had concluded. Maybe the heat would be off by then.

In February 1937 the county prosecutor in charge of Lima sent Hoover photos of Effinger for use on wanted posters. "There is a great amount of rumor in this vicinity that members of the police department and high city officials are members of the Black Legion," said Prosecutor Robert Jones. "The Black Legion is reputed to be so large in this section that one cannot hazard a guess as to whom might be depended upon." Once more Hoover responded: Not our jurisdiction. Effinger stayed hidden for more than a year. In December 1937 he reemerged. A trial was scheduled for 1938 on the syndicalism and bomb charges. It was delayed several times. Finally, in May 1939, the prosecution said its witnesses had left the state, couldn't be located, or were unwilling to testify. The case was dismissed. Effinger would never face trial. "They're scared he'll expose too many big shots—that's why," legion spy Fred Gulley told an FBI agent who questioned him in prison.

Labor, leftist, and civil rights activists would have loved most to prove that two of their fiercest enemies—the ardently anti-union Col. Pickert and hard-boiled Harry Bennett of Ford—were among the shadowy figures pulling Black Legion strings. Those who spoke with Bert Effinger had trouble accepting that he was the driving force behind an organization so large. He and founder Dr. Billy Shepard were, one observer noted, "small-town men with horizons that extend no farther than their front porches."

Those who suspected a cover-up could ponder a tangled web of connections. There was the link between Col. Pickert and attorney Harry Z. Marx. There was Harry Bennett's relationship with assorted officials, including Pickert, Mayor Couzens, and Judge Jim Chenot, the former Republican prosecutor who headed the one-man grand jury. There was Clyde Markland, brother of Mayor Markland, who served as Chenot's clerk until his attendance at legion meetings became public and he was forced to resign. There was H. O. Weitschat, the governor's general secretary who represented him before the grand jury; Weitschat's brother had been a legion member. There was attorney Louis Colombo Jr., who was attached to the Chenot jury. His father represented Ford and knew Bennett well. "It is just possible that the reason why the Ford Motor Company was never linked with the Black Legion was that Ford's attorney's son was in this position," wrote Maurice Sugar in his "Memorandum on the Black Legion."

In 1979, forty-some years after the Black Legion had been dragged into the light, history professor Peter H. Amann interviewed one of the key figures in the investigation, sheriff's department detective Mickey Farrell. Almost everyone else affiliated with the case had died by then. Farrell told Amann that for decades he kept a confidential, multipage list that contained 2,000 names of men whom local police had tied to the Black Legion. By the time Amann interviewed the deputy, Farrell had destroyed the list. Amann asked him whether a thorough investigation of the legion had been done.

"No, no, no, no," Farrell said. "They had a lot of big wigs. . . . If they'd have really investigated it, there'd have been a lot of big timers with their heads off. . . . In fact, the commissioner of police, who was a very good friend of mine, he was hooked into it. A lot of other big ones, too."

———

In May 1938, after most of the trials had been held, Captain Marmon was still trying to get the FBI to investigate. He thought he had found a way. He went to the Detroit office of the bureau and informed the agent in charge that Roy Pidcock had been killed en route to Canada's Fighting

Island. The agent reported to J. Edgar Hoover that Marmon had insisted "that the Detroit River was considered the high seas as far as federal jurisdiction is concerned, and that if this crime, as alleged, did occur as claimed, this would constitute a violation over which this bureau would have jurisdiction."

Hoover asked the attorney general's office for direction. It was decided that the U.S. attorney in Detroit should explore the issue. The attorney decided that a murder at high seas may have been committed and a probe should be initiated. This led to an FBI interview with Dayton Dean in prison in December 1938. Among the revelations: Dean told the agent that not only were Col. Pickert and Prosecutor McCrea members of the legion, but also that Governor Frank Fitzgerald and other high-ranking politicians had belonged. Dean also described what he had heard about the Pidcock killing. These details were included in a twenty-eight-page report, which also looked into whether the agency had jurisdiction. Local FBI agents felt they did and wanted to investigate. They sought permission from their director to conduct more interviews and they outlined a variety of leads to be followed up on by other bureau offices.

J. Edgar Hoover responded with a scathing letter. "The Bureau is unable to understand why your division should conduct any investigation with regard to the question of jurisdiction," he wrote. He went on to point out minor discrepancies between the words of Captain Marmon and Dayton Dean and used them as justification to scuttle further interviews. There was no need, in other words, to speak with the men that Dean and others had identified as responsible for Pidcock's death. Hoover said the probe should have been terminated at the first appearance of inconsistencies in the report of "Captain Marmon or his alleged informant, Dayton Dean." For all practical purposes the letter quashed further investigation.

No other Black Legion crimes would be prosecuted and thousands of legionnaires would go on with their lives, their secrets safe, their identities hidden, their covert midnight meetings receding into memory. For Captain Marmon and everyone else the dark trail ended there.

Epilogue

In the long shadows of late afternoon, a cool breeze jangles a wind chime and rustles the faded American flags that mark the graves of veterans. On this April day I'm at St. Mary's Cemetery in Pinckney, Michigan. At the spigot a man in his sixties fills a water bucket. He's wearing a blue service station shirt with "Steve" stitched in white on a patch above his left pocket. I figure he's a local.

"Is this the old mill pond?"

He looks up at the placid, marshy body of water beyond us.

"Yep, that's it," he says.

While not visible from Main Street, the pond dominates the landscape of Pinckney. On the north side it borders the school grounds and a city cemetery. On the west it sidles alongside Cedar Lake Road, and here, to the south, it edges up to the Catholic cemetery.

"I hear there's a deep sinkhole out there."

He shrugs. "I don't know about that," he says.

I'm trying to be nonchalant with my questions.

"Where's Nash Bridge?"

"Never heard of it," he says.

He turns off the spigot.

"How about Silas Coleman?"

"Who?"

"Coleman. Silas Coleman?"

"Is he buried here?"

"Nah, he died in the marsh years ago."

He shakes his head and excuses himself. I don't mention the six or seven bodies that were supposedly dumped in the pond.

Pinckney sits twenty miles northwest of Ann Arbor in a region speckled with lakes and ponds. Some carry the names of long-ago property owners, like Gallagher, Zukey, Winans, and Rush. A couple, Oneida and Mohican, honor tribes. Others—Strawberry Lake, Triangle Lake, Half-Moon Lake, and, in three uninspired cases, Crooked Lake—attest to geographic shapes. And then there are Buck, Bass, Pickerel, Gosling, Wild Goose, and Coon, all evoking the wildlife that once drew vacationers like Harvey Davis and Dayton Dean to the log cabins and cinder-block cottages that have mostly been replaced by large, modern homes. In 1925 the *Pinckney Dispatch* counted fifty-five lakes in a tourism-minded survey. Among them was Nigger Lake, where blacks vacationed. That one, thankfully, is no longer on the map, not by that slur anyway.

Within the village limits only one body of water really matters: Mill Pond—or as old-timers call it, Ford Mill Pond, for Henry Ford. Now a shadow of its earlier self (the dam broke decades ago and later a housing development encroached), the pond begins a fraction of a mile from the town square with its war memorial, commemorative gazebo, and senior center. A hawk's-eye mural of the village, featuring the body of water, decorates the exterior of the center.

The Black Legion did not slip instantly from the public consciousness. In the 1930s it spawned works of art: novels, plays, and at least two movies, one a major release starring Humphrey Bogart. It reverberated for years after the Silas Coleman and Charles Poole murder trials. It surfaced in news reports of court appeals and parole requests. It flared occasionally in accusations during legislative hearings and political campaigns. Its taint hounded some of those who had been muddied by allegations. In December 1936 a Pontiac fire captain who had grown tired of being teased after his name appeared in a grand jury report shot the co-worker who had been harassing him. He then took his own life.

What became of those who appear on these pages?

Major-General Bert Effinger tried to reorganize his secret society under a new name, the Patriotic Legion of America. He invited American-born Catholics to join his crusade against blacks, Jews, and communists. The organization did not survive. But Effinger did—into his eighties, never serving a day in prison.

State commander Arthur Lupp was paroled in 1938 just before Christmas. He also lived to be an old man. Urban Lipps and Ervin Lee saw their sentences commuted in the 1960s. Gangly Harvey Davis did not. He died in prison.

Rebecca Poole, fearful of the legion's reach, sent her daughters to Tennessee to be raised by her mother. After five or six years, they reunited in Michigan, where some of her descendants still live.

No record of Silas Coleman's family could be found.

Attorney Maurice Sugar rose to become legal counsel of the United Auto Workers, serving into 1946. His and his wife's names have been carried forward through the work of the Maurice and Jane Sugar Law Center for Economic and Social Justice.

Highland Parker publisher Art Kingsley died before all of the legion's legal cases concluded. He perished in a 1937 fire, likely the result of his own smoking. Employees purchased his newspaper company and continued publishing for decades.

Ecorse mayor William Voisine had a colorful career in politics—both before and after his prison sentence on corruption charges. "Sure, I stole a little in those days," he admitted. "I took from the rich and gave to the poor." The evidence showed he gave handsomely to himself as well.

Prosecutor Duncan McCrea also served time in prison for malfeasance. The man who ran against him (and lost) in 1936 prosecuted the case. Col. Heinrich Pickert served as police commissioner until 1939. He remained active in public life. When he died, city flags flew at half-staff.

Former governor Wilber Brucker, who had spoken to the Wolverine Republican League, defeated Senator James Couzens in the primary but was beaten in the general election in a Roosevelt-led Democratic landslide. In 1955 Brucker became secretary of the army under President Dwight Eisenhower. Mickey Cochrane's friend Emmett "Rosie" O'Donnell soared to the rank of four-star general and commander of the Pacific Air Forces.

Malcolm Bingay and Harry Salsinger remained active journalists until their deaths in the 1950s. Salsinger was posthumously given the Baseball Hall of Fame's Spink Award, the sport's highest honor for writers. Bingay died at his desk while composing his final "Good Morning" column.

During pennant races the *Free Press* sometimes resurrects Iffy the Dopester, using the original line drawing that accompanied Bingay's contributions.

Gerald Ford and Ronald Reagan, of course, became presidents of the United States; Ernie Harwell, a radio legend.

Father Solanus Casey, thirty-eight years after his death, was declared "venerable" by Pope John Paul II. It is the second of three steps toward sainthood in the Catholic Church.

Father Charles Coughlin's reputation has, justifiably, fared less well. He stayed on the air into 1942 until his increasingly strident views during World War II prompted his bishop to silence him. Coughlin disappeared from the radio, suddenly resuming more humble duties as the ordinary parish priest of the Shrine of the Little Flower. The church still stands along Woodward Avenue.

Henry Ford outlived his son Edsel, who succumbed to cancer in 1943 at age forty-nine. Edsel's death allowed Harry Bennett to strengthen his grip on the Ford Motor Company—until the Ford family rallied around Edsel's oldest son, Henry II. "Hank the Deuce" became president in 1945 and fired Bennett, who moved to the West Coast and lived a mostly quiet retirement painting seascapes.

Hank Greenberg and Charlie Gehringer had brilliant careers in the major leagues, both ascending to the Baseball Hall of Fame. Gehringer skipped his induction; he got married instead. In June 1983 the Tigers retired their numbers on the same day. They both returned to the ballpark for the honor.

Schoolboy Rowe played for fifteen years professionally, often plagued by arm troubles. At fifty he died of a heart attack. He was still writing love notes to his Edna, who kept them in a box with his good-luck charms. She never remarried.

Detective Jack Harvill was recognized as National Police Officer of the Year in 1936 for his work in breaking the Black Legion case. He eventually became superintendent of the Detroit Police. In 1942 Captain Ira Marmon retired from the Michigan State Police, the first man to do so.

The Red Wings won the Stanley Cup again in 1937, but the Tigers wouldn't capture another World Series title until 1945 and the Lions would come up empty until the 1950s. Though other sports towns have tried to claim the mantle of City of Champions, none has ever matched Detroit's achievement of three major professional sports titles within one season.

Detroit emerged from the Great Depression as strong as ever. During World War II it earned the designation "Arsenal of Democracy" for its contributions to the war effort. The automotive industry rebounded and flourished and the city's population continued to grow, peaking at more than 1.8 million in the 1950s. Then the decline began, leaving Detroit a half-century later with fewer than 700,000 residents and stretches of landscape pocked by vacant lots and abandoned homes and factories. More recently signs of a revival have appeared downtown and in other nearby areas.

Olympia Arena is gone. So is the Little Stone Chapel. The neighborhoods of Black Bottom and Paradise Valley have mostly disappeared. The Brewster Center, where Joe Louis first trained, is closed and deteriorating, but plans have been put forward to save it.

Navin Field became Briggs Stadium, which became Tiger Stadium. The last season of baseball was played there in 1999. Elden Auker threw out the ceremonial first pitch at the final game. The ballpark has since been demolished, but its field remains, with visitors coming daily to pay homage. Some park along Cochrane Road. The diamond is maintained by a group of volunteers who call themselves the Navin Field Grounds Crew.

At Holy Sepulchre Cemetery in Southfield, two bronze tiger statues, green with age, stand guard over a family mausoleum. It is there that Frank Navin rests. In peace, one presumes—his dream eternally realized.

And what of Joe Louis, Mickey Cochrane, and Dayton Dean?

Joe Louis went on to become the world heavyweight champion, holding the title longer than anyone, nearly twelve years. After the loss to Max Schmeling, he won his next thirty-four bouts, including their rematch. A tribute to him—a massive statue of his fist—hovers above a patch of cement in the middle of an intersection in downtown Detroit.

Mickey Cochrane returned as the player-manager of the Detroit Tigers. The following season he was struck in the head with a pitched ball. Players did not wear helmets in 1937 and the impact nearly killed him. He managed again but was never the same. A year later Walter O. Briggs fired Cochrane. The darkest moment of Cochrane's life, however, was yet to come. In 1945 his son, Gordon Jr., died in military action while serving as a US private in Holland. In the years after, Cochrane worked a variety of jobs, some in baseball. He eventually bought a ranch in Wyoming and escaped to it when time allowed.

Dayton Dean tried to have his conviction overturned but never succeeded. He regretted ever having heard of the Black Legion, lamenting that he had been a dupe, a goat, and a pawn in someone's else plan. He died in prison in 1960. By then he had surrendered to one of the legion's dreaded "isms": Catholicism. He had converted.

At the library, at the town hall, in and around Pinckney, I asked strangers about the Ford Mill Pond, the sinkhole, Nash Bridge, and the Black Legion. No one could answer my questions. Their voices and their expressions revealed not a hint of familiarity. They didn't know of what I spoke. Why would they? It's been eighty years since Silas Coleman's bullet-pierced body was found on the edge of the pond. Generations have come and gone.

I am in the cemetery now. Following a snowy Michigan winter, it remains dotted with evergreen blankets from last Christmas. But signs of spring abound. Dozens of birds are chirping, twittering, and cooing and the trees have finally begun to bud. The rods of loosestrife are already bright purple. The Canada geese have returned as well. Two honk loudly, wings thrashing, as they splash-land on the pond. Dayton Dean's claim of a watery burial ground, like much surrounding the Black Legion, was never fully investigated. It long ago descended into its own murkiness.

On this day the pond looks more placid and serene than it ought, given the secrets it may still hold.

Acknowledgments

For more than a decade, I have been working in spurts and flourishes on *Terror in the City of Champions*. Although I set the project aside for several years, I never stopped pondering it or feeling the pull of its gravity. It is a tale that deserved to be told and I hope I have done it justice.

Along the way I have been fortunate to have the support of many people, none more important to me professionally than Philip Spitzer, my agent and friend. I will always be indebted to Philip, whose advice, encouragement, and loyalty have been unwavering in my years as an author. It has been a pleasure working with him. (Thank you also to Lukas Ortiz of the Spitzer Literary Agency.) Further I am grateful to editor Keith Wallman of Lyons Press for recognizing the value and potential in this book and for his guidance along the way. Fellow writers Ian Thibodeau, Tim Wendel, and Taylor Stanton have also offered valuable assistance and my peers at the University of Detroit Mercy—especially Dr. Vivian Dicks, professor Jason Roche, Dr. Roy Finkenbine, Dr. Mark Denham, and Fr. John Staudenmaier—have been generous with their expertise and encouragement. Writer Richard Bak deserves a special acknowledgment for repeatedly going the extra mile to assist me. He is the most prolific author on subjects related to Detroit, including the Tigers, Joe Louis, and Henry Ford. His work deserves a wider audience. Author Charles Avison also merits a nod for his energetic efforts to bring attention to the City of Champions era.

Anyone who writes authoritatively about the Black Legion owes a debt to historian Peter H. Amann and attorney Maurice Sugar, both of whom devoted years to researching the organization and left their files accessible to all at the Walter P. Reuther Library. In particular I drew upon Sugar's extensive news clippings and Amann's oral histories and collection of Michigan State Police reports. I would also like to thank these individuals for their helpful contributions, both large and small: Greg Bishton, Jamie Bishton, Sara Cochrane Bollman, Basil Mickey Briggs, Holly Campbell, Mark Jerome Cavanagh, Barbara Chenot, Elizabeth Clemens, Mary Teresa Coulter, Nancy Durston, Lisa Edmondson, Ned Garver, Rick Gehringer, Dennis Hurkett, Danielle Kaltz, Maurice Kelman, Robert Krajenke, Christian Kraus, Nancy Kreider, Cassidy Lent, Gloria Lewis, Amy Marsh, Jessica Masten, Marti Morris, David Nantais, Francis Parker, Chris Pidcock, Lois Ralph, Amy Reytar, Barbara Rock, Matt Rothenberg, Carl Scheib, Bobby Shantz, Linda Ann Shaw, Patterson Smith, Garnett Stokes, and the late Fr. Leo Wollenweber.

Finally, I offer my heartfelt appreciation (and love) to my partner in life, Beth Bagley-Stanton, always my first reader; my caring and talented sons, Taylor, William, and Zack (and daughter-in-law Molly Heinsler); my friend Mike Varney; and my whole extended family. *Terror in the City of Champions* marks my first book since the death of three people dear to me whose devotion was unconditional: my mother-in-law, Marjorie Bagley; my oldest sister, Janis Stanton-Peterson; and my father and hero, Joe Stanton. They are part of this work too.

Notes

All direct quotes that appear in *Terror in the City of Champions* have been sourced on the following pages. I've also supplied citations where materials were difficult to find, where information was potentially controversial, or where I felt explanations were necessary. The only abbreviations used in these notes are for the three Detroit daily newspapers, which are referenced extensively: *DFP* for *Detroit Free Press*, *DN* for *Detroit News*, and *DT* for *Detroit Times*.

Part I: Something Afoot, 1933–1934
Mickey and Dayton

3. Mickey Cochrane arriving in Detroit: *DFP*, *DN*, and *DT*, December 15–17, 1933.

3. "a soul of torment": *New York Daily News*, August 29, 1934.

3. Mickey Cochrane biography: Numerous sources, including Bevis's *Mickey Cochrane*, Newcombe's "Black Mike of the Tigers," and Salsinger's *DN* profile, August 21, 1934.

4. Car sales fell by four million: Holli, *Detroit*, 126.

5. "If baseball is a sport . . .": Lieb, *The Detroit Tigers*, 196–97.

5. Frank Navin biography: Numerous sources, including Lieb, *The Detroit Tigers*; *Detroit News Tribune*, October 10, 1909; *DN*, February 24, 1918; *DT*, October 1, 1922; and *New York Times*, November 14, 1935.

6. "He put on one of the greatest examples . . .": Bevis, *Mickey Cochrane*, 48.

6. "Men fall naturally into his groove . . .": *DN*, July 1, 1934.

6. Navin borrowed $100,000: *DN*, July 1, 1934.

7. Stomach ailments: *DN*, November 13, 1935, and *DFP*, November 14, 1935.

7. "I wish I could let my feelings . . .": Bak, *A Place for Summer*, 119.

7. Scene inside Navin's office: *DN*, December 17, 1933.

7. "Now we can shove him off . . .": *DFP*, December 16, 1933.

9. "Why Detroit? . . .": *DFP*, April 10, 1934.

9. "In the South they had labor trains . . .": Moon, *Untold Tales, Unsung Heroes*, 80.

9. "It is a city of strangers . . .": Davis, "Labor Spies and the Black Legion," 171.

9. "They are everywhere . . .": Dos Passos, "Detroit City of Leisure," 281.

10. Walbri Court Apartments: Author interview with Basil "Mickey" Briggs.

11. Dayton Dean biography: Numerous news sources, plus Dean's "Secrets of the Black Legion."

11. "We shot them down. . . . I always obey orders.": *DN*, June 4, 1936.

12. Dayton's Dean's Black Legion initiation: Dean, "Secrets of the Black Legion," 5.

14. "It was his religion, his whole life . . .": *DT*, June 6, 1936.

A Friend Disappears

15. "to get a good rest": *DN*, January 4, 1934.

Spring in Lakeland

16. Lakeland hotel scene: *DFP*, March 11, 1934.

17. "What do you say if we all sing 'Mammy'?": Ibid.

17. "There's never been another like him": *DT*, September 24, 1934.

17. "perfect model for the [clerical] collar ads": Ibid.

17. Charlie Gehringer biography: Numerous sources, including Skipper's *Charlie Gehringer* and Stanton's *The Road to Cooperstown*.

18. "I had to pick a team . . .": *DFP*, March 18, 1934.

18. "Like most members of his race . . .": Ibid.

18. "Dah she comes . . .": *DFP*, March 11, 1934.

19. Sewell-Greenberg bus incident: Based on several sources, including A. B. "Happy" Chandler Oral History Collection, Truett "Rip" Sewell interview.

20. "You're better than any team . . . all these years": *DN*, June 30, 1934.

20. "You've been a second-division . . . any ball club": Ibid.

20. "It feels like it's . . .": *DFP*, March 13, 1934.

21. "They've been babied so much . . .": *DN*, August 14, 1934.

21. "He is no star . . .": *DFP*, March 17, 1934.

Major-General Bert

22. Origins of the Black Legion: For a thorough, authoritative account of the legion's beginnings and the roles of Shepard and Effinger, see Amann's "Vigilante Fascism."

22. "I will shoot square with everybody . . .": *Lima Sunday News*, August 12, 1934.

24. "The first prerequisite of a prospective member . . .": *DN*, August 26, 1936.

25. "Nobody wants to see a red flag . . .": *DN*, June 5, 1936.

25. "But not good enough . . .": Anonymous, "I Was a Captain in the Black Legion," 129.

26. "When men have pledged themselves . . .": *DN*, May 26, 1936.

26. "I have had many disappointments . . .": Lupp letter to Arthur Cross, dated February 3, 1936, Michigan State Police files, Amann Collection, Box 5A.

28. Chief Charles Barker who: *DFP*, June 16, 1936.

28. RED'S SLAYING STILL MYSTERY: *DN*, December 23, 1933.

28. "in fact, to all the plants that had strikes . . .": *DN*, June 2, 1936.

A Future Together
30. John Bielak's life and murder: Numerous sources, including *DN* and *DFP*, March 16–17, 1934; *DN*, June 1, 1936; *DT*, June 2, 1936; *DN*, June 19, 1936; and *DN*, August 27, 1938.

The Bee Is Buzzing
32. "We're running out everything . . .": *DFP*, April 22, 1934.
32. "That'll just about cost you . . .": Ibid.
32. "Now fellows, we're down here . . .": *DN*, March 22, 1934.
33. "Willing? Why, I'll be sitting . . .": *DFP*, April 19, 1934.
33. decanter through a train window: *DFP*, July 27, 1934.
33. "his fate is in the lap of the gods . . .": *DFP*, March 27, 1934.
33–34. "This is my thirty-first year . . .": *DN*, March 21, 1934.
34. "Not so hard . . . been able to do that": *DFP*, March 28, 1934.
34. "a pack of lies": *DN*, May 18, 1937.
34. "There isn't a pitcher . . .": *DN*, April 7, 1934.
34. "I've never seen anything like it": *DFP*, April 15, 1934.
35. "The championship bee is buzzing . . .": *DFP*, April 22, 1934.
35. "When the rest of the fellows . . .": *DFP*, July 29, 1935.
35. "He's the nearest . . . same way": *DFP*, April 22, 1934.

Neither Threats Nor Bribes
36. Art Kingsley biography: Several sources, including *DN*, December 19, 1979, and Loren Preeter oral history, Amann Collection, Box 15.
36. Plots against Kingsley: These are divulged in numerous newspaper stories, including *DN*, June 12, 1936, as well as in testimony related to *Wilson vs. Highland Park*, a case before the Michigan Supreme Court in 1938, Amann Collection, Box 3.
36. "The whistle means your paper is on the porch": *Highland Parker*, March 31, 1932.
37. "He is not very smart": Ibid.
37. Politicians Cannot Muzzle This Newspaper: Ibid.
37. "Neither threats nor bribes . . . vastly better equipped . . . may be quite correct": Ibid.
37. "I shall do what I think is right": Ibid.
37. "a damn Jew . . . hook out of his nose": *Highland Parker*, March 3, 1932.
37. "for any office in this democracy": *Highland Parker*, March 31, 1932.
37. "Intolerance of race or religion . . .": Ibid.
37. "not an intellectual giant . . .": *DN*, June 13, 1936.
38. "Sacrificed at the altar of political ambition": *Highland Parker*, January 5, 1933.
38. "I have always been critical . . . mayor of any city": *DN*, June 16, 1936.
38. charge of criminal libel: *Highland Parker*, June 18, 1936.
39. "through a window with a rifle . . .": *DN*, January 27, 1937.
39. "There's your man": *DN*, June 13, 1936.
41. Shall "Dictator" Kingsley Run . . .: Fake paper, Amann Collection, Box 9.
41. Arlington Jones incident: *DN*, July 7, 1936, and *Wilson vs. Highland Park*.

It Hurt for Days

43. "Boy, I'm just telling . . . I like to died": *DFP*, May 8, 1934.
43. longing for Edna: Ibid.
43. "I'm going to surprise all of you guys": Ibid.
44. "Unless the [Tigers] change their ways . . .": *DFP*, May 22, 1934.
44. son's bike was stolen: *DN*, May 1, 1934.
44. Yacht club quotes and scene: *DFP*, May 27, 1934.
45. "I want to apologize for saying that . . .": Ibid.
46. "baby-face Negro": *DFP*, March 2, 1934.
46. "The Ku Klux Klan stopped them . . .": Barrow and Munder, *Joe Louis*, 26.
46. "When he hit you, it hurt for days": Roberts, *Joe Louis*, 16.
47. "the most promising heavyweight prospect": *Los Angeles Times*, June 22, 1987.
47. "the classiest and most finished boxer": *DN*, April 7, 1934.
47. "distinct handicap . . . vigor out of the ball players": *DN*, May 5, 1934.
47. "If we finish our present swing through the east . . .": *DFP*, June 12, 1934.
48. "This sort of stuff belongs in a Class B league . . .": *DN*, July 1, 1934.
49. "chief squanderer . . . burning deck": Ibid.
49. "dizzy": *DFP*, July 2, 1934.
50. "All I wanted to do is to get that fellow . . .": Ibid.
50. "like a freshman footballer . . .": *DFP*, July 3, 1934.
50. "I guess I had it coming": *DN*, July 2, 1934.
51. "thoroughly chastened . . . case of the blues": *DFP*, July 25, 1934.

The Little Stone Chapel

52. Heinrich Pickert biography: Numerous sources, including *DN*, March 15, 1934, and June 5, 1934.
52. "No one can tell what patience . . .": *DN*, July 3, 1931.
52. "Gum and police work . . .": *DN*, April 3, 1934.
53. "all the time": *DN*, October 10, 1934.
53. "teaching, living, talking, and breathing": Ibid.
53. "The appalling thing . . . a showdown soon": Ibid.
54. child lost for nine hours: *DFP*, June 3, 1935.
55. "I believe in doing what's right . . .": *DT*, June 1, 1936.
56. "Nothing could stop him . . .": *DT*, June 2, 1936.
56. Police initiated into the legion: *DN*, June 27, June 30, and July 1, 1936, and *DFP*, July 1–2, 1936.
57. "meet a bunch of American fellows . . .": *DN*, July 1, 1936.
57. "very strenuous speaker . . . fear in any man": *DFP*, July 2, 1936.
57. "somebody might get hurt": *DN*, July 1, 1936.
57. "But I was afraid they would consider . . .": *DN*, June 30, 1936.
58. Hit-and-run deaths: *DN*, April 17, 1934.
58. Ralph Wilson killing: *DFP*, April 7, 1934.
58. "You'll never get me": *DFP*, March 27, 1934.
58. "shoot at a person who is running . . .": *DN*, January 27, 1936.

59. "many of the teachings would frighten . . .": *DFP*, April 17, 1934.
59. Col. Pickert soon joined the effort: *DFP*, April 19, 1934.

The Superstitious Schoolboy and His Gal
60. collection of good-luck charms: *DN*, September 1, 1934.
60. Rogell stepped on third base: *DFP*, July 26, 1934.
60. Black Betsy: *DN*, August 29, 1934.
60. He insisted on being in that seat: *DFP*, July 22, 1934.
61. Schoolboy Is Invincible: *DFP*, July 29, 1934.
61. "Young Master Rowe can't pitch nine full innings . . .": *New York Daily News*, July 31, 1934.
62. "Rowe pitched one of the greatest . . .": *DN*, August 18, 1934.
63. "Frank Merriwell in the flesh": *DFP*, August 2, 1934.
63. "Man Mountain from Arkansas": *DN*, May 28, 1934.
63. "The Pygmy from El Dorado": *DFP*, August 2, 1934.
63. "Today they're pitching . . . he'll be immortal, too": *DN*, August 25, 1934.
63. "handsome in the athletic way . . .": *Philadelphia Inquirer*, August 29, 1934.
64. "has practically a fool-proof face": *DN*, August 25, 1934.
64. "He's becoming nervous": *DFP*, August 29, 1934.
64. "He will break Rube . . .": Ibid.
64. "Rowe probably will not be beaten . . .": Ibid.
64. "The man had been crying": *New York Daily News*, August 29, 1934.
64. "Aww, you can't miss, kid . . .": Ibid.
65. Rowe looked haggard: *DFP*, August 30, 1934.
65. "How's he look? . . . as he goes along": *New York World-Telegram*, August 30, 1934.
65. "You need some help. . . . Get to it": Ibid.
65. "I guess it was just not my day": *DFP*, August 30, 1934.
65. "too many colored people . . .": Lester, *Black Baseball's National Showcase*, 44.
66. Mollenhauer fire: *DT*, June 13, 1936; *Pontiac Press* (MI), June 24, 1936; and *DFP*, June 25, 1936.
67. "I've been knowing Edna ever since we were kids": *DT*, August 31, 1934.
67. Rowe on Rudy Vallee show: *DN*, August 31 and September 2, 1934.
68. "My name is Edna Mary . . .": *DT*, September 16, 1934.
68. love story was sweet, true, and endearing: Author interviews with Greg and Jamie Bishton, grandsons of Schoolboy and Edna Rowe.
68. sodas and sundaes: *DN*, September 21, 1934.
68. "I know everybody in the town . . .": *DT*, August 29, 1934.

Happy Rosh Hashanah, Hank
69. all of whom gently encouraged him: *DN*, September 11, 1934.
69. "Happy New Year, Hank": *DFP*, September 9, 1934.
69. "You tell Henry Greenberg . . .": *DN*, September 11, 1934.
70. "In a game such as this . . .": *DT*, September 10, 1934.

70. "I hope I did . . . on my conscience": *DN*, September 11, 1934.

70. "celebrated Rosh Hashana . . . civic duty": Ibid.

70. "a truly great competitor . . . very fine chap": Ibid.

70. "Oi, Oi, Oh, Boy!": *The Sporting News*, September 12, 1934.

71. "They seemed surprised I didn't have horns . . .": Ritter, *The Glory of Their Times*, 311.

71. "My religion was seen . . .": Ibid., 328.

71. Tanton Apartment residents: *Detroit City Directory 1935*.

71. "There was a sign there . . .": Auker, *Sleeper Cars and Flannel Uniforms*, 99.

71. "mixed . . . he's not all Jewish": Bennett, *Ford*, 83.

71. Effinger had some ideas: Maurice Sugar Collection, Sugar Memo, Box 18, and FBI files, August 7, 1936, letter from agent H. H. Reinecke to J. Edgar Hoover.

72. "This time it's different . . .": *DN*, September 17, 1934.

72. "I wish I had 100,000 . . .": *DN*, September 23, 1934.

73. "They're the best of them all": *DN*, September 12, 1934.

73. "Keep your chin up, lad . . .": *DN*, September 19, 1934.

74. "I hope you win that pennant, Mr. Navin": *DFP*, September 18, 1934.

74. "You don't think . . . get past those fielders": *DT*, September 18, 1934.

74. "So many things can happen . . .": *DFP*, July 25, 1934.

75. "I've been on four championship clubs . . .": *DT*, September 25, 1934.

75. "If we don't win the pennant . . .": *DN*, September 23, 1934.

75–76. "world's best batboy": *DN*, September 30, 1934.

76. "Yes, sir, you've got a great pitcher . . .": *DT*, August 30, 1934.

76. "I'm going to make a prediction . . .": *DN*, September 25, 1934.

Oh, Those Dean Boys

77. Hotel scene with Dean brothers: *DN*, October 3, 1934.

77. "I know just what you want me to say . . .": Ibid.

78. "You're telling the genuine truth, Diz": Ibid.

78. "never saw a city wilder": Frisch, *Frank Frisch*, 173.

78. "Detroit is as crazy about the Tigers . . .": *New York Evening Journal*, October 3, 1934.

79. "All the boys flocked around him": *DFP*, August 17, 1935.

79. "I think the Tigers are not as good . . .": *DN*, October 4, 1934.

80. "Henry Ford's big plant slipped by . . .": *DN*, October 5, 1934.

80. "a yell that nearly stopped the tower clock": Ibid.

81. playing on a broken ankle: Bak, *Cobb Would Have Caught It*, 268.

81. "a tongue lashing": Lieb, *The Detroit Tigers*, 208.

82. Tigers Insist It's in the Bag: *DN*, October 8, 1934.

82. "We now cheerfully eat those words": *DT*, October 8, 1934.

83. "I don't care who pitches": Ibid.

83. Mickey the Manager: *News-Week*, October 6, 1934.

83. "We thought Detroit was a madhouse . . .": Frisch, *Frank Frisch*, 174.

83. Don't win or else: *DFP*, May 5, 1935.

84. What Happened to Rowe's Hand?: *DN*, October 11, 1934.

84. "unparalleled": Frisch, *Frank Frisch,* 174.

84. "To hell with $50,000 . . .": Lieb, *The Detroit Tigers*, 43.
85. "I watched the crowd and Medwick . . .": *DFP*, October 10, 1934.
85–86. Charlie Jacobs spotted an opportunity: *DN*, October 7, 1935.
86. "Those coarse and vulgar Cardinals . . .": *DN*, October 10, 1934.
86. "I never knew a city to take . . .": Frisch, *Frank Frisch*, 176.
86. "If the spirit engendered . . .": *DN*, October 10, 1934.
86. "There are no regrets in the hearts . . .": Ibid.

The Attorney Down the Street

87. Maurice Sugar biography: Numerous sources, including Sugar Collection book files, Boxes 1–7 and 118, and Sugar's "Memorandum on the Black Legion," Box 18, as well as Johnson's *Maurice Sugar*.
88. "There are a thousand times more illegal arrests . . .": Sugar Collection, Box 118.
89. *"To hell with your plan of starving . . .":* Sugar Collection, Box 14.
89. *"There's a cry that starts them shaking . . .":* Ibid.
89. bought the Portsmouth football team for $15,000: Willis, *Dutch Clark*, 180.
90. "We'd get 5,000 people . . .": *DN*, September 10, 1971.
90. Even Coughlin would hype the team: *Milwaukee Journal*, November 20, 1934.
90. Each game cost about $8,000 . . . : *DN*, October 13, 1934.
90. "like a rabbit in brush . . .": Dow, "The Lions' Dutch Clark," 1.
92. "Is Greenberg in the house? . . .": *DN*, March 5, 1935.
92. Gehringer heard rumors: *DFP*, January 15, 1935.
93. Clifton raced to Navin Field uninvited: *DFP*, January 19, 1935.
93. "He turned out to be my guiding light": Kelly, "Flea Clifton," 136.
93. his ma was strangled: Bak, *Cobb Would Have Caught It*, 243.
93. "Let me go to camp . . .": *DFP*, March 10, 1935.
94. one of her teenage daughters complained: *DT*, June 7, 1936.
94. "I gritted my teeth . . .": Dean, "Secrets of the Black Legion," 35.
94. "Fordissimus": Davis, "Labor Spies and the Black Legion," 170.
95. "At last I had witnessed . . .": Stevens, "Detroit the Dynamic," 190.
95. "upholding a rule of terror and repression": *DN*, October 10, 1976.
95. "inhuman brute": Sugar Collection, draft of autobiographical manuscript, Boxes 118–119.
95. In Bennett's estimation, he was closer to Henry: Bennett, *Ford*, 1.
95. characterization of Harry Bennett: Numerous sources, including Lacey's *Ford*, Babson's *Working Detroit*, Bennett's *Ford*, Bryan's *Henry's Lieutenants*, and McCarten's "The Little Man in Henry Ford's Basement."
95. "I am Mr. Ford's personal man": McCarten, "The Little Man in Henry Ford's Basement," 7.
95. strangled with his own necktie: Lacey, *Ford*, 360.
95. "pool hall clientele, the air thick with menace": Lacey, *Ford*, 368.
95. "right beside the garage . . .": Ibid.
95. released from prison into his care: Babson, Biddle, and Elsila, *The Color of Law*, 54.

96. "They're a lot of tough bastards . . .": McCarten, "The Little Man in Henry Ford's Basement," 10.

96. Harry Bennett's castle home: *DN*, October 10, 1976.

96. convince Cochrane to run for sheriff: McCarten, "The Little Man in Henry Ford's Basement," 10.

96. "Uncle Harry": Author interview with Sara Cochrane Bollman.

97. admiring "yes" men: *DFP*, March 15, 1936.

PART II: GRAND PLANS, 1935
A New Year

101. "My life is just about perfect . . .": *DFP*, January 1, 1935.

101. Crime statistics . . . : Ibid.

101. "no home, no job, and no visible means of support": Johnson, *Maurice Sugar*, 159.

102. "The Brown Bomber": *DFP*, January 5 and January 12, 1935.

102. "We want Mickey": *DFP*, January 3, 1935.

102. "A lot of baseball men are predicting . . .": *DFP*, January 5, 1935.

102. Cochrane's gun request: *DN*, January 6, 1935.

Mr. Hoover, Investigate

103. William Guthrie ordeal: *DN*, June 18 and July 30–31, 1936.

104. "A man carrying a red lantern . . .": *DN*, July 21, 1937.

105. "to inject typhoid germs into bottles of milk": *DN*, August 5, 1936.

105. "class enemies": Ibid.

105. "It might wipe out the whole city": Ibid.

106. "They did it in Russia with 30,000 . . .": Crowley, "Black Legion Secrets Never Before Told," 86.

106. "the greatest menace . . .": *DFP*, March 16, 1935.

106–7. "This capitalist system . . . an immense danger": Ibid.

107. "an alleged man of God . . . figure of the priesthood": Ibid.

107. "of passion and prejudice": Ibid.

107. "toxic twaddle . . . John St. Loe Strachey": Ibid.

107. "I have authorized no one . . . stupid thing to do": Ibid.

108. "working men . . . general membership meetings": *DFP*, March 15, 1935.

108. "The club has operated under various names . . .": *DFP*, April 8, 1935.

108. "in more or less constant jeopardy": Report of postal inspector J. F. Cordrey, February 23, 1935, FBI files.

109. "If they resign or abandon the organization . . .": Ibid.

109. "and state there is no indication . . .": J. Edgar Hoover's handwritten April 8, 1935, note related to March 19, 1935, memo from Department of Justice, FBI files.

109. "In view of the fact that it is alleged . . .": Memo from Attorney General William Stanley to J. Edgar Hoover on April 15, 1935, FBI files.

110. Plot against Maurice Sugar: Numerous sources, including *DN*, June 12, 19, and 29, 1936, and *DT*, April 14, 1937.

111. Fake Communist Party pamphlet: *DN*, August 3, 1936.
112. "Clarence Darrow urges election of Maurice Sugar": *DN*, March 31, 1935.

Harry's Caravan
113. "How many pitchers . . . and then some": *DN*, March 4, 1935.
113. "The men who have established themselves . . .": Ibid.
114. Navin had occasionally sent money: *DFP*, March 7, 1935.
114. saved his life by getting him medical treatment: Ibid.
114. "a flock" of teeth: *DN*, March 2, 1935.
114. one-thirty-second Cherokee: Bak, *Cobb Would Have Caught It*, 252.
114. They wouldn't speak for the entire 1935 season: *DT*, October 9, 1935.
114. "a grim little fellow . . .": Lieb, *The Detroit Tigers*, 201.
114. Lakeland clubhouse description: *DN*, March 4, 1935.
115. "That's a bet, Mike": *DFP*, February 20, 1935.
115. "That's the thing that makes stars . . .": *DFP*, March 5, 1935.
115. "The big dream lures him": *DFP*, January 13, 1935.
116. "Gerald Walker remains . . .": *DN*, March 7, 1935.
116. "The Mississippi Hard Head": *DFP*, March 8, 1935.
116. "We didn't win the World Series . . .": *DFP*, January 30, 1935.
116. "We'll win again unless . . .": *DN*, March 2, 1935.
116. informed Grantland Rice: *DFP*, March 29, 1935.
117. "Luck is a big thing in baseball . . .": *DN*, March 1, 1935.
117. "Hal Trosky, who is a much better . . .": *DFP*, March 28, 1935.
117. "blood in his eye": Ibid.
117. "To hell with Owen . . .": *DFP*, March 23, 1935.
117–18. "is the kind of man who would make . . .": *DFP*, February 3, 1935.
118. "If you really ain't gonna be another Jack Johnson . . .": Louis, *Joe Louis*, 36.
118. tried to sign him to professional contracts: *Michigan Daily*, January 4, 2007.
118. Harry Bennett's caravan to the game: *DFP*, April 14, 1935.
119. "We want them all wild . . .": Ibid.
119. Louis Sherry death and investigation: The information was culled from FBI files, and *DFP*, *DN*, and *DT* stories April-June 1935 and May-July 1936.
119. Dayton Dean's wife would suggest: *DT*, June 5, 1936.
119. "We believe a satisfactory explanation . . .": *New York Sun*, June 5, 1936.
119. "I would like to know . . .": Dr. Bicknell letter, May 25, 1936, FBI files.
120. "Navin Field fans are ever ready . . .": *DFP*, April 14, 1935.
120. "A lot of things . . . something unexpected happens": *DFP*, April 14, 1935.

The Radio Priest
121. ten million to thirty million listeners: "Father Coughlin," 34.
121. "from the more humble walks of life": *DN*, April 25, 1935.
121. "of such mellow richness . . .": Stegner, "The Radio Priest and His Flock," 232.

122. "two pied pipers": *DFP*, March 5, 1935.

122. "lunatic fringes": Ibid.

122. "It is not exaggeration to say that . . .": Ibid.

122. "ridiculous rumor . . . that Father Coughlin is . . .": Ibid.

122. "comic-opera, cream-puff general": *DFP*, March 13, 1935.

122. "a political corpse . . .": Ibid.

122. "political termites": Ibid.

122. 80,000 on an average week: "Father Coughlin," 34.

123. "a just, living, annual wage": Joe Brown Collection, Box 7.

123. "fair profit": Ibid.

123. "There are men in this audience tonight . . .": *DT*, June 5, 1936.

123. "For years the laboring man has endeavored . . .": *DN*, April 25, 1935.

123–24. "As a result of that statement, many more . . .": *DN*, July 26, 1930.

124. "animated not with malice but mercy . . .": *DFP*, April 25, 1935.

124. "Jewish gold": Doherty, "The Amazing Career of Father Coughlin," 44.

124. "feed and fan flames of anti-Jewish feeling": *DN*, March 14, 1935.

124. "an atom of sincerity in his entire system": *DN*, July 3, 1934.

124. "Free speech is a wonderful thing . . .": Ibid.

124. region's most prominent antisemite: For thorough explorations of Ford's antisemitism, check Baldwin, *Henry Ford and the Jews*, and Woeste, *Henry Ford's War on Jews*.

124. "bigoted about Jews . . .": Bennett, *Ford*, 83.

125. THE INTERNATIONAL JEW—THE WORLD'S PROBLEM: *Dearborn Independent*, May 22, 1920.

125. Adolf Hitler, whose waiting room . . .: Baldwin, *Henry Ford and the Jews*, 172.

125. would become allies: Ibid., 297.

125. "the worst physical beating . . .": Marcus, *Father Coughlin*, 15.

125. "No change today . . .": Ibid., 24.

126. Casey All-Brothers Nine: Odell, *Father Solanus*, 35.

126. stubbornly refusing a mask: Ibid., 38.

126. "simply of the bankers": Casey, *Letters from Solanus Casey*, 42.

126. "my enthusiasm for him . . .": Ibid.

126. "prophet": Crosby, *Thank God Ahead of Time*, 131.

126. "gullibility [that] . . . was able to be exploited . . .": Ibid., 215.

126. Frank Murphy . . . Alex Groesbeck: Author interview with Brother Leo Wollenweber of St. Bonaventure Monastery.

126. Andre Bessette meeting: Wollenweber, *Meet Solanus Casey*, 78.

127. "kept press": Basso, "Radio Priest—In Person," 97.

127. "the voice of the people": *Milwaukee Journal*, May 23, 1935.

127. "All these disturbing voices . . .": *Brooklyn Daily Eagle*, May 24, 1935.

The Killing of Silas Coleman

128. He preferred blacks not be in his world at all: *The Afro-American*, August 1, 1936.

128. Harvey Davis biography: Numerous sources, including *DN*, June 4 and 25, 1936.

129. "I want to shoot a nigger": *The Afro-American*, August 1, 1936.

129. "Hey, Sid ...": *DN*, July 26, 1936.
129. "Let's get the hell out of here": *The Afro-American*, August 1, 1936.
129. "Well, I don't see no use wasting ...": Dean, "Secrets of the Blank Legion," 35.
129. POLICE OFFICER'S SHOOTING OF CRAZED ...: *Highland Parker*, April 4, 1935.
130. "Shooting a human being to death ..." Ibid.
130. "get hold of a colored guy": *DN*, July 21, 1936.
130. "a little excitement": Ibid.
131. "A guy can't get a word in edgewise ...": *Los Angeles Times*, May 22, 1935.
131. Jesse Owens at Ferry Field: McRae, *Heroes Without a Country*, 38–47; *DFP*, May 25, 1935; and *Los Angeles Times*, May 25, 1985.
132. Silas Coleman killing: Numerous sources, including *DN*, July 21 and 28, 1936; *DFP*, November 26, 1936; *Pinckney Dispatch*, May 29 and June 5, 1935.
133. "Get your guns, you fellows ...": *DN*, July 22, 1936.
133. "Don't see any boat fishing out there": *DN*, July 28, 1936.
133. "like a deer": *DN*, July 21, 1936.
133. "Don't let that nigger get away": *DN* and *DT*, November 26, 1936.
134. "or it will be too bad for you": *DN*, July 22, 1936.
134. "the bullet-riddled body of a Negro ...": *DFP*, May 27, 1935.
134. "The crime of murder is no novelty in Detroit ...": *Pinckney Dispatch*, June 5, 1935.

Worries

135. "worried about his failure": *DFP*, May 23, 1935.
135. "to bolster his morale": Ibid.
136. "We've got to do something": *DFP*, May 28, 1935.
136. "the human slingshot ...": *DFP* April 8, 1934.
136. "thoughtful and observant": *DFP*, May 1, 1935.
136. "thoughtful, wide-awake": *DFP*, May 27, 1935.
136. "Hank puts more thought, effort ...": *DFP*, April 8, 1935.
137. "I don't think Carnera can fight ...": *New York Daily News*, June 21, 1935.
137. "When he does that to me, I'll be right in there ...": *DFP*, May 13, 1935.
137. "I started noticing some things I thought ...": Louis, *Joe Louis*, 48–49.
137. Lena Horne: Louis, *Joe Louis*, 56.
138. "I hope Joe can take us around ...": *DFP*, June 16, 1935.
138. "It was twenty-five years ago when Jack Johnson ...": *DFP*, June 25, 1935.
138. "He sure is a wonderful man ...": *DFP*, June 22, 1935.
138. MEET JOE LOUIS: *DFP*, June 24, 1935.
138. "Joe just whipped him badly": Barrow and Munder, *Joe Louis*, 50.
138. "There was so much noise ...": *DFP*, June 26, 1935.
138. "He won! He won! He won!": *DT*, June 26, 1935.
139. "I've been in a nightmare ... even pitching": *DFP*, June 12, 1935.
139. Entertained Harry Bennett: *DFP*, June 13, 1935.
139. "Look out, Yanks, there's a bengal loose ...": *DFP*, July 10, 1935.
140. "I don't want no celebration ...": *DFP*, July 2, 1935.
140. "All I can say is I'm glad to be home": *DFP*, July 3, 1935.

140–41. "Hi there, fellows. . . . Sign this, will you, Rowe": *DFP*, August 25, 1935.

141. "I guess they take experience . . .": *DFP*, June 30, 1935.

141. "How many does Gehrig have?": Ibid.

142. "But there are limitations . . .": *DFP*, July 5, 1935.

142. "The only solution is to cancel the game . . .": *DN*, July 10, 1935.

142. Hank Married? Tiger and Blond Don Sage Grins: *DFP*, July 9, 1935.

142. "You can light your cigar . . .": *DFP*, July 11, 1935.

142. Will Rogers's news reports: Smallwood and Gragert, *Will Rogers' Daily Telegrams, Vol. IV*, 309–311.

143. Will Rogers's death: Ketchum, *Will Rogers*, 383–394, and *DFP*, August 17, 1935.

143. "He loved and was loved by the American people": *DFP*, August 17, 1935.

143. "We all tried to get him not to go . . .": *DFP*, August 16, 1935.

143. "There isn't a man in the world . . .": *DFP*, August 10, 1935.

143. "But if the Yankees can't win . . .": Ibid.

143. "It seems that a member of our club has been killed": *DFP*, August 17, 1935.

143. "I guess when your number comes up . . .": Ibid.

144. "These things like injuries . . .": *DFP*, August 17, 1935.

144. "curl up and crackle": *DFP*, August 24, 1935.

144. "I just love to hear Mike cuss . . .": Ibid.

Unwanted Attention

145. "You'd see men walking down the street . . .": Ernie Navarre oral history, Amann Collection, Box 15.

146. "an undercurrent": William Mellus oral history, Amann Collection, Box 15.

146. "a stormy petrel in Ecorse politics": *Wyandotte Herald*, August 9, 1935.

146. James Bailey house fire: Maurice Sugar's "Memorandum on the Black Legion," Sugar Collection, Box 18.

147. "Why not get rid of him? . . . bomb him": *New York Sun*, June 5, 1936.

147. Bombing of Mayor Voisine's home: *DFP*, August 7–8, 1935, and *Wyandotte Herald*, August 9, 1935.

147. "So far as I know, I haven't an enemy in the world . . .": *DFP*, August 8, 1935.

148. Albert Bates scene and quotes: *DFP*, August 14–15, 1935, *DN*, May 24, 1936, and *DT*, May 25, 1936.

149. Spooky Hoods Found in Auto: *DFP*, August 14, 1935.

149. Black Legion arrest in Adrian: *Adrian Daily Telegram*, August 21 and 28, 1935, and FBI reports of August 31 and October 16, 1935, FBI files.

150. "very stout": FBI report of October 16, 1935, FBI files.

150. "one of the highest officers of the Black Legion": Ibid.

151. "Bill won't be in office after tonight . . .": *DN*, June 5, 1936.

151. "There is room for only one 'ism' in America . . .": *DN*, May 3, 1935.

151. "This insidious propaganda of communism . . .": Ibid.

151. "An effort of the great barons . . . terms of the bill": Ibid.

151. "To my mind he is the best advised man . . .": Benson Ford Research Center, Ford Family Papers, personal correspondence.

Zero Hour

153. "No, no, no": *DFP*, August 27, 1935.

153. "The team went east and came back in second place": Ibid.

153. "The only way for the Tigers to lose . . .": *DFP*, August 25, 1935.

153. "Great as your team is today . . .": *DFP*, August 27, 1935.

154. "Those guys make me sick": *DFP*, August 28, 1935.

154. Meeting with J. Edgar Hoover: National Archives, J. Edgar Hoover scrapbooks.

154. "Listen, Mr. Hoover . . .": *DFP*, September 12, 1935.

154. Gehringer and Al Capone: Bak, *Cobb Would Have Caught It*, 187.

154. "After getting an eyeful of the machinery . . .": *DN*, September 12, 1935.

155. "General Upps . . . Ike White": FBI report, May 24, 1935, FBI files.

155. "lost his leg in a gun battle with the Purple Gang": Ibid.

155. "leave the house for a half hour": Ibid.

155. "the only registered communist . . .": Ibid.

155. "a modern two-family dwelling": FBI report, June 24, 1935, FBI files.

156. "This man derided both political . . .": Letter to J. Edgar Hoover, April 26, 1935, FBI files.

156. "I assume that it is of interstate character . . .": Ibid.

156. "Lixto": Anonymous, "I Was a Captain in the Black Legion," 54.

156. "If you don't go . . .": Ibid.

157. "I like to died": *DFP*, September 8, 1935.

157. "Sleeping powders—they're only a joke": *DFP* September 11, 1935.

157. "But we haven't won . . . beat us now": *DN*, September 13, 1935.

157. "In fact, every time Joe comes . . .": *DN*, September 14, 1935.

158. "Champions—Detroit Is Proud of You": *DN*, September 22, 1935.

158. "These Tigers are not my champions": *DN*, September 23, 1935.

158. "These two men gave me the greatest break . . .": Ibid.

Louis vs. Baer

159. Black Bottom and Paradise Valley: Description culled from various sources, including Williams, *Detroit*, and Bak, *Turkey Stearnes . . . and Joe Louis*.

159. "Housing is one of the basic . . .": *DFP*, September 10, 1935.

159. "We all knew him . . .": Moon, 30.

160. "because they churned ice cream on Sunday": Moon, *Untold Tales, Unsung Heroes*, 111.

160. "What impressed this observer . . .": *Chicago Daily Tribune*, September 8, 1935.

160. "Now, Louis of his own initiative . . .": Ibid.

160. "What am I going to do to Baer . . .": *DFP*, September 24, 1935.

161. "We aren't going to let Joe do it . . .": *DN*, September 21, 1935.

161. "When will you be married? . . . we hope to have a quiet affair": *Chicago Daily Tribune*, September 8, 1935.

161. "Maybe Joe shouldn't marry . . .": *DFP*, September 21, 1935.

161. "Marva was too beautiful . . .": Louis, *Joe Louis*, 70–71.

162. "These are the gloves we'll use . . .": *DFP*, September 25, 1935.

162. "Give Max anything he wants . . .": Ibid.

162. "He'll slaughter me . . . not quitting now.": Schaap, *Cinderella Man*, 268.
162. "scared to death": Louis, *Joe Louis*, 72.
163. "Although Joe Louis is colored . . .": Mitchell, "Joe Louis Never Smiles," 239.
163. "fell like a marionette whose string had snapped": *DFP*, September 25, 1935.
163. "It was twice as noisy . . .": *DN*, September 25, 1935.
163. "He's the Brown Embalmer now": Ibid.
163. "Something had popped loose, all right . . .": Wright, "Joe Louis Uncovers Dynamite," 22.
164. "Since President Lincoln freed the slaves . . .": *DFP*, September 30, 1935.

World Champions
165. "Where've you been . . . do me any good": *DN*, October 3, 1935.
166. "The Babe wants his drink": *DFP*, October 3, 1935.
166. "Knowing the Tigers personally . . .": Ibid.
166. "If you play the same confident brand . . .": *DFP*, September 28, 1935.
167. "Grimm's Fairy Tale": *DN*, October 1, 1935.
167. "Greenberg's bat . . .": *DN*, October 2, 1935.
167. "Greenberg will be a star . . .": Ibid.
167. The Cardinals had told them so: *DFP*, October 5, 1935.
167. "were a bunch of tough SOBs": Greenberg, *Hank Greenberg*, 78.
167. "especially vicious": Ritter, *The Glory of Their Times*, 329.
167. "Jew this and Jew that": Greenberg, *Hank Greenberg*, 78.
168. "Those ladies in the boxes . . .": *DFP*, October 5, 1935.
168. "The trick is to make the umpire . . .": *DN*, October 8, 1935.
168. "Some of the words shouldn't be printed . . .": Greenberg, *Hank Greenberg*, 79.
168. "hay-pitching, coon-hunting . . .": *Time*, October 7, 1935.
168. "Boy, you certainly tied a knot . . .": *DN*, October 3, 1935.
168. Ernie Wettler story: *DN*, October 4, 1935.
169. "frail looking": *DT*, October 8, 1935.
169. "Little Tennessee Tom": Ibid.
169. "not much bigger than a hickory bootjack": *New York World-Telegram*, October 8, 1935.
169. "skinny . . . slender, wiry": *DN*, October 4, 1935.
169. "about as big as thirty cents . . .": *The Sporting News*, March 14, 1946.
169. "doesn't look like he could break . . .": *New York World-Telegram*, October 8, 1935.
169. "We had Greenberg's goat . . .": *Chicago Daily News*, October 7, 1935.
169. "I knew they couldn't keep us down forever": *DFP*, October 4, 1935.
170. "Never mind about the train . . . I'll be okay, Joe": Ibid.
170. "Mickey, my wife is pregnant . . .": Author interview with Basil Mickey Briggs.
170. "You know what this means . . . in twenty minutes": *DFP*, October 5, 1935.
171. "Did you order Owen . . . I alone": *DN*, November 14, 1935.
172. "used blasphemous language . . . on both sides": *DFP*, October 5, 1935.
172. "Pappy's in the poorhouse . . .": Bak, *Cobb Would Have Caught It*, 248.
172. "It looks like they don't need me": *DN*, October 5, 1935.

172. "I'll wait until the numbers go up . . .": *DFP*, October 7, 1935.

173. "The crowd oozed confidence . . .": *DFP*, October 7, 1935.

173. "That guy is as game as they come": Ibid.

173. "He's the best ball player all around": Ibid.

174. "Go away, Doc . . . hope you can make it": *DFP*, October 8, 1935.

174. "Was that my daddy?": *DN*, October 9, 1935.

176. "Without question, I am the most pleased . . .": *DFP*, October 8, 1935.

176. World Series victory and celebration: Multiple sources, including *DFP*, *DN*, and *DT*, October 7–9, 1935.

177. "The Leaning Tower can now crumble . . .": Ibid.

177. "We graybeards of the years . . .": *DN*, October 8, 1935.

177. "It was Detroit's salute to America . . .": *DFP*, October 8, 1935.

177. "I can now die in peace": *DN*, November 16, 1935.

Amid the Joy, Punishment

178. "Your foreman wants to see you . . .": *DN*, July 30, 1936.

178. "I know what you want . . .": Ibid.

180. "a terrible, shameful sight": Letter to Marmon from X-9 informant, July 3, 1936, Michigan State Police files, Amann Collection, Box 5A.

180. Harley Smith beating: *DN*, May 27, 1936.

180. "die for the Red, White, and Blue . . .": *Washington News*, June 3, 1936.

181. Denver Carter beating: Michigan State Police report, May 25, 1936, Amann Collection, Box 5A.

181. Paul Every beating: *DFP* and *DN*, May 24, 1936.

181. Alfred Roughley disappearance: *DFP*, July 2, 1936.

181. Alexander Murdy disappearance: *DT*, June 2 and 10, 1936, and *DN*, June 10, 1936.

The Pastor Who Said No

182. "*When we get wise and organize* . . .": Sugar Collection, Box 14.

182. Plot against Maurice Sugar: Numerous sources, including *DN*, June 19 and 29, 1936, and *DT*, April 14, 1937.

183. "The automobile manufacturers of this city . . .": Sugar Collection, Box 10.

183. "I say that the unemployed of this city . . .": Ibid.

183. "reactionary Republican": Ibid.

183. "denounce and ridicule procedure under our Constitution . . .": Ibid.

183. "Upton Sinclair still loves Roosevelt . . .": *DN*, November 4, 1935.

184. "I'm sorry for the state of the brains . . .": Ibid.

184. "Vote for Comrade Sugar . . .": Fake pamphlet, Sugar Collection, Box 19.

184. Seize Sugar Literature: *DN*, November 4, 1935.

184. "On the walls were pictures of Lenin . . .": Ibid.

184. "It's a last-minute move . . .": Ibid.

184. "There was nothing of an incriminating nature": *DFP*, November 5, 1935.

185. "One of our party sections is bombed . . .": *DFP*, September 7, 1935.

186. "If you'd ever been to a meeting and seen . . .": *DN*, June 9, 1936.
186. "I told them that I had a gun . . .": Michigan State Police report, June 8, 1936, Amann Collection, Box 5A.
186. VFW members in Sandusky: *DN*, May 28, 1936.
187. Rev. Ralph C. Montague initiation: *DN*, May 28 and June 5, 1936.
187. "outspoken . . . square-jawed": Ibid.
187. "despicable and un-American": Ibid.
188. "String him up . . . I'm prepared to die": Ibid.

Uncle Frank
189. Frank Navin's death: Numerous sources, especially the *DFP*, *DN*, and *DT*, November 13–15, 1935.
189. "good for my liver": *DN*, November 14, 1935.
190. "I'll never forget our dressing room . . .": *DN*, October 9, 1935.
190. "the luckiest and happiest boy in the world": Ibid.

Come to Detroit, Lindbergh
192. "We've lost our last game . . .": *DN*, November 18, 1935.
192. "kings of athletics": *DN*, October 13, 1935.
193. "a genius of baseball": *DFP*, November 14, 1935.
194. "Our business association always had been a fine one . . .": Ibid.
194. Description of Walter O. Briggs, his homes, his wealth, and his personality: Various sources, including author interview with one of his grandsons, Basil Mickey Briggs.
195. "unorthodox . . .": *DN*, July 1, 1934.
195. "highly emotional and extremely aggressive": *DN*, July 23, 1934.
195. "unlike any other man . . .": *DN*, September 26, 1934.
195. "moved to bitter resentment": *DN*, September 29, 1934.
195. "not exactly in the mood . . .": *DN*, July 3, 1934.
195. "speaking in mournful tones": Ibid.
195. "When everything is rosy and treasure trove . . .": Newcombe, "Black Mike of the Tigers," 80.
195. "He is taciturn, surly, sullen . . .": *DFP*, November 24, 1935.
195. "elements of greatness": Ibid.
195. "It may be that responsibility . . .": Ibid.
195. Schmeling in Pompton Lakes: *DFP*, December 9, 1935.
196. "Massa Joe": Ibid.
196. "Nobody can hit like Louis . . .": *DFP*, December 14, 1935.
196. "There isn't a fighter in the game right now . . .": *DFP*, December 17, 1935.
197. "New York was no match": *DN*, December 16, 1935.
197. "Detroit is a City of Champions . . .": *DFP*, December 17, 1935.
197. Texas Ranger: *DN*, December 8, 1935.
197. meandering, cross-country drive: Al Simmons in a letter to F. C. Lane, December 3, 1934, F. C. Lane Papers.

198. "When we got on the train . . .": *DFP*, December 11, 1935.
199. "Had I known he was moving to England . . .": *DFP*, December 24, 1935.
199. Rudolph Anderson death: *DN*, December 16–17, 1935, and *DFP*, May 25, 1936.

Part III: Joy and Terror, 1936
Case Closed
203. Plots against Mayor Voisine: Numerous newspaper stories aided in the description of these events, but the key source was testimony in the *People vs. Pettijohn and Madden* case, Amann Collection, Box 3.
203. "the one that is here to do the job": *People vs. Pettijohn*, Amann Collection, Box 3.
203. "I did not come here to fool . . .": Ibid.
203. Clarence Oliver house shooting: *DN*, June 12, 1936.
205. "I can promise you that your prints . . .": *DFP*, March 17, 1936.
205. Fire at Shrine of the Little Flower: Details in press reports differed. I relied on the account written by Coughlin himself and published days after the fire in the church bulletin, *Shrine Herald*, March 22, 1936.
205. "the entire church was a fiery furnace": *Shrine Herald*, March 22, 1936.
205. "the building which I loved more than all . . .": Ibid.
206. "our little shingle church": Ibid.
206. "I do not know what caused the fire . . .": Ibid.
206. "was writing his head off . . .": Bingay, *Detroit Is My Own Hometown*, 84.
207. Player nicknames: These appear throughout Iffy the Dopester's columns in 1934 and 1935.
207. "We won't do so badly with York . . .": *DFP*, March 11, 1936.
207. "I can't see why the Tigers aren't . . .": *DFP*, March 22, 1936.
208. "Mickey's weakness is that he loves his friends . . .": *DFP*, March 15, 1936.
208. "If Frank Navin had lived . . .": *DFP*, March 22, 1936.
208. "The club is a vast impersonal organization . . .": *DFP*, March 23, 1936.
208. "Mr. Briggs has only owned the ball club . . .": *DFP*, March 26, 1936.
208. "This public-be-damned gag went out of fashion . . .": *DFP*, March 27, 1936.
209. "keep the public informed . . .": *DFP*, April 5, 1936.
209. "All is not peace and contentment . . .": *DFP*, March 29, 1936.
209. Abraham Lincoln on Fighting Island: *Toledo Blade*, February 13, 2008.
209. "white, desolate moonscape": *DFP*, June 7, 2009.
209. Pidcock case: Details drawn from Michigan State Police reports and memos of Captain Ira Marmon, Amann Collection, Boxes 4 and 5A, as well as news reports and various 1938 FBI reports.
210. "I can't tell you about it . . .": *DN*, June 7, 1936.
211. FBI agent visits Effinger: All quotes come from agent N. E. Manson's report, April 14, 1936, FBI files.
212. "completes the investigation": J. Edgar Hoover memo to Joseph B. Keenan, assistant to the attorney general, April 22, 1936, FBI files.
212. evening of May 2: *DN*, August 4, 1936.

City of Champions

214. "If a player or an official can disregard taunts . . .": *DN*, January 21, 1936.
214. "That wasn't necessary . . . you know how it is.": *DN*, January 6, 1936.
215. "I couldn't sleep last night in New York . . .": *DFP*, March 14, 1936.
215. "You can eat yourself out . . . that bulging stomach?": *DFP*, March 16, 1936.
216. "Jack, you've got a great team here . . .": *DFP*, March 20, 1936.
216. SPIRIT OF REAL CHAMPIONS . . .: *DN*, March 20, 1936.
216. "Emulating the example of the Tigers . . .": Ibid.
216. "play like hell . . . no more on Tuesday afternoon": *DFP*, March 24, 1936.
216. "just an earnest, everyday workman": *DFP*, March 26, 1936.
217. "My boys are just like kids . . .": Ibid.
217. "It was a crime for either team to lose.": Ibid.
217. "stood there a helpless little old man . . .": *DFP*, April 8, 1936.
217. "We'd rather lose with the old guy . . .": Ibid.
218. "Go to it, boys. It's our night": *DFP*, April 13, 1936.
218. "Upon what meat does our city feed . . .": *DN*, April 13, 1936.
218. "unduplicated distinction . . .": Ibid.
218. "The Sports Capital of the World": Ibid.
218. WHOLE NATION CHEERS CITY'S CHAMPIONS: *DT*, April 16, 1936.
218. "It is swell to be home . . .": Ibid.
218. "Keep it up, Tigers": *DN*, April 14, 1936.
219. "I've been watching hockey for nine years . . .": *DN*, January 20, 1936.
219. "Providing Charlie Gehringer or Billy Rogell . . .": *DFP*, April 14, 1936.
219. "Good God, we had to get all the police . . .": Barrow, *Joe Louis*, 53.
220. Conversation with Henry Ford at the train station: *DT*, April 18, 1936.
221. "I'm not a champion yet but I hope to be": *DT*, April 19, 1936.
221. "the greatest gathering of champions": Ibid.

Rumors

223. out in the mess was Roy Pidcock: *DFP*, June 6, 1936, and Michigan State Police report, June 3, 1936, Amann Collection, Box 5A.
223. "They are going to get me and you, too": Ibid.
223. "I love everybody": Ibid.
223. Black Legion had infiltrated his group: *DN*, June 8–9, 1936.
224. Findlater Temple details: *DN*, May 22, 1936, and *DFP*, May 23, 1936.
224. "The sooner the New Deal is rooted out . . .": *DN*, April 17, 1936.
224. "put the Wolverine League . . .": Floyd Nugent letter, April 30, 1936, Amann Collection, Box 13.
225. Marx's office was Wolverine League headquarters: Ibid.
225. Victor Nicholas Schultz addressed the crowd: *Milwaukee Journal*, June 7, 1936.
225. Black Legion meeting of May 12 and Charles Poole plot: Based on court testimony and dozens of newspaper stories in *DFP*, *DN*, and *DT*, May through September 1936.
227. "If the organization is any good . . .": *DN*, September 13, 1936.
227. "I'd like to kill him myself": *DN*, September 14, 1936.

228. "A fellow hardly knows how he gets into these things": *DT*, June 7, 1936.
229. "No. I'm not Poole . . . Out on the west side": Meehan, Harvill, and Farrell, "The Inside Story of Michigan's Black Legion Murder," 6.

Poole and Pidcock

230. Poole talking baseball: *DT*, June 7, 1936.
230. "all washed up": *DFP*, May 2, 1936.
230–31. "That's as far down the lineup as we can go . . .": *DFP*, May 15, 1936.
231. Cecil Pidcock had come up from Toledo: Michigan State Police report, June 3, 1936, Amann Collection, Box 5A.
231. "something fishy": Sugar Collection, Box 23.
232. "What is this going to be, a party . . .": *DN*, September 18, 1936.
232. "To all that know me, I love you all . . .": *DN*, June 1, 1936.
232. The abduction of Roy Pidcock: This scenario is based on the reports of Captain Ira Marmon as described in various Michigan State Police reports and memos, Amann Collection, Box 5A.
233. "You're a dirty liar . . . to do it again": *DN*, September 18, 1936.
234. AGAIN THE G-MEN SCORE A TRIUMPH: *DFP*, May 23, 1936.
234. "Poor Charlie. To think that two . . .": Meehan, Harvill, and Farrell, "The Inside Story of Michigan's Black Legion Murder," 5.
235. "Tennessee Slim": Ibid., 5.
235. decided he had taken his own life: *DT*, June 1, 1936.

Secrets

236. "Charles was good to me . . .": *DN*, June 5, 1936.
236. Jack Harvill biography: *DN*, December 7, 1968, and Harvill family history by Jean Harvill Gallagher.
237. "Nobody is going . . . know these people": Meehan, Harvill, and Farrell, "The Inside Story of Michigan's Black Legion Murder," 35.
238. POOLE A VICTIM OF BLACK LEGION: *DN*, May 22, 1936.
238. SIXTEEN OFFICERS . . .: *Daily Leader* (Mt. Clemens, MI), May 22, 1936.
238. MURDER UNMASKS POLITICAL ACTIVITY . . .: *DFP*, May 23, 1936.
238. Col. Pickert hearing: *DN*, May 22, 1936, and *DFP*, May 23, 1936.
238. "In the interest of good law and order . . .": *DN*, May 19, 1936.
238. Marx represented Pickert: *DT*, May 22, 1936, and Kahn, *High Treason*, 206.
239. Dean had seen Pickert: Letter from agent John Bugas to J. Edgar Hoover, December 12, 1938, FBI files.
239. Pickert membership card: Alfred E. "Mickey" Farrell oral history, Amann Collection, Box 15.
239. Sugar apartment visitors: Maurice Sugar's "Memorandum on the Black Legion," Sugar Collection, Box 18.
239. "This was his moment of glory": Farrell oral history, Amann Collection, Box 15.
239. "big fool": *DN*, June 2, 1936.

239. "It looks like an underhanded way of . . .": *DFP*, May 23, 1936.

240. "I don't remember what my clients told me . . .": *DT*, May 25, 1936.

240. "I have never heard any hint that a terrorist group . . .": *DFP*, May 23, 1936.

240. "It isn't a small clique inside the club . . .": *DFP*, May 25, 1936.

240. "Some well-meaning but stupid men . . .": Ibid.

240. "What if I am the leader?": *DFP*, May 26, 1936.

240. "I want the statement refuted that we are interested . . .": Ibid.

240. "I hope those damn fools . . .": Ibid.

241. Peg-Leg White on his farm: *DN*, June 20, 1936.

241. "I'd be ashamed to admit I belonged . . .": Ibid.

241. Lupp interview in prosecutor's office: *DFP, DN, DT*, May 26, 1936.

Black Legion Hysteria

244. "The row of manacled Black Knights . . .": Davis, "Labor Spies and the Black Legion," 169.

245. "My boy couldn't have done what they say . . .": *DT*, May 27, 1936.

245. "I can't say that the signature . . .": *DFP*, May 27, 1936.

245. McCrea newsreel interview of Lupp: *DT*, May 26, 1936.

246. THE BLACK LEGION MAKES KLAN LOOK LIKE CREAM PUFF: *DN*, May 31, 1936.

246. "The Black Legion probably is the craziest . . .": *DT*, May 28, 1936.

247. "I have ordered the police commissioner . . .": *DT*, May 25, 1936.

247. "Dayton always said it was a shame . . .": *DT*, June 4, 1936.

247. Dorothy Guthrie assault: *DFP* and *Washington Times*, June 18, 1936.

247. "You don't know anything": *DFP*, June 18, 1936.

248. "It seems you can't tell where . . .": *DN*, June 5, 1936.

248. "My life is ruined": *DN*, June 9, 1936.

248. "Some of the defendants awaiting trial . . .": *DN*, June 14, 1936.

248. "Two years ago, I didn't have a gray hair . . .": *DN*, June 13, 1936.

248. "I made up my mind they would . . .": *DN*, August 5, 1936.

249. Estimates of legion size: *DN*, May 31, 1936.

249. "We thought for years that things such as . . .": *DFP*, June 2, 1936.

249. "Dear enemy. You are to die soon . . .": Michigan State Police report, June 15, 1936, Amann, Box 5A.

249. "Beware! Black Legion!": Michigan State Police report, June 23, 1936, Amann, Box 5A.

250. "Aw, we wouldn't have dropped him . . .": *Washington Times*, June 6, 1936.

250. "Think you know too much . . .": *Washington Post*, October 21, 1936.

250. "Black Legion Game": *DFP*, June 30, 1936.

250. "A veritable nationwide Black Legion hysteria . . .": *Toledo Blade*, May 29, 1936.

250. Nelson Harding editorial cartoon: *Washington Times*, June 1, 1936.

250. "Indeed, when I looked at a photograph . . .": *New York World-Telegram*, May 29, 1936.

251. "springs from an inferiority complex . . . are not of the elect": *Washington Star*, June 14, 1936.

251. "stripped of their hoods . . .": *Washington Post*, May 25, 1936.
251. "Homicidal fanatics of the Black Legion type . . .": *Washington Times*, May 29, 1936.
251. "a strange and particularly evil manifestation . . .": *New York Herald-Tribune*, October 1, 1936.
251. "a new zoological specimen . . . mockery of 'justice'": *New York Daily Mirror*, May 25, 1936.
251. "Outside the grooves of his prejudices . . .": Eliot, "Behind the Black Legion— What?" 29.
251. "the diseased minds of fanatics . . .": *DN*, June 6, 1936.
251. "The responsibility for this shameless . . .": Ibid.
251. "fall to pieces as soon as it . . .": *Brooklyn Daily Eagle*, June 7, 1936.
251. "Bosh!": *DFP*, May 26, 1936.
252. "There are indications that several Michigan . . .": *Boston Herald*, June 10, 1936.
252. "J. Edgar Hoover says the federal government . . .": *Washington Star*, May 28, 1936.
252. "If the state inquiry reveals kidnapping . . .": *Chicago Daily Times*, May 29, 1936.
252. "The sooner this thing is dragged out . . .": *New York Post*, May 28, 1936.
252. "lawlessness": *DN*, May 29, 1936.
252. "I advised her that in the absence . . .": Memo from agent R. B. Hood to Edward Tamm, assistant FBI director, May 29, 1936, FBI files.
252. "unduly alarmed": Ibid.
252. "John Dillinger was a gentleman . . .": Letter to J. Edgar Hoover, May 23, 1936, FBI files.
253. "Decent Michigan people would welcome . . .": Letter to J. Edgar Hoover, May 25, 1936, FBI files.
253. "show these outlaws . . .": Letter to J. Edgar Hoover, May 27, 1936, FBI files.
253. "Certainly this organization is a far greater . . .": Letter to J. Edgar Hoover, May 26, 1936, FBI files.
253. "Organization intends harm to President . . .": Telegram to J. Edgar Hoover, May 25, 1936, FBI files.
253. "a savvy Connecticut Yankee": *Chicago Daily Times*, June 5, 1936.
253. "He knows he's got a good thing . . .": Ibid.

Frenzied Nerves
255. Mickey Cochrane's nervous breakdown: Numerous sources, especially press reports in the *DN*, *DT*, and *DFP*, June 3–10, 1936.

Dayton Dean and the Negro Reporter
257. The Dean-Cowans interview: The scene was adapted from *The Afro American*, August 1, 1936.
258. "just for the hell of it": *Daily Leader* (Mt. Clemens, MI), July 21, 1936.
259. "I'm afraid Dean is confirming anything . . .": Ibid.

The Captain

260. Ira Marmon biography: Several sources, including *DN*, July 12, 1943, and author interview with Marmon granddaughter Barbara Rock.

261. "quiet . . . unobtrusive . . . determined": *Michigan State Digest*, June 25, 1942.

261. "wise and smart": Farrell oral history, Amann Collection, Box 15.

261. Frieda rattled his nerves: Author interview with Marmon granddaughter Barbara Rock.

262. Pickert and McCrea disputes: *DFP*, May 26, 1935, and March 12, 1936.

262. as many as fifty deaths: Numerous news stories, including *DFP* and *Washington Post*, May 25, 1936.

262. "Pidcock had been out of work . . .": *DN* and *DT*, June 1, 1936.

263. "He had been a communist . . .": *DN*, June 1, 1936.

263. "There have been several bodies . . .": Marmon memo to commander, June 10, 1936, Amann Collection, Box 4.

263. "A lot of people are going to disappear . . .": Anonymous, "I Was a Captain in the Black Legion," 55.

264. "It looks as if Oakland County . . .": Marmon memo to commander, May 29, 1936, Amann Collection, Box 4.

264. Irvine Wurm incident: Michigan State Police report, May 30, 1936, Amann Collection, Box 5A.

264. "extra confidential" X-9 proposal: Letter to Marmon from informant X-9, July 3, 1936, Michigan State Police files, Amann Collection, Box 5A.

265. certain the legion had killed Roy Pidcock: Various news accounts, including *DN*, June 7, 1936, and *Wyandotte Herald*, June 5, 1936, as well as numerous Michigan State Police reports, Amann Collection, Box 5A.

265. Hazen Branch death: *Wyandotte Herald*, January 31, 1936.

265. Charles Allran death: *Wyandotte Herald*, January 17, 1936.

265. Alexander Murdy death: *DFP*, May 25, 1936; *DT*, June 2, 1936; and *DN* and *DT*, June 10, 1936.

265. Jerome Wolf death: *DN*, June 4, 1936, and *New York Times*, May 25, 1936. Note: His name was spelled "Wolfe" in news stories, but in letters to Michigan officials his son spelled it "Wolf."

265. Howard Curtis death: *DFP*, May 27, 1936; *DN*, May 28, 1936; and *Milford Times*, October 19, 1934, and May 29, 1936.

265. Vernon Dodge death: *DN*, June 1, 1936.

265. R. T. Philip death: *DFP*, May 27, 1936.

265. Walter Fisher death: Ibid.

265. Cornelius Vanderveen death: *DFP*, May 30, 1936.

265. Oliver Hurkett death: *DT*, May 26, 1936; *DFP*, May 27, 1936; and author interview with relative Dennis Hurkett.

266. "a certain official . . .": Crowley, "Black Legion Secrets Never Before Told," 82.

266. "exaggerated accounts": Ibid.

266. "innumerable indictments the entire work . . .": Ibid.

Wyoming
267. "It is painful to watch the creeping shadows . . .": *DN*, June 10, 1936.

267. "Cochrane has been doing . . .": *DT*, June 5, 1936.

267. "a highly nervous temperament": *DN*, June 10, 1936.

267. "terrific mental pressure": Ibid.

267. "aggravated by a Detroit newspaper columnist . . .": Ibid.

267. "It has been no fault of Mickey's . . .": *DFP*, June 21, 1936.

267. Cochrane's activities in the hospital: Ibid.

268. "Louis inside of five": *DFP*, June 18, 1936.

268. "Louis in three": Ibid.

268. "Two rounds": Ibid.

268. "condemned man": *DFP*, June 19, 1936.

268. "I think I can lick Max": *DFP*, June 18, 1936.

268. collapsed and died of heart attacks: Roberts, *Joe Louis*, 121–122.

268. "It's the greatest place on earth": *Weston County Gazette* (WY), May 21, 1936.

269. LAST ROUNDUP?: *Prescott Evening Courier* (AZ), July 16, 1936.

269. Bennett had played a role: Bak, *Cobb Would Have Caught It*, 81.

The Cover-Up
270. "refuse anyone the right": *DFP*, July 26, 1936.

270. "Absolutely, I do.": *Pinckney Dispatch*, July 29, 1936.

271. Effinger was gone—a fugitive: *Cleveland Plain Dealer*, August 26, 1936.

271. "No organization like the Black Legion . . .": *DFP*, June 13, 1936.

271. "as a public servant sworn to uphold the law": *DT*, May 26, 1936.

272. "I don't care who they are . . .": Ibid.

272. "There probably would have to be an overt . . .": *DN*, May 27, 1936.

272. "The danger of uncovering ramifications . . .": *Christian Century*, June 17, 1936.

272. "They were told that I was a member . . .": *DN*, June 14, 1936.

273. "We have had several big names . . .": *DT*, May 28, 1936.

273. For his silence about Pickert's membership: Farrell oral history, Amann Collection, Box 15.

273. "He said the orders for the death . . .": Peg-Leg White statement to constable Roy Bucy, Amann Collection, Box 2.

274. "same large grocery orders . . . prodigious eater": Letter to J. Edgar Hoover from editor James Blissell, October 21, 1936, FBI files.

274. "There is a great amount of rumor . . .": Letter to J. Edgar Hoover from Allen County prosecutor Robert Jones, February 28, 1937, FBI files.

274. "They're scared he'll expose too many . . .": Fred Gulley statement to Michigan State Police, March 29, 1938, Amann, Box 5A.

274. "small-town men with horizons . . .": *DN*, May 31, 1936.

275. Weitschat's brother: Michigan State Police report, June 5, 1936, Amann Collection, Box 5A.

275. "It is just possible that the reason . . .": Maurice Sugar Memo, Sugar Collection, Box 18.

275. "No, no, no, no . . .": Farrell oral history, Amann Collection, Box 15.

276. "The Bureau is unable to understand why . . .": J. Edgar Hoover letter to agent John Bugas, December 28, 1938, FBI files.

276. "Captain Marmon or his alleged . . .": Ibid.

Epilogue

278. Pontiac fire department murder-suicide: *DN*, December 5, 1936.

279. "Sure, I stole a little . . .": *DN*, September 28, 1956.

Bibliography

ARCHIVES, PAPERS, AND COLLECTIONS

Benson Ford Research Center, The Henry Ford, Dearborn, MI
- Henry Ford and Ford Family Papers
- Ford Reminiscences Oral Histories

Giamatti Research Center, National Baseball Hall of Fame, Coopers-town, NY
- Charlie Gehringer Collection
- F. C. Lane Papers
- Player clipping files

Louie B. Nunn Center for Oral History, University of Kentucky Libraries
- A. B. "Happy" Chandler Oral History Collection

National Archives, Records of the Federal Bureau of Investigation, College Park, MD
- J. Edgar Hoover's Scrapbooks, 1913–72

University of Detroit Mercy Library, Detroit, MI
- Influence of Father Coughlin Collection
- Shrine Herald Collection

Walter P. Reuther Library, Wayne State University, Detroit, MI
- Peter H. Amann Collection
- Joe Brown Collection
- Father Charles Coughlin FBI Files
- Maurice Sugar Collection

NEWSPAPERS
In the 1930s three English-language daily newspapers covered Detroit: the *Free Press*, *News*, and *Times*. All three dailies proved invaluable to my research. I scoured thousands of issues. In addition, the following papers were helpful. Other Michigan newspapers: *Adrian Daily Telegram*, *Daily Leader* (Mt. Clemens), *Highland Parker*, *Milford Times*, *Oxford Leader*, *Pinckney Dispatch*, *Pontiac Press*, and *Wyandotte Herald*. New York: *Daily Mirror*, *Daily News*, *Evening Journal*, *Herald-Tribune*, *Post*, *Sun*, *Times*, and *World-Telegram*. Washington, D.C.: *News*, *Post*, *Star*, and *Times*. Chicago: *Daily News*, *Daily Times*, and *Daily Tribune*. Other newspapers: *Afro-American* (Baltimore), *Boston Herald*, *Brooklyn Daily Eagle*, *Cleveland Plain Dealer*, *Lima News* (OH), *Los Angeles Times*, *Milwaukee Journal*, *Philadelphia Inquirer*, *Prescott Evening Courier* (AZ), *Toledo Blade* (OH), and *Weston County Gazette* (WY).

PUBLIC RECORDS
The Freedom of Information Act is a critical and sometimes underappreciated tool that allows all of us access to the records of our government. It was through the act that I obtained copies of more than nine hundred pages of FBI documents related to the Black Legion. These proved vital.

WEBSITES
I continually found helpful, reliable information at baseball-almanac.com, baseball-reference.com, historicdetroit.org, and retrosheet.org.

BOOKS, PAMPHLETS, AND MAGAZINE AND JOURNAL ARTICLES
Adamic, Louis. "Hill-Billies Come to Detroit." *Nation*, February 13, 1935.

Allen, Frederick Lewis. *Since Yesterday: The 1930s in America*. New York: Harper & Row, 1939.

Amann, Peter H. "Vigilante Fascism: The Black Legion as an American Hybrid." *Comparative Studies in Society and History* (July 1983): 490–524.

Ambrogio, Anthony, and Sharon Luckerman. *Cruisin' the Original Woodward Avenue*. Charleston, SC: Arcadia, 2006.

Anderson, William M. *The Glory Years of the Detroit Tigers, 1920–1950*. Detroit: Wayne State, 2012.

Angelo, Frank. *On Guard: A History of the Detroit Free Press*. Detroit: Detroit Free Press, 1981.

Anonymous. "I Was a Captain in the Black Legion." *True Detective Mysteries*, December 1936 and January 1937.

Astor, Gerald. *And a Credit to His Race: The Hard Life and Times of Joseph Louis Barrow.* New York: Saturday Review, 1974.

Auker, Elden. *Sleeper Cars and Flannel Uniforms.* Chicago: Triumph, 2001.

Avison, Charles. *Detroit City of Champions.* Detroit: Diomedea, 2008.

———. *Detroit City of Champions: The Players.* Detroit: Diomedea, 2013.

Babson, Steve. *Working Detroit.* New York: Adama, 1984.

Babson, Steve, Dave Biddle, and David Elsila. *The Color of Law.* Detroit: Wayne State, 2010.

Bak, Richard. *Cobb Would Have Caught It.* Detroit: Wayne State, 1991.

———. *Joe Louis: The Great Black Hope.* New York: Da Capo, 1998.

———. *A Place for Summer: A Narrative History of Tiger Stadium.* Detroit: Wayne, 1998.

———. *Turkey Stearnes and the Detroit Stars.* Detroit: Great Lakes, 1995.

Baldwin, Neil. *Henry Ford and the Jews: The Mass Production of Hate.* New York: Public Affairs, 2001.

Barrow, Joe Jr., and Barbara Munder. *Joe Louis: Fifty Years an American Hero.* New York: McGraw-Hill, 1988.

Basso, Hamilton. "Radio Priest—in Person." *New Republic*, June 5, 1935.

Bennett, Harry, as told to Paul Marcus. *Ford: We Never Called Him Henry.* New York: Tor, 1987.

Bevis, Charlie. *Mickey Cochrane: The Life of a Baseball Hall of Fame Catcher.* Jefferson, NC: McFarland, 1998.

Bingay, Malcolm W. *Detroit Is My Own Home Town.* New York: Bobbs-Merrill, 1946.

———. *Of Me I Sing.* New York: Bobbs-Merrill, 1949.

Bryan, Ford R. *Henry's Lieutenants.* Detroit: Wayne State, 1993.

Cabadas, Joseph P. *River Rouge: Ford's Industrial Colossus.* St. Paul, MN: Motorbooks, 2004.

Casey, Bernadine, ed. *Letters from Solanus Casey.* Detroit: Father Solanus Guild, 2000.

Clinansmith, Michael S. "The Black Legion: Hooded Americanism in Michigan." *Michigan History* (Fall 1971): 243–62.

Cochrane, Mickey. *The Fan's Game.* Cleveland: SABR, 1992.

"Coughlin: 23,000 Applaud the Fighting Priest, Two Rebuke Him." *News-Week*, June 1, 1935.

Crosby, Michael. *Thank God Ahead of Time.* Quincy, IL: Franciscan, 2000.

Crowley, David H. "Black Legion Secrets Never Before Told." *True Detective Mysteries*, December 1936.

Davis, Forrest. "Labor Spies and the Black Legion." *New Republic*, June 17, 1936.

Dean, Dayton. "Secrets of the Black Legion." *Official Detective Stories*, October 1, 1936.

Derum, James Patrick. *The Porter of Saint Bonaventure's.* Detroit: Fidelity, 1972.

Doherty, Edward. "The Amazing Career of Father Coughlin." *Liberty*, January 5, 1935.

Dos Passos, John. "Detroit City of Leisure." *New Republic*, July 27, 1932.

Dow, Bill. "The Lions' Dutch Clark." blog.detroitathletic.com, January 23, 2012.

Eliot, George Field. "Behind the Black Legion—What?" *Liberty Magazine*, September 5, 1936.

"Father Coughlin." *Fortune*, February 1934.

Feldman, Doug. *September Streak: The 1935 Chicago Cubs Chase the Pennant*. Jefferson, NC: McFarland, 2003.

Ferkovich, Scott, ed. *Detroit: The Unconquerable*. Phoenix: SABR, 2014.

Fine, Sidney. *Frank Murphy: The Detroit Years*. Ann Arbor: University of Michigan, 1975.

Fox, Craig. *Everyday Klansfolk: White Protestant Life and the KKK in 1920s Michigan*. East Lansing: Michigan State, 2011.

Freedman, Lew. *Joe Louis: The Life of a Heavyweight*. Jefferson, NC: McFarland, 2013.

Frisch, Frank. *Frank Frisch: The Fordham Flash*. Garden City, NY: Doubleday, 1962.

Garraty, John A. *The Great Depression*. New York: Harcourt, 1986.

Goll, Ralph. "Ripping the Black Mask from Detroit's Terror Legion." *Daring Detective*, August 1936.

Greenberg, Hank, with Ira Berkow. *Hank Greenberg: The Story of My Life*. Chicago: Triumph, 1989.

Heidenry, John. *The Gashouse Gang*. New York: Public Affairs, 2007.

Helmer, William, with Rick Mattix. *Public Enemies: America's Criminal Past, 1919–1940*. New York: Checkmark, 1998.

Henrickson, Wilma. *Detroit Perspectives: Crossroads and Turning Points*. Detroit: Wayne State, 1991.

Holli, Melvin, ed. *Detroit*. New York: New Viewpoints, 1976.

Holway, John. *Voices from the Great Black Baseball Leagues*. New York: Dodd, Mead & Co., 1975.

Johnson, Christopher. *Maurice Sugar: Law, Labor, and the Left in Detroit 1912–1950*. Detroit: Wayne State, 1988.

Kahn, Albert E. *High Treason: The Plot Against the People*. New York: Lear, 1950.

Kavieff, Paul R. *Detroit's Infamous Purple Gang*. Charleston, SC: Arcadia, 2008.

———. *The Purple Gang: Organized Crime in Detroit 1910–1945*. Fort Lee, NJ: Barricade, 2005.

———. *The Violent Years: Prohibition and the Detroit Mob*. Fort Lee, NJ: Barricade, 2001.

Keegan, Tom. *Ernie Harwell: My Sixty Years in Baseball*. Chicago: Triumph, 2002.

Kelly, Brent. "Flea Clifton: Lifelong Disciple of Ty Cobb." *Sports Collectors Digest*, July 15, 1994.

Kessler, Ronald. *The Bureau: The Secret History of the FBI*. New York: St. Martin's, 2002.

Ketchum, Richard M. *Will Rogers: The Man and His Times*. New York: Touchstone, 1973.

Krauss, Henry. *Heroes of the Unwritten Story: The UAW, 1934–39*. Chicago: University of Illinois, 1993.

Lacey, Robert. *Ford: The Men and the Machine*. Boston: Little, Brown, 1986.

Lee, Albert. *Henry Ford and the Jews*. New York: Stein and Day, 1980.

Lester, Larry. *Black Baseball's National Showcase: The East-West All-Star Game, 1933–1953*. Lincoln, NE: Bison Books, 2002.

Lieb, Frederick G. *The Detroit Tigers*. New York: Putnam, 1946.

Lodge, John C. *I Remember Detroit*. Detroit: Wayne State, 1949.

Louis, Joe, with Edna and Art Rust Jr. *Joe Louis: My Life*. New York: Harcourt Brace Jovanovich, 1978.

Lundberg, Alex, and Greg Kowalski. *Detroit's Masonic Temple*. Charleston, SC: Arcadia, 2006.

Marcus, Sheldon. *Father Coughlin: The Tumultuous Life of the Priest of the Little Flower*. Boston: Little, Brown, 1973.

Mason, Philip P. *Rumrunning and the Roaring Twenties*. Detroit: Wayne State, 2005.

McCarten, John. "The Little Man in Henry Ford's Basement." *The American Mercury*, May and June 1940.

McRae, Donald. *Heroes Without a Country: America's Betrayal of Joe Louis and Jesse Owens*. New York: Ecco, 2002.

Meehan, Charles, Jack Harvill, and Alfred Farrell. "The Inside Story of Michigan's Black Legion Murder." *Official Detective Stories*, September 1936.

Messick, B. Morris. "The End of the Black Legion." *The National Police Officer*, July 1936.

Mitchell, Jonathan. "Joe Louis Never Smiles." *The New Republic*, October 9, 1935.

Moon, Elaine Latzman. *Untold Tales, Unsung Heroes: An Oral History of Detroit's African American Community, 1918–1967*. Detroit: Wayne State, 1994.

Morris, George. *The Black Legion Rides*. New York: Workers Library, 1936.

"Mumbo Jumbo." *Time*, June 8, 1936.

Navarre, John. "Unmasking the Black Legion." *Real Detective*, September 1936.

Newcombe, Jack. "Black Mike of the Tigers." *Sport*, April 1960.

Odell, Catherine M. *Father Solanus: The Story of Solanus Casey*. Charlotte, NC: Our Sunday Visitor, 1995.

Olander, Oscar. "Black Legion Secrets Never Told Before, II." *True Detective Mysteries*, November 1936.

Pickert, Heinrich. "Black Legion Secrets Never Told Before, I." *True Detective Mysteries*, October 1936.

Piel, Henry W. "Secrets of the Black Legion." *Inside Detective*, September 1936.

Poremba, David Lee. *Detroit: 1930–1969*. Charleston, SC: Arcadia, 1999.

———. *Detroit: City of Champions*. Charleston, SC: Arcadia, 1998.

Ritter, Lawrence S. *The Glory of Their Times*. New York: William Morrow, 1992.

Roberts, Randy. *Joe Louis: Hard Times Man*. New Haven: Yale University, 2012.

Rosengren, John. *Hank Greenberg: The Hero of Heroes*. New York: New American Library, 2013.

Schaap, Jeremy. *Cinderella Man: James J. Braddock, Max Baer, and the Greatest Upset in Boxing History*. New York: Houghton Mifflin Harcourt, 2005.

Skipper, John C. *Charlie Gehringer*. Jefferson, NC: McFarland, 2008.

Smallwood, James M., and Steven K. Gragert, eds. *Will Rogers' Daily Telegrams, Vol. IV: The Roosevelt Years, 1933–35*. Stillwater, OK: Oklahoma State University, 1979.

Spivak, John. "Who Backs the Black Legion?" *New Masses*, June 16 and 23, 1936.

Stanton, Tom. *The Road to Cooperstown*. New York: Thomas Dunne, 2003.

Stegner, Wallace. "The Radio Priest and His Flock." *The Aspirin Age, 1919–1941*. New York: Simon and Schuster, 1949.

Stevens, James. "Detroit the Dynamic." *American Mercury*, November 1935.

Thomas, Richard W. *Life for Us Is What We Make It: Building Black Community in Detroit, 1915–1945*. Bloomington, IN: Indiana University, 1992.

Vincent, Fay. *The Only Game in Town: Baseball Stars of the 1930s and 1940s Talk About the Game They Loved*. New York: Simon and Schuster, 2006.

Warren, Donald. *Radio Priest: Charles Coughlin, the Father of Hate Radio*. New York: Free Press, 1996.

Wilkinson, Ellen. "Detroit Through Socialist Eyes." *The Living Age*, May 1935.

Williams, Jeremy. *Detroit: The Black Bottom Community*. Charleston, SC: Arcadia, 2009.

Willis, Chris. *Dutch Clark: The Life of an NFL Legend and the Birth of the Detroit Lions*. Lanham, MD: Scarecrow, 2012.

Wilson, Edmund. "Detroit Paradoxes." *The New Republic*, July 12, 1933.

Woeste, Victoria Saker. *Henry Ford's War on Jews*. Stanford, CA: Stanford University, 2012.

Wollenweber, Leo. *Meet Solanus Casey: Spiritual Counselor and Wonder Worker*. Ann Arbor: Charis, 2002.

Wright, Richard. "Joe Louis Uncovers Dynamite." *New Masses*, October 8, 1935.

INDEX

A

Adams, Jack, 45, 215–19, 221

Allran, Charles, 265

All-Star Game, 141, 198

Amann, Peter H., 275

American League, 7, 19, 48, 61–62, 64, 120, 141–42

American Legion, 53, 151, 225

American Vigilante Intelligence Federation, 151

Anderson, Rudolph, 199

Angstadt, Earl, 178

Armour, Edward, 129

Armstrong, Louis, 159

Auker, Elden, 33, 62, 71, 85, 91, 135, 156–57, 169, 171, 176, 281

Aurie, Larry, 216

Averill, Earl, 219–20

B

Baer, Max, 18, 137–38, 157, 159–63

Bailey, James, 146

Baker, Del, 61, 171, 269

Baltimore (Maryland), 8

Banks, Newell W., 192

Bannerman, John "Scotty," 132, 227, 231

Bannister, Harry, 63

Barber, Red, 171

Barker, Charles, 28

Barrow, Clyde, 109, 249

Barrow, Deleon, 219

Barrow, Eulalia, 138

Barrow, Joe Louis. *See* Louis, Joe

Barrow, Vunies, 46

Barry, Marty, 218

baseball, 5

superstition in, 60

Bates, Albert, 147–48, 199

Battle of the Overpass, 95

Behrendt, Sheriff, 272

"Be a Man," 89

Bennett, Harry, 25, 75, 89–90, 94–97, 102, 118–19, 120, 124–25, 139, 166, 190, 207, 219, 221, 238, 256, 269, 274–75, 280

Benny, Jack, 219

Benson, Elmer, 253, 271

Berriman, Stanley, 259

Bessette, André, 126

Bicknell, Nathan, 119

Bielak, Dolores, 30

Bielak, John "Jack," 28, 30–31, 236, 241, 262–63, 265, 270

Bingay, Malcolm "Iffy the Dopester," 5, 9, 86, 97, 154, 193, 195, 206, 267, 279–80

critical turn of, 208–9

Iffy craze, 207

Birkie, Hans, 102

Blackburn, Jack "Chappie," 110, 118, 160

Black, Julian, 110, 162

Black Legion, xii–xiii, 22, 27–29, 31, 53, 66, 68, 78, 89–90, 106–8, 112,

123, 128, 146, 149, 154–55, 199,
203, 206, 209–12, 223–25, 227,
238, 240–242, 256, 260, 269, 280,
282
African Americans, attitude toward,
257–58
antisemitism of, 71–72
arson squad, 184–85
as baseball fans, 178–79
Black Oath, 14, 24, 41, 104, 150,
185–87, 228, 272
communism, opposition to, 24–26,
185
cover-up, 266, 270–71, 273–75
expansion of, 23, 53
federal investigations, lack of into,
109, 253–54, 274–76
floggings, as punishment, 179–81,
247
in Ford Motor Company, 119–20
intimidation methods, 247–50
interrogation process, 12–13
investigations into, 244–53, 261–66
leftists, dislike of, 25
Little Stone Chapel, 54–57, 87, 103,
110, 152, 281
"Lixto order," 156
municipal power of, 38
origins, 23–24
press coverage, 251–52
prosecution of, 273
rejection of, 186–88
Secret Agent X-9 informant, 263–65
as secret society, 13
spies of, 150
works of art inspired by, 278
and "zero hour," 156.
See also Wolverine Republican
League
Black, Leslie, 110–11, 150, 225, 239,
272
Black Sox scandal, 95
Blissell, James, 274

Bogart, Humphrey, xiii, 278
Boston (Massachusetts), 8
Boston Bruins, 214
Boston Red Sox, 47, 62, 70, 117, 139,
153, 158, 230
Boston Tea Party, 24
Bourke-White, Margaret, 95
Bowman, Scott, 219
Braddock, Jimmy "Cinderella Man,"
138, 161–62, 195
Branch, Hazen, 265
Bridges, Tommy, 17, 33, 62, 71, 83,
85, 91, 136, 141, 144, 148, 169,
174–77, 190
Briggs, Mirt, 10
Briggs, Spike, 10, 170, 194
Briggs, Walter O., 5–6, 10, 17, 54, 75,
88, 110, 158, 170, 193–94, 198,
207, 220, 281
Brooklyn Dodgers, 192–93
Brooks, Lillie, 46
Brooks, Pat, 46
Broun, Heywood, 250
Brown, Natie, 109
Brown, Joe E., 79, 83
Brown, Monroe, 101
Brown, Mordecai "Three Finger," 135
Brucker, Wilber M., 151, 224–25, 272,
279
Bruneteau, Mud, 217
Bucy, Constable R., 273
Buick, David Dunbar, 9
Bullet Club.
See Black Legion
Burns, Jack, 49
Burnstein, Joseph, 10

C
Cagney, James, 79, 162
California, 184
Canada, 145, 260
Cantor, Eddie, 124
Capone, Al, 154, 249

Carlisle, John, 241
Carmichael, John, 216
Carnera, Primo, 132, 136–38, 162
Carroll, Denny, 19–20, 61, 73, 81, 114, 166, 170, 173–74
Carter, Denver, 181
Casey All-Brothers Nine, 126
Casey, Father Bernard "Solanus," 125–26, 280
Cavarretta, Phil, 168
Cesnovar, Mike, 114
Chegwidden, William, 57
Chenot, "Big Jim," 261, 275
Chevrolet, Louis, 9
Chicago (Illinois), 9, 161, 250, 261
Chicago Bears, 91, 192–93
Chicago Blackhawks, 214, 216
Chicago Cardinals, 192–93
Chicago Cubs, 47, 167–68, 171–75, 190
Chicago White Sox, 148, 191
Chrysler, Walter, 9, 79
Cicotte, Eddie "Knuckles," 95
Cincinnati Reds, 118
Citizens Committee, 28
Civic Pride Association, 75
Clark, Earl "Dutch," xi, 90–91, 193
Clark, George "Potsy," 90, 192, 221
Clark, Lefty, 40
Cleveland (Ohio), 8
Cleveland Indians, 47, 61–62, 117, 153, 218–20
Clift, Harlond, 61
Clifton, Herman Earl "Flea," 33, 60, 82, 91, 93, 120, 135, 143–44, 171–72, 174
Cobb, Ty, 4–7, 18, 54, 93, 168, 190, 207, 234
Cochrane, Archie, 96
Cochrane, Joan, 8, 73–74, 158
Cochrane, Gordon Jr., 8, 44, 73–74, 282
Cochrane, Mary, 8, 92, 220

Cochrane, Gordon Stanley "Mickey," xi, 5, 7–8, 10–11, 16–21, 28, 34–35, 40, 43–51, 54–55, 61–62, 64–65, 69, 73–76, 79–81, 83–86, 90, 91–92, 94, 96–97, 102, 113, 115, 116, 118–20, 135–36, 139, 141, 153–54, 158, 162, 165, 167–71, 174–77, 190–91, 193–94, 197, 199, 206–9, 219–21, 227, 230, 268–69, 279, 282
  background of, 3–4
  as Black Mike, 195
  coaching style of, 32
  firing of, 281
  nervous breakdown, 255–56, 267
  "skull sessions," 33
  temperament, 3, 6, 195
  as worrier, 143–44, 156–57
Cohan, George M., 166
Colburn, Harry, 248, 249
Coleman, Donald, 132
Coleman, Eulah, 132
Coleman, Silas, 130, 154, 199, 204, 225, 236, 270, 273, 277–79, 282
  murder of, 132–34, 258–59
Collier, Jelly, 19
Colombo, Lou, 118, 275
Colombo, Louis Jr., 275
The Coming Struggle for Power (Strachey), 106
Comstock, William, 75
Conference for the Protection of Civil Rights, 238
Cordrey, J. F., 108–9, 155
Corum, Bill, 78, 169
Coughlin, Father Charles, 18, 57, 80, 90, 106, 126, 151, 169, 238, 249
  anti-Jewish bigotry of, 71, 124–25
  fame of, 123
  National Union for Social Justice, 121, 123, 127, 205
  as powerful, 122

Shrine of the Little Flower, 107, 110, 123, 185, 205–6, 280

Couzens, Frank, 75, 139–40, 246, 264, 275

Couzens, James, 10, 79, 224, 264, 279

Cowans, Russell J., 160, 257–59

Cox, Thomas, 178

Cronin, Joe, 48, 141, 153

Crosby, Michael, 126

Crowder, Alvin "General," 79, 113, 144, 172–73, 209

Crowley, David, 266, 271–72

Cubs (Negro league baseball team), 20

Cuddy, Jack, 169

Cummings, Homer S., 251, 253–54

Currier, William, 205

Curtis, Howard, 265

D

Daily Worker (newspaper), 252

Darrow, Clarence, 88, 112

Davey, Martin L., 271

Davis, Forrest, 9, 244

Davis, Harry, 19

Davis, Harvey, 58–59, 110, 130, 151, 212, 245, 278–79
    African Americans, hatred of, 128–29, 257
    arrest of, 148, 150, 237
    Coleman murder, 132–34, 199, 204, 225
    physical description of, 55
    Poole murder plot, 212, 225–28, 231–33, 239
    Voisine murder plot, 147, 184, 203–4

Davis, Ruth, 128

Dean, Dayton, 24, 29, 51, 54, 59, 94, 104, 110–12, 115, 117, 123, 128–30, 151, 182, 184–86, 199, 212–13, 223, 227, 245, 278
    background, 11
    Black Legion, as public face of, 248
    and Coleman murder, 132–34, 258–59
    confessions of, 237, 239, 247–48, 257–59, 273, 276
    death, 282
    as good soldier, 11
    joins Black Legion, 12–14
    Kingsley plot, 14, 39–41, 56
    physical description of, 55
    Poole plot, 212–13, 227, 229–33, 239, 259
    Sugar plot, 152
    Voisine plot, 203–4

Dean, Dizzy, 19, 76–79, 81–82, 85, 92, 153–54, 166, 173

Dean, Paul, 76–78, 81, 92, 117, 153–54, 173

Dearborn Independent (newspaper), 125

Demaree, Frank, 175

Dempsey, Jack, 162, 196

Detroit (Michigan), xiii, 4, 101, 124, 155, 177, 222–23, 249
    as Arsenal of Democracy, 281
    as baseball crazy, 75, 78
    Black Bottom neighborhood, 46, 138, 159–60, 281
    as boom town, 8–9
    as City of Champions, 197, 218, 280–81
    Jewish community in, 69–71
    as "kings of athletics," 192
    Paradise Valley neighborhood, xii, 138, 159, 281
    police brutality, toward blacks in, 129
    police presence in, 58
    police raids, 58–59
    sports trifecta in, xi

Detroit Athletic Club, 75

Detroit Lions, xi, 74, 89–91, 118, 192–93, 196–97, 216, 219, 280

Detroit Red Wings, xi, 214–18, 280

Detroit Tigers, xi, 3–7, 21, 33–35, 43–44, 47–49, 60–65, 67–70, 90, 92–93, 102, 113–14, 116–17, 119–20, 125, 139, 144, 148, 153–54, 158, 178, 192, 198, 207, 209, 216, 218, 220, 230–31, 255–56, 269, 280–81
  All-Star Game, 141
  black fans of, 20
  future of, 193, 194
  Joe Louis, as fan of, 140, 157
  slump of, 135–36, 157
  Tiger mania, 50, 72–76
  in World Series, 77–86, 165–77
Dickstein, Sam, 253
Dillinger, John, 22, 58, 109, 249, 252
DiMaggio, Joe, 198, 267
Dixie Oils softball team, 192
Dodge, Horace, 9
Dodge, John, 9, 106
Dodge, Matilda, 106
Dodge, Vernon, 265
Doljack, Frank, 32, 43, 73, 83
Donoghue, Joseph Patrick, 73
Dorais, Guy, 96
Dos Passos, John, 9
Dotten, Paul, 57
Dougherty, Dennis, 251
Doyle, Lucius, 133, 270
Drukenbrod, M. F., 35
Dugan, Joe, 125
Durocher, Leo, 76
Dyer, Braven, 131
Dykes, Jimmy, 197–98

E
Earle, George, 251
Eckhardt, George, 107, 240
Ecorse (Michigan), 145–46
Edgar, W. W., 268
Edison, Thomas, 54
Effinger, Guy, 108
Effinger, Mrs., 211

Effinger, Virgil "Bert," 22–27, 29, 56, 71, 106, 108–9, 150, 154–55, 211–12, 223, 240, 249, 251, 264, 273, 278
  dismissal of case against, 274
  as fugitive, 271, 274
  indictment of, 271
Egan, Wish, 61, 69, 102, 125
Eisenhower, Dwight D., 279
Eliot, George Fielding, 251
Ellington, Duke, 159
Ellmann, James, 37
End Poverty in California (EPIC), 183
English, Woody, 172
Ernest, Ray, 180–81
Europe, 9, 124
Evans, Billy, 84, 193
Evans, Harlow, 57
Evans, Hiram, 252
Every, Paul, 181

F
Fard, Wallace, 59
Farrell, Mickey, 234–35, 237, 239, 273, 275
Fay, Stan, 119
Federal Bureau of Investigation (FBI), 205, 211–12, 254, 271, 274–76
  Black Legion, investigation into, 150, 154–56
  and G-Men, 109, 234, 251–53
Field, Stanley, 250
Fighting Island (Ontario), 209, 262–63, 275–76
Fischer, Carl, 113, 135
Fisher, Walter, 265
Fitzgerald, Frank, 271–72, 276
Fleeson, Doris, 253
Fleischer, Nat, 46–47, 268
Fleming, Whitney, 11–12
Floyd, Pretty Boy, 109
football, 90
Ford, Clara, 75, 220

Ford, Edsel, 25, 74–75, 79, 95, 280
Ford, Eleanor, 74
Ford, Gerald, 118–19, 131, 138, 280
Ford, Henry, 9, 25, 36, 44, 58, 62,
    68–69, 74, 79–80, 95–96, 110,
    123, 132, 151, 220, 224, 231, 278,
    280
    antisemitism of, 71, 124–25
Ford, Henry II, 280
Ford Hunger March, 25, 28, 88, 95
Ford Motor Company, 119–20, 130,
    270, 275, 280
    Rouge plant at, 94–95
Ford, Josephine, 74
Ford, William Clay, 74
Fox, Pete, 33, 43, 48, 62–64, 80, 91, 114,
    116, 135, 169, 174, 198–99, 230,
    255
Foxx, Jimmie, 45, 72, 115, 167, 198
Franklin, Rabbi Leo, 69–70
Frawley, William, 166
French, Larry, 174–75
Frick, Ford, 172
Friends of the Soviet Union, 88
Frisch, Frankie, 78–79, 82–84, 86
Frye, Clarence, 248
Fulton, Clyde, 242–43
Futch, Eddie, 46

G
Galan, Augie, 175
Gallagher, Michael, 10, 18, 249
Gallico, Paul, 61, 85, 137, 196
Gardner, Carrie, 133
Gehrig, Lou, 4, 18, 72, 92, 115, 141,
    167
Gehringer, Charlie, xi, 7, 32–34, 43,
    48–49, 61, 62, 73, 75, 78, 80–81,
    82, 84, 91–92, 113, 136, 141, 144,
    154, 168–69, 171, 173, 175–76,
    190, 198, 207, 209, 219–20, 230,
    280

background, 17–18
    as devout Catholic, 17
    "Gehringer at Bat" (radio program),
       18
General Motors, 183
Gill, Agnes, 227, 235
Gill, Herschel, 226
Gnau, Russell, 118, 219, 256
Goldwater, Barry, 96
Goodfellow, Ebbie, 214, 216, 218–19
Gorman, Tommy, 217
Goslin, Leon "Goose," 20, 33, 35, 43,
    48–49, 75, 77, 80–84, 91, 113–14,
    116, 135, 154, 168, 171, 173,
    175–77, 190, 209
Grange, Red, 91
Great Depression, xi, 4, 6, 9, 25, 44, 75,
    78, 126, 241, 281
Green Bay Packers, 118, 192–93
Greenberg, Hank, xi, 17–18, 33, 43–44,
    48–49, 61–63, 68, 73, 75, 78,
    80–84, 92, 114–15, 117, 136, 140,
    144, 154, 157, 166, 196, 198, 209,
    220, 230, 260, 267, 280
    All-Star Game snub, 141–42
    anti-Semitism toward, 71
    faith of, as issue, 19, 69–72
    injury to wrist, 169–70, 172–74
    pay raise, issue over, 207–8
    verbal attacks on, 167–68
Greene, Sam, 177, 195
Grieve, Curly, 268
Grimm, Charlie, 167–69, 171–72
Groesbeck, Alex, 126
Grove, Lefty, 63
Guinyard, Fred, 160
Gulley, Fred, 150–51, 178–79, 274
Gulley, Mary, 150
Guthrie, "Doc," 247
Guthrie, Dorothy, 247
Guthrie, William, 103–5
Gutowsky, Art, 197

H

Hackett, Joseph "Honest Joe," 41
Hack, Stan, 174–75
Hagen, Walter, 75, 166, 192
Hainsworth, George, 217–18
Halas, George, 91
Hammett, Dashiell, 263
Harding, Nelson, 250
Harding, Warren, 52
Harridge, William, 141–42
Hart, Albert Bushnell, 251
Hartnett, Charles Leo "Gabby," 169
Harvill, Andrew Jackson "Jack," 234–37, 239, 257, 280
Harvill, Hildegard, 237
Harwell, Ernie, 171, 280
Haskin, Frederic J., 251
Hatter, Clyde, 114
Hauptmann, Richard, 154, 244
Hawley, Dite, 180
Hayworth, Ray, 91, 170–71
Hearst, William Randolph, 106, 110, 112, 247
Heilmann, Harry, 7, 68, 125
Heinrich, Thomas, 149
Helmsley, Rollie, 49
Hemingway, Ernest, 162
Herman, Billy, 174
Hepner, Roy, 39, 110, 149–50
Highland Parker (newspaper), 36, 39
Hilliard, Harriet, 77
Hinchey, Harold, 134
Hitler, Adolf, 106, 125, 183, 196
Hoffman, John A., ix, 246, 273
Hogan, Elmer, 119
Hogsett, Elon, 33, 71, 85, 113–14
Holst, Doc, 217
Holy Sepulchre Cemetery, 281
Hood, Richard, 252
Hoover, Herbert, 52, 162
Hoover, J. Edgar, xiii, 23, 109, 119–20, 154, 156, 166, 168, 211–12, 234, 251–53, 271, 274, 276

Horne, Lena, 137
Hornsby, Rogers, 50
Howell, Dixie, 114, 120
Hudson Motor Company, 28
Hurkett, Oliver, 265
Hyatt, Ralph, 228, 235

I

Illinois, 23, 53
Indiana, 23, 53, 155
The International Jew (Ford), 125
Irvin, Dick, 218
Isserman, Rabbi Ferdinand M., 124
It Can't Happen Here (Lewis), 250

J

Jacobs, Charlie, 85–86, 173
Jacobs, Mike, 109–10
Japan, 4, 92
Jeffries, Jim, 138
Jennings, Hughie, 16, 33, 35
Jentsch, Paul, 56
Joe Louis Boosters Club, 161
John Paul II, 280
Johnson, Hugh, 122
Johnson, Jack, 110, 118, 137–38, 162–63
Jones, Arlington, 41–42
Jones, Robert, 274
Jung, Harry A., 151
The Jungle (Sinclair), 183
Jurges, Billy, 174–75

K

Kahlo, Frida, 25
Keane, W. E., 169
Keating, Father Cyril, 205
Kelly, Father Columban F., 253
Kelly, Machine Gun, 109
Kelly, Pete, 218
Kentucky, 146
Kerr, Andy, 215
Kessler, Gene, 268

Kieran, John, 195
Kilgallen, James, 244
King, Allen, 118
Kingsley, Art, 14–15, 36–37, 56, 130,
    204, 225, 243, 248, 259, 273, 279
    murder plot against, 38–42
Kingston, Robert, 56–57
Kipke, Harry, 45, 96, 118, 139, 221
Kirby, Rollin, 250
Klein, Chuck, 175
Klem, Bill, 77
Knacker, Ida, 245
Knights of Columbus, 249
Knott, Jack, 49
Knudsen, William, 10
Kuenzel, William, 90
Ku Klux Klan (KKK), 12, 23, 27, 46,
    125, 241, 246–47, 252
Kuney, Lavon, 149–50

L
Lada, Steve, 263
La Guardia, Fiorello, 76
Lake, Austen, 267
Landis, Kenesaw Mountain, 79, 86,
    158, 167
Lane, Ruby, 226–27, 235
Larkin, Steve, 32–33, 44, 113
Lazlo, Steve, 133
LeDuc, Harry, 218
Lee, Charles, 101
Lee, Ervin, 132, 225, 227, 229, 232–33,
    239, 279
Lesinski, John Sr., 119
Levinsky, King, 140, 147, 157
Lewis, Herbie, 219
Lewis, Sinclair, 250–51
Liddy, Ralph W., 244
Lieb, Fred, 114
Lima (Ohio), 154
Lincoln, Abraham, 209
Lindbergh, Charles, 199
Lindemeyer, Ernest, 56

Lindstrom, Fred, 173
Link, Harry, 191
Lipps, Urban, 228–30, 232, 239, 279
Lissner, Will, 244
Little, Earl, 29
Little, Louise, 29
Lombard, Carole, 79
Long, Doc, 160
Long, Huey, 106–7, 122, 157
Lorance, James Roy, 132–33, 225
Louisiana, 155
Louis, Joe, xi, 8, 46–47, 59, 101–2,
    109–10, 131–32, 136, 139–40,
    143, 147, 157, 159, 166, 192,
    195–97, 216, 218–19, 221, 257,
    267, 269, 281
    Baer, bout with, 160–63
    as black hero, 137–38, 163–64
    marriage of, 161
    public image of, 117–18
    Schmeling, bout with, 268
    as worldwide sensation, 195
Loveland, B. F., 147
Lukin, Elie, 189
Lupp, Arthur F., 26–27, 29, 38–40, 103,
    104–5, 110–11, 155–56, 186, 233,
    241–43, 245–46, 263, 279
Luther, Joseph, 151

M
MacFarland, J. P., 211
Mack, Connie, 3, 6, 45, 48, 64, 92,
    153
    public persona of, 44
Mackey, Howard, 210
Malcolm X, 29
Manson, N. E., 211–12
Mantle, Mickey, 170
Manush, Heinie, 7
Marberry, Fred, 32, 82, 113, 135
Marchuk, George, 28, 236, 262–63, 265,
    270
Margolis, Rabbi William, 107

Markland, Clyde, 275
Markland, N. Ray, 14, 37–42, 272, 275
Marmon, Ira Holloway, 260–66,
    270–71, 274–76, 280
Marmon, Leon, 261
Marmon, Lillian, 261
Marmon, Owen, 261
Marquard, Rube, 64
Marshall, Donald, 130
Martin, Andrew, 149–50
Martin, Pepper, 76, 84
Marx, Harry Z., 150, 225, 238, 240,
    272, 275
Marxism, 106
Massie, Frank, 129–30
Mathewson, Christy, 63
Maurice and Jane Sugar Law Center
    for Economic and Social Justice,
    279
McCarthy, Joseph, 47
McCoy, Kid, 95, 219
McCrea, Duncan, 42, 241–42, 246, 248,
    253, 258, 261–62, 266, 270–73,
    276, 279
  Black Legion membership of, 245
McCutcheon, Charles, 104–5
McDonald, Bucko, 215–16
McDonald, Harry A., 76
McGrath, Edward J., 15
McLemore, Henry, 80
McManis, John E., 214
McNamee, Graham, 91, 171
McNichols, John, 38
Meehan, Charles, 234–35, 237, 239
Medwick, Joe "Ducky," 76, 85–86, 117,
    167, 173
Mellus, William, 146
Metcalfe, Ralph, 258
Michaelson, Sidney, 15
Michigan, 9, 23, 53, 155, 184, 240, 246,
    248–49, 265
Miller, Bing, 64
Millman, Harry, 233

Modglin, Lloyd, 57
Mollenhauer, William, 66
Montague, Ralph C., 187–88
Montreal Maroons, 216
Moody, Lester, 151
Moran, W. H., 253
Morgan, Chet, 114, 116, 135
Moriarty, George, 167–68, 172, 190
Murdy, Alexander, 181, 263, 265
Murphy, Frank, 18, 95, 126, 149, 264
Mussolini, Benito, 106

N
Nacker, Clarence, 11
Nagurski, Bronko, 91
National Hockey League, 214
National Labor Relations Board, 95
National League, 19, 61, 153
National Rifle Association, 223
Nation of Islam, 59
Native Son (Wright), 250
Navarre, John, 101, 233–34, 241–42,
    248, 263
Navin, Charles, 61, 69, 193–94
Navin, Frank, 3–4, 6, 16–17, 33–35,
    44, 47, 50, 60, 69, 72, 74–75,
    80, 82–84, 93, 102, 110, 115,
    117, 120, 153, 158, 166, 171–72,
    176–77, 189–90, 193–95, 197,
    208, 219, 281
  background of, 5
  death of, 191
  horses, raising of, 5
  as poker face, 7
Navin, Grace, 166, 189, 191, 194, 220
Nazi Germany, 124
Negro leagues, 19, 140
Nelson, Baby Face, 109
Nelson, Ozzie, 77
Ness, Thomas, 180
New Deal, 183, 224
The New Deal in Money (Coughlin),
    124

Newman, Harry, 196
New York Giants, 76, 196–97
New York Yankees, 47, 49, 61–62, 64, 69, 74, 117, 139, 153, 157–58, 198, 231
Nixon, Robert, 250
Norris, James, 214, 218
Nugent, Floyd, 225

O
O'Connell, William, 127
O'Donnell, Emmett "Rosie," 119, 268, 279
O'Donovan, Constance, 192
Ohio, 9, 23, 53, 146, 155
Olander, Oscar, 263–65
Olds, Ransom, 9
Oliver, Clarence, 128–29, 203
Olmsted, Frederick Law, 222
O'Rourke, Margaret, 11, 56, 94, 119
Owen, Marv, 33, 43, 48–49, 61, 63–64, 70, 72, 85, 91, 117, 135, 171–72, 174, 176, 255
Owens, Brick, 84, 168
Owens, Jesse, 130–32, 258

P
Packard, James, 9
Palmer, Thomas, 10
Parker, Bonnie, 109, 249
Parker, Harold, 73
Parker, Salty, 114
Patriotic League of America, 278. See also Black Legion
Pegler, Westbrook, 79, 86
Penland, Mamie, 178
Penland, Robert, 178–79, 273
Penner, Joe, 74
Pennsylvania, 23
Perkins, Cy, 61, 64–65, 83, 92, 197
Perroni, Patsy, 102
Peterman, Cy, 63

Pettijohn, Jesse J., 146, 203–4, 225
Pettinger, Gord, 214–15
Philadelphia Athletics, 3–6, 44–45, 47–48, 63–65, 139, 153, 255
Philip, R. T., 265
Phillips, Red, 61
Pickert, Heinrich, 57–59, 80, 89, 101, 139–41, 184–85, 199, 225, 238–39, 262, 272–76, 279
    police brutality, claims of, 53
    policing, attitudes toward, 52–53
    protesters, hard line against, 53
    Red Squad, 53
Pickert, Julie, 53
Pidcock, Cecil, 231
Pidcock, Nellie, 209–10, 223, 231
Pidcock, Roy, 209–10, 223, 231–32, 235, 254, 262, 265, 275–76
Piet, Tony, 144
Pittsburgh (Pennsylvania), 8
Pitts, Edgar, 161
Pius, Pope, 251
Politzer, Esther, 192
Poole, Charles, 235–36, 261, 273, 278
    murder plot against, 212–13, 230–34, 237–40, 244, 248, 259, 262
Poole, Mary Lou, 213, 228
Poole, Rebecca, 212–13, 226–28, 234, 236, 248, 279
Post, Wiley, 142–43
Powell, Jake, 230
Powers, Jimmy, 3, 64
Pratt, George, 56
Pressnell, Glenn, 91
Prohibition, 8, 58, 145, 261
Proletarian Party, 10
Purple Gang, 10, 27, 155, 233, 261
Purnell, "King Ben," 261

Q
Quindt, John George Jr., 185–86
Quindt, John George Sr., 223

R

Raft, George, 79, 166
Reagan, Ronald, 171
Reiber, Frankie, 114, 256
Reinecke, H. H., 205
Retzlaff, Charley, 196
Revere, Paul, 24
Rice, Grantland, 79, 116, 138–39, 163, 177
Richards, George, 89–91, 139
Rivera, Diego, 25, 94
Roberts, R. E., 253
Robinson, Bill "Bojangles," 143
Robinson, Edward G., 162, 190
Robinson, Wilbur, 186, 225
Roby, Doug, 119
Rockne, Knute, 32, 167
Rockwell, Tod, 50
Rogell, Billy, 33, 43, 48, 60–61, 73, 81–82, 91–92, 157, 174, 219, 255
Rogers, Will, 54, 77, 79, 142–43
Roggin, Joe, 72, 170, 174, 190, 198, 230
Roginski, Joey.
    See Roggin, Joe
Roosevelt, Eleanor, 159
Roosevelt, Franklin D., 106, 121–22, 126–27, 143, 183, 219–20, 224, 253
Roosevelt, G. Hall, 89
Roughley, Alfred, 57, 181
Rouse, Charles, 128, 130, 132
Rowe, Edna Mary, 91, 135–36, 139, 165, 260, 280
Rowe, Lynwood "Schoolboy," xi, 20–21, 33–34, 43–44, 64, 67–68, 73, 75–76, 79–80, 82, 84–86, 91, 114–15, 138–39, 141, 156–57, 165–66, 169, 171–72, 176–77, 190, 207, 209, 220, 230, 260
    complete-game shutout, 62
    death of, 280
    end of winning streak, 65
folk hero status, 63
popularity of, 66
slump of, 135–36
as superstitious, 60–62
threats against, 83
Rowe, Lynwood Jr., 138–39
Roxborough, John, 110, 139
Runyon, Damon, 169
Rushing, Lowell, 148–49, 212–13, 226–27, 237, 245
Rushing, Marcia, 226–28, 234–35, 237, 245
Rushing, Owen, 226, 234, 237, 245
Russia, 88, 106, 151
Ruth, Babe, 7, 47, 63, 72, 92, 125, 132, 162, 166, 173

S

Salsinger, H. G. "Harry," 6, 47, 70, 113, 116, 142, 168, 193, 195, 197, 206, 267, 279
Sarber, Jess, 22
Schmeling, Max, 47, 195–96, 267–68, 281
Schuble, Heinie, 44, 115, 135, 171
Schultz, Victor Nicholas, 225
Schussler, Chris, 8
Schwartz, Perrin, 205
Second Amendment, 211–12
Sewell, Rip, 19
Shanley, George, 28
Sharkey, Jack, 162
Sharp, Eugene, 110, 224–25
Shaver, Bud, 82, 218, 267
Shelley, Hugh, 114
Shepard, Billy, 23–24, 108, 154, 274
Sherman, Gene, 228–29, 235, 237
Sherry, Louis, 119
Shettleman, Fred, 233
Shinaberry, Elsworth, 149–50
Simmons, Al, 267
Sinclair, Upton, 183–84

Simmons, Al, 92, 141, 191, 197–98, 207, 209, 230
Smith, C. E., 155
Skinner, Edna Mary, 66–68, 75, 79–80, 86.
   See also Rowe, Edna Mary
Smith, Gordon, 39
Smith, Harley, 180
Smith, Normie, xi, 216–18
Smith, Red, 169
Smythe, Conn, 217
Socialist Labor Party, 10
Social Justice (magazine), 205
Soldati, Arlo, 46
Sorrell, Johnny, 219
Sorrell, Vic, 64, 71, 82, 91, 113
"The Soup Song," 89
Sparrow, Riley, 25
Spears, Joan, 134
Spreksel, Frieda, 261
Stainback, Tuck, 172
Stanley, William, 109
Stark, Dolly, 172
Stars (Negro league baseball team), 19
Stegner, Wallace, 121
Stevens, James, ix
St. Louis (Missouri), 8, 46
St. Louis Browns, 47, 49, 61, 158
St. Louis Cardinals, 19, 61, 76, 116–17, 153, 166, 175
   in World Series, 77, 79–86
Stone, Bucky, xii
Stone, Clements Maximilian, xii
Strachey, Evelyn John, 106–7
Stull, I. M.
   See White, Isaac "Peg-Leg"
Suffrin, Harry, 73
Sugar, Jane, 87–88, 152
Sugar, Maurice, 87–89, 101, 106–7, 152, 183, 186, 204, 221, 225, 238–39, 248, 259, 273, 275, 279
   campaign appearance, disruption of, 110–11

death threats against, 182
   fake campaign literature planted, 184
   murder plot against, 112, 151
Sullivan, Joe, 114, 190
Swanwick, Charles, 38
Sweet, Ossian, 88, 101
Swing, Raymond Gram, 107

T
Tamm, Edward, 252
Tears, Johnny, 161
Tebbetts, Birdie, 114
Tennessee, 146
Thompson, Dorothy, 252
Thumim, Joseph, 69
Tolan, Eddie, 143, 192
Toronto Maple Leafs, 217–18
Trosky, Hal, 117
Trotter, Marva, 161, 163
Tunney, Gene, 162
Tyson, Ty, 68, 158, 173–74, 190

U
United Auto Workers (UAW), 28, 252, 279
United States, 88, 106, 123–24, 246, 249
Uzcudun, Paulino, 195–96

V
Vallee, Rudy, 67, 190, 219
Vanderveen, Cornelius, 265
Van Dusen, Charles, 10
Victory, James, 88, 111
Voisine, Bill, 146, 150, 179, 225, 248, 259, 273, 279
   murder plot against, 147, 151, 184, 203–4
Voisine, Bobby, 147

W
Wade, "Whistling" Jake, 114
Wadelik, Wanda, 30

Walker, Gee, 17, 19, 32–33, 44, 48–51, 80, 82, 91–93, 114, 116, 120, 136, 165, 171, 174, 176, 198–99, 230–31
Walker, Gerald, 116, 120
Walker, Hubby, 135
Walker, Jerry, 165
Walker, Mike, 165
Walker, Sherman, 164
Walters, Phillip, 262
Waner, "Big Poison," 77
Waner, "Little Poison," 77
Ward, Charles P., 18, 116
Ward, Willis, 131
Warneke, Lon, 168
Washer, George, 14
Washington Senators, 48, 62, 79, 144, 153
Waters, Ethel, 138
Watkins, Wattie, 73
Weitschat, H. O., 275
Wellman, Frances, 179
Wellman, Rudyard Kipling, 179
West, Mae, 77
West Virginia, 23, 146
Wettler, Ernie, 168–69
Wheeler, Rosa Lee Kirkman, 159
White Angel (film), 108
White, Isaac "Peg-Leg," 27–29, 104, 155, 179, 241, 263, 270, 273–74
White, Jo-Jo, 43, 73, 80, 84, 91, 114, 116, 135, 169, 172, 174, 190, 199

White, Rev. Sam Jacob, 55
White Russians, 25
White, Teddy, 27
Wilde, Max, 268–69
Williams, Joe, 169
Willis, Whitey, 72, 75–76
Wilson, Ralph, 58
Wilson, Woodrow, 185
Windsor (Ontario), 8
Wise, Rabbi Stephen, 124
Wolf, Jerome, 265
Wolverine Republican League, 31, 224–25, 237–39, 272, 279
   See also Black Legion
Women's City Club, 53
Wood, Gar, 192, 221
Woodruff, Harvey, 160
Woollcott, Alexander, 107
Wright, Richard, 163
Wurm, Irvine, 264

Y
York, Rudy, 207
Young, Cy, 63
Young, Bobbie, 216
Young, Doug, 216
Young, Doug Jr., 216
Young, Mrs. Doug, 216
Young, Helen, 142

Z
Zerilli, James, 47

ABOUT THE AUTHOR

Tom Stanton is the author of four other nonfiction books, among them the critically acclaimed memoir *The Final Season* and the Quill Award finalist *Ty and The Babe*. A journalist for more than thirty years, he founded, owned, and edited a group of suburban Detroit newspapers winning state and national press awards, including a Knight-Wallace Fellowship at the University of Michigan. Stanton teaches journalism at the University of Detroit Mercy. He and wife Beth Bagley-Stanton live in New Baltimore, Michigan.